W9-CDA-438

Boston Sites & Insights

Boston Sites
& Insights

COMPLETELY REVISED AND UPDATED

AN ESSENTIAL GUIDE
TO HISTORIC LANDMARKS
IN AND AROUND BOSTON

Susan Wilson

FOREWORD BY James Carroll

BEACON
150

Beacon Press BOSTON

BEACON PRESS
25 Beacon Street
Boston, Massachusetts 02108-2892
www.beacon.org

Beacon Press books
are published under the auspices of
the Unitarian Universalist Association of Congregations.

07 06 05 04 03 8 7 6 5 4 3 2 1

This book is printed on acid-free paper that meets
the uncoated paper ANSI/NISO specifications for
permanence as revised in 1992.

Library of Congress Cataloging-in-Publication Data
Wilson, Susan (Susan Carolyn)
Boston sites and insights : an essential guide to historic
landmarks in and around Boston / Susan Wilson ;
foreword by James Carroll.—Rev.
pbk. ed.
p. cm.
ISBN 0-8070-7135-8 (pbk. : alk. paper)
1. Boston (Mass.)—Guidebooks. 2. Historic
sites—Massachusetts—Boston—Guidebooks. I. Title.
F73.18.W55 2004
917.44'6104—dc22 2003022385

Book design and typesetting by Boskydell Studio

Cover photographs (left to right):
The Shaw / 54th Regiment Memorial; the Massachusetts
State House; David Connor performing as Paul Revere for tour
groups and special events (he can be contacted through the
Old North Church or the Paul Revere House).

Contents

PART SIX: The Green, Green Grass of Home
PARKS, PLAYGROUNDS, AND OPEN SPACES   273

Foreword

"The chief means of moral education," Alisdair MacIntyre wrote, "is the telling of stories." *Boston Sites and Insights* is a book of stories about the city of Boston. Though it poses at the most obvious level as the commentary of a wise, witty, and well-informed tour guide, Susan Wilson's book is implicitly a reflection on the moral education of America's founding city, and therefore, in some way, of the nation itself.

Americans, unlike citizens of other countries, are bound together as a people by the future, not the past. An immigrant can arrive here with the hope that she can become an American, and with the full expectation that her children will. No such thing is possible for newcomers to Germany, say, or France or China. That is true not primarily because other countries are by definition xenophobic, but because their national ethos is tied more to the past than the future. The refrain of the Fleetwood Mac song used by Bill Clinton as a campaign anthem, "Don't stop thinking about tomorrow," expressed a deep strain in the American psyche, one of the elements that makes us an open people, and a hopeful one.

But you can't know where you're going if you don't know where you come from. For more than three centuries, newly arrived Americans have needed to fold into their own personal histories—histories of persecution often, of pogroms, of famine, of slavery, of flight—the history of the people who preceded them here. First, of course, the native peoples; then the English, Dutch, French, Spanish, the kidnapped Africans, then the rest of us.

The chief means of the moral education of Americans as Americans has been the telling of stories—of the Pilgrim encounters with the Massachusett Indians, of Paul Revere's ride, of the Underground Railroad, of the wagon trains moving west. As befits a vast country and a diverse people, the reach of this narrative seems almost endless, but, in fact, there is a soul to the American story, and it resides in Boston.

When John Winthrop pointed to what we now know as Bunker Hill in Charlestown and invoked the biblical image of the "City on a Hill," he was hoping that the settlement itself would exemplify what made the New World different from the Old. Boston, with its bookish air, narrow streets, tidy row houses, and lively ethnic neighborhoods, is often described as a European-like city, but it is the place, more than any other, in which America invented itself. That heritage, of course, has put a special burden on subsequent generations of Bostonians to be part of the constant reinvention that history requires of this country. It is a burden we have not always carried gracefully.

Visitors to Boston, to its shrines and markers, its monuments and waterfront, gaslights and brick sidewalks, marvel that its charm is real, the creation not of theme park entrepreneurs but of humans who have lived here. We live here still, of course, and we still create according to who we are. Now a bit more than half of us are white, a quarter are black, 15 percent are Hispanic, and nearly another 10 percent are Asian. Other divisions by class, culture, and turf are, as always, palpable in Boston. But, to use a local image, such differences are like spokes coming out of a hub, which is the right we all have to call this city ours.

Boston takes such rights very seriously. Revolutionary Boston—the Old State House, Faneuil Hall, the Freedom Trail—is a wonder, especially for the way it still enables Irish or Italians or European Jews or Asians or Haitians to identify with that original band of Anglo-Saxons who created America's first character ideal. Yet in the nineteenth and early twentieth centuries the image of those first English heroes was revered in ways that seemed to disqualify such newcomers from every joining them as equals.

The stones of this city tell the African-American version of this story, too, from the nation's first black slaves imported by the pious Winthrop to the Revolution's first martyr, Crispus Attucks, to Beacon Hill's African Meeting House, where the overthrow of slavery was plotted. The descendants of slaves who came to Boston during the great twentieth-century migration met the resistance of the remnant Puritan culture as all immigrants had, but blacks also met resistance from the immigrants themselves, a story that shadows Boston still. But the democratic meaning of that initial revolutionary impulse remains the measure of the city's soul. Now the story of numerous once-despised groups is as central to the city's story as their present and former neighborhoods are to its geography. And the "moral" of such education is crystal clear: the city founded by outcasts, and built by other outcasts, must welcome outcasts now.

Among Boston's citizens, from whatever outcast cadre they descend, a rank individualism has been a common note. Individualism looked like courage when it prompted the first settlers to come here, like treason when it stirred the colonial merchant class to rebel, like nobility when it was preached as abolition, like Yankee thrift when the Boston oligarchy opted out of public investment. In our own time, that individualism has tested the limits of our city's social cohesion as class conflict and racism have seemed to dominate politics and news. That is part of the story, too, as evident, say, when we look again at the hill in Charlestown that first inspired Winthrop, then inspired the minutemen who held their fire until they saw the whites of British eyes, then inspired the fiercest opponents of busing for integration. Now the obelisk on Bunker Hill stands as a monument to many things, not the least of which is the city's new commitment to racial harmony.

Boston's most familiar places reward such close examination. Its theaters, cemeteries, art museums, parks, libraries, ballparks, universities, and churches all have stories relating aspects of the one story that, in its triumph and also defeat, makes us a people. The story makes us Boston.

As you will shortly find, Susan Wilson is the master of that story. She has collected here not just fresh retellings of the old yarns—Mrs. Gardner's strange house, the confusion between Breed's Hill and Bunker's, the Brahmin at Friday Symphony—but an offering of closely researched new versions of Boston sagas that even lifelong residents will find illuminating. This is a book for visitors, certainly—the best introduction to the "sites" I know of. But its "insights" add up to a kind of biography of the city, an account of a life still being lived.

This is a collection, as we began by saying, of Boston's best stories; a summary of all that this city has taught us, for better and for worse; a precis of the many reasons we—and our whole nation—have for treasuring Boston; a justification, one could even say, for the fact that we love it so.

JAMES CARROLL
Boston, Massachusetts
October 2003

Preface

In April 1994, the first edition of *Boston Sites and Insights* was released by Beacon Press. Over the ensuing months and years, I was continually thrilled to discover how significant this volume—my first published book— had been to so many different people. Yes, there were the tourists, the tour leaders, and the tour-guide classes that used it as their reference book and personal encyclopedia of historical Boston sites; that, of course, was wonderful but was also, in a way, to be expected.

What delighted me even more was finding that secondary schools and colleges had used *Sites and Insights* to study Boston and American history, or had used individual chapters as a basis for field trips; that the Boston Public School system had used it to teach literacy to teenage students; that it was *the* most referenced book on Boston history in the *Boston Globe* library; that local folks felt it was a book for them as much as it was for visitors to Boston; and that numerous research librarians, journalists, and resident historians kept it on their desks—as a quick, dependable source of impeccably researched facts, dates, names, and stories—in places as diverse as the Massachusetts Historical Society, the Boston Athenaeum, the Boston Public Library, Boston National Historical Park, and the *Boston Globe*.

Having mentioned the *Boston Globe* twice, I must step back and give credit where it is surely due. I was a regular contributor to the *Globe* from 1978 through 1996, first as an arts and entertainment critic and then, during my final nine years there, as a feature writer specializing in lengthy columns on Boston history. (In my former life, I had accumulated a B.A., M.A., and A.B.D. in history and taught history at the secondary school and college levels before abandoning that career due to a lack of jobs and a personal restlessness.)

As a result, *Sites and Insights* actually made its debut in 1987, as a monthly feature column in the *Globe*. The idea behind the column was quite simple: to explore historic treasures in the Greater Boston area, from public buildings, museums, and parks to houses of worship and centers of literature, arts, and entertainment. The intent of the column—and the intent of this book that grew from them—was to observe Boston's rich past in a way that was both accessible to the general public and enlightening to serious students of history. Boston, after all, is the ultimate walking town, with many of its most illustrious sites surprisingly close to one another. I wanted to engage the reader's imagination and to encourage both Bostonians and Boston visitors to discover—or rediscover—the history around them.

One goal for *Sites and Insights* was to dig deeper than the Boston guide-books currently on the market. This meant not only spending time physically exploring each site—through interviews, archival research, and other detective work—but also, in the process, unearthing long-lost facts, debunking tired legends, and finding interesting anecdotes and tales that brought each site to life. In both the column and the book, a deliberate effort was made to acknowledge that Boston's history was molded by women and men of all socioeconomic classes and a multitude of races, religions, and national origins.

Time, of course, passed. And though the fifty landmarks selected for the book all had their roots firmly planted in Boston history, they were all living, growing sites as well—meaning, of course, that the 1994 edition of *Boston Sites and Insights* eventually became dated. During the spring and summer of 2003, with encouragement and support from Joanne Wyckoff and Brian Halley of Beacon Press, I went about updating every single chapter. Packets went out to all fifty sites, with annotated requests for corrections and contemporary materials. Thanks to the willing assistance of more than one hundred individuals—staff, friends, and knowledgeable colleagues connected with each of the sites—every chapter was read, reread, edited, commented on, corrected, altered, and expanded. Site visits were also made to places I hadn't frequented in recent years, or which had changed substantially since my last visits.

Though managers and fans of many other historical sites had requested inclusion in the book over the years, we opted to stay with the original fifty. Of those fifty, most are in Boston and its immediate environs; when out-of-town sites appear, it's because their stories were deemed unique and vital to understanding the area's heritage. All of the sites selected had to be old—really, really old; an institution or area first developed in the 1930s, for instance, was much too new to deal with in this particular volume. The sites also had to exist in their original form, at least to the extent described by the late Dan Coolidge in his discussion of the Old South Meeting House: "There's been an awful lot of replacement of the fabric of the Old South," Coolidge once explained. "But the space is really just the same. It's what Buckminster Fuller called the 'Model T Syndrome.' You know, where over the auto's life you get a dent in the bumper and replace it. You put on new wheels . . . you replace and repair the parts bit by bit until many of them are not the original. But it's still very much a Model T!"

As in the first edition, this tenth anniversary edition of *Boston Sites and Insights* is full of some of Boston's most precious Model Ts, and many of its most precious memories. Still, it's only one small segment—a starter package, if you will—of the many historic and cultural sites Boston has to offer those who are willing to read, wonder, and wander.

Susan Wilson
Cambridge, Massachusetts
October 2003

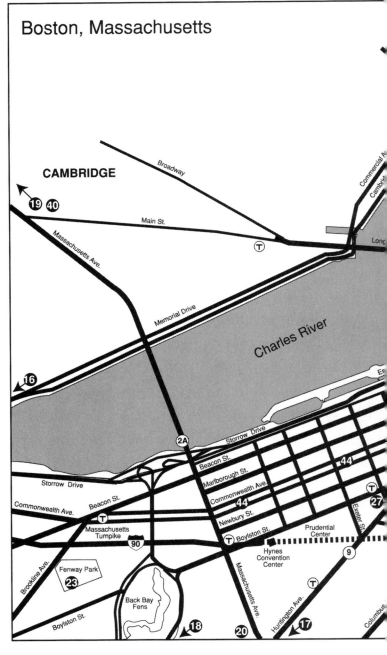

Boston, Massachusetts

CAMBRIDGE

Broadway

19 40

Main St.

Massachusetts Ave.

Memorial Drive

Charles River

16

2A

Storrow Drive

Beacon St.

Marlborough St.

Commonwealth Ave.

44

Storrow Drive

Beacon St.

Commonwealth Ave.

Newbury St.

Massachusetts Turnpike

90

Boylston St.

Prudential Center

27

Hynes Convention Center

9

Brookline Ave.

Fenway Park

23

Back Bay Fens

Boylston St.

18

20

17

Massachusetts Ave.

Huntington Ave.

Long

Commercial

Cambri

44

Exeter St.

Columbu

Es

City Map Sites

Numbers correspond to chapters.

1 The Old State House
2 Faneuil Hall
3 The Old South Meeting House
4 The Paul Revere House
6 The Bunker Hill Monument
8 The State House
9 USS *Constitution*
11 The First Church in Roxbury

12 King's Chapel
13 The Old North Church
14 Trinity Church
15 The Granary Burying Ground
16 Mount Auburn Cemetery
17 The Museum of Fine Arts
18 The Isabella Stewart Gardner Museum
19 Harvard University Museums and
    Memorial Hall
20 Symphony Hall
21 The Colonial Theatre

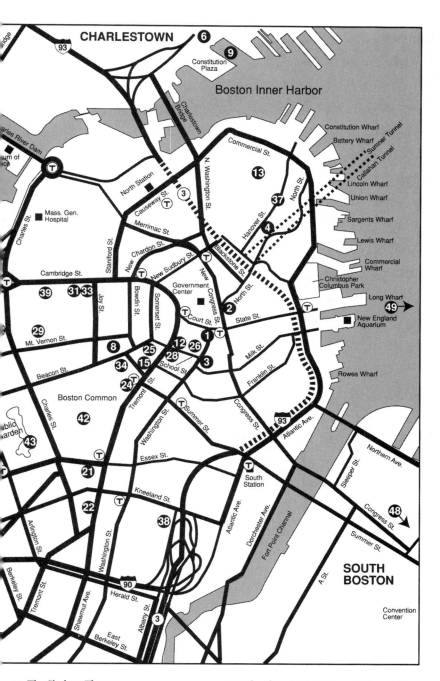

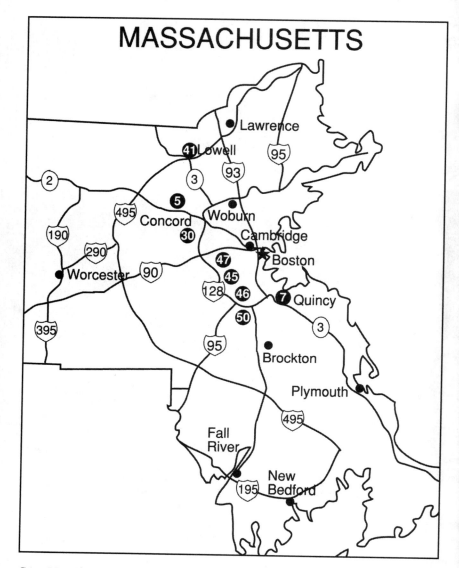

MASSACHUSETTS

State Map Sites

Numbers correspond to chapters.

5 Minute Man National Historical Park
7 Adams National Historic Site
30 Walden Pond
41 Lowell National Historical Park
45 The Arnold Arboretum
46 Franklin Park
47 The Frederick Law Olmsted National Historic Site
50 Blue Hills Reservation

PART ONE

Politics as Usual

THE FREEDOM TRAIL AND BEYOND

THOUGH THE HISTORY of Boston is close to four centuries long, one particular segment of that past is better known and more widely chronicled than any other. The last third of the eighteenth century and the opening of the nineteenth—often referred to as the American Revolutionary and Early National periods—are perennially linked with the town of Boston in the popular imagination.

Boston's political history actually began in 1630, when John Winthrop and the Puritans of the Massachusetts Bay Company first settled the Shawmut peninsula. They originally called it Trimountain before settling on the name Boston. These English colonists were not the first people to live in the area. Native American tribes, including the Wampanoag, Nipmuck, and Massachusset, had inhabited various parts of eastern Massachusetts for thousands of years. A variety of European voyages of discovery had passed through the Boston area as well, perhaps as early as Leif Eriksson's in the eleventh century, but with great regularity throughout the sixteenth and early seventeenth centuries. In 1620, the people we now know as the Pilgrims—who, like the later Puritans, were seeking religious freedom—had established the first permanent English settlement in New England at Plymouth, to the south of Boston.

During the seventeenth century, the English colonists of Puritan Boston were concerned with survival and growth—with laying foundations for religious, political, and economic patterns of life. Throughout that century, arguments continually arose over religious issues. By the eighteenth century, new and different growing pains gradually became apparent. As the British colonies prospered and expanded far away from the mother country, certain colonists grew to resent control by the British monarch and Parliament, particularly in the area of taxation without representation. The result was the American War for Independence.

Many of the men and women who helped incite the Revolution lived, worked, and worshipped in Boston—in buildings and churches and on open lands that we can still observe and visit today. Patriot Paul Revere made his home in Boston's oldest neighborhood, the North End. That quaint structure is now the oldest wooden dwelling standing on its original site in the city. During the 1760s and 1770s, Sam Adams, Joseph Warren, James Otis, John Hancock, and their radical patriot colleagues delivered orations, rallied crowds, and fanned the flames of revolution in still-extant sites like the Town House (today's Old State House), Faneuil Hall, and the Old South Meeting House. When fighting finally broke out between Britain and the colonists in April 1775, it happened in the suburban towns of Lexington and Concord—on lands now commemorated in Minute Man National Historical Park. From there, hostilities moved back to Charlestown, where the Battle of Bunker Hill erupted two months later.

As men like Sam Adams were intently severing connections with English sovereignty and rule, others, like his cousin John Adams, were working to create a new American nation and forge ties with amicable international neighbors. John Adams and his wife, Abigail—credited by some as one of America's first active and outspoken feminists—lived south of Boston in the town of Quincy, in homes now preserved as part of Adams National Historical Park. Once the war was over and American independence was officially recognized by Great Britain, the Adams family provided the young nation with two of its early presidents, John and John Quincy Adams. In 1789, John Adams was the nation's first vice president under George Washington. Washington, of course, had also spent considerable time in Boston as commander in chief of the Continental army.

When President Washington decided to build a U.S. Navy in the 1790s, that was partly accomplished in Boston—in the form of USS *Constitution*, which remains the oldest fully commissioned warship afloat in the world. Meanwhile, the rapid growth of the commonwealth of Massachusetts and its government necessitated a move from the Old State House to a new one, built atop the venerable slope known as Beacon Hill. In other cities, older buildings were often demolished to make way for the new. In Boston, however, an unusual number of original structures—from the Old State House and Old South Meeting House to Old City Hall—were preserved for posterity after their replacements were built.

The first ten chapters of this book describe many of these Revolutionary-era sites and their stories. Included as well is the tale of how these landmarks were eventually linked to form the most famous historic walking tour in the world—Boston's Freedom Trail. You'll find three other Freedom Trail sites—the Old North Church, King's Chapel, and the Granary Burying Ground—in Part 2, since I thought it appropriate to include churches having active modern congregations with other houses of worship and cemeteries.

1 The Old State House

PEOPLE HAVE called this antique structure a variety of names over the past three centuries—from the New Town House, the Province House, and the Court House to City Hall, the State House, and even the Temple of Liberty. But Philip Bergen, former librarian of the Bostonian Society, has an even more interesting epithet for one of Boston's most eclectic buildings. "I like to call it the oldest historic subway kiosk in the United States!"

It's true. Boston's oldest public building has housed the State Street "T" (subway) stop in its sub-basement since 1903—a downtown station where the Orange and Blue lines still meet. But the "kiosk" above, popularly known today as the Old State House, is not your ordinary public transportation entranceway. Within its walls, colonial patriot and lawyer James Otis argued against the Writs of Assistance and helped pave the road for the Revolution. Just outside those same walls, the 1770 Boston Massacre set the revolutionary spirit ablaze. And from the building's second-floor balcony, the Declaration of Independence was first read aloud to the town of Boston.

Located at the intersection of State and Washington streets, the Old State House alternately served Boston as a courthouse, a primeval stock exchange, a city hall, the seat of British royal governors, and, as the name implies, as the seat of the Massachusetts state government. Though the structure houses a fascinating museum of Boston and American Revolutionary-era history today, it's still called the Old State House to differentiate it from the "new" Massachusetts State House on Beacon Hill, which itself is more than two centuries old (see Chapter 8). But that's getting a bit ahead of our story.

As with most public buildings of the period, the edifice built on the corner of Cornhill and King streets (now Washington and State) in 1713 was specifically designed to be a multipurpose structure. The previous building, the wooden Town House built through the bequest of Puritan trader Robert Keayne in 1657, had housed merchants downstairs and governing bodies above—housed them, that is, until it was destroyed in the Great Fire of 1711. Hence, when the New Town House was built on the old one's ashes, everyone assumed it too would serve a variety of community needs.

The New Town House was wisely constructed with red brick rather than flammable wood and financed by the royal province, Suffolk County, and the town of Boston—all of which planned to use its several chambers. William Payne was credited as the builder; the designer, if there was one, remains unknown.

Like the original Town House, the new one had a "merchants' exchange" on the first floor. A precursor of today's stock exchange, it was a place

The majestic spiral staircase is a literal centerpiece of the Old State House— the stage on which many dramatic scenes from Boston history have been played.

where traders talked shop, swapped information, and received up-to-date news on prices and commodities. The building's location was ideal for such endeavors: the waterfront and Long Wharf, where most ships' captains first stopped in Boston, was close by at the time. Over the next hundred and fifty years, Long Wharf all but disappeared, as periodic landfill projects extended the mainland and State Street into Boston Harbor. Today's financial district, incidentally, grew up around that old merchants' exchange.

Other early uses of the first floor, where several exhibit rooms and a museum shop stand today, were provincial and county records offices and a post office. Meanwhile, the third-floor attic—now a curatorial office—housed the Boston Board of Health, for which Paul Revere worked during 1799 and 1800. The building's basement served variously as a warehouse, a wine cellar, and, possibly, a fire station. John Hancock rented space there in 1766, probably to store his imported merchandise.

The balcony, which opened out from the second floor, had many functions as well. Beneath it lay a granite platform and steps where at least one colonial forger was forced to stand with a large paper on his chest that read, "CHEAT." From the balcony itself, news items were read, often to the accompaniment of trumpet and drum. New laws, new wars, new governors, new monarchs, and recently deceased monarchs were all heralded there.

The second floor—which now contains several museum galleries and a multipurpose hall—was an epicenter of thunderous argument and theatrical antics throughout the eighteenth century. The east end, from which the balcony opened, harbored the council chamber of British royal governors. At the west end was a small court chamber. Between the two was the large Representatives Hall, where the Massachusetts Assembly met, steadily earning itself a reputation as the most independent and outspoken of colonial legislatures.

Visitors to the second floor now see a room with changing exhibits on Boston history, plus several smaller chambers and a nineteenth-century spiral staircase. There's no trace today of the gallery built there in 1766, an interior balcony that was used to pack crowds of vociferous citizens into Massachusetts Assembly meetings—a vital element in building support for the eventual revolution. (That 1766 gallery, incidentally, was the first of its kind in any legislative assembly in the English-speaking world.)

In 1761, the second floor became the stage on which one of the most dramatic events associated with the Old State House was acted out. It was then that lawyer James Otis, Jr., made a blazing eight-hour speech against the Writs of Assistance, which authorized royal authorities to enter private buildings and ships to search colonial property for smuggled goods.

"Otis was a flame of fire," recalled John Adams in reminiscences he penned half a century later. "With a promptitude of classical allusions, a depth of research, a rapid summary of historical events and dates . . . and a torrent of impetuous eloquence, he hurried away everything before him. . . . Then and there was the first scene of the first act of opposition to the arbitrary claims of Great Britain. Then and there the child Independence was born."

Otis, as it turned out, lost the battle but won the war. His case failed, and the Writs of Assistance continued to be implemented. But the revolutionary spirit was ignited, coming to fruition fifteen years later.

Like many historic figures, Otis had his idiosyncrasies. George Washington had malodorous, ill-fitting wooden dentures; Benjamin Franklin allegedly sired a large brood of illegitimate children (a claim largely debunked by modern historians). Otis, for his part, had a tendency toward mental instability. Although he had been known for erratic behavior, self-contradiction, nonsensical chatter, and periodic melancholia over the years, the final blow, quite literally, came in September 1769, when an angry British officer, John Robinson, cracked Otis on the head in a local tavern. From that point on, observed Adams, Otis rambled and wandered "like a ship without a helm." Fourteen years later the glorious old patriot died—as he himself had predicted—after being struck by lightning while watching a summer thunderstorm in Andover.

The other legendary event most closely associated with the Old State House—the Boston Massacre of 1770—took place below the building's historic balcony. The approximate site is marked by a small circle of stones on the traffic island facing that balcony. Historic accounts of the incident are as varied and contradictory as the people who wrote them; an abbreviated, eclectic version follows.

Tensions were high between the red-coated British "regulars" stationed in Boston and the local residents. Some radicals—like Sam Adams, John's rabble-rousing cousin—fanned every flame they could, hoping to incite outright American rebellion. On Monday, March 5, 1770, a young wig-maker's apprentice kept pestering a British officer about an unpaid barber bill, although the bill was paid and the officer even had a receipt. A soldier (perhaps the same one) eventually butted the taunting kid with his mus-ket. Crowds began to assemble and the situation grew to a standoff as a few more soldiers arrived and the growing crowds got rowdy.

Church bells began ringing, and someone yelled "Fire!" (Ringing bells were often used as fire alarms.) Why and exactly when the bells were rung, incidentally, are widely argued points. They may have been ringing to an-nounce the impending danger, much like a modern siren; or they may not have started tolling until *after* the shout of "Fire!" Whatever the order of events, the British soldiers fired their guns, and five men eventually died from the wounds inflicted. Among the dead was an African-American for-mer slave named Crispus Attucks.

Patriot activists milked the incident for all it was worth. Paul Revere made and distributed his famous engraving of the "massacre," closely based on Henry Pelham's original, featuring the Old State House in the back-ground. The factually inaccurate image was used as propaganda to push the colonies closer to rebellion.

Today, people can still experience the Boston Massacre. Every year on March 5, the event is reenacted outside the Old State House by the Mass-achusetts Council on Minutemen and Militia and His Majesty's Fifth Reg-iment of Foot. Inside the Old State House, visitors can see Paul Revere's original Massacre engraving, as well as a number of Massacre-related items, including the coroner's report on Crispus Attucks and a musket be-lieved to have been used in the attack.

Once the rebellion was under way, the State House was host to another historic event—the first local reading of the Declaration of Independence. Though dated July 4, 1776, the text had taken considerable time arriving from Philadelphia. Finally, on July 18, the revolutionary document was read from the second-floor balcony. Later that evening, the carved figures of the royal lion and unicorn were torn down from the roof. Each year that reading is repeated on Independence Day, with the same Old State House balcony as its stage. Rooftop replicas of the lion and unicorn, however, are not pillaged following the modern-day ceremonies but remain intact as re-minders of pre-Revolutionary days.

After the reading of the Declaration of Independence, the onetime town, province, and courthouse officially became the Massachusetts State House. Meanwhile, King Street was renamed State Street, symbolically making royalty give way to the new republic. Cornhill's name was eventu-ally changed, too, in honor of the first U.S. president. In 1789, George Washington proudly rode a white horse down the long highway from Boston Neck to the Old State House as he made his first official entrance into Boston as president,.

A year before, on February 6, 1788, the Massachusetts Convention had ratified the United States Constitution in an official ceremony inside the

Old State House. Two hundred years later to the day, the U.S. Postal Service issued a twenty-two-cent stamp commemorating the anniversary of that event. The image was a 1793 engraving of the Old State House, designed by Richard Sheaff of Needham.

It was not long before the Commonwealth of Massachusetts outgrew the cramped quarters of this old building. Architect Charles Bulfinch was commissioned to design a new state house on John Hancock's former Beacon Hill properties. In 1798, with great pomp and procession, the state government officially moved from the old to the new structure.

From 1798 until 1881—when the old State House became a museum site operated by the Bostonian Society—the aging structure endured a variety of incarnations, face-lifts, and fires, as well as structural and decorative changes. Boston bought the building from the state in 1803. Between 1830 and 1841 it served as Boston's city hall and underwent a Greek Revival renovation still evident in its interior columns and curved doors. It was during that period, in 1835, that abolitionist William Lloyd Garrison was chased through Boston streets by an angry mob hoping to lynch him for his radical views; Garrison fled into the south entrance of the Old State House, finding shelter and support there from Mayor Theodore Lyman, Jr.

Save for that eleven-year stint as City Hall, the Old State House was primarily a commercial center for much of the nineteenth century, leased by the city to sundry shops and offices. By 1870, fifty of those tiny offices filled the small building; meanwhile, shopkeepers plastered the exterior with billboards, giving it a cheesy, carnival look.

The outside of the Old State House, by the way, was not always the natural red brick we see today. Though much of the brick dates from the original 1713 structure, it was painted a variety of stone, buff, and ochre colors for decades. Only in 1909 was the brick restored to its natural shade.

A fortuitous combination of good fate and good friends has been responsible for the endurance of the Old State House into the twenty-first century. Fire, of course, was a major threat since the beginning. Not only did fire create the space where the Old State House was built, when flames engulfed the 1657 wooden Town House in 1711, but fire also caused major damage to the new brick-based building, especially in 1747 and 1921.

An even greater threat to the Old State House, however, was public apathy and antagonism. As the building became an eyesore toward the end of the nineteenth century, some citizens wanted to raze it altogether. They argued that removing the building would eliminate the horrendous downtown traffic jams, which had been escalating even in the late 1800s. They reasoned further that the Old State House was no longer a "genuine relic" worth preserving, since it had been rebuilt and renovated so many times. At one point during the debate, the city of Chicago offered to buy the old building and move it brick by brick to the shores of Lake Michigan—giving it the honor it deserved. The threat apparently worked.

The historic structure's Boston saviors were noted antiquarian William Whitmore and a group that would later be known as the Bostonian Society. Though the building is still owned by the city of Boston, the Bostonian Society—the only organization solely committed to interpreting and preserving Boston history—has operated the Old State House as a museum since 1882. It was most recently reopened to the public in 1992 following a $7 million, eighteen-month structural renovation funded through the National Park Service. Meanwhile, a Bostonian Society campaign raised money for sparkling new exhibits, programs, and collections management.

Today, the Old State House is a fascinating potpourri of many architectural styles and multiple incarnations. Walls, staircases, roofs, and artifacts have come and gone—as have objects closely associated with the building's history. Those models of the lion and unicorn, for example—the symbols of British royalty that were torn down by jubilant Bostonians when independence from Britain was declared—were replaced for a century by carved scrolls. When the structure opened as a museum in 1882, however, replicas of the old creatures were put back in place.

By contrast, the carved wooden Sacred Cod, first installed in the Old State House in 1784 as "a memorial of the importance of Cod Fishery to the welfare of the Commonwealth," left and never returned. In 1798, the wooden fish was ceremoniously moved to the new State House, where it hangs today in the assembly hall of the House of Representatives.

Plenty of other historical objects are found in the newly redesigned, accessible, and interactive Old State House museum today. Permanent exhibits on the first floor explore Boston during the Revolution, as well as the history of the Old State House. In the second-floor galleries are changing exhibits featuring topics such as Boston's architectural history, the Great Fire of 1872, Boston's West End, and John Hancock and his family. An introductory video, located in a small first-floor chamber near the gift shop, is the perfect way to begin your visit.

Over its almost three hundred years of existence, the Old State House has played host to a variety of historical figures. One of the building's most unlikely, in a sense, was Britain's Queen Elizabeth II, who visited on July 11, 1976, thus becoming the first British sovereign to visit Boston. Participating in America's official bicentennial celebration, Her Majesty noted that colonial patriots like Paul Revere and Samuel Adams would surely have been surprised at her honored presence there—the queen is, after all, the great-great-great-great-granddaughter of King George III, who reigned over Britain and her colonies during the American War for Independence.

"But perhaps they would also have been pleased," she added with a royal grin.

THE ESSENTIALS

Address: Old State House Museum and Shop, corner of Washington and State streets, Boston. Bostonian Society Library, 15 State Street, 3rd Floor, Boston 02109. Two other retail stores at Quincy Market and Faneuil Hall, Boston. **Telephone:** (617) 720-1713 or (617) 720-3292. **Website:** www.bostonhistory.org. **Visitor Information:** The Old State House is open from 9:30 A.M. to 5:00 P.M. daily; closed Thanksgiving, Christmas Day, and New Year's Day. Small admission fee. Audio guides and printed material available in five languages. Gallery tours by appointment. Wheelchair lift and doorbell on Washington Street entrance; inside, only the first floor is wheelchair accessible.

The Bostonian Society Library is open from 9:30 A.M. to 4:30 P.M., Tuesday through Thursday; closed major holidays. Wheelchair accessible via entrance on Devonshire Street.

The Old State House is a stop on the Freedom Trail (see Chapter 10).

2 Faneuil Hall

YOU'D THINK the first question most visitors would ask when entering historic Faneuil Hall would be, "Why is it called the Cradle of Liberty?" Actually, some do come with a sense of the great events that happened in this hallowed structure: "Is this the place where patriot Sam Adams made all those Revolutionary speeches?" Indeed it is. And a statue of old Sam stands proudly in the building's backyard.

Still, one of the single commonest queries encountered there by National Park Service rangers is how to pronounce the dang thing (or, at least, how the building acquired such a curious name). Over the years, folks have come looking to find Filene Hall, Filene's Basement, Fenway Hall, Fanooly, and Finneal, not to mention a place called Nathaniel Mall.

As it turns out, Faneuil Hall was named for the man who paid for its construction in 1742, the local merchant Peter Faneuil. According to Boston tradition, it's pronounced *Fan*-el or *Fan*-yuhl, though Faneuil's French Huguenot ancestors undoubtedly said Feh-*noy*. Young Peter Faneuil and his peers added to the confusion, since his anglicized name, "P. Funel," was originally engraved on his tombstone in the Granary Burying Ground.

The hard-to-pronounce hall that Faneuil built soon became a landmark of American history. It is the place where Samuel Adams regularly advocated the overthrow of tyrannical British rule, where William Lloyd Garrison appealed for an end to slavery, where Susan B. Anthony denounced the second-class status of women, where Suzette LaFlesche, an Omaha, advocated Native American rights, and where John F. Kennedy gave his final preelection speech in 1960. Today Faneuil Hall can still be rented as a meeting place or political pulpit, but it's also regularly used for activities as diverse as concerts, commencements, debates, awards ceremonies, tours, memorial services, lectures, and naturalization services. In fact, one of the few things you specifically *can't* do in this building is plot to overthrow the government. Rules have obviously changed in Faneuil Hall since 1776.

Meanwhile, the lower level of the building remains true to its legacy as Boston's first major marketplace building—it's filled with a broad variety of shops. The structure's fourth floor has a historic use as well: the Ancient and Honorable Artillery Company, the first military company chartered in Western Hemisphere, still maintains a headquarters and museum in a spot they've occupied since 1746.

The man responsible for Faneuil Hall, Peter Faneuil (1700–1743), was a scandalously wealthy man by the time he was forty—reputedly the richest in all of Boston. He hadn't expected to gain his wealth by inheriting his uncle Andrew's fortune. Andrew Faneuil was a shipping magnate and landowner whose chosen heir was his nephew Benjamin, Peter's brother. But Andrew's will specifically forbade his heir to marry, and young Benjamin made the mistake of ignoring that instruction. As a result, Benjamin inherited just five shillings—essentially, pocket change—from Uncle Andrew. Young Peter, who remained single all his life, got the lion's share instead.

Peter Faneuil proved as talented at spending his fortune as he was in abstaining from nuptials. He was not an attractive fellow, to be sure; a contemporary source described him as "a fat, squat, lame man, hip-short with a high shoe." But he became Boston's "jolly bachelor," fond of the high life, prominent display, madeira wines, and his Tremont Street mansion with its seven acres of gardens.

He was also a bright merchant and an attentive public benefactor. One of his major concerns was the anarchistic method of food marketing in Boston. During the seventeenth and early eighteenth centuries, vendors would scatter throughout town, selling at irregular sites with irregular hours; others would travel from house to house, peddling from carts. Peter Faneuil was among those who advocated a permanent downtown market where buyers could take care of all their needs at once—the precursor of modern one-stop shopping.

So Faneuil made the town an offer it couldn't refuse: he would build an open marketplace structure in downtown Dock Square and donate it to the city. Actually, the town could refuse the offer—and almost did. The final vote at town meeting was 367 yeas to 360 nays. (Many merchants feared that the competitive nature of central markets would drive down their prices and profits; a group of them had already defeated another attempt at a Boston marketplace several years earlier.)

Almost as an afterthought, Faneuil also proposed that an auditorium, or meeting hall, be built on the second floor of his new marketplace. This would provide Boston with its own version of the English guildhall, in which official meetings of the town's voting citizens were held. Boston, one of the king of England's first and finest colonies, had the most democratic government of its time. Until 1822, local decisions were made in town meetings, where voters assembled, debated, and decided the issues. Before Faneuil Hall was built, such gatherings were often held in borrowed "meetinghouses," as Puritan churches were called, or the small Town House (the precursor of the Old State House). Hence, the great second-floor chamber at Faneuil's new hall became Boston's first and only "town meeting hall."

The completed 1742 building, designed by artist John Smibert, was considered quite beautiful in its day. It was two stories high, with elegant side arches, a beautiful Georgian design, and open arcades on the ground-floor merchant level. Red Medford brick, imported English glass and metal trim, and a gilded grasshopper weather vane all added to its allure.

Six months after the hall's completion, Peter Faneuil died of "too much good living" at the age of forty-three. A public memorial was held for him in the hall. His brother Benjamin and Benjamin's wife, Mary, inherited the rest of Peter's wealth, while the city kept the building.

Sculptor Anne
Whitney's statue of
Revolutionary-era
activist Sam Adams
stands guard
behind Faneuil Hall.

So much did the town love Faneuil Hall, in fact, that it rebuilt the building when it burned down in 1761, financing the project by public lottery. In 1805, Boston paid to double the hall's size to today's heftier proportions and hired celebrated architect Charles Bulfinch to oversee the restoration. The cost of $56,700 was covered partly by the sale of Fort Hill and partly by taxation. Not until 1898 did the Bulfinch Faneuil Hall of 1805–6 undergo major structural changes. At that time, the city appropriated $104,500 to update, fortify, and fireproof the aging building, and to provide it with new furniture.

The most recent renovation of the building was essentially completed in 1992. This $6 million overhaul improved wheelchair access, added elevator service to all four floors, made the restrooms more accessible, repaired the roof, restored exterior brick and woodwork, reinforced the structure, plastered and repainted the interior, updated electrical and mechanical systems, improved the heating, added much-needed air conditioning as well as new sound and light systems, rehabilitated and redesigned the ground floor, and conserved the Hall's largest piece of artwork, *Webster's Reply to Hayne.*

*

Since its earliest days, Faneuil Hall was a space for all seasons and all reasons. Peter Faneuil, for example, was the first but not the only Bostonian to lie in state in the hall. The body of Crispus Attucks—an African-American killed in the 1770 Boston Massacre—was taken there on the way to the Granary Burying Ground. The bodies of Wendell Phillips, Daniel Webster, and other charismatic orators who once spoke at Faneuil Hall were also laid out there for crowds to mourn.

Despite its many and varied functions, it was certainly the hall's constant use by a cast of American Revolutionary–era characters that earned Faneuil Hall its everlasting nickname, the Cradle of Liberty. Beginning in 1763, patriot Sam Adams and his colleagues ushered in the greatest period of town meetings in Boston history—thereby making Faneuil Hall a focus of revolutionary activity. Adams, James Otis, Dr. Joseph Warren, and other "Sons of Liberty" could often been seen there, arguing against such British impositions as the 1764 Sugar Act, the 1765 Stamp Act, the 1767 Townshend Acts, or the 1773 tax on tea. In 1772, a meeting within the hall created the first "committees of correspondence" in the colonies. When such meetings grew too large for the hall, incidentally, they were often hustled over to the larger space at the Old South Meeting House. Sometimes, however, more heated assemblages spilled into violent episodes in the streets.

Supervisory park ranger John Manson also loves to point out the ironies in Faneuil Hall's history: Nineteenth-century abolitionists like William Lloyd Garrison and Frederick Douglass held forth there, but the Faneuil family fortune was partly earned from the slave trade. Susan B. Anthony, other suffragists, and modern-day women's rights advocates met there; on the other hand, so did the Massachusetts Association to Oppose the Further Extension of Suffrage, in 1915. Patriots assembled at Faneuil Hall to protest unfair British taxation, but Faneuil family boats were among those pillaged in the Tea Party affair; moreover, members of our own Internal Revenue Service have met there to honor their most efficient tax collectors! Colonial patriots partied and celebrated there; so, too, did British soldiers, who used Faneuil Hall as a barracks and a theater during their occupation of Boston.

Other than some Medford brick on the exterior back wall and the weather vane, none of the original 1742 building remains today. That vane, however, is one of Faneuil Hall's most distinctive touches. Peter Faneuil copied the hall's grasshopper from vanes atop the London Royal Exchange and his uncle's mansion. Periodically refurbished over the years, the thirty-eight-pound, fifty-two-inch grasshopper is considered an original: it still has a copper interior, a gilded exterior, glass-doorknob eyes, and a copper vest, into which "time capsules" are periodically tucked.

Designed by Shem Drowne, the grasshopper has left its perch more than once over the centuries. It hopped off during a 1755 earthquake, was knocked off during an 1889 flag-lowering, and was removed several times for repairs. It was also stolen once, in 1974. After a weeklong, citywide search—and the retrieval of twenty-eight other stolen weather vanes in the course of that search—the gilded grasshopper was located under a pile of flags in the Faneuil Hall cupola. (The reason for the grasshopper's flight has never been discovered.) The grasshopper's most recent excursion was out for regilding, and over to the Museum of Fine Arts, Boston, where it briefly sat on display during the 1990–92 renovation of Faneuil Hall. It was one of the rare opportunities Bostonians have had to meet the gilded insect almost eye to eye—since its normal perch is eighty feet above ground level.

Many of the distinctive features of today's Faneuil Hall originated in the Bulfinch enlargement of 1805–6. During that renovation a third story was added, and floor space was doubled as the building was widened. Doric and Ionic columns were added inside—typical of the Federalist neoclassical style that Bulfinch preferred and that is so apparent in his architectural masterpiece, the Massachusetts State House on Beacon Hill.

Bulfinch also created the galleries that circle the Great Hall, providing a place where women could watch lectures, debates, and other goings-on down below. Women, of course, could not vote in town meetings, since eighteenth-century law specified that only male, property-owning, church-going citizens over the age of twenty-one could vote. (It is assumed that most, if not all, of these males where white as well.) Historical statistics show that those stipulations eliminated 90 percent of the population.

Most of the artwork that graces the interior of the Great Hall is from the nineteenth and twentieth centuries. Much of it was not created for Faneuil Hall and was first displayed elsewhere. The "artificial stone" eagle on the back gallery, for example—molded from a mixture of lime putty and pulverized marble—was made for a State Street bank in 1798, then moved to the Great Hall when the bank building was demolished in 1824. The large clock set below the eagle was the 1850 gift of Boston schoolchildren, purchased with their pennies. Two paintings that once hung in the Great Hall —images of the British monarch George III and of Peter Faneuil—are gone, probably whisked away during the British evacuation of Boston in 1776. In their place are portraits of a host of men linked with Faneuil Hall's past.

While the nineteenth-century paintings and busts in Faneuil Hall are originals—including G.P.A. Healy's mammoth 1850 *Webster's Reply to Hayne,* immortalized in social studies textbooks across the nation—the eighteenth-century images are copies, mostly done in oils. During the centennial celebrations of 1876, the original oils—colonial portraits of Revolutionary heroes—were moved to Boston's Museum of Fine Arts, where they remain to this day. Part of the rationale was that the artworks were endangered in a firetrap like Faneuil Hall (unfireproofed, remember, until 1898); part, too, was Boston's fine new art museum provided better access and display for the paintings.

Some artistic enigmas to ponder: Why was Washington's horse painted with his backside facing the viewer in Gilbert Stuart's painting? John Manson's theory is that the painter was in a rush to finish the work so borrowed the idea from a Rubens painting, without much thought as to the consequences. (Others suggest it was designed to draw attention to Washington rather than the steed.) And why, in Dennis Malone Carter's 1857 *Retreat from Breed's Hill,* do all the soldiers have the same face? A commentary on brother fighting brother? Or perhaps on the family of man?

"The family of man" is an accurate phrase to use at Faneuil Hall, since of the multitude of historic busts and paintings displayed in the Great Hall only one depicts a woman—the renowned feminist editor, suffragist, abolitionist, and women's rights advocate Lucy Stone (1818–1893). A bust of Stone, sculpted by Lloyd Lillie (who also did the Red Auerbach and James Michael Curley near Fanuel Hall, and nineteen feminists at Seneca Falls), was installed in 2001. She was the first woman to organize a meeting at Faneuil Hall; at that 1873 event, dubbed the New England Women's Tea Party, Stone and an animated overflow crowd complained that one century after the Boston Tea Party and America's War for Independence, women were still suffering "taxation without representation," since they were denied the right to vote.

Another long-overdue figure in Faneuil Hall was that of escaped slave, radical abolitionist, and progressive editor Frederick Douglass (ca. 1817–1895). Installed in 1995, and also crafted by Lloyd Lillie, the bust is dedicated to Mary Shannon, the beloved executive secretary of the Boston Art Commission and advocate for public art, who passed away in 1994.

On the fourth floor, two stories above the Great Hall, is the home of the Ancient and Honorable Artillery Company of Massachusetts. The company was chartered in 1638 and began lodging at Faneuil Hall in 1746, just four years after it was built. Today, the company maintains there a meeting hall, a library, and a museum of military history, which contains antique and modern firearms, flags, and other artifacts.

Meanwhile, down below, twentieth-first-century merchants carry on their business in the old marketplace as merchants did in 1742. The setting has changed: old arcade entrances have been replaced by doors and walls, and the many scattered stalls of yore are now divided into larger areas for a variety of new shops and services. An information desk staffed by National Park Service rangers is also located on the market level, as is an elevator with access to all floors. Unlike many Boston historic buildings, Faneuil Hall has never been in danger of demolition—perhaps because of these merchants, who have always provided a visible reminder of Peter Faneuil's wish and his legacy.

"Besides, the merchants here have always paid rent," observed one former tenant. "And that may make this the only self-supporting monument in America!"

THE ESSENTIALS

Address: 0 Dock Square, Boston, MA 02109; at the head of Faneuil Hall Marketplace, Dock Square, Boston. **Telephone:** National Park Service office, (617) 242-5675; city superintendent, (617) 635-3105; Ancient and Honorable Artillery Company, (617) 227-1638; Boston National Historical Park Downtown Visitor Center, (617) 242-5642. **Websites:** www.nps.gov/bost/Faneuil_Hall; Ancient and Honorable Artillery Company: www.ahacsite.org. **Visitor Information:** Great Hall open 9:00 A.M. to 5:00 P.M. daily except Thanksgiving, Christmas Day, and New Year's Day, or during city-sponsored events. Free. Interpretive talks every half hour, 9:30 A.M. to 4:30 p.m. Copies of *Boston Town Crier* contain news of Boston National Historical Park and seasonal events; available at Faneuil Hall, NPS visitor centers, and cooperating sites on the Freedom Trail. Wheelchair access via elevator on ground floor; restrooms accessible.

Faneuil Hall is a site on the Freedom Trail (see Chapter 10) and the Boston Women's Heritage Trail (see Chapter 36).

3 The Old South Meeting House

THOUGH IT'S lodged amid the noisy bustle of Boston's Downtown Crossing shopping district, the Old South Meeting House retains the proud look and aura of a bygone era. As the second home to one of Boston's earliest Puritan congregations, the meetinghouse was first and foremost a church. Outside, you can still see its soaring white steeple pointing toward the heavens. Inside are other vestiges of that sacred, historic past—numbered box pews, wraparound balconies, a chandelier, Doric columns, a lofty preaching pulpit, and multipaned window sashes.

But the building's importance to American history isn't merely religious. It was here, in December 1773, that patriots gathered to protest the British tax on tea and Samuel Adams gave the secret signal to descend on Griffin's Wharf, where they threw the biggest Tea Party in history.

It was also on this site that black poet Phillis Wheatley worshipped, Ben Franklin was baptized, General George Washington bemoaned the British desecration of the town, Boston's "Mother Goose" sang hymns, Joseph Warren decried the horrors of the Boston Massacre, and twentieth-century free-speech advocates held court. It was here, too, that the movement to preserve historic urban structures won its first victory, more than a century ago.

Despite its obvious importance—and despite ongoing lectures, concerts, educational programs, and special events at the Old South Meeting House today—an unsettling number of Bostonians and tourists know surprisingly little about the building and its history. Henry Lee, a longtime member of the Old South Association, suggests, "For long periods of time the Old South was a well-kept secret. Unlike the Paul Revere House, USS *Constitution*, and even the Old State House, it's one site on the Freedom Trail that doesn't have instant recognition."

One of the greatest misconceptions about the meetinghouse relates to the building's function. With a belfry and steeple outside and pulpit and pews inside, it certainly *looks* like a church. But though it began its life as a Puritan house of worship, it hasn't served as a church since 1872.

The valuable downtown corner of Milk and Washington streets, where Old South has stood since 1729, was once Governor John Winthrop's garden. (Winthrop served as colonial governor of Massachusetts for four terms between 1630 and his death in 1649.) In 1669, the Reverend John Norton's wife, Mary, held the title and donated the plot to a Puritan offshoot group who called their congregation the Third Church of Christ. On the site this dissident congregation of twenty-eight built a medieval-looking place of worship remembered as the Cedar Meeting House.

The group's split from Boston's original First Church arose from a complex theological argument over baptism and membership rights known as the "halfway covenant." Theological arguments were very much a part of daily life in seventeenth-century Boston. Staunch Puritans and even later Congregationalists, for example, banned Christmas celebrations as "pagan rituals" adopted by Roman Catholics. Moreover, the Puritans felt that musical instruments—including organs—defiled the pure word of God and had no place in church.

The Cedar Meeting House endured until 1729, when its growing congregation—popularly known as the Old South Church by then—tore it down, replacing it with a newer, larger, brick building. This simple, elegant Georgian structure opened for religious services on April 26, 1730—and is essentially the one we know today as the Old South Meeting House.

It's true that the authentic-looking pews were crafted in 1947, and the belfry is empty: Old South's original bell was discarded after it cracked while tolling an 1815 fire alarm, and its replacement was moved to a new Copley Square church in 1872. Still, a good deal of the building's fabric and furnishings—including the exterior brick walls, wooden elements of the steeple, the weather vane, and the southeast stairs between the east galleries—has remained from the original building, constructed between 1729 and 1770. The 1768 tower clock, for instance, is still in place. Its archaic mechanism of brass, wood and iron rods, gears, braces, and pendulum—

The Old South Meeting House survived British abuse, the Great Fire of 1872, and the wrecking ball of downtown developers.

installed by Gawen Brown in pre-Revolutionary times—still keeps excellent time.

Over the years, Old South has been an ever-evolving building, decorated and redecorated to fit changing tastes, styles, and uses. During the nineteenth century, for example, its red brick exterior was covered with white or gray paint, and the normally plain interior walls and ceilings were festooned with gaudy Victorian trompe l'oeil paintings. In the 1870s, the U.S. Post Office turned it into a wide-open mail-sorting and shuffling room and even added two unsightly chambers off the sides of the slim front tower. Those bulky exterior chambers were removed after the postal service departed for more permanent quarters in 1876.

Thanks to historical research, today's Old South is much closer in substance, style, color, and form to the eighteenth-century meetinghouse begun in 1729. Though the architect or master craftsman who designed the Old South remains unknown, the skilled individuals who worked on it included masons Joshua Blanchard and Nathanael Emmes (both men carved their initials in cornerstones). The builders and designers were probably influenced by other Boston church designs of the time, which in turn were inspired by the London churches of Christopher Wren. The Old South's interior, however, was clearly based on that of the 1669 Cedar Meeting House, which it was built to replace.

The Old South congregation wanted their meetinghouse to be as simple, unadorned, and pure as their services (although the congregation's affluence was apparent in the building's vast size and high spire). Hence the building was constructed plain, long, and low, with simple red brick laid in an alternating pattern called Flemish Bond. The roof was slate—sturdy enough to survive the 1744 earthquake, albeit with major repairs. The windows were clear glass, not stained. The tower—topped by a belfry, steeple, bull's-eye windows, and gilded weather vane—reached 183 feet skyward.

The Georgian exterior was matched by stark classical detail inside. Pews were built both in the slip and the box styles; the former were long, narrow seats, while the latter were private rectangular enclaves, each protected by a low wall and a latching half door. Those box pews were rented to wealthier families, who decorated them to fit their individual tastes with, for example, special fabrics, varied seating arrangements, assorted shelves, and foot warmers. The two layers of upstairs galleries included seating for "less desirable" elements of Boston society: slaves, servants, the town poor, and teenage boys.

Up front, of course, was the pulpit. The version in place today is the 1857 pulpit, buttressed by the central "wineglass" portion of the one donated in 1808. (After 1872 there was no pulpit whatsoever in the meetinghouse; during restorations executed in 1910, however, portions of the 1857 and 1808 pulpits were merged and reinstalled.) Ministers preached from the Old South pulpit for the building's first 143 years—though fiery orators of all types have held forth there over the centuries. From eighteenth-century radicals like Sam Adams and Joseph Warren to twenty-first-century figures like Al Gore, Coretta Scott King, and David McCullough, speakers have regularly used this meetinghouse to discuss, debate, and disseminate both religious and secular issues and information. (Two lecture series hosted by the Old South over the years have been their own Middays at the Meeting House and the prestigious Ford Hall Forum, Boston's oldest institution for the discussion of ideas.)

Whereas eighteenth- and nineteenth-century speakers counted on good lungs, the fine old sounding board above the pulpit, and window light to make themselves heard and seen, modern orators usually use the Old South's state-of-the-art sound and lighting systems—installed as part of the building's massive $7.2 million renovation of the mid-to-late 1990s. Today's lecturers have another advantage: they can keep track of the time using the replica of the 1805 Simon Willard clock that hangs on the south gallery's balustrade. In early days, however, ministers' sermons were timed by a large hourglass—which was flipped several times, incidentally, since Sunday services lasted up to six hours.

Faneuil Hall was often the venue of choice for Bostonians to gather and debate the topics of the day. But until that public hall was enlarged to its present size (in the Charles Bulfinch project of 1805–6) the Old South Meeting House was the town's largest and most accessible indoor space. Hence, both before and since 1806, the grand auditorium at Old South has remained Boston's prime space for public meetings and cultural events when Faneuil Hall is unavailable or under repair. This was the case just prior to the Revolution, and again when Faneuil Hall closed for major renovations from 1990 to 1992.

Today, the multimedia exhibit "Voices of Protest" and the audio installation "If These Walls Could Speak" tell the stories of compelling figures from Old South's past, such as African-American poet and slave Phillis Wheatley and George Robert Twelves Hewes, a participant in the Boston Tea Party. Other figures, like Boston mayor James Michael Curley and birth control advocate Margaret Sanger, reveal the controversial history of free speech that continues to this day.

The controversy for which Old South will always be remembered, of course, is as a center for the debate that preceded America's War for Independence. Three favorite stories in particular illustrate Old South's role in that heated pre-Revolutionary discourse:

The first tale concerns the gathering of a reported five thousand men who crammed into the hall on December 16, 1773, shortly before embarking on the Boston Tea Party. Since the building's legal capacity is now just 650 people—plenty of space for the concerts, theatrical presentations, lectures, and even weddings that take place there today—historians can't quite account for that five thousand figure. Some joke that Americans were smaller in the eighteenth century—a popular myth with virtually no historic basis; others say that colonial observers tended to vastly overestimate crowds. The galleries were also bigger at the time.

Colonials might also have been wedged in the windows, as they were when a second well-known Revolutionary event took place in 1775. Dr. Joseph Warren reportedly had to climb through the pulpit window to give Old South's annual Boston Massacre Oration, since the crowd had already completely filled the building. Warren was ready for one of the bravest

speeches of his life—and theatrically dressed for the occasion in a Ciceron-
ian toga.

The third story is much less amusing for lovers of Boston's historic
structures. In 1775, when British forces occupied the city, their troops took
over Old South, ripped out most of its interior furnishings, chopped up the
old pews and pulpit for firewood, and turned the hall into a riding school
for General John Burgoyne and his horses. After the British had been
forcefully evacuated from the city in 1776, General George Washington
viewed and reviled the ruin. "My wife swears she can still smell the British horses in the stairwell!" once insisted Lowell Warren, former president of the Old South Association and a collateral descendant of General
Warren.

Still, the Revolution was not the roughest period for the Old South.
There was the Great Fire of 1872, a massive blaze that consumed sixty
acres and 776 buildings between Washington Street and the harbor.
Miraculously, the meetinghouse sustained only minor exterior damage.
But even before the fire broke out, the Old South congregation had voted
to build a new church in the Back Bay—the Copley Square structure now
popularly known as the *New* Old South Church. With that congregation
went many precious artifacts and furnishings—including the bell from the
now-empty belfry—as well as title to valuable real estate the church had
acquired.

Once the Old South Meeting House was no longer occupied by a congregation, savvy developers began plotting to demolish the aging building
and use its prime downtown acreage for commercial pursuits. In 1874, the
land sitting under Old South was valued at $400,000 (a vast sum in that
day's dollars). But the public outcry over plans to level this historic building began one of the proudest moments in Boston and American history.

Within the museum's creatively crafted audio and multimedia exhibits
is the story of the saving of the Old South Meeting House: Philanthropist
Mary Hemenway, a supporter of the (then) innovative kindergarten movement, led the effort to save the Old South from the wrecker's ball. Hemenway not only donated substantial money and time to preserving the building but also established Old South's earliest American history educational
programs for both teachers and students, collectively called Old South
Work, in 1883. Meanwhile, several of Boston's most preeminent citizens—
such as Wendell Phillips, Julia Ward Howe, James Russell Lowell, and
Ralph Waldo Emerson—climbed to the pulpit for public readings of their
works and to plead for the building's preservation. (Visitors can still listen
to some of Phillips's impassioned oratory in "If These Walls Could Speak.")
Local citizens, especially women from Boston's "better" families, rallied
and organized countless community fairs, balls, and fund-raisers. Finally,
in 1877, the Old South Association was formed—a private, nonprofit organization that continues to operate the Old South Meeting House to this
day.

The late historian Walter Muir Whitehill, former president of the Old
South Association, best summarized America's first urban historic preser-
vation success when he called the saving of Old South "the first instance in
Boston where respect for the historical and architectural heritage of the

city triumphed over considerations of profit, expediency, laziness and vulgar convenience."

Since 1878 the Old South has been a museum. Until new, modern exhibits were installed in the late twentieth century, however, that museum remained a curious nineteenth-century-style "reliquary" containing a hodgepodge of interesting but sometimes strange objects encased in dark, low boxes. Today, the most fascinating of those artifacts have been integrated into colorful interactive multimedia displays. Among them: a vial of tea leaves from the Boston Tea Party; a tea set fused into a Dali-esque whole by the 1872 fire; John Hancock's lap desk; and an original volume of Phillis Wheatley's 1773 poetry book, *Poems on Various Subjects, Religious and Moral*. (Wheatley, incidentally, has grown into one of Old South's favorite historic foremothers; the tale of her arrival in colonial Boston on a slave ship, her membership in the Old South congregation, and her accolades as the first African-American to publish a book of poetry have made her a popular and perennial role model for schoolchildren and adults alike.)

Today Old South still faces challenges of survival. Granted, its recent three-year, $7.2 million renovation—which included massive structural improvements, new subterranean office and classroom space, mechanical and systems upgrades, increased wheelchair access, and the new exhibits— was a giant step into the twenty-first century. But will its vibrant array of programs and publications, and its secure place on the Freedom Trail, the Boston Women's Heritage Trail, and the Literary Trail, ensure that the building is preserved for generations of history lovers to come?

Bostonians should heed the words spoken by Wendell Phillips in his 1876 plea to save the Old South: "I can only say we come here to save what our fathers consecrated to the memories of the most successful struggle the race has ever made for the liberties of man. You spend half a million for a school-house. What school so eloquent as these walls?

"The saving of this landmark is the best monument you can erect to the men of the Revolution."

THE ESSENTIALS

Address: 310 Washington Street, Boston, MA 02108. Located at Downtown Crossing, corner of Washington and Milk streets, on the Freedom Trail. **Telephone:** (617) 482-6439. **Website:** www.oldsouthmeetinghouse.org. **Visitor Information:** Open 9:30 A.M. to 5:00 P.M. daily, April through October; open 10:00 A.M. to 4:00 P.M. daily, November through March; closed Thanksgiving, Christmas Eve, Christmas Day, and New Year's Day. Small admission fee.

Ongoing programs include Middays at the Meeting House, Music at the Meeting House, Paul Revere Lecture Series, Boston Spring Lecture Series, and the annual Boston Tea Party Re-enactment. See website for times and topics.

The Old South Meeting House is a site on the Freedom Trail (see Chapter 10), the Boston Women's Heritage Trail (see Chapter 36), and the Literary Trail of Greater Boston. Special tours also available through the Old South itself; call for details. Building and restrooms are fully wheelchair accessible.

4 The Paul Revere House

THE SOMEWHAT SMALL, dark clapboard house at 19 North Square is an odd sight amid the tall brick buildings of the North End. And given the structure's almost medieval demeanor, it should come as no surprise that it's the only seventeenth-century wooden dwelling still standing on its original site in downtown Boston. The building's main claim to fame, however, is that the illustrious Revolutionary War hero Paul Revere owned and lived in the house from 1770 to 1800.

Today, more than 200,000 guests annually visit Revere's former abode, now a beautifully maintained museum operated by the Paul Revere Memorial Association. Most visitors presumably come to learn more about the Boston patriot and his famous "midnight ride." In the process they learn about "the man behind the myth," about family and home life in colonial America, and about the War for Independence—while discovering the multicultural heritage of one of Boston's oldest neighborhoods.

Paul Revere was not born at 19 North Square, nor did he die there. He bought the home in 1770 at the age of thirty-five. By then he was an established silversmith, a trade learned from his French immigrant father, Apollos Rivoire. The house was sturdy if not terribly stylish (it was already ninety years old when he purchased it), and the neighborhood was perfect for Revere's needs.

North Square, also known as Clark's Square, was a long, narrow triangle just a block from the busy waterfront docks and taverns. In the late eighteenth century, the square had occasional markets, a town pump, a watch house, and a meetinghouse. Revere's neighbors included mast makers, spinsters, a soap boiler, government officials, and merchants. Moreover, his own silversmith shop was at the head of Clark's Wharf, just a short walk away.

Only five months after his first wife, Sarah, died of childbirth complications in 1773, Revere married his second wife, Rachel Walker. Though his remarriage may seem hasty by contemporary standards, it was in keeping with the custom of the time; most eighteenth-century men and women remarried as soon as possible after the death of a spouse, to provide care and support for their large families.

The stocky, dark, hardworking Revere eventually fathered sixteen children, eight with each wife. It was a reasonable number, considering the high childhood mortality rate of the time, and the fact that his oldest and youngest children were thirty years apart. Coincidentally, everything his offspring did seemed to happen in fives: Revere had five children living with him when he moved to the North Square; five children died before their fifth birthdays; only five outlived him; and between five and eight lived with him in the North Square house at any given time. The last fact

The "Best Chamber" at the Paul Revere House is decorated with furniture and furnishings typical of a successful late eighteenth-century middle-class artisan like Revere.

helps answer one common query of Revere House visitors: How did the whole family fit in these four rooms? All sixteen Revere children never simultaneously lived under the same roof. Moreover, Revere's home had a third-story addition at the front—an addition that was removed during the renovations of 1906–8. A wooden lean-to outside the Revere kitchen also added space, but that structure too is long gone.

Just as surprising to visitors as Revere's family life are the real facts about his role in the American War for Independence. Contrary to popular belief, Revere wasn't considered a hero in his own time. Furthermore, Henry Wadsworth Longfellow's legendary 1861 poem, "Paul Revere's Ride" —which helped make both Revere and Longfellow household names—was inaccurate at best.

> Listen, my children, and you shall hear
> Of the midnight ride of Paul Revere,
> On the eighteenth of April, in Seventy-five;
> Hardly a man is now alive
> Who remembers that famous day and year. . . .

One, if by land, and two, if by sea;
And I on the opposite shore will be,
Ready to ride and spread the alarm
Through every Middlesex village and farm. . . .

Revere did ride into the countryside on the night of April 18, 1775, to warn colonists that the British regulars were coming. But so did William Dawes, Samuel Prescott, and some three dozen other men whose names just weren't as easy to rhyme as *Revere*. The message they were all delivering was that the redcoats, camped out on Boston Common, were traveling "by sea," that is, across the Charles River to Cambridge. From there, they would march to Concord to seize and destroy colonial stores of arms. Revere, as it turns out, boated to Charlestown, then borrowed a steed. He was captured on the way to Concord, however, so never finished his ride. Dr. Prescott did, and the colonists in the countryside were duly warned—and prepared—for the battles of Lexington and Concord, which ensued the following morning (see also Chapters 5 and 13).

Visiting the Revere House today, one quickly realizes that Revere was equally—if not more—important as an "industrial revolutionary." In a lighted display case are samples of what Revere did best—metalwork. He fashioned silver into spoons, bowls, tea sets, and dental wiring. He created copper plates to reproduce political cartoons and engravings. He cast bells large and small, including an enormous 1804 specimen on display in the courtyard outside the house. Nine hundred and fifty-nine bells in all, from cowbells to the church bell at King's Chapel, were made in his family's foundry between 1792 and 1828.

Though history books often call Paul Revere a silversmith, his contemporaries used the term *goldsmith*. During Revere's time, American goldsmiths like himself worked largely in silver, while their British counterparts still made much from gold; British clients apparently had lots more money to spend than their colonial cousins.

In his later years, Revere became a true industrialist, rolling sheet copper at his Canton mill—copper that covered, among other things, the bottom of "Old Ironsides" and the top of the new State House. By that time, the busy entrepreneur had moved from North Square into a larger house on Charter Street. But the story is there in Revere's old home. Incidentally, the Revere firm's descendant company, Revere Copper Products, Inc., is still in business.

Though most visitors come to 19 North Square to learn more about Paul Revere, the Revere House is much more than the colonial silversmith's onetime abode. Its history began in 1676, when one of Boston's many "Great Fires" consumed much of the North End, clearing the land it later occupied. (The house destroyed in that blaze was owned by Puritan minister Increase Mather, whose son Cotton Mather gained later notoriety for his vocal support of the Salem witchcraft trials and executions.)

Some four years after the fire, the structure that would become the Revere House was built. It was purchased by a wealthy merchant named Robert Howard in 1681. Though it looks downright primitive by contemporary standards, the house was considered spacious and modern in the late seventeenth century. The asymmetrical building had a steeply pitched roof with a prominent front overhang above the second story. Light filtered in through the diamond-paned casement windows, while broad, open fireplaces heated the major chambers. Covering the house's heavy timber frame was clapboard siding. The foundation was fieldstone, the shingles wood. (Such wooden construction was soon to become obsolete, by the way, since several devastating fires eventually convinced Bostonians that brick and stone structures had better survival rates in a congested urban setting.)

At the Revere House today, visitors see an amalgam of Howard's early colonial period and Revere's Revolutionary-era occupancy, which began ninety years later. True to Howard's time is the house's current two-story construction; as noted above, when Revere was in residence, a third-story addition was attached at the front. While three of the house's chambers reflect Revere's decor and furnishings, the fourth—a large first-floor room called the Hall—is set up to simulate Howard's era.

The Hall's odd-looking furniture—which some visitors perceive as Oriental or Spanish—is typical of the late seventeenth century, as are the bare floors and rug-covered tables. Several of the house's oldest items are also exhibited in the Hall, including a hand-colored 1635 Dutch map. (In early colonial times, maps were much more common as wall decorations than paintings or drawings.) On the other hand, the Hall also houses some historical incongruities. The beautiful exposed post-and-beam house frame, for example, would have been cased sometime in the eighteenth century—after Howard's occupancy but before Revere's. Moreover, the Hall's seventeenth-century kitchen fireplace doesn't belong there; the original survives in the fieldstone cellar, an area now closed to the public.

In the rest of the house, the furniture and furnishings are those of a successful middle-class artisan like Paul Revere. Six of the items on display, including a veneered bow-front dresser, an upholstered chair, and a sewing table in the upstairs "Best Chamber," are Revere family pieces.

The owner of the house two doors away was Nathaniel Hichborn, Revere's first cousin. "Whenever there are Hitchbourn [*sic*] names in Boston," wrote Revere biographer Esther Forbes, "there were sure to be Reveres nearby." So it is in the Granary Burying Ground in death, and so it was on the cobbled streets of North Square in life.

Boatbuilder Hichborn bought the handsome three-story brick mansion two doors down from Revere's house a few years after cousin Paul moved in. The English Renaissance structure, sometimes labeled early Georgian, was built for glazier Moses Pierce around 1711. Though the homes were but thirty years apart in construction (separated by a third house, where the Revere courtyard and herb gardens sit today), they were worlds apart in style.

The Revere House's wood exterior and craggy angles stand in sharp contrast to the Hichborn's brick walls, low roof, shallow-arched window crests, and relative symmetry. The huge old fireplaces in Paul's place looked archaic next to the smaller, heat-efficient, painted ones at Nathaniel's. (Neither house had any indoor amenities more convenient than a chamber pot.)

Operated by the Paul Revere Memorial Association since 1970, the Pierce-Hichborn House offers guests a fascinating architectural and cultural comparison to Revere's. It also provides office space for site staff and an education center for small classes. Unlike those at the Revere House, all Pierce-Hichborn House tours are guided and take place on a set schedule.

Between their eighteenth-century lives as patriot residences and their twentieth-century incorporation as museums, the Revere and Hichborn houses filled other important social functions. During the nineteenth century, the center of Boston's upper- and middle-class life shifted from the North End to other sections of town. The North End, in turn, began playing host to new generations of immigrants (see Chapter 37). Irish, Jewish, Portuguese and (finally) Italian newcomers crowded into the increasingly impoverished neighborhood. Houses like the Hichborn and Revere became tenements upstairs and shops downstairs. Had they not been adaptable to tenement life, the two homes might have met the wrecking ball long before the turn of the century.

The account of the Paul Revere House in the *Milton Record* of 1905 would hardly be recognized today: "It's a quaint, dirty, dilapidated wooden building with queer chimneys and overhanging upper story. . . . The lower floor is occupied by a Hebrew green grocery shop while the upper two floors are ordinary North End tenements." Among the retail stores that set up on the ground floor of the Revere House in the 1800s were a candy store, the Banca Italiana, F.A. Goduti cigars, and a Jewish vegetable shop.

In order to ensure that the former Revere house would not be destroyed, John P. Reynolds, Jr., a Revere great-grandson, bought it in 1902. Over the next few years, the Paul Revere Memorial Association was organized, and architect Joseph Chandler was hired to restore the building. On April 18, 1908, the hundred and thirty-third anniversary of the overblown "midnight ride," the house officially opened its doors to the public as a museum.

Today, the Paul Revere Memorial Association sponsors historic research, publishes popular and scholarly works, oversees the house's furnishings, mounts rotating exhibits, creates afternoon activities for youngsters, and offers a variety of educational programs for children and adults. In one popular school program, "Paul Revere: The Man Behind the Myth," students examine letters, advertisements, and reproduction artifacts, looking for clues about Revere's personality and his contributions to the Revolution, as well as his large family and many business ventures.

Revere House education programs also focus on the North End's rich cultural history, examining its various immigrant groups. Director Nina Zannieri even admits that the thought of redecorating one of the rooms in the Revere House—presumably the "Children's Room"—as a nineteenth-century tenement space has a certain appeal. It would certainly fit into her underlying philosophy.

"In our presentations we try to talk about how the house was used during, before, and after Revere. Not to denigrate Paul Revere, an important person whose business career requires much more study, but these houses are dynamic, not static. Some people may prefer houses that deal with an isolated time frame. But ours really reflect change."

THE ESSENTIALS
Address: 19 North Square, Boston, MA 02113. **Telephone:** (617) 523-2338. **Website:** www.paulreverehouse.org. **Visitor Information:** Open 9:30 A.M. to 5:15 P.M. daily, April 14 to October 31; 9:30 A.M. to 4:15 P.M. daily the rest of year. Revere House tour is self-guided, with interpreters on duty. The only guided tours are at Pierce-Hichborn house; call for information and times. Small admission fee for each house; combination tickets available. Both houses partly wheelchair accessible, with assistance; call for further information.

The Paul Revere House is a site on the Freedom Trail (see Chapter 10) and the Boston Women's Heritage Trail (see Chapter 36).

5 Minute Man National Historical Park

ANYONE WHO'S ever attended an American grade school knows at least *something* about the historic towns of Lexington and Concord. Those two suburban towns—located less than twenty miles northwest of Boston—are generally associated with the opening battles of the American War for Independence, and with the famed "shot heard 'round the world." For some, the names elicit visions of colonial resistance to British aggression on Concord's North Bridge or the Lexington Green; others remember bands of minutemen and British redcoats exchanging fire as the British regulars marched back toward Boston down the long Battle Road.

Aside from these basic facts, however, misconceptions about the battles at Lexington and Concord—and about what really happened on that fateful day of April 19, 1775—do abound. Fortunately, Minute Man National Historical Park exists to bring the true history of the early days of the Revolution to life—if, indeed, that can be done. The problem is, of course, that discrepancies are numerous between even the most astute chroniclers of American history. How many soldiers were involved in the skirmishes? What were their motives? Where was "the shot" fired, and by whom? On these points and many others, accounts by Concord historians often disagree with those of historians from Lexington, Massachusetts accounts conflict with Virginian ones, and American records contradict those of the British. Keeping those limitations in mind, here is a brief outline of April 19, 1775.

Trouble had been brewing between England and its American colonies long before 1775—and long before the famous Boston Tea Party of 1773, the Boston Massacre of 1770, and earlier protests against "taxation without representation." In fact, the far-off colonists—more precisely, the white, wealthy, male colonists with voting privileges—had actually experienced a great deal of autonomy during Boston's hundred and fifty-odd years of growth. But when Britain tried to tighten royal control over the colonies,

Each year on Patriots' Day, costumed re-enactors recreate the battles at Lexington and Concord that marked the beginning of the American War for Independence.

whether with words, regulations, or fairly insignificant taxes, many colonists balked. Radicals like Samuel Adams and John Hancock fanned the flames of revolution, milking every minor incident they could to incite the colonists to revolt. Until 1775, however, their efforts had little effect.

When British general Thomas Gage decided to send seven hundred "redcoats" into the Concord countryside on April 19, 1775, it wasn't an invasion or a battle he had in mind. The British knew that the colonists had been storing arms in that rural town, and they marched out the eighteen miles from Boston Common to seize and destroy those stores. Without arms, there could be no revolution, no battle, no bloodshed.

Numerous in-town tip-offs led Paul Revere, William Dawes, and their colleagues to ride into the countryside, warning Lexington and Concord residents of the secret British mission. Although Revere alone received the popular credit, thanks to Henry Wadsworth Longfellow's beloved but inaccurate "Paul Revere's Ride," the man who actually got the word to Concord was twenty-nine-year-old Dr. Samuel Prescott—since Dawes was forced to turn back and Revere was captured (the site of that capture is marked in stone along Route 2A, between the park's Minute Man Visitor Center and Hanscom Drive).

It's probable that neither side intended to fight, draw blood, or kill "the enemy," but they did so nonetheless. The first bloody encounter on April 19 was at Lexington Common, where Captain John Parker and his seventy-seven militiamen met the seven hundred British troops at dawn. A shot was fired by someone—perhaps a British regular, perhaps a colonist. At the end of much confusion, British fire, and unheeded commands, eight Americans lay dead.

After moving on to Concord, the British began collecting and burning any colonial army supplies they could find. Colonial militiamen on the heights above Concord saw the fires and smoke and erroneously assumed their homes were being destroyed. That assumption led to an encounter at the North Bridge—an encounter only a few minutes long—leaving two dead on each side. It was the first time Americans fired a volley at the British; Concord's Major John Buttrick gave the order.

The longest, deadliest part of the day was the running battle along the Battle Road, as minutemen and militia from surrounding communities joined the attack on the British regulars, who gradually retreated to Bunker Hill. Visitors can still explore these battle sites—beginning with Meriam's Corner and moving through Brooks Hill, the Bloody Angles, the Bluff, Fiske Hill, and beyond—aided by detailed park maps, brochures, booklets, displays, and knowledgeable interpreters.

The British were surely surprised by the fighting abilities of their colonial counterparts, but they were also grossly outnumbered. By day's end, some 3,500 militiamen had battled some 1,700 redcoats (which included reinforcements). An estimated 94 colonials were killed, wounded, or missing, compared to 273 British troops.

Contrary to popular belief, the colonial militiamen were neither superior marksmen nor guerrilla fighters hiding behind a thick forest of trees as the British column marched down the road. One historian has estimated that the colonials hit their mark with maybe one out of every three hundred musket balls. Furthermore, most of the trees thickly lining park roads today were not there in 1775. All the land was bare of trees by then, since townsfolk needed firewood for fuel. Hence, when the militiamen fired at the British regulars marching down the road, they were running through open pastures, meadows, fields, and home lots—interspersed with occasional orchards and woodlands—and darting behind homes, rocks, and bushes.

While popular histories often paint the colonial fighters who flocked to battle on April 19 as a bunch of untrained, ragtag farmers, that was hardly so. From earliest colonial times, Massachusetts settlements and towns had their own militias, a necessity since there was no standing army. In general, every able-bodied man between sixteen and sixty was a militia member. "They drilled once or twice a year," adds park ranger Mark Nichipor, "whether they needed it or not."

Clearly, such minimal drilling was not enough to make a skilled army. Hence, in 1774, when the strain between Britain and the colonies was reaching a dangerous level, the Suffolk Resolves asked each town to set aside one quarter of their militia force as "minutemen," a skilled group of soldiers who could muster at a moment's notice. Though in appearance the regular militia and the minutemen were identical, the minutemen were generally younger, better organized, and better trained. (All the Concord minutemen and militia who turned out for the April 19 fight billed the town for their services, as was the custom for such work.)

In sum, these farmers were fighters, too, and many of them had honed their battle skills in the French and Indian War twenty years earlier. Though they lacked the sparkling uniforms of the British regulars, large numbers of them came to the April 19 encounters clean-shaven and sporting their best clothes. "The Acton Minute Men Company stopped on the way to powder their hair white," reveals Nichipor, "and one guy from Danvers turned out for muster in his wedding clothes!"

Since 1963, costumed "minutemen" have periodically visited Minute Man National Historical Park, recreating and commemorating historic events. They also make appearances around the country and the world, often for civic and charity purposes. Each group represents an area town, and membership is based on interest rather than direct lineage. Though participation in these groups peaked during the bicentennial era, new, younger patriots continue to join each year.

Although the war contributions of minute- and militiamen are well documented, women played a role at Lexington and Concord as well. Women were not only the linchpin of the home economy, but essential to the war effort; they helped enforce embargoes on British goods, protected military stores from the British, and actively supported military activities.

Furthermore, according to volunteer Gene Prowten, who helped organize the modern-day Boxborough Minute Men, "If there hadn't been women, there wouldn't have been a nineteenth of April!" It seems that Dr. Samuel Prescott was out courting one Lydia Mulliken the night Revere and Dawes began their ride from Boston. Miss Mulliken's father apparently threw paramour Prescott out—which resulted in his meeting the two alarm riders and then taking the warning on to Concord.

Three objects closely identified with the start of the Revolutionary War in Lexington and Concord are sources of patriotic pride—and occasional confusion.

The Minute Man statue that stands majestically by North Bridge was commissioned by the town of Concord for the 1875 centennial. The seven-foot bronze "embattled farmer" was the work of sculptor Daniel Chester French. French, who later gained worldwide fame for statues like the seated Lincoln in the (Washington, D.C.) Lincoln Memorial, was just twenty-four years old at the time. For the minuteman, his first monument contract, he used the classic Roman statue known as the Apollo Belvedere —a plaster cast of which was at the Boston Athenaeum—plus several living men as models. He was paid just a thousand dollars plus expenses for the work, though the exposure and experience were priceless.

Another minuteman statue stands on Lexington's town green, where Massachusetts Avenue meets Bedford Street in the town center. Crafted by Henry Hudson Kitson in 1900, this spirited fighter represents Captain John Parker, who lined up his militiamen on Lexington Common for the first encounter with British troops on April 19. The statue's "minute man" designation is not quite accurate, however. Despite the 1774 Suffolk Resolves, Lexington had not yet organized or financed such a unit from its militia by April 1775; unless the term is used loosely to mean "citizen-soldier," Parker, his seventy-seven courageous soldiers, and the statue are not technically minutemen.

Then there's the North Bridge. It's not the *"Old"* North Bridge—though plenty of people call it that—and it isn't the bridge on which the battle was fought. The present North Bridge is a 1956 creation by the Massachusetts Department of Public Works, though it is constructed on the site of the original. It's higher than the 1760 bridge—which may help it survive the floods that have always plagued the slow-moving Concord River—but looks similar to its historic ancestor. The model for this incarnation was Amos Doolittle's engraving, a copy of which hangs in the Concord Museum at the intersection of the Cambridge Turnpike and Lexington Road. The 1760 bridge was not destroyed by the British, though they did tear planks from it to stave off the minutemen on April 19. It was, however, dismantled in 1793, when many roads in the area were realigned. The next bridge on the site was an elaborate Victorian version built for the 1875 centennial. That and two subsequent commemorative bridges were damaged and removed before the current one was built.

Minute Man National Historical Park was established by an act of Congress and entrusted to the National Park Service in 1959 to commemorate the events of April 19, 1775, and the opening battle in the American War for Independence. Though best known for the small area near the North Bridge and the Minute Man statue, the sprawling 971-acre park has much, much more to offer visitors. The best way to begin discovering the park is actually from the Minute Man Visitor Center off Route 2A in Lexington. There, a twenty-five-minute multimedia show entitled "The Road to Revolution" gives a stirring account of the battle and sets the tone for exploring the park. Park rangers can direct you to period buildings and to a number of lesser-known but equally engaging sites along the Battle Road. The North Bridge area, at the far western end of the park, is especially interesting if visitors hike up the winding dirt road to the nearby North Bridge Visitor Center and park headquarters in the 1911 Buttrick Mansion.

In recent years, the park has completed a variety of projects aimed at better protecting its significant cultural resources, improving opportunities for visitors to understand the events of the American Revolution and the colonial era, and developing new facilities. The feel of colonial times has been recreated by the restoration of the eighteenth-century landscape, with its varied patterns of tilled fields, pastures, meadows, orchards, gardens, and woodlots. In addition, segments of the original Battle Road that diverge from the modern Route 2A have been closed to vehicular traffic.

The park has also made major improvements in interpretation, educational outreach, and visitor access. Along the five-mile Battle Road Trail, a linking network of foot and bicycle trails accessible to wheelchairs and strollers has made it possible for visitors to leave their cars behind and experience the New England landscape. (In winter, the trail is not plowed, making it ideal for cross-country skiers.) The trail system, marked with outdoor exhibit panels and granite mile markers, follows segments of stone fences and other features used for cover by the American militia as it fired on the retreating column of redcoats. The trail network also introduces broader themes, from changes in the landscape caused by glaciation to changes brought about by human use, all helping to put the events of April 19, 1775, in a more comprehensible context.

The Battle Road, North Bridge Visitor Center, and the Wayside Barn ("Home of Authors") have also been redesigned. The historic Meriam House, site of the start of the running battle after the North Bridge fight, has become a visitor contact station; at key locations, including the Ephraim Hartwell Tavern, visitors now meet costumed interpreters who demonstrate Revolutionary-era militia activities and trades. A varied program of educational offerings has also been developed cooperatively with regional school systems.

Exploring the battles at Lexington and Concord need not end within the park itself. Although the park's collections include only a few artifacts related to April 19, 1775, other area museums, libraries, and collections contain a wealth of interesting items. Treasures at the Concord Museum, for example, include one of the two lanterns used at the Old North Church to signal British movements, while the Lexington Historical Society has pistols dropped by British major John Pitcairn when his horse bolted at a volley of musket fire. Battle exhibits focusing on Lexington are displayed at the National Heritage Museum, and the pride of the Bedford Library is the flag that the Bedford minutemen reportedly carried with them to the North Bridge in 1775.

THE ESSENTIALS

Address: North Bridge Visitor Center, 174 Liberty Street, Concord, MA 01742. Park runs along Route 2A through the towns of Concord, Lincoln, and Lexington. **Telephone:** North Bridge Visitor Center, (978) 369-6993; Minute Man Visitor Center, (781) 862-7753. **Websites:** www.nps.gov/mima; www.nps.gov/mima/wayside. **Visitor Information:** Park open daily until sunset, year-round. Visitor center open 9:00 A.M. to 5:00 P.M. daily, April through October. Reduced hours or days November through March; call or visit website for current information. Closed Thanksgiving, Christmas Day, and New Year's Day. Free. (Fees are charged for personally guided tours arranged in advance for organized groups, and for educational programs conducted for school groups.) Call for hours, and for schedules of guided walks, talks, and audiovisual displays. Both visitor centers and their restrooms, as well as the Battle Road Trail and the Wayside Barn, are wheelchair accessible; best wheelchair access to North Bridge is from Monument Street parking lot; paths and trails throughout park vary in accessibility, depending on surface, slope, and steps.

6 The Bunker Hill Monument

IT'S JUST about as strange a site as you could imagine: right in the middle of what was once a working-class, largely Irish Boston neighborhood stands a 221-foot-tall Egyptian obelisk memorializing a British military victory.

One of eight historic sites that make up Boston National Historical Park, and one of the Freedom Trail's most distinctive stops, the Bunker Hill Monument commemorates the Battle of Bunker Hill, fought on June 17, 1775. Though that bloody encounter is widely remembered as the first decisive battle of the American War for Independence, the fact is the American colonists actually *lost* to their British foes. So why build a spectacular monument to a seemingly sad defeat?

Two months after the running battle at Lexington and Concord (see Chapter 5), the colonists moved to occupy the hill on which the monument now stands. British troops made three assaults on the rebels, though their first and second efforts ended in British retreats. The third British assault knocked the colonists off the hill and out of Charlestown altogether.

As defeats go, however, the Battle of Bunker Hill was a glorious one. An army of provincial New England farmers had repelled two out of three British attacks, decimating the well-trained "redcoats'" ranks before their own final retreat. Colonial resentment of British oppression swiftly crystallized after this bloody encounter, unleashing a full-fledged Revolutionary War.

Britain's pyrrhic victory is only one of several curious or forgotten facts, misnomers, and misquotes associated with the Battle of Bunker Hill. The name, for example, is dead wrong. It should be *Bunker's* Hill, named for George Bunker, a rich landowner who moved to Massachusetts from England in 1634. That detail turns out to be irrelevant, however, since the battle was actually fought—and the monument stands—on Breed's Hill. Bunker's Hill is a half mile to the northwest, where Saint Francis de Sales Church stands today.

Moreover, the most famous quotation to emerge from historical accounts of the battle—"Don't fire 'til you see the whites of their eyes"—is of dubious authenticity at best. While some historians attribute it to colonial colonel William Prescott, others insist the words were General Israel Putnam's. No one knows who, if anyone, used the phrase that day. In any case, it wasn't original; it had been an oft-quoted Prussian military order for three decades before the Revolutionary War broke out.

None of these minor historical mishaps seems to have fazed public interest in the site, nor dampened New England pride in the name Bunker Hill. Attracting almost 200,000 visitors every year, the monument is also the center of celebrations every June 17. A long-standing Suffolk County holiday, the annual observance of Bunker Hill Day rounds out a gala

Colonial colonel
William Prescott
wields his saber at the
base of the towering
Bunker Hill Monument.

Charlestown weekend filled with splashy parades, traditional flag raisings, military salutes, and assorted festivities.

Long before the Battle of Bunker Hill, the Charlestown peninsula was known primarily as a pleasant place to pass through. The glaciers had passed through, for instance, leaving three distinctive drumlins, or hills, behind. The Pawtucket Indians had passed through, naming the land Mishawum, or "great spring." John Winthrop's Puritan settlers also passed through, departing largely because the spring wasn't all that great (presumably, it was then unpotable). Since fresher water was available on the nearby Shawmut peninsula, Winthrop et al relocated there in 1630, eventually renaming it Boston (see Chapter 29).

In the century before the Revolution, however, Charlestown developed into a prosperous seaport and a center of American economic independence. Paul Revere borrowed a horse in Charlestown to make his 1775 ride to the Lexington countryside. (A wayside marker close to USS *Constitution* shows the site where Revere came ashore after rowing to Charlestown from the North End.) Charlestown was also the area that British troops—

sequestered in Boston after Lexington and Concord—meant to fortify as a hedge against colonial aggression.

Placing troops on the three strategic hills overlooking Boston—Breed's and Bunker's in Charlestown and Dorchester Heights—was what British lieutenant general Thomas Gage should have done; major generals William Howe and Henry Clinton pressed him to do so. When Gage didn't move, however, Colonel William Prescott did. On the night of June 16, 1775, the Pepperell farmer and his ill-trained provincial troops moved quietly through the night toward Breed's Hill. There they swiftly and silently built an earthen fort called a redoubt and prepared to defend their position when the sleeping British soldiers awoke.

No one knows why Prescott advanced and built on Breed's Hill rather than Bunker's. Perhaps he thought Breed's provided a better defensive position or closer firing range. Perhaps his fellow officers, including many not from Boston, didn't know one hill from the other. (British maps interchanged the names of the two hills, or called all three of Charlestown's mounds "Bunker's Hill.")

However it was, the bloody encounter that ensued the next day was forever known as the Battle of Bunker Hill. That encounter was the deadliest of the Revolutionary War. By the end of a siege that lasted less than two hours, Charlestown's grassy slopes were littered with some 1,500 bodies, and most of its 400 buildings were burned.

British casualties outnumbered colonial ones two to one. An estimated 500 colonials and 1,034 British soldiers died, despite the colonists' inferior weaponry—marginally accurate muskets and no bayonets. According to legend, British troops had twice the manpower of their colonial foes; many popular accounts state that 1,000 colonists battled 2,200 British soldiers. New research, however, suggests that more than 2,000—and perhaps as many as 5,000—New Englanders came to fight that day.

Even if the colonists weren't outnumbered, their fight was still impressive. "The actual numbers probably don't matter," explained Tom Brown, professor emeritus in American History at the University of Massachusetts at Amherst. "The rule of thumb is that the attacking force should outnumber the defenders three to one. The British failed to do that."

No one will debate that Britain paid dearly for that victory on the hill. The British carried off their dead, interring many in the Boston Common burying ground. British major John Pitcairn, shot by a free black American named Peter Salem, fell into his own son's arms. Pitcairn was buried, ironically, in a crypt below the Old North Church on Salem Street—the same church from which, two months earlier, two lanterns had warned the colonists of the British attack "by sea." (In 2003, an exciting new study sponsored by the National Park Service, *Patriots of Color*, showed that Peter Salem was hardly the only black colonist who fought at Bunker Hill; it is now known that perhaps as many as 150 Native Americans and African-Americans participated in the fight, literally changing the face of that battle in the annals of history.)

Of all the colonial soldiers who died that day, the most prominent was Dr. Joseph Warren—a highly respected patriot, organizer, orator, doctor, and writer, known by many British as the most troublesome of all the rebellious colonists. So dearly was the patriot doctor missed that in 1794 fellow members of the local King Solomon's Lodge of Free and Accepted Masons erected an eighteen-foot wooden Tuscan pillar atop Breed's Hill in his memory. The monument, inscribed to honor "Major-General Joseph Warren and his Associates," was the first Bunker Hill monument on this site. A replica stands inside the base of the current granite obelisk.

The present Bunker Hill Monument began in a controversy and ended in a bake sale. The controversy erupted in 1818, when Major General Henry Dearborn published a pamphlet of his recollections of the Battle of Bunker Hill. Dearborn claimed that Colonel John Stark and his New Hampshire regiments were never given adequate credit for their major role; moreover, he insisted that the revered Revolutionary hero General Israel Putnam was cowardly in that battle and incapacitated by a gall bladder attack for most of the day. The full truth of who did what—when, where, and how—amid all the confusion of the battle will never really be known.

The outcries that ensued over Dearborn's claims brought back fading memories of the colonists' valiant defense at Bunker Hill, the fiftieth anniversary of which was seven years away. Meanwhile, acreage atop Russell's Pasture, as the old battleground was then called, had come up for sale. Dr. John Collins Warren, a distinguished surgeon and nephew of the late Joseph Warren, bought the first three acres. Soon, with the formation of the Bunker Hill Memorial Association, some fifteen acres were in hand.

Realizing that the aging Marquis de Lafayette had planned a trip to the United States to celebrate the fiftieth anniversary of America's War for Independence, the association arranged to have that venerable military ally participate in a ceremony to lay the cornerstone of a new, larger monument on Bunker Hill. The ceremony took place in 1825 and featured an oration by Daniel Webster. Forty elderly Bunker Hill veterans attended the event.

It wasn't until eighteen years later, on June 17, 1843, that the 221-foot, 6,700-ton granite monument was finally dedicated—with another oration by Daniel Webster, and thirteen *extremely* elderly Bunker Hill veterans in attendance. The lapse of time was due not so much to the difficulty of building the obelisk—though it was a landmark construction feat—as to finances.

The Bunker Hill Memorial Association had held a competition for an architectural plan. In the final selection for monument design, the Egyptian obelisk was chosen over the column form. The obelisk had been popular in Egyptian, Greek, and Roman cultures as a symbol of heroism, glory, and death. Most recently it had reappeared in the West with nineteenth-century Egyptian and Greek Revival styles.

A granite quarry was purchased in Quincy for a mere $325. Meanwhile, engineer Gridley Bryant developed "the first commercial railroad in America" to carry the huge twelve-foot blocks of dressed granite to a wharf on the Neponset River. From there the blocks were barged to Charlestown. Those early railroad cars were horse drawn, and the whole process was fairly traumatic for the granite. Eventually, overland oxcarts were brought in to finish the hauling job.

Much to the dismay of supervising architect Solomon Willard, expenses mounted exponentially. Donations came in, large and small, and eleven of the original fifteen surrounding acres were sold to raise funds. Still the money wasn't enough. When, in 1840, it looked as though the half-completed obelisk was never going to be finished, the women took over.

Sarah Josepha Hale, "America's first woman editor," ran the Boston-based *American Ladies Magazine.* Grandstanding from her journal and inspiring newspapers to do the same, Hale and a small army of women organized "the Fair," a spectacular weeklong cake, cookie, handcraft, and curio sale held in the new Quincy Market near Faneuil Hall. The women netted an unprecedented $30,035.53, which, along with two other major contributions from individuals, enabled the monument to be completed soon thereafter. In all, the monument cost $156,218.14 to build, with all but $7,000 raised by public subscription.

In the century and a half since its dedication, the towering Bunker Hill Monument has endured numerous changes. For one thing, it has changed hands several times. Bankrupted by the costs of their investment despite a long-standing ten-cent admission fee, the Bunker Hill Memorial Association turned the monument over to the Metropolitan Parks Commission (later the Metropolitan District Commission) in 1919. The commission also found the property too costly to maintain well, and, finally, during the 1976 bicentennial, transferred it to the National Park Service.

Physically, the site has had its ups and downs. A steam-propelled "elevator" that existed from 1842 to 1844—used first for hauling granite, then briefly adapted for people—is long gone. Now it's 294 huffing, puffing steps to the top. Statues of Prescott and Warren are displayed outside the monument base and inside the adjacent 1903 marble lodge, but many of the old firearms, paintings, and other artifacts once shown in the monument or lodge are stored elsewhere.

Today, there are a variety of ways to learn more about the infamous military encounter. At the monument itself, National Park Service rangers tell the story of the battle in hourly talks, using a series of dioramas in the lodge for illustration.

A few blocks away, at 55 Constitution Road, is the Bunker Hill Pavilion, which houses the National Park Service Navy Yard Visitor Center as well as "The Whites of their Eyes," a multimedia surround-sound show on the Battle of Bunker Hill operated by Historic Tours of America—the same folks who bring you the Old Town Trolley. (The pavilion and show were originally created by Raytheon for America's bicentennial.)

The old Bunker Hill Museum at 43 Monument Square, run since 1976 by volunteers from the Charlestown Historical Society (CHS), is now slated to be rehabilitated and reinvented as a National Park Service interpretive center for Bunker Hill, developed in partnership with the CHS and a major contribution from the Masons. (That new facility, which will include original artifacts, the above-mentioned dioramas, and sound-and-light animation, is scheduled to open by 2005, along with completion of repair work to the Bunker Hill Monument, its grounds, and surrounding lighting; wheelchair access to all the Bunker Hill sites will also be greatly improved.)

The monument's cultural and symbolic life has also changed. The Bunker Hill memorial was the first monument built through public donations, and it was the country's first publicized tourist attraction. Before 1885, it was the first and most prominent monument in the country—*the* American obelisk. In that year, however, the Washington Monument in Washington, D.C.—an obelisk grander and 335 feet taller than Bunker Hill's—was dedicated. Once the Washington Monument became the national symbol, only Bostonians kept the Charlestown obelisk first in their hearts.

But which Bostonians? That, too, has evolved over the decades. Originally built by Federalist party members—wealthy, upper-class merchants, bankers, and manufacturers—the Bunker Hill Monument later came to be identified with the Whig party. When Charlestown became a working-class Irish area, the obelisk became a "democratic" symbol. "Even during the Boston busing crisis of the early 1970s," explained Professor Tom Brown, "Charlestown people opposed to busing invoked the Bunker Hill Monument. They said that they, just as in 1775, were resisting outside tyrannical authority. Since its inception, people have spoken about being, or acting, 'under the shadow of the Bunker Hill Monument'"

At turn of the twenty-first century, controversy again erupted at Bunker Hill when, as part of Boston's Big Dig, a glorious new ten-lane cable bridge—which mirrored the obelisk form of the Bunker Hill Monument—was built across the Charles River. Certain members of the community were at arms over whether to name the bridge for Bunker Hill or for the recently deceased regional director of the Anti-Defamation League, Leonard Zakim. The compromise was to call it the Leonard P. Zakim Bunker Hill Bridge. Then came the Krzysztof Wodiczko public art installation of September 1998, during which the artist repeatedly projected a sixteen-minute videotape onto the monument, featuring huge talking heads of Charlestown residents discussing their murdered family members and urban violence today. The artwork—which sought to link the violent sacrifices and symbols of freedom during the American Revolution with those of the modern day—enraged some Charlestown locals but was praised by others as one of the most amazing projects ever witnessed.

All of which goes to show that the Bunker Hill Monument is a living symbol—not a dead artifact—and arguably the liveliest symbolic site in Boston!

THE ESSENTIALS

Address: Monument Square, Charlestown, MA. Boston National Historical Park Headquarters, Charlestown Navy Yard, Boston, MA 02129. **Telephone:** (617) 242-5641. **Website:** www.nps.gov/bost. **Visitor Information:** Monument open 9:00 A.M. to 4:30 P.M. daily. Lodge/exhibit area open 9:00 A.M. to 5:00 P.M. daily except Thanksgiving, Christmas Day, and New Year's Day. Extended summer hours mid-June to Labor Day: Monument open 9:00 A.M. to 5:30 P.M.; lodge/exhibit area open 9:00 A.M. to 6:00 P.M. daily. Free. Ranger-conducted battle talks given hourly, 10:00 A.M. to 4:00 P.M., except at 1:00 P.M. Musket-firing demonstrations given on the half hour, 10:30 and 11:30 A.M., 1:30, 2:30 and 3:30 P.M., Friday through Sunday, mid-June to Labor Day. Grounds wheelchair accessible via a fairly steep paved ramp from main entrance; lodge/exhibit area ramp available by asking ranger to open gate by monument; restrooms accessible; monument itself not wheelchair accessible.

The Bunker Hill Monument is a site on the Freedom Trail (See Chapter 10).

Renovation and rehabilitation of the monument and lodge in 2004 and 2005 may affect visitor access to these sites. A new visitor facility, located across Monument Square in the old community museum, is scheduled to open by or before summer 2005. Wheelchair access to all these related sites will be enhanced by these renovations.

7   Adams National Historical Park

IF YOU'RE looking for the history of the American Revolution, the city of Quincy is not the first place you might consider. Yet in downtown Quincy, only ten miles south of Boston via the Southeast Expressway (Route 3), is a bucolic thirteen-acre spread of gardens, rolling lawns, and scattered structures known as Adams National Historical Park. This beautiful old South Shore estate was once home to two eminent patriots, John and Abigail Adams. Moreover, two of the site's smaller, more rustic structures are the birthplaces of John and John Quincy Adams, the first father and son to become presidents of the United States. The Quincy site also illuminates the stories of many more members of the Adams family—an illustrious political dynasty that lived and worked the land there from colonial times through 1927.

John Adams (1735–1826), known as the level-headed counterpart to his radical cousin Sam Adams, was a member of the First and Second Continental Congresses, the first vice president of the United States, and the second president of the new nation. Adams was the patriot lawyer who argued the Boston Massacre case in court and garnered European support for the American cause on numerous diplomatic missions abroad. Meanwhile he wrote a Constitution for the Commonwealth of Massachusetts and helped Thomas Jefferson fine-tune the Declaration of Independence.

Equally revolutionary was John's wife, Abigail Smith Adams (1744–1818), one of America's earliest and most notable women of letters. (Adams staff are cautious about using the word *feminist* to describe Abigail, though others readily employ the term.) In marriage, Abigail and John were partners and equals. Beginning with John's departure for the First Continental Congress in 1774, Abigail took sole charge of hearth and home, effectively balancing child-rearing with managing the family farm and business. When the American War for Independence began, Abigail opened her home as a sanctuary for soldiers and refugees from Boston. While her husband was serving the nation at home and abroad, she constantly wrote to him of personal and political matters—from the gory details of the Battle of Bunker Hill to tales of melting down her pewter spoons to mold bullets for patriot guns.

The most quoted of Abigail's letters to John was written in March 1776,

The "Old House" at Adams National Historical Park is famous for its beautifully landscaped grounds and gardens, and for honoring two centuries of Adams family history.

when she advised her husband and his colleagues to think through the implications of their declarations of independence: "By the way, in the new code of laws which I suppose it will be necessary for you to make, I desire you would remember the ladies and be more generous and favorable to them than your ancestors! Do not put such unlimited power into the hands of the husbands. Remember all men would be tyrants if they could. If particular care and attention is not paid to the ladies, we are determined to foment a rebellion."

Tales of John and Abigail, of course, are only part of the allure of Adams National Historical Park. The most logical place to start a tour is at the National Park Service Visitor Center located at 1250 Hancock Street. Chronologically speaking, the next stop would be a small triangle of land at 133–141 Franklin Street. There sit the birthplaces of John Adams and John Quincy Adams, two modest wood-frame houses that later generations would describe as in the New England "saltbox" style. Though the rambling acres of farmland that once surrounded these homes are long gone, the houses' significance and charm remain intact. They are the two oldest surviving presidential birthplaces in the United States—and the site where the Adams saga began.

The John Adams Birthplace had several owners before his father, Deacon John Adams, bought the house in 1720. William Needham had been granted the land in 1640, though the 1681 structure that sits there today was built by a subsequent owner, Joseph Penniman. While living in this home, Deacon John's wife, Susanna, bore three sons. The eldest became our second president. Though Deacon John died in 1761, both this and the neighboring house continued to be used by Adams family members into the early nineteenth century.

Seventy-five feet away stands the John Quincy Adams Birthplace, a structure built by Samuel Belcher in 1663 and sold to Deacon John in 1744. When Deacon John died, his son John inherited this home. John and Abigail subsequently lived there through the births of five children and the period of colonial upheaval and war. The couple's second child was future president John Quincy Adams, born in 1767. It was in this home that Abigail raised her family, managed the Adams farm and business, molded pewter bullets, and wrote her voluminous war correspondence to her husband. Though John was frequently away on political missions, he too put the stamp of history on this site: he wrote the Massachusetts State Constitution in his law office on the first floor.

Sparsely furnished with colonial period pieces and reproductions, these two modest houses offer visitors a telling glimpse of daily life in early New England. National Park Service rangers enjoy explaining to guests how twentieth-century phrases originated in seventeenth century life. The colonial table was called a board, for example, because that's what it was— a big, long board; so the expression "room and board" meant a room to sleep in and a board to eat on. Generally, the family would sit on a long common bench along the side of the board, while the father would sit at the end in a chair; hence, "chairman of the board." The phrase "sleep tight" also came from a piece of early American furniture: mattresses were supported by crisscrossed ropes underneath, and sleeping simply wasn't comfortable unless the ropes were kept taut.

John and Abigail Adams did not live in this rustic simplicity forever. Though John was a farmer at heart, his fame and fortune were constantly growing. (His fortune, alas, never kept pace with his fame.) In 1785, John was appointed the first U.S. minister to Britain's Court of Saint James. Weary of long wartime separations, Abigail and the family decided to join John in Europe. Upon their return in 1788, the Adams family moved into a larger, more elegant home about two miles away—the mansion at 135 Adams Street, now known as the Old House. This house, along with its surrounding outbuildings, country gardens, and rolling greens, is the centerpiece of the Adams site today.

When visitors stop by the Old House, however, they are not seeing the Adams mansion as it looked in the days of John and Abigail. The home and its environs are more like an archeological dig, reflecting layer upon layer of changes, renovations, and additions.

When John and Abigail settled at the Old House, the land was known as the Vassall-Borland estate, a farm that once included more than forty

acres. The seven-room home they found there had been built by West Indies sugar planter Leonard Vassall in 1730–31. When the Adamses arrived
in 1788, they envisioned it as a working farm, filled with orchards, gardens,
and serenity. John named the place Peacefield, partly for that serenity and
partly for the treaty of peace he had recently negotiated abroad. Abigail
called it "a wren's house," since it was significantly smaller than the mansion they had left behind in England.

The couple furnished the Old House with secondhand furniture from
John's missions abroad. Many of these original pieces are still in the house
today. Abigail also began adding chambers and halls to their small, low-
ceilinged abode—a practice followed by Adams descendants. By 1927, the
original seven-room house had grown into a twenty-one-room mansion.

John and Abigail were the only Adamses to live in the Old House year-
round; later generations tended simply to spend the summer there. The
second-generation owner, John Quincy Adams (1767–1848), was too involved in politics to give the house as much time and care as his parents
did. Still, when not away fulfilling his duties as president, foreign diplomat,
or member of Congress, John Quincy loved to experiment with planting
trees on the grounds. Like his father, he used the home as a "summer
White House."

Charles Francis Adams (1807–1886) was the third generation to run the
Adams estate. Although this skilled U.S. congressman and diplomat initially considered demolishing the house and starting from scratch, Charles
Francis settled for beautifying and altering the original site. Under his
guidance, John and Abigail's working farm took on the demeanor of a Victorian gentleman's country estate. The old farm buildings on the east lawn
were torn down and a wood fence was replaced with a stone wall. Charles
Francis also built the magnificent Stone Library to house his family's overflowing book collection, and he added the carriage-house complex, providing quarters for the coachman and a stable for horses.

When the fourth generation of Adamses took charge, a few final alterations were made. While author Henry Adams visited and wrote there at
times—he finished his nine-volume *History of the United States* at the Old
House—it was his brother Brooks Adams who acted as official caretaker
and brought the estate into the twentieth century.

After the eccentric Brooks died in 1927, the clock stopped, as it were, on
the Adams estate. The house, furnishings, gardens, outbuildings, and
grounds that visitors see today are essentially the same as they were the
day Brooks passed on—a gloriously agreeable clutter of art, artifacts, porcelain, plantings, and chambers that reflect four generations of Adams
family living, and three different centuries of style.

Among the fascinating sights you'll see on a Park Service tour of the Old
House:

- The Paneled Room, to the left of the front entrance, was part of the
original house. Though later generations admired the rich mahogany
walls, Abigail whitewashed them to make the room brighter for her
guests.

- The Long Room was part of Abigail's east-wing expansion of the house. The nine Louis XV chairs were brought back by John from his service as minister to The Hague. Though some of the chairs look "normal," several have unusually puffy seats—designed to accommodate the overflow of ladies' hoopskirts. "The furnishings here are like global maps," explains chief of interpretation Caroline Keinath, referring to the wonderful hodgepodge of historic styles in the Long Room. "And the paintings of family and friends that line the walls are like today's photograph albums."
- John's Study, upstairs, includes his desk, where he wrote to his close friend Thomas Jefferson. Literate and lingering correspondence was an Adams family specialty. In 1813, John wrote to Jefferson, "You and I ought not to die, before we have explained ourselves to each other." Thirteen years later, on July 4, 1826—the fiftieth anniversary of the Declaration of Independence on which they'd worked together—both Jefferson and Adams died, unbeknownst to each other.
- Abigail passed away in her Dutch bed in the President and First Lady's Bedroom; John saw his last light of day in the study.
- The circle of several flatirons heating in the Laundry were used by the servants who worked under Brooks Adams. He required his staff to follow his example and change clothing three times daily—white attire in the morning, gray at midday, and black at night—which must have kept them ironing all day.
- The Kitchen is outfitted with eight bells, installed by Charles Francis Adams. Each bell was connected to a different chamber, and each had a different tone, enabling servants to know which room required attendance. (The bells have sometimes inspired folks to joke about the *other* Addams family, of comic strip and movie fame, responding with, "You rang?")

When Brooks Adams died in 1927, the Old House came into the hands of the Adams Memorial Society, who opened it to visitors for nineteen years. In 1946, the society turned the property over to the National Park Service, which has operated the Adams estate ever since. In 1979, the two birthplaces were reunited with the Old House as part of the Adams National Historical Park and restored to their colonial appearance.

Today, the Adams site maintenance staff takes gentle care of the historic structures and grounds. Regular duties can involve anything from identifying historic plant species and clipping the ancient box hedge to grading the driveways or reshingling Brooks Adams's doghouse, the smallest of the site's eleven historic structures. Meanwhile, the administrative, management, cultural resource, and interpretive divisions are often at work on new projects. Most of the house's 78,000 historic objects, for example, have been cataloged on the computer. The Park works with the Quincy community on various special events during the year, linking the area's historic sites. Tours and interpretation are offered to visitors at the United First Parish Church at 1306 Hancock, which contains the crypt of the two Adams presidents and their wives. Information is also provided at the National Park Service Visitor Center on Hancock Street.

Meanwhile, Adams National Historical Park remains "a beautiful landscape and a country setting" in the eyes of Caroline Keinath. "It chronicles nearly two hundred years of Adams history, but unlike many other historic sites, it's not a museum or a public hall. It's a home." And quite a revolutionary home, at that.

THE ESSENTIALS

Address: Adams National Historical Park (Old House) and Visitor Orientation Center (in historic 1873 Carriage House), 135 Adams Street, Quincy, MA 02169. John and John Quincy Adams Birthplaces, 133 and 141 Franklin Street, Quincy. National Park Service Visitor Center, 1250 Hancock Street, Quincy, MA 02169. **Telephone:** Visitor Center, (617) 770-1175; Carriage House Visitor Orientation Center, (617) 745-0926; administrative headquarters, (617) 770-1177. **Website:** www.nps.gov/adam. **Visitor Information:** Open 9:00 A.M. to 5:00 P.M. daily, April 19 through November 10. Admission fee for visitors seventeen year of age and older; National Park passes accepted. Guided tours only; last tour begins 4:05 P.M. Parking and accessible restrooms at visitor center; validated parking in visitor center garage. Free trolley transportation between sites. Restrooms at visitor center and Visitor Orientation Center only. Limited wheelchair access to ground floors of homes via moveable ramps; no upstairs access. Please call for details.

8 The State House

To SOME, the Massachusetts State House is just a lovely landmark—a glittering golden dome on Beacon Hill, overlooking Boston Common. But take one step inside this Freedom Trail attraction and you'll find a wealth of history at hand. Over here, for example, the Marquis de Lafayette walked when he came to Boston to help lay the cornerstone for the Bunker Hill monument. Over there is where legions of young Union soldiers stood, receiving arms, ammunition, and other equipment before embarking for the bloody American Civil War. And that's only the beginning. Protesters and presidents, abolitionists and antiabortionists, Native American chiefs and "Indian fighters," senators and suffragists have all been through these marbled halls and elegant chambers since the "new" State House doors first opened on January 11, 1798.

Some of the history inside these old walls is in the form of fascinating tales told by well-versed guides and informative guidebooks. But much of that history is in more tangible form—statues, models, plaques, paintings, furnishings, chambers, and artifacts that bring the past into the present day. Herewith our unorthodox guide.

It wasn't simply that the Old State House, built in 1713 on Cornhill and King streets (now Washington and State), was getting too small to house the expanding state government; after the American Revolution, state leaders wanted an official edifice that properly reflected the grandeur of our prosperous new republic.

Meanwhile, young Charles Bulfinch—Boston's first native-born professional architect—had been traveling in Europe from 1785 to 1787, thanks to an inheritance from a wealthy uncle. Architectural historians believe that Bulfinch's designs for the State House, first submitted when the architect was only twenty-four years of age, were derived from buildings he observed firsthand in London. Certainly he was influenced by English neoclassical style, as evidenced in the State House facade we see today.

Of course, a site for the new State House had to be chosen as well. Many Boston locations, as well as spots in faraway towns like Watertown and Worcester, had been considered. But John Hancock's family cow pasture—with its overview of Boston from the summit of Beacon Hill—was the first choice and was eventually purchased for the project. The cornerstone for the State House was laid near the top of the pasture on July 4, 1795, by colonial patriots Samuel Adams and Paul Revere. That symbolic stone was hauled in by fifteen white horses, representing the thirteen original states plus two new ones, Vermont and Kentucky. The new Massachusetts State House—featuring the distinctive dome, tall white columns and trim, and red-brick facade we all recognize today—was officially completed on January 11, 1798. The cost was the wonderfully curious sum of $133,333.33—not so wonderful, of course, to those who thought the price tag exorbitant.

Though the Bulfinch State House was much larger and grander than its predecessor, it was not long before the government began outgrowing even these quarters. Throughout the nineteenth and early twentieth centuries, land purchases increased the building's original 1.6-acre lot to its current 6.7 acres. Each of the major new wings and renovation projects—completed in 1831, 1856, 1895, and 1917—was intended to be architecturally "subservient" to the original design. A small-scale model of the original 1798 Bulfinch facade, minus the subsequent additions, can be seen just outside the State House's Doric Hall.

Many of the original columns, including those on the facade and in Doric Hall, were hewn from enormous pine trunks carved on the State House lawn. As fireproofing of the building became a growing concern in the late nineteenth century, these wooden pillars were eventually replaced by steel and plaster facsimiles.

Other cosmetic and structural changes over the past two centuries have included both color and composition. The distinctive red-brick exterior, for example, was painted alternately white and yellow for many years, beginning in 1825; only in 1928 was the last coat of yellow sandblasted off, revealing the original red brick, which has been maintained ever since.

A gaggle of great writers, from Shakespeare and Chaucer to Alain de Lille and John Lydgate, have all noted in one way or another that "all that glitters is not gold." While they were not discussing the Massachusetts State House in particular, they might as well have been.

Though internationally renowned for its distinctive gold dome, the State House has actually been gilded for only two-thirds of its life. The thirty-foot-high cupola, with a diameter of fifty feet, began as uncovered, lead-colored wood. When that surface began to deteriorate, Paul Revere and Sons covered it with copper in 1802. Not until 1874 was expensive

The distinctive golden-domed Massachusetts State House sits above Boston Common, at the crest of Beacon Hill.

twenty-three-carat gold leaf added over the copper-sheet base, though such a project had been debated for years. The cost in 1874 was $2,862.50. In 1969, when gold was selling for forty dollars an ounce, the same job ran up a bill of $36,443.00. By the time of the most recent regilding in 1997, the price tag was a hefty $300,000.00.

The dome has not always been gold in the twentieth century, either. During the blackouts of World War II, for example, it was camouflaged with battleship gray paint.

Visitors can visit the second and third floors in the State House with or without the aid of a tour guide. The logical starting place—and the spot to pick up guides and guidebooks—is at the Tours and Information Desk on the second floor, in Doric Hall. Doric Hall, the main reception room, is named for the ten not-quite-Doric columns scattered within. For the past two centuries, Doric has been used for countless special events, from banquets and press conferences to swearings-in and military munitions distribution. Despite all that activity, the front doors to Doric Hall are opened only on three occasions—when a U.S. President visits, when a foreign head of state comes to call, and when a governor leaves office. As you climb the stairs at the end of Doric Hall, you move out of the original Bulfinch building and enter the 1895 addition, designed by Charles Brigham. There, the small Bartlett Hall commemorates William Francis Bartlett, a Civil War general then only in his twenties. Though he had lost a leg in the war, Bartlett had his men regularly strap him on his horse so he could continue leading his troops; respected by both the North and South (Confederates were instructed not to fire on the brave, honored hero), he declined offers to serve in political office and died at thirty-six. The next, larger room, once called the Senate Staircase Hall, was renamed the Civil War Nurses' Hall in 1985. It boasts Bela Pratt's dramatic 1914 sculpture of an army nurse in action, plus the most impressive marble floor in the building (six types of exotic marble are inlaid there).

The Hall of Flags—also known as Memorial Hall—is a circular room surrounded by columns of Sienna marble. On display is a small sample of the more than four hundred flags once carried into battle by Massachusetts soldiers, from the Civil War to Vietnam. Though the hall once exhibited the original banners—many of them badly frayed and mended with mesh —those were moved to climate-controlled vaults in 1987. Despite these currently shown banners' deceptively real appearance, they're actually just life-size backlit transparencies. It's hoped that the originals will some day be returned to display.

The loveliest mosaic at the State House is certainly the beautiful marble work in the Grand Staircase Hall floor. The most curious display may well be the stained-glass window on the staircase landing, which shows the evolution of the state seal. It seems ironic, of course, that a Native American is depicted on the official state emblem, considering their historic mistreatment in Massachusetts and across the nation. But the tale is even stranger than the image.

On the original emblem, created in 1629–30, an Indian in a leaf skirt implores, "Come Over and Help Us," presumably asking to be educated and Christianized by the new English colonists. The London artist commissioned to draw the Native American had never seen one, so he apparently copied a drawing in Sir Walter Raleigh's book on Venezuela. According to Russell Peters's book *The Wampanoags of Mashpee*, the most recent incarnation of the state seal Indian is not much more historically accurate. When Harvard anthropologist Charles Willoughby was commissioned to create a better emblem in 1897, he could not find an appropriate-looking model among the Mashpees of Cape Cod or the Ponkapoags in the Blue Hills. He found his "ideal" Native American at the Parker House in Boston —a tall, strong, long-haired, high-cheekboned man named Little Shell. As a result, Little Shell, an Ojibway from Lake Superior, became immortalized on the Massachusetts seal, along with the new state motto, "By the sword we seek peace, but peace only under liberty."

The most controversial artwork in the State House is probably the giant clock suspended in the magnificent, renovated Great Hall. The cavernous hall itself—decorated in tricolored marble and topped by a vaulted skylight—was opened in 1990 for official state functions and receptions. The clock, designed by New York artist R. M. Fischer at a cost of $100,000, was commissioned in 1986. Unfortunately, it arrived at a time when fiscal belt-tightening was de rigueur in the Commonwealth—thereby minimizing local appreciation of the clock's unusual postmodern design. It is now well received by all who visit.

Other than the golden dome, the two symbols most frequently associated with the State House are the pine cone and the Sacred Cod. The pine cone—often mistaken as a pineapple by visitors—is the gilded figure atop the dome. The cone was given this prominent position to remind citizens of the importance of lumbering in the state's economy. Lumbering in Massachusetts may sound an unfamiliar note, until you remember that the current state of Maine was part of Massachusetts until 1820.

The Sacred Cod, suspended in the public gallery above the House of Representatives, is part of a delightful fish story. The four-foot-eleven-and-a-half-inch good-luck Cod is carved from pine and is older than the State House itself. Though the fish's exact age is unknown, it certainly existed prior to 1784. John Rowe, a well-known Revolutionary-era gentleman—merchant, selectman, representative, activist, and patriot—donated the Cod to the Old State House "as a memorial of the importance of the Cod Fishery to the welfare of this Commonwealth." Rowe himself is memorialized today in the downtown wharf that bears his name. He was remembered by his contemporaries for his actions and ideas, including the suggestion that tea be thrown into Boston Harbor. (Rowe himself was part owner of one of those Tea Party ships.)

When the House of Representatives moved from the old to the new State House in 1798, the Sacred Cod was carried along. In 1933, the famous fish was carried a bit farther, when members of the Harvard Lampoon cod-napped him. He was stolen again, and found again, in 1968.

Both the House and Senate chambers, located on the third floor of the State House, are beautifully decorated rooms with public galleries and plentiful historic tales. Moreover, modern history is being made in those active chambers today—at least *some* of the time. Meanwhile, there are literally hundreds of other rooms in the State House where business goes on as usual day after day, from offices and storage areas to restrooms, hearing committee rooms, and ceremonial and reception halls.

The Sacred Cod, Great Clock, and state seal are not the only pieces of art in the State House. Quite the contrary; visitors soon discover that the historic building's interior and exterior provide a veritable museum of historic architecture, painting, sculpture, and odd artifacts. The problem with this museum—not unlike the problem with government and politics—is a dearth of femininity.

The State House's chambers, halls, and beautifully landscaped lawn, for example, are filled with marvelous busts and larger-than-life memorials to men who molded the state's growth. In 1990, a statue of President John F. Kennedy became the newest addition to an array that includes educator Horace Mann, orator Daniel Webster, patriot-governor John Hancock, Supreme Court Justice Louis Brandeis, and—boldly facing the State House from across Beacon Street—the valiant all-black 54th Regiment being led into battle by Robert Gould Shaw during the Civil War. Though the aforementioned all have strong local connections, representations of men less related to Boston history—like Washington, Lincoln, and David and Goliath—also abound.

But where are the women? On the front lawn are two statues of brave, powerful seventeenth-century leaders, Anne Hutchinson and Mary Dyer; the first was banished from Massachusetts for her religious beliefs, and the second was hanged for hers. Inside the State House are two installations as well—artist Bela Pratt's statue of an anonymous nurse aiding a wounded

Civil War soldier, and *Hear Us,* the newest addition to the State House art collection. Installed in 1999, *Hear Us* began bridging the State House statue gender gap by depicting six women at once—Dorothea Dix, Lucy Stone, Sarah Parker Remond, Josephine Ruffin, Mary Kenny O'Sullivan, and Florence Luscomb. All six of these heroes made contributions to Massachusetts government, championing causes that ranged from women's suffrage and the proper treatment of the mentally ill to racial equality and good working conditions for women and children.

Meanwhile, the halls and chambers of the State House fairly burst with two-dimensional faces and scenes from our past. Portraits of every Massachusetts governor can be found in the building, mostly hanging about the hallways, with a few notable exceptions. Governor Mitt Romney, for example, has a portrait of former governor John Volpe suspended over the fireplace mantel in his office. When Jane Swift was chief executive, she displayed Winthrop Murray Crane (like her, a governor from western Massachusetts) in the same spot. William Weld placed an image of Governor James Michael Curley there, and Michael Dukakis chose Governor Samuel Adams. Each incumbent governor is encouraged to place his or her favorite predecessor in that honored spot.

Among these paintings as well, women are hard to find. A nameless group of sorrowful soldiers' mothers graces one canvas, and women are alluded to in the spread of the *Milestones on the Road to Freedom* murals in the House of Representatives chamber. In one image, Judge Samuel Sewall is seen repenting his part in the 1692 Salem witchcraft trials and regretting the innocent women and men hanged because of this "error."

Throughout the decades, the stunning State House has retained a substantial hold on the city. The nineteenth-century "Boston Brahmin" Oliver Wendell Holmes, who was known to have something to say about virtually everything, called the State House "the hub of the solar system." Over the years, faulty collective memory and overzealous egos have altered his original quote to "Boston is the hub of the universe." Holmes died in 1894, but Bostonians still call their city "The Hub" today.

If Boston is the hub, incidentally, the golden dome must be the hubcap of the universe. At least mapmakers seem to see it that way. When you're driving along and spot a highway sign that reads "Boston, 75 miles," the distance is not measured to the city limits or some arbitrary central location; it's the distance in miles to—you guessed it—the dome of the Massachusetts State House.

THE ESSENTIALS

Address: State House Tours Division, Office of the Secretary of the Commonwealth, Room 194, State House, Boston, MA 02133. **Telephone:** Tour and other information, (617) 727-3676. **Website:** www.state.ma.us/sec/trs. **Visitor Information:** Free guided tours offered Monday through Friday between 10:00 A.M. and 3:30 P.M. Reservations required. Tours last 30 to 45 minutes. Self-guided tours also available; building open 9:00 A.M. to 5:00 P.M. Closed on all major federal and state holidays. Main entrance to the State House is at Beacon and Park streets; bounded also by Derne, Bowdoin, and Joy streets. Enter through east wing entrance near General Joseph Hooker Statue; check in with Tours and Information desk on second floor in Doric Hall. Gift cart open 10:00 A.M. to 4:00 P.M., also in Doric Hall. Handicapped entrance on Bowdoin Street; most of building, and restrooms, are wheelchair accessible. Public restrooms on first floor.

The Massachusetts State House is at the intersection of Boston's major historic walking tours: it is a stop on the Freedom Trail (see Chapter 10), the Boston Women's Heritage Trail (see Chapter 36), and the Literary Trail of Greater Boston, and it faces the Shaw/54th Memorial, the starting point of the Black Heritage Trail (see Chapter 35).

9 USS *Constitution*

WITH MORE than a half million guests each year, "Old Ironsides" is Boston's most frequently visited historical landmark. Having celebrated its two hundredth birthday in 1997, it is also the oldest fully commissioned warship afloat in the world. The ship's official name, of course, is USS *Constitution*.

Whether taking a guided tour of the ship or visiting the USS *Constitution* Museum, many first-time visitors to the Charlestown Navy Yard still inquire about the names. "Why was it named *Constitution*?" After the document, it seems, which was ratified a decade before. "Why did they call the frigate 'Old Ironsides,' when the ship is clearly made of wood?" Answering the latter inquiry takes a bit more explaining.

The nickname originated in the ship's heyday, during the War of 1812. A sailor—Yankee or British, depending on your historical source—watched shots from the British warship HMS *Guerriere* bounce off the side planking of *Constitution*. He allegedly exclaimed, "Huzza! Her sides are made of iron!"—an understandable error, since the ship's wooden sides were painted black and appeared indestructible. The name "Ironsides" stuck. A good thing, incidentally, since *Constitution*'s earlier nickname was the comical "Ship of Patches," after its frequently torn sails, which were constantly being stitched back together.

It is somewhat amazing that USS *Constitution* was built at all, since the leaders of the newly formed United States didn't even want to have a navy. The Revolution was a vivid but distant memory. The nation had created its first Constitution—the document, that is—and elected its first president. America was happily at peace, while Britannia continued to rule the waves with a proud navy of some 1,500 vessels.

But economic reality was about to alter American complacency. In the early 1790s, Barbary Coast pirates persistently preyed on U.S. merchant ships in the Mediterranean. President George Washington and Congress responded by ordering six frigates to be built in major ports along the eastern coast. From Portsmouth, New Hampshire, to Norfolk, Virginia, construction began on ships respectively named *Constitution, Congress, President, United States, Constellation,* and *Chesapeake.* Though construction was stalled midway (because of the threat of peace!), the ships were eventually built, and the U.S. Navy was born.

Constitution was built in Edmund Hartt's shipyard, where the North End's U.S. Coast Guard Support Center stands today. The design was developed by Joshua Humphreys, who got the credit, and Josiah Fox, who did not. Colonel George Claghorn was appointed the ship's "constructor," and a masterly job he did. In the words of the USS *Constitution*'s retired schoolmaster Leon Kaufman, the ship was deliberately "overbuilt and oversailed." In essence, that meant that though *Constitution* was much thicker, heavier, broader, and sturdier than other forty-four-gun warships of the period, it was exceptionally swift as well.

The ship's speed was enhanced by hull lines designed to be as svelte as those of the later clipper ships, and by close to an acre of flaxen sailcloth spread over thirty-six sails. Its sturdiness came from superior strains of wood. Tall pines felled in Unity, Maine, then towed to Boston became the masts. The mainmast was 220 feet high, only a foot shorter than the Bunker Hill Monument. The frame used durable live oak timbers from Georgia, and the outside was covered with New England white oak.

The omnipresent Paul Revere, who protected our State House dome with copper in 1802, sheathed *Constitution*'s bottom in copper as well. Revere's bill, which covered spikes, rods, and other bronze and copper fas-

"Old Ironsides," in the beautifully renovated Charlestown Navy Yard, is Boston's most frequently visited historic landmark.

tenings, was $3,820.33—a pittance compared to the total construction cost of $302,718.00.

The launching of such a phenomenal frigate should have been marked by festivities and delight. Instead, it was plagued with disasters that some superstitious sailors considered bad omens. The launch was initially set for September 1797, but *Constitution* quickly jammed as it slipped toward the sea. It wasn't until the ways were adjusted to a steeper incline—and the tide was adequately high—that a successful launching followed on October 21, 1797. Equally ominous, according to Kaufman, was that *Constitution* was christened by a man, Captain James Sever. "All ships have been christened by women since Helen of Troy," explained Kaufman, "so many assumed *Constitution* to be a hard luck ship."

Despite the dubious start, USS *Constitution* proved more than a match for other nineteenth-century naval vessels. In eighty-four years of service, the heavily armed floating fortress won forty-two battles, captured twenty vessels, was never defeated in battle, and was never boarded by enemy troops save for prisoners of war.

Though its active wartime duties began soon after 1797—first with a quasi war against France in the West Indies and later with the plundering pirates of the Mediterranean—*Constitution* earned undying fame in the War of 1812. The biggest battles are the stuff history classes are made of:

- On August 19, 1812, under the command of Captain Isaac Hull, it had a glorious, victorious mid-Atlantic clash with HMS *Guerriere,* a captured French warship that became the pride of Her Majesty's Navy and then the prey of America's expertly run superfrigate.
- On December 29, 1812, under commanding Captain William Bainbridge, *Constitution* defeated the warship HMS *Java* off the Brazilian coast only five months after the defeat of the *Guerriere.*
- Its last great fight of the war, when *Constitution* outmaneuvered and defeated the British ships HMS *Cyane* and HMS *Levant,* was on February 20, 1815, under the command of Captain Charles Stewart.

All of this was astounding, incidentally, since vessels in Her Majesty's Navy were not expected to be beaten in one-on-one encounters with ships of their own class.

War is generally not a laughing matter, but the sailors on "Old Ironsides" did get some amusement during the 1812 battle with *Guerriere.* Leon Kaufman, who lectured to USS *Constitution* crews on the ship's history for some three decades, explained that the rotund Captain Isaac Hull—said to be the finest sailor the ship ever had—was in charge of the frigate at the time. Officers' breeches in those days were skintight, and when the fighting captain bent down to yell "Fire!," his pants split and the sailors howled with glee. That didn't prevent them from firing the ship's many stout carronades and long guns on command—and vanquishing *Guerriere* in an astonishing thirty-five minutes.

A less amusing but equally strange detail of history concerns *Constitution* sailors who died at sea. The dead were stitched up in their sleeping hammocks with thirteen stitches, the last of which went through the seaman's upper lip. The reason, apparently, was to make sure the sailor was really deceased; some illnesses, like epilepsy, can simulate death, and sailors were known to feign death to escape naval duties.

War was certainly not *Constitution's* only mission, though it tended to dominate the ship's early days. For many years and many long stretches, the vessel was laid up in dry dock, awaiting or getting repairs, while serving as a symbolic inspiration to a growing world power. At other times, the active ship was involved in peacetime missions and humanist endeavors.

From 1835 to 1855 in particular, USS *Constitution* was involved in numerous battle-free voyages. One was a spectacular round-the-world journey under the volatile "Mad Jack" Percival in 1844–45. Pope Pius IX stepped on board when the ship visited Naples in 1849. Today, we're used to pontiffs jet-setting around the globe; in 1849, however, Pius made headlines as the first pope to enter what was technically U.S. territory, the deck of Old Ironsides.

Constitution's last trip abroad was in 1878, when it carried American exhibits to the Paris World Exhibition. The vessel's last major trip under the power of its own sails was in 1881, though "assisted" excursions followed, including Captain Gulliver's cruise of major American seaports, which began in 1931.

Old Ironsides saw duty as an antislaving ship from 1852 to 1855. As part of the African Squadron, *Constitution* was supposed to stop the capture of slaves off the west coast of Africa, but it proved no match for the fast, small schooners used as slavers. During a renovation of the ship in 1927, stores of extremely durable but hard-to-find live oak were found stored in Pensacola, Florida. The precious timber had been cut by the navy in 1856 using slave labor, then left unused and forgotten. Hence, wood cut by slaves was used to refurbish an antislaving vessel.

It's impossible to give exact figures, but no more than 18 percent of the wood on the ship we visit today is the original 1797 fabric. Almost two centuries of periodic renovation and repair have left few of the frigate's initial wooden or metal parts intact. Surprisingly, the few vestiges left of the old structure are probably under, not over, the water line. Briny seawater is a superb preservative, while fresh water and man-made acid rain will both quickly rot a ship. Part of the preservation process for *Constitution* once included packing salt between the vessel's ribs so that any fresh rainwater seeping in became a saline solution. This practice stopped on the frigate after the 1970s, however, when the salt began to solidify and lose its effectiveness.

Though preserving Old Ironsides for posterity seems imperative today, that sentiment wasn't always true. Some insiders have even half kidded that *Constitution* defended the country more than the country defended *Constitution*. As early as 1830, less than two decades after the ship's victories in the War of 1812, the first talk of scrapping the vessel began. It was Oliver Wendell Holmes, Sr., a Harvard student at the time, who first came to the rescue. Though the decision to save the ship had reportedly already been made, Holmes stirred up popular support for the project when he published his famous poem "Old Ironsides" in 1830. Money was soon found, and refurbishing begun.

The next time the ship was in financial danger, in 1897, Representative John F. Fitzgerald—President Kennedy's maternal grandfather and later, the mayor of Boston—successfully lobbied Congress for repairs. Still, USS *Constitution* needed even more work if it was to survive another century. By 1905, some had suggested Old Ironsides be used for naval target practice out at sea. The public protested again, and Congress appropriated $100,000 for more repairs.

The cycle was repeated in the late 1920s, when the ship's condition looked hopeless once more. This time, kids across America collected pennies and nickels in a people's campaign to save the ship. Ordinary citizens collected most of the money, and Congress made up the difference. The repair bill ran close to a million dollars.

Today, the U.S. Navy has assumed full responsibility for the frigate, including all repair work. The last significant dry-dock and inspection period was completed for the ship's bicentennial in 1997: between July 1992 and March 1996, *Constitution* underwent a $12 million, U.S. Navy–funded restoration and rehabilitation, which returned the ship to its 1812 appearance (the most historically accurate configuration presented in perhaps a century). The next major overhaul is planned for 2007, in preparation for the two hundredth anniversary of the War of 1812.

Old Ironsides itself is open year-round, and the thirty-minute guided tours—given by friendly, eloquent sailors dressed in either 1812 or modern uniforms—are among the most interesting and informative given at any historical landmark. The nearby USS *Constitution* Museum is also a must-see. Housed in a renovated 1832 pump house and opened in 1976, it offers a broad glimpse of American life and culture in the Federal period. Throughout the year, teacher workshops, lecture series, living history programs, and guided tours for school groups are part of the museum's ambitious activities.

Thanks to a major renovation during the 1991–92 year and ongoing exhibit updates, the museum excels at visually demonstrating just how *Constitution* was constructed and sailed. Its collection of three thousand original artifacts and hands-on displays are wonderful ways to understand sailing life at the turn of the nineteenth century. Equally wonderful are the museum's friendly, well-informed "living exhibits," model shipbuilders who construct meticulously detailed wooden ships and gladly answer questions for visitors.

Other treasures worth visiting in the Charlestown Navy Yard are USS *Cassin Young*—a World War II destroyer that was launched in 1943 and fought in the 1945 invasion of Okinawa—as well as seasonal offerings like the imposing old Commandant's House, an informative exhibit about the Navy Yard and the people who worked there over the decades ("Serving the Fleet"), and the National Park Service Visitor Center, which includes "The Whites of Their Eyes," the classic multimedia presentation on the Battle of Bunker Hill.

Though folks come to see it every day of the year, Old Ironsides certainly gets its biggest photo opportunity every Independence Day. Since 1975, visitors have flocked to watch its gala July Fourth "Salute to the Nation" turnaround in Boston Harbor. While generally the most widely publicized, it's not the ship's only annual cruise; turnarounds are actually scheduled seven to ten times each summer. Since *Constitution* hasn't been able to sail under its own power for eons (1997, when the ship sailed solo in celebration of its two hundredth birthday, being a notable exception), the frigate is escorted by tugboats.

Incidentally, many people are unaware that anyone from anywhere in the world can sail on Old Ironsides' Fourth of July turnaround; access is via lottery, found on the ship's website. The number of guests on any given cruise can sometimes be as many as nine hundred, though only one portion of those slots is allocated to lottery winners.

THE ESSENTIALS

Addresses: USS *Constitution,* Charlestown Navy Yard, Boston, MA 02129; USS *Constitution* Museum, P.O. Box 1812, Building 22, Boston National Historical Park, Charlestown Navy Yard, Boston, MA 02129. **Telephone:** Ship, (617) 242-5671; museum, (617) 426-1812; Charlestown Navy Yard Visitors Center, Boston National Historical Park, (617) 242-5601. **Websites:** www.oldironsides.com; www.ussconstitutionmuseum.org; www.ussconstitution.navy.mil/visitorinfo. **Visitor Information:** Ship open May through October, Tuesday through Sunday, 10:00 A.M. to 3:50 P.M.; November through April, Thursday through Sunday, 10:00 A.M. to 3:50 P.M. Free guided tours, daily, every half hour, 10:30 A.M. to 3:30 P.M. *For security and other reasons, ship's hours can change at any time; check website or call before visiting.*

The USS *Constitution* Museum, located across the yard, open daily 9:00 A.M. to 6:00 P.M., May 1 through October 15; 10:00 A.M. to 5:00 P.M., October 16 to April 30. Closed Thanksgiving, Christmas Day, and New Year's Day. Admission currently free to all; donations requested. Top deck of ship is wheelchair accessible via ramps; guided tours are not accessible, though special lectures can be requested. Museum is fully wheelchair accessible, including bathrooms. A full video "tour" of interior of ship can be seen in the museum. The Charlestown Navy Yard Visitor Center and its bathrooms are also accessible. There is no longer public parking inside Charlestown Navy Yard. Validated parking/reduced rates at the nearby Nautica Parking Garage are available at the museum.

The ship and museum are stops on the Freedom Trail (see Chapter 10).

10 The Freedom Trail

FROM A purely business perspective, its credentials are impressive: it's known as Boston's most popular tourist attraction and one of the most innovative concepts designed in the history of American tourism. Most of its fans are oblivious to such economic considerations—and simply know that Boston's popular Freedom Trail is red, revolutionary, and two and a half miles long.

The *red* part is a long, thin line: a stretch of inlaid bricks and overlaid

Boston's Freedom Trail, founded in 1951, is red, revolutionary, and two-and-a-half miles long; the route is embedded in city sidewalks, like this plaque in front of the State House.

paint that meanders down select Boston sidewalks, spruced up as needed by the Boston Department of Public Works.

The *revolutionary* aspect involves the sixteen sites linked by that line: from simple ground markers, eerie graveyards, and lofty old churches to majestic buildings, a rambling park, and a sturdy old naval frigate. In theory, at least, each of these historic landmarks played a significant role in America's rebellious beginnings.

Though *two and a half miles* sounds intimidating at first, it's really not. Yes, the full Freedom Trail does connect downtown Boston to the North End, then goes on to the Charlestown Navy Yard and the Bunker Hill Monument. While that seems like something of a hike for inexperienced walkers, the overview of Boston history is well worth the effort. The venerable trail—overseen at various points by National Park Service rangers, city rangers, the Freedom Trail Foundation, U.S. Navy officers, site personnel, and plenty of tourists—is one of the safest strolls around. Moreover, you can walk any single portion of the two-and-a-half-mile strip you'd like. Some three million people do just that each year.

Perhaps the best thing about the Freedom Trail is that it can be an inexpensive and entertaining educational experience for all ages; free self-guiding maps are available from National Park Service Visitor Centers and from many of the sites, and free tours are given by National Park Service interpreters. Guidebooks are available in area stores, and private tours—such as those given by the Freedom Trail Foundation using costumed characters from the colonial era, or those offered by Boston by Foot, which emphasize architectural history—offer visitors other perspectives.

In some ways, the Freedom Trail is as old as Boston itself. The Common, for example, was marked off in 1634, only four years after the town was founded. A year later, Boston opened its first public school. By 1661, the town boasted three urban burial grounds, followed by numerous churches, homes, meetinghouses, and public buildings. Many disappeared with time. But others survived—and played a role in the start of the American Revolution.

Though the sites were there for centuries, it wasn't until 1951 that *Boston Herald–Traveler* editor and daily columnist William Schofield (1909–1996) offered his own "revolutionary twist" to these landmarks. After discussions with Bob Winn, a member of the Old North Church who loved to regale visitors with tales from Boston history, Schofield wrote several editorials in his own Have You Heard column. His argument was that Boston had an unusual concentration of sites sacred to our nation's beginnings but that tourists often visited just two or three of these spots and missed the full story. Since so many of these landmarks were located within easy walking distance of one another, Schofield concluded, why not "connect the dots" with a walking tour—and call it the Freedom Trail? (Actually, he dabbled with "Puritan Path," "Liberty Loop," and "Freedom's Way" before the final moniker was devised.)

Boston mayor John B. Hynes picked up on Schofield's challenge, and the trail took shape. At first it was little more than a series of painted plywood markers. By 1953, forty thousand people were walking the Freedom Trail each year, so the city commissioned sturdier metal signs in their stead.

Under the care and guidance of the local businessman and philanthropist Richard Berenson (1909–1990), the trail began to mature through the late fifties and sixties. (It was Berenson's idea, for example, to add the distinctive red line.) As is still true today, Berenson and his colleagues' successes with the trail were the result of cooperative efforts between the public and private sectors.

In 1958, the Advertising Club of Greater Boston and the Greater Boston Chamber of Commerce were persuaded to adopt the trail as a permanent joint community service project. The John Hancock Insurance Company agreed to donate $10,000 for the first brochures. Businesspeople and bankers made charitable contributions. The city agreed to lay the paint-and-brick line. And the Freedom Trail Committee, which later became the Freedom Trail Foundation, was established, with Berenson as its chair.

By 1966, the first Freedom Trail information center was opened on the Common, distributing maps to the annual half million visitors who were then walking the trail. Among that period's most unusual Freedom Trail fund-raising efforts was a 1967 bean-eating benefit sponsored by the Boston Rotary Club. Some 22,000 people paid $25,000 to eat nine tons of Boston baked beans, serenaded by an eleven-piece banjo band and the veteran local TV personality Rex Trailer.

"Boston's Freedom Trail is unique in that it is probably the only do-it-yourself tour in the world that actually works," wrote a local columnist in the early 1970s, punctuating his statement with the tentative, "Well, maybe!"

Despite all the Freedom Trail's successes and support, all was not yet perfect.

Public toilets were too rare, and tourists sometimes got lost. People argued about which sites were appropriate for the revolutionary route. The modern Boston surrounding the sites was a mess as it moved from disrepair to citywide rebuilding projects. Several of the sites were closed on Sundays, and all had different visiting hours.

For better or worse, the sixteen participating sites were, and still are, a mix of city-, state-, and federally owned units, along with buildings belonging to or managed by various churches, private nonprofits, and historic associations. Some of the sites' personnel and managers proved less cooperative than others in dealing with the groups created to oversee the trail. The Chamber of Commerce, the Advertising Club, and the original Freedom Trail Committee eventually assumed lower profiles, and they were replaced by today's maze of institutions: the Freedom Trail Foundation, which specializes in educational and promotional projects; the city's Freedom Trail Commission, which oversees physical maintenance and determines the route; the Greater Boston Convention and Visitors Bureau; and the sites themselves.

In 1974, thanks to the persistence and vision of Berenson, U.S. congressman Joseph Moakley, and others, yet another group joined the fray. Boston National Historical Park, run by the National Park Service, was established. Today, the Park Service and its rangers are a visible presence along the trail. The National Park Service Visitor Center, at 15 State Street, is a full-service resource for tourists, offering free maps, a bookstore, restrooms, and guided Heart of the Freedom Trail tours each day during the summer. The Park Service works cooperatively with several of the sites and has helped procure millions of dollars in federal funding to revamp decaying historic structures. The Park Service also participates in active school programs with cooperative sites, like the popular "People and Places," geared to the third- and fifth-grade curriculum in the Boston public schools.

Meanwhile, the separate Freedom Trail Foundation sponsors "Walk into History"—guided tours led by colonial characters in period costume— as well as private family tours, school field trips, group tours, and a portable audio tour. The Foundation also created "Let Freedom Ring!," a family celebration held each year during April school-vacation week. (Most of the sites on the trail, of course, have their own array of programs, events, and special offerings, as described in chapters 1–4, 6, 8, 9, 12, 13, 15, 26, and 42.)

Opinions vary as to the best way to walk the Freedom Trail. Some people enjoy looking at just the outside of each of the sixteen sites, which allows them to complete the trail in about two hours. Others prefer to linger inside each structure, making the excursion last a full day or more. Guided tours, for the most part, tend to be ninety-minute "samplers" of specific portions of the trail.

If you choose to use the National Park Service's annotated map (free) or their beautifully crafted, colorfully illustrated handbook *Boston and the American Revolution* (not free), there is yet another way to approach the trail: by following four "chapters" in Boston and American history, organized by geographic location and theme. Chapter 1, for example, is called "Revolution of Minds and Hearts" and suggests how the intellectual and social grounds for revolt were laid in Boston, while viewing related sites from Boston Common to King's Chapel. Chapter 2 takes guests from the Old South Meeting House to Faneuil Hall, delineating the story called "The People Revolt." The third and fourth chapters, "Neighborhood of Revolution" and "Boston Goes to War," span Freedom Trail sites in the North End and Charlestown, ending with USS *Constitution* and the War of 1812.

Where's the best place to start? It depends on which approach you choose. Many people begin at the Common and end at Old Ironsides—an order followed by most guidebooks. Others reverse the route. Their rationale: since the last tour group enters Old Ironsides at 3:50 P.M., if you make USS *Constitution* the last stop of the day and you happen to get off schedule, you might just miss the boat.

There are other methods, too. Folks who come to the Boston National Historical Park Visitor Center for tours may begin at the nearby Old South Meeting House or Old State House. Boston by Foot Tours, on the other hand, often depart from the statue of Samuel Adams behind Faneuil Hall.

With all that in mind, here's a brief synopsis of the sixteen official sites. Many of them offer self-guided or interpreter-guided tours or talks inside. Small admission fees are charged at the Old South Meeting House, the Old State House, and the Paul Revere House; those three sites also offer a joint ticket option. The others are either free or have suggested donations.

The forty-eight-acre **Boston Common** is America's oldest green. Purchased in 1634 as common land for Boston's townspeople, it initially served as a cow pasture, military training field, and public hanging site. During the Revolution, British regulars camped and trained there—and were buried there after the disastrous Battle of Bunker Hill.

The majestic, gold-domed "new" **Massachusetts State House** opened in 1798. Designed by the celebrated Boston architect Charles Bulfinch, it houses the Sacred Cod and the refurbished Hall of Flags.

The striking, white-steepled **Park Street Church,** built in 1809, stands on "Brimstone Corner"—which alludes to both the fiery sermons heard inside and the gunpowder once stored below. It was there that William Lloyd Garrison gave his first antislavery address and the song "America" was first performed.

Next door is the **Granary Burying Ground,** named for a huge grain-storage building that once fed the poor near this site. It's now an outdoor museum of funerary folk art and a veritable who's who of Revolutionary-era names, including Paul Revere, John Hancock, Samuel Adams, and the victims of the Boston Massacre.

When Paul Revere died in 1818, his demise was tolled by the "passing bell" at **King's Chapel.** The bell itself had been recast by Revere's own foundry in 1816, a sweet-sounding addition to this 1754 stone chapel. Built as New England's first Anglican Church and once the house of worship of choice for royal governors, King's Chapel became America's first Unitarian church after the Revolution.

The adjacent **King's Chapel Burying Ground** is filled with feisty seventeenth-century Puritans, who surely turned in their graves when the Anglicans set up shop next door. Despite the confusing similarity of their names, these two sites are unrelated.

On the sidewalk behind King's Chapel is the site of another "American first"—the colonial precursor to the famous Boston Latin School. Marked by a folk-art mosaic, the memorial to the **First Public School** rests near the bronze statue of its most illustrious dropout, Ben Franklin.

Farther down School Street is the **Old Corner Bookstore** building, now home to Historic Boston Incorporated and several retail shops. Built in 1718 as an apothecary, it gained renown in the nineteenth century as a magnet for esteemed authors like Ralph Waldo Emerson, Henry Wadsworth Longfellow, Nathaniel Hawthorne, and Harriet Beecher Stowe.

Near the bookstore building stands the **Old South Meeting House,** where several thousand rowdy revolutionaries assembled before descending to Griffin's Wharf for the Boston Tea Party in December of 1773. Despite centuries of wear and tear—including its conversion by British soldiers into a horse stable and riding school during the Revolution—the Old South has survived.

The **Old State House,** built in 1713, was the first seat of Massachusetts state government. Colonial patriot James Otis argued against the Writs of Assistance there, and the Declaration of Independence was first read to Bostonians from its balcony.

Below the balcony of the Old State House lies the trail's most treacherous stop, the site of the **Boston Massacre.** A circle of stones on a traffic island marks where British regulars fired on a snowball-hurling colonial mob, killing five colonists. Sam Adams blatantly exploited the incident to fan revolutionary flames.

Across State Street and a short walk down Congress Street lies **Faneuil Hall.** Renovated and reopened in 1992, the 1742 building has long been known as the Cradle of Liberty—and America's foremost historic meeting, market, and military hall.

From the Faneuil Hall Marketplace area—an extremely popular complex of shops, cafés, and quality fast food stands—the trail loops under the elevated Central Artery and through a slice of the Big Dig (when the latter is completed, the trail will eventually cross a park at this site). Visitors will now find themselves in the North End, home of the **Paul Revere House.** Built in 1680, it's the oldest house in downtown Boston and the place where Revere lived when he made his famous ride of April 18, 1775. From the steeple of the Episcopalian **Old North Church,** the city's oldest standing house of worship, two lanterns were hung that same night, warning Charlestown citizens that the British were approaching Concord "by sea."

The North End's **Copps Hill Burying Ground** was a final resting place for colonists, though irreverent redcoats used it as a target practice site, cannon emplacement, and lookout. Across the harbor, in Charlestown, stands the soaring obelisk commemorating the Battle of Bunker Hill. Though it rests on Breed's Hill, where the battle was fought, it's called the **Bunker Hill Monument.**

In the nearby Charlestown Navy Yard, which was decommissioned in

1974, floats the Freedom Trail's most visited site, the mammoth **USS Constitution,** as well as the privately run **USS Constitution** **Museum.** Built in 1797, Old Ironsides won battles against the Barbary pirates and against the British in the War of 1812. The wonderfully informative and interactive museum is a perfect complement to a visit aboard the ship. There is also a National Park Service Visitor Center in the Navy Yard, in case you missed the downtown branch at 15 State Street.

Despite five decades of improvement and change, the Freedom Trail is not yet perfect. Not only is there no single desk marked "The Buck Stops Here," there's no buck—no annual city budget, no endowment fund, and no large financial source to regularly pay for major improvements.

Thanks in part to an intensive series of focus-group meetings conducted in 1996—called the Freedom Trail Task Force and utilizing the talents and insights of almost a hundred community volunteers—the sites, the National Park Service, the Freedom Trail Foundation, the City of Boston, and the Commonwealth have all made concerted efforts to work together and implement change. Among the most visible improvements are the development of thematic chapters in the trail (as noted above), sponsorship of special events, new signage, new maps and guidebooks, website development, a more permanent red line, colonial-costumed tour guides, antenna audio guides, and improved wheelchair access.

There's still a ways to go, of course. More explicit, perhaps even multilingual, signs would be useful, and wheelchair access is still not what it could be. Road renovations and mazes created by the Big Dig will, one hopes, soon be a thing of the past. A comprehensive urban design study would enable better planning of revitalization efforts. And a new, more modern visitor center—one employing multimedia audiovisual presentations and other new technology to illustrate Boston history—would help enhance the Freedom Trail experience. The latter two, of course, may well be possible once the Artery Project is completed.

And yes, there's just one more problem, as noted by the "Father of the Freedom Trail" in the last interview he ever gave. During that conversation, Bill Schofield was asked if the Freedom Trail he conceived in 1951 was now perhaps passé.

"No way is it obsolete," Schofield adamantly responded. "I think [the Freedom Trail] is one of the things that can help to maybe bring this city back to what it should have been. And, well . . . I haven't seen it in years, but remembering what it used to be like, what it needs more than anything is a couple of toilets!"

THE ESSENTIALS

Addresses: Two-and-a-half-mile red line begins on Boston Common, ends at the Navy Yard and Bunker Hill Monument in Charlestown. Boston National Historical Park Visitor Center: 15 State Street, Boston, MA 02108. The Freedom Trail Foundation: 3 School Street, Boston, MA 02108. **Telephone:** Boston National Historical Park Visitor Center, (617) 242-5642; Greater Boston Convention and Visitors Bureau, (617) 536-4100; the Freedom Trail Foundation, (617) 227-8800. **Websites:** www.nps.gov/bost; www.thefreedomtrail.org. **Visitor Information:** Trail itself always there for self-guided walking tours.

National Park Service offers free maps, and free daily 90-minute tours, from April through November, starting at Boston National Historical Park Visitor Center, 15 State Street, Boston. Maps and information also available at Greater Boston Convention and Visitors Bureau information kiosk near the Park Street subway station on Boston Common, and at the NPS Visitor Center at the Charlestown Navy Yard. Most Freedom Trail sites open roughly 9:00 A.M. to 5:00 P.M. year-round. Admission to most sites free; three have nominal fees and offer a joint ticket. Trail is fairly wheelchair accessible if curb cuts not blocked; minor rerouting necessary in North End. All Freedom Trail sites are at least partially accessible, some with assistance; visitor centers have wheelchair-accessible restrooms.

The private, nonprofit Boston by Foot offers Heart of the Freedom Trail tours, which focus on architectural history: (617) 367-2345; 24-hour Hot Foot Line (617) 367-3766; www.bostonbyfoot.com; special tours are also offered by the Freedom Trail Foundation (see above); fees are charged for these tours.

PART TWO

From Here to Eternity

HOUSES OF WORSHIP AND
HOMES FOR THE DEAD

I N T H E eighteenth century, during the stormy years that preceded the Revolutionary War, Boston gained a reputation as a center of political sedition. Just a century before, however, the same town was known for its religious repression—a product, pure and simple, of the Puritan presence.

When the Puritans of the Massachusetts Bay Colony first settled Boston in 1630, they were seeking religious freedom. Liberated from the shackles of the Church of England, the colonists began establishing their own houses of worship. Unfortunately, they also created a Puritan theocracy as intolerant as the Anglican society from which they had fled. Their meetinghouses—used for both town and church matters—were created in simple, stark fashion rather than the ornate architectural styles associated with Anglicanism and Roman Catholicism. Harvard College, founded in Cambridge in 1636, was intended to train the colony's ministers. Boston Latin School, today a public school for academically outstanding high school students, prepared young men to go to Harvard.

Meanwhile, church attendance was mandatory, sermons were long, and burial was an altogether unholy affair. Throughout the colonial period, corpses were buried in downtown graveyards like King's Chapel, Copp's Hill, and the Granary. Not until 1831, with the advent of Mount Auburn Cemetery in Cambridge, were cemeteries designed as gardens of bucolic charm.

As various groups of Puritans broke off to colonize other areas around Boston, their first order of business was building a meetinghouse. That house immediately became the First Church—like the First Church in Roxbury, begun in 1632—a naming practice that ultimately created a plethora of "First Churches" throughout New England. When schisms within a particular church occurred, groups would create Second and Third churches. The dissident Third Church of Christ, for example, broke from Boston's original First Church over a theological controversy known as the "halfway covenant." They established their own independent meetinghouse in 1669, and by 1729 had built a structure still known and loved today as the Old South Meeting House.

Some dissidents came from within the church. Anne Hutchinson preached a "covenant of grace" and the equality of men's and women's souls. For these heresies she was banished to Rhode Island (see Chapter 26). Other dissidents came from outside the church. If they appeared to accept the Puritan faith, as did the "praying Indians" of "apostle" John Eliot, their lives might be saved; if they refused to convert, however, they might be hanged on Boston Common. Such was the tragic fate of the Quaker Mary Dyer, as well as countless Native Americans, supposed witches, pirates, and other so-called infidels.

Despite that early Puritan stranglehold, other religious groups filtered into Boston and eventually prospered. By 1685, much of the town was either Congregational (the later generations' name for Puritan), Baptist, or Quaker. By 1688, even the Anglican Church had gotten its first real foothold in the Hub. The original King's Chapel was built on the corner of School and Tremont streets, displacing part of the town's first Puritan graveyard. The rapidly growing Anglican congregation of King's Chapel spawned two more of Boston's most cherished churches as well. In 1723, their parishioners helped build Christ Church in the North End—today popularly known as the Old North Church. In 1733, a third Anglican Church, called Trinity, absorbed the next overflow. That building was the granddaddy of the magnificent 1877 Trinity Church, which graces Copley Square to this day.

The last great change for these churches began near the end of the eighteenth century—and was partly inspired by ideals unleashed in the Revolution. In 1785, under the guidance of the Reverend James Freeman, the Anglican King's Chapel became the first official Unitarian Church in America. Buoyed by the popular liberal preachings of William Ellery Channing, Unitarianism swept through New England, which explains, in part, why so many structures built as Puritan churches are Unitarian-Universalist today.

Meanwhile, Boston's rapidly growing community of free blacks was asserting its independence as well. African-Americans had always been allowed in white churches, but only tucked away in the back galleries, out of sight of both congregation and preacher. By the early nineteenth century, this too began to change. Free Boston blacks built their own African Meeting House in 1806. Today, it's the oldest standing black church built primarily by free blacks in the nation. Other African-American citizens joined their white comrades in protesting segregated churches like the Charles Street Meeting House, which was eventually purchased by a Black Baptist congregation (see Part 5, "The Many Faces of Boston," for these and related stories).

Boston churches and their congregations changed hands, shape, styles, and neighborhoods throughout the nineteenth and twentieth centuries. The influx of Irish immigrants in the mid-nineteenth century, for example, created numerous Catholic churches, while newly arriving German and Eastern European Jews built or adapted synagogues near their new homes (see Chapter 39, "The Vilna Shul"). Old houses of worship sometimes succumbed to one of Boston's periodic "Great Fires," or adapted to different uses as their congregations moved to larger structures in more fashionable, and more convenient, parts of town.

The end result for Boston? A mosaic of engaging structures and sites with an endless stream of tales, both secular and religious, to share.

11 The First Church in Roxbury

STANDING ATOP a lightly wooded hill overlooking John Eliot Square, the First Church in Roxbury is a stunning sight. Prim, grand, and gracious—and guarding an enviable panoramic view of Boston proper—the white clapboard meetinghouse looks like the quintessential New England village church.

It is, in fact, just that. But the First Church in Roxbury also boasts an unusually distinguished past. Dating back to 1631, it is the third oldest congregation in the present-day city of Boston. And though four previous church buildings stood on this site, the 1804 structure we see today is the Hub's oldest wood-frame church. John Eliot, famous for his ministry to the Indians, preached and taught here, in one of the building's more primitive incarnations. William Dawes began his own famous "midnight ride" here, to warn patriots that the British regulars were coming, while Paul Revere made a parallel ride from Charlestown. Revere himself left his mark here in the form of a huge church bell cast in his family's Canton foundry. That bell still hangs in the belfry—as impressive an ornament as the church's Simon Willard clock and Hook & Hastings organ.

Only the best was good enough for Roxbury's very first church.

The first people to come to the First Church were the Puritans of the Massachusetts Bay Colony, who arrived on the eastern shores of Massachusetts in 1630. In the course of the first year, small groups broke away from this core, dispersing into seven distinct communities. On the north shore they had already founded Salem, and on the south, Dorchester. In between were the Puritan settlements of Boston, Medford, Charlestown, Watertown, and Roxbury.

William Pynchon led one such group into the craggy land on the neck of the Boston peninsula. Because of the hilly uplands, ledges, and the distinctive textured rock they called puddingstone, the settlers named their town Rocksbrough, also spelled Rocksborough, or Rocksbury. The town, incorporated on September 28, 1630, included 10,686 acres. The town center developed in a small area of high ground at modern John Eliot Square. Since a meetinghouse was essential to Puritan life—providing a space for both town and church matters—and since church attendance was mandatory, work on the first First Church building began immediately.

Though records on this period are few, historians believe that the original meetinghouse, completed in 1632, was a simple log cabin with a thatched roof and clay floors. The first pastor was the Reverend Thomas Weld, an English university graduate descended from an ancient Saxon family and an ancestor of William Weld, who became governor of Massachusetts more than three and a half centuries later.

Known to his Roxbury flock as "a painful preacher"—then a term of re-

The community-centered First Church in Roxbury looks like the quintessential New England village church.

spect—Weld helped to edit the original *Bay Psalm Book,* the colonies' first collection of metrical versions of the psalms, which became more popular than any other English Psalter. He was also a member of the first board of overseers at Harvard College, founded in 1636. Less laudable from a modern perspective is his active part in the 1637 sedition trial of Anne Hutchinson; as a result of her "unorthodox" religious views and these subsequent trials, Hutchinson was banished from the commonwealth. The large Weld family also owned slaves, as did other rich seventeenth-century Roxbury landowners like the Dudleys and Williamses.

In less than a decade, the Reverend Weld returned to England, eventually becoming chaplain to Oliver Cromwell.

The most famous preacher to emerge from First Church was Weld's colleague and successor John Eliot (1604–1690), long remembered as the saintly "apostle to the Indians." Eliot worked alongside Weld as church teacher and editor of the *Bay Psalm Book,* then stayed with First Church for fifty years after Weld's departure. In 1645 he helped establish the "Free Schoole in Roxburie," later known as the Roxbury Latin School.

Unlike most of his contemporaries, Eliot believed that New England's Native Americans were people—people who could and should share the

Puritan gospel and covenant. One of his rationales may seem curious today: Eliot believed these natives were part of the Lost Tribes of Israel, and that their language included traces of Hebrew, the true tongue of God.

In a day and age when many Puritans thought nothing of killing or enslaving American Indians—or hanging Quakers simply because of their beliefs—Eliot's mission, begun in 1646, was clearly radical. He learned the native language, taught many Native Americans the English alphabet, translated the Bible into Algonquin, and began setting up communities for Christian Native Americans. The first such town was founded in Natick in 1651 and the second at Ponkapoag, on the modern site of Ponkapoag Golf Course in the Blue Hills Reservation.

Today we realize that imposing the white man's culture and religion on these Native Americans showed a cruel lack of respect and recognition for their culture. In Eliot's world, however, it was an earnest attempt to civilize and save "the heathens." John Eliot has been memorialized in the area in a variety of ways, including Eliot Square, Eliot Street, Eliot Hall, and the Eliot School in Jamaica Plain. His remains were buried in what's now known as the Eliot Burying Ground, on the corner of Washington and Eustis streets in Roxbury.

One interesting footnote to the Eliot story: According to historian Samuel Eliot Morison, the "Indian Bible" had trouble with words or concepts for which there was no Algonquin equivalent. For instance, apparently the native word for "virgin" was little known and little used; hence, wherever that word appeared in the text, Eliot translated it using a more common Algonquin term that meant "a chaste young man."

During Eliot's tenure at the First Church in Roxbury, the congregation outgrew its first structure and built a bigger one, in 1674. This second house was razed in 1741 and replaced by an even larger, more elegant church building. Throughout this period, the First Church maintained its role as both civic center and religious meetinghouse. Therefore it was not unusual that the third First Church stored grain in its loft and gunpowder in the roof beams and steeple. That gunpowder led to disaster when, in 1743, a foot-warming stove in one of the pews set the church ablaze only two years after it was built.

The fourth First Church emerged from the rubble in 1746 and survived the rigors of the Revolution—despite a cannonball that blasted through its belfry during the siege of Boston. In 1803, that sturdy structure was torn down and its timber sold for six hundred dollars so that the beautiful white Federal-style building we know today could be built. Many irate parishioners complained of the decision to build yet another First Church when the last one was still sound. One mused in his diary, "Whether every generation grows wiser or not, it is evident they grow more fashionable and extravagant."

This fifth and present meetinghouse, dedicated June 7, 1804, was unarguably both fashionable and extravagant. The design was adapted from Timothy Palmer's First Unitarian Church in Newburyport; architect William Blaney oversaw the Roxbury construction. Built on mortared rubble stone and granite, the structure was braced with heavy timber walls covered with wooden clapboard. The classical front entrance had finely arched doorways and a beautiful Palladian window. Directly above, a storied steeple rose in five sections, from clock tower to belfry, attic to dish-cover dome, finally ending in a swallowtail banner weather vane. One reviewer called it "a virtual museum of Federalist architecture and antique decorative art." And that was true, both inside and out.

The interior was more ornate than that of the Newburyport meetinghouse on which it was based. It included multiple columns, white box pews with mahogany armrests, and a curved symmetrical pair of stairs leading to either side of the gallery. Among the furnishings were a grand chandelier, the Paul Revere bell, and two clocks designed by the famous clockmaker Simon Willard. Though the interior underwent major remodeling in 1835, 1857, and 1888, the exterior has remained essentially unchanged.

In 1876, a modest parish house, Putnam Chapel, was built behind the white clapboard church. Though most of that building's historical elements were lost in a devastating 1983 fire, Putnam Chapel is still the center of First Church daily activities.

For almost four centuries, the five different structures that have housed the First Church in Roxbury have been a living stage for the play of Boston history. In the seventeenth century, the acts included preaching Christianity to the Native Americans, creating the *Bay Psalm Book* and the "Indian Bible," establishing America's first Protestant Sunday school, and helping to build centers of education like Roxbury Latin School and Harvard College.

During the eighteenth century, the First Church naturally became a stage for scenes from the War for Independence. As noted earlier, William Dawes began his famous ride there. Moreover, because of its elevated location and unencumbered view of nearby Boston, Eliot Square was frequently used for militia training and musters after 1762.

Patriot general John Thomas, who commanded the first brigade under Major-General Artemus Ward, made his headquarters at the Dillaway-Thomas House, across Roxbury Street on Eliot Square. The grounds and meetinghouse of the First Church itself were occupied by patriot troops. To help minimize the inevitable devastation, which reached its height during the eleven-month British siege of Boston, the First Church parish committee removed the pews and bell. As it happened, British cannonballs periodically punctured the church, the area in and near John Eliot Square was severely damaged, and many of Roxbury's woodlands were cut for firewood.

As the nineteenth century and the new republic dawned, so too did theological reforms. The Congregational Church of colonial days declined—mired, as it was, in Puritan severity and Calvinist conservatism—while the liberal ideas of William Ellery Channing and the Unitarian movement found increasing favor with Boston churchgoers. This movement eventually transformed Protestant religion in New England, and the Reverend Eliphalet Porter quietly steered Roxbury's First Church through the first and roughest periods.

In 1975, the church merged into the Benevolent Fraternity of Unitarian Churches, now doing business as the Unitarian Universalist Urban Ministry. Today, the First Church embraces Unitarian Universalism in its small congregation that includes members who are black and white, gay and straight, old and young, female and male, and from a variety of ethnic backgrounds and economic classes.

Recent decades have seen equal doses of sorrow and joy at Roxbury's aging First Church. In 1954, Hurricane Carol tore off the church's bell tower. Meanwhile, congregations declined, neighborhoods changed, tensions rose, and internal problems hurt the church. The area was victimized by vandalism and arson: between 1978 and 1983 alone, three major fires ravaged Eliot Square. As a result, Putnam Chapel was gutted, the meetinghouse suffered major water damage, and the famous Hook & Hastings organ, purchased in 1883, was rendered inoperable.

Happily, a 1990 matching grant from the Massachusetts Historical Commission's Preservation Projects Fund helped pay for $170,000 worth of exterior rehabilitation. Funds were also raised to minimally refurbish the chapel. And though it would take another $150,000 to restore the organ fully, enough money was collected to make it playable.

One item that has survived intact it is the Simon Willard wall clock that was hung in the church in 1806. Although the clock now in the gallery is actually a replica of the original, the switch was not one caused by fire or destruction; instead, it was one of the last acts by church leaders before the merger of the First Church into the Benevolent Fraternity. (The rare original clock was moved to the Willard Clock Museum in Grafton, Massachusetts, where it may be viewed today.)

As of mid-2003, construction of a Youth Education Center was well under way and expected to be completed by year's end. The center is positioned to connect the chapel and church and will include an elevator and updated bathrooms—thereby making all three buildings wheelchair accessible. The UU Urban Ministry raised $2.3 million to build the new structure and to make renovations to the old meetinghouse.

So bit by bit, with help from parishioners and friends, grants, donations, and rental fees, the work is being done. Meanwhile, the First Church's first priority is building and sustaining a community of faith and action. Its staff reaches out to community youth and helps to develop programs like the Stand High/Stand United weekend enrichment activities, and On TRAC, an after-school program operated as a partnership with the BELL (Building Educated Leaders for Life) Foundation.

"The updated facilities, continued renewal of the surrounding neighborhood, and devotion of people who care," says James H. Staton, associate director of the UU Urban Ministry, "can give great hope for the evolution of a vital congregation in this sacred, historical place."

THE ESSENTIALS

Address: First Church in Roxbury, 10 Putnam Street, Roxbury, MA 02119; located in John Eliot Square, Roxbury, Boston; bounded by Dudley, Roxbury, and Putnam streets. Unitarian Universalist Urban Ministry, 110 Arlington Street, Boston, MA 02116. **Telephone:** main church number, (617) 445-8393; programs, (617) 427-2255; UU Urban Ministry, (617) 542-6233. **Websites:** www.uuum.org; www.firstchurchroxbury.org. **Visitor Information:** Church open for services 11:00 A.M., Sundays. Free. Occasional tours given; call for information. Putnam Chapel open evenings for youth outreach programs. Meetinghouse and chapel are wheelchair accessible via elevator in new Education Center; accessible bathrooms in Putnam Chapel and Education Center.

12 King's Chapel

MAYBE George Washington slept here. Then again, maybe not. But it really doesn't matter, since so many *other* historically significant events have taken place within King's Chapel's dark granite walls.

For starters, the downtown chapel with the "sawed-off steeple" is an architectural wonder. Built in 1754—around and on top of its congregation's previous church—King's Chapel was based on a "mail order" design and crafted with the first granite dug from the not-yet-famous Quincy quarries. Its original organ was the first to be permanently installed in a church in British America, and the chapel's exceptional musical programs included the American debut of Handel's *Messiah*. The building served as the first Anglican church in New England and later as the first Unitarian Church in America (explaining, in part, the church's unique formal liturgy and its Unitarian Universalist congregation's continued use of the Anglican-based *Book of Common Prayer*).

Tucked away in its subterranean chambers are the tombs of a multitude of colonial souls, while upstairs King's Chapel's religious services have inspired and consoled a broad spectrum of humanity, including British redcoats, plundering pirates, Boston Brahmins, repentant prisoners on their way to the hangman's noose, and a host of everyday people. Throughout it all, the chapel's chiming bells—especially the sweet-sounding one recast by Paul Revere in 1816—have tolled the end of major wars and the death of prestigious leaders.

As for George Washington, who knows if he dozed off here? He did come to a concert at the chapel during a visit to Boston in 1789 and sat in the eminently comfortable, regally decorated, boxed-off Governor's Pew. He also attended services here years earlier while serving in the French and Indian War. Religious services were known to last for hours in those days; and what did or did not happen to the comfortably cushioned General Washington was apparently not recorded for posterity.

You can find King's Chapel on the corner of Tremont and School streets. It's interesting to note that the story of King's Chapel—and, in many ways, the story of colonial Boston—actually begins with those three simple words: *King's, Tremont,* and *School.*

Tremont, for example, is a contraction of *Trimountain,* or "three mountains." When the Puritans of the Massachusetts Bay Colony arrived in Boston in 1630—escaping, among other things, the oppressive "popery" of the Church of England—they found a pear-shaped peninsula with a distinctive

Beautiful King's Chapel was New England's first Anglican and, later, America's first Unitarian house of worship.

mountain ridge running through its center. Three hills made up this ridge, individually known as Pemberton Hill, Mount Vernon, and Beacon Hill and collectively known as the Trimountain. The colonists called their peninsula Trimountain for a brief period before changing its name to Boston. As for the three hills, Beacon was eventually pared down some sixty feet and used for landfill in Boston's mudflats, while the other two disappeared altogether.

School Street, once called Latin School Street, was named for Boston's— as well as America's—first public school, built in 1645; it's commemorated by a folk-art memorial set in the sidewalk behind King's Chapel. When the original small wooden chapel was replaced by today's larger stone structure, its congregation snatched land away from the Latin School property. In return for this land, King's Chapel built the displaced school a new home, where the Omni Parker House stands today. (Boston Latin School still exists; its current home is in the Fenway). Among the Latin School's alumni were Samuel Adams and John Hancock, men who would eventually rebel against English sovereignty in the colonies.

The name King's Chapel comes from the British monarch James II (not, as a visiting child once surmised, from Martin Luther King, Jr.). It was during James II's brief reign (1685–89) that Britain began tightening its control over the American colonies. Part of that crackdown meant building a church for loyal Anglicans living in Boston—a group that included royal governors, British soldiers, and certain local merchants.

It was difficult for King James and his Boston emissaries to buy land for the Anglican Church, especially since those emissaries were the despised Royal Governor Edmund Andros and the detested Reverend Robert Ratcliffe, Boston's first Anglican minister. The Puritans, as noted earlier, had deliberately left the Church of England six decades before, and their descendants were understandably loath to sell precious downtown Boston real estate to support an Anglican establishment.

Rather than face failure, the resourceful Governor Andros expropriated a prime parcel of land at the intersection of Tremont and School streets. The land was already in use as a burying ground owned by the city. Perhaps assuming that it would be easier to dislodge the dead than the living, the governor seized the land by eminent domain. By 1688, many of the dead had presumably been reinterred elsewhere, and the original King's Chapel was built on part of that site. The portion of the burying ground that remained, incidentally, is still owned by the city (and legally unconnected to the adjacent King's Chapel). An ironic twist, since the Puritans interred there would have been outraged at the idea of spending eternity next to an Anglican Church.

Though christened as King's Chapel, the original wooden church was renamed Queen's Chapel during the reign of Queen Anne (1702–14). It was not long before the building (by either name) was bursting at the seams with a growing congregation; less than sixty years after its construction, plans to build the larger, more elegant granite church we know today were already in the works.

Building funds, as ever, were hard to come by, despite the chapel's royal connections. Fortunately, in 1749 the talented Peter Harrison of Newport, Rhode Island, agreed to design a Georgian chapel for the Anglicans for nary a shilling. (In the mid-eighteenth century, architecture was still a gentlemen's hobby and not a paying profession; fortunately, Harrison was ably supported by his wealthy wife.)

Designing King's Chapel, as it turned out, was an easy job. The church's building committee mailed its size requirements and a request for "Symmetry and Proportion" to Harrison. Harrison, who had a sizable architectural library to draw from, mailed back detailed plans, which borrowed liberally from designs of certain London churches, including Sir James Gibbs's St. Martin-in-the-Fields in Trafalgar Square. It's not clear whether Harrison, who later gained fame for his Newport mansions, ever saw the empty site. But the builders in Boston employed his plans, ultimately with great success. In order to keep the church open as much as possible during the five-year construction process, the workers built around the old wooden structure, gaily passing leftover segments out the windows as they progressed.

The exterior of the new chapel was rough-hewn granite from Quincy (then Braintree), the first use of the stone that would later be used in the Bunker Hill Monument, the Parker House, Quincy Market, Fort Warren, and other Boston buildings. Since the Quincy quarries were yet to be dug, surface granite was used, shaped into four-foot blocks by a process of heating the stone and then dropping cannonballs it.

Two major exterior sections deviated from Harrison's plans. Due again to lack of funds, the steeple was never finished—thereby giving it the distinctive, truncated, "half-steeple" look we see today. Money was also lacking for the front portico and its twelve twenty-five-foot Ionic columns. Those were added in 1789—after the Revolution, when the chapel had evolved into America's first Unitarian church—but added on a tight budget. Since rock was costly, the massive columns were built of wood, then disguised as stone. A close inspection reveals the wooden beams underneath, with some chinks corroding away, gnawed by the elements.

Though Harrison gave King's Chapel a rustic and dark exterior, the Georgian interior was all brightness and light. Harrison's design lined the galleries with matching pairs of Corinthian columns, which draw the eye up to the vaulted arches. King's Chapel tour guides often bring visitors to one particular such column on the edge of Pew 24. There, a small door opens on one side, revealing a shallow closet where the pew's owners could store personal belongings; on the other side, a similar hatch exposes the enormous tree trunk from which the column was hewn.

Though the parishioners of King's Chapel were originally offered free stone to make these columns, they declined the gift because they could not afford the shipping or masonry costs. The huge pine trees used instead were officially sent from the royal forests in York, Maine. (An interesting footnote: it was illegal for anyone to cut wood from the king's forests in Maine without royal permission; only trees accidentally felled by wind could be taken without punishment, giving us the word *windfall* for unexpected good fortune.)

Echoing the ceiling's upward sweep is a wineglass-shaped pulpit built by Peter Vintoneau, complete with sounding board above and reading and clerk's desk below. The 1717 pulpit—like the communion table in the chancel behind—is among the objects remaining from the original wooden chapel. Over the centuries, church leaders from virtually every faith have spoken from the elegant elevated podium. Thanks in part to the chapel's excellent acoustics, a microphone has never been necessary to spread the Word all the way back to the organ and choir loft in the rear gallery.

Above the chancel is another Georgian touch, Harrison's fan-shaped Palladian window. Behind the central shutters lies hidden a perennial point of contention, a German-made glass window painted with the image of Christ. Donated by merchant and banker John Amory Lowell during the Civil War, the image was considered inferior artwork by many Unitarian parishioners. "It's terribly ghastly . . . and not even real stained glass," confided one longtime church member while awaiting the chapel's weekly Wednesday noontime service. Though the glass panel has been covered in various ways much of its life—some claim it's simply to block the late-morning sunlight during Sunday services—it is always open on Easter Sunday. According to the Reverend Earl Holt, King's Chapel's minister, the image of Christ was retained when the glass panels on either side were removed. "It has been typical and consistent over the years," he explains, "for the building to be maintained as it was."

Representations of Christ—whether poorly executed or expertly done—are not often found in Unitarian churches today. Though the church has Protestant roots, contemporary Unitarian Universalists often shy away from using formal Christian ceremonies and symbols. This Unitarian church, however, is unique—as its guides will explain in detail—at once "Unitarian in theology, Anglican in liturgy, and congregational in church government." Though occupation by the Church of England and the link with the British crown officially ended after the American Revolution—when the Reverend James Freeman helped pioneer changes in liturgy and doctrine that made King's Chapel America's first Unitarian Church—the chapel has retained reminders of its historic Anglican roots.

As a result, many items reflecting the congregation's Anglican heritage are still in use. The antique communion table donated by British monarchs William and Mary, for example, is employed for monthly communion services. Within the comfortably cushioned wooden box pews can generally be found a Holy Bible and a hymnal, along with a volume entitled the *Book of Common Prayer According to the Use in King's Chapel;* the latter is an Anglican/Episcopalian text, revised to date nine times by the parish, most recently in 1986. Royal crowns and miters adorn the handsome loft organ; and the "Governor's Pew," once dismantled as an affront to democratic seating, was rebuilt in 1928. Furthermore, the name King's Chapel remains, although it was changed to Stone Chapel from 1776 to the 1830s due to ardent anti-British sentiments.

In recent decades, a gradual democratization has helped to dispel the chapel's old aura of wealth and Brahminism. A century and more back, well-to-do parishioners bought pews for exclusive use by their families. Owners would outfit their pews with shelves, umbrella stands, fabrics, stools, small foot stoves, and varied seating arrangements. (If the backward-facing benches seem odd, remember that parents of yore found it a convenient setup for watching their children during two- or three-hour services, and for keeping everyone's feet cozy.) Today the church owns these pews, which are open to all.

Although its religious history fascinates, visitors to King's Chapel will find other interesting items as well. In the rear gallery, for example, sits the chapel's sixth organ, built by Charles Fisk. The original King's Chapel housed the first church organ in New England; the walnut-stained case of this present organ—a wonderful mechanical action instrument—is a replica of that first one, which occupied this space in the 1750s. The chapel's active musical life includes some sixty concerts and recitals per year, coordinated by organist and musical director Heinrich Christensen, who conducts the renowned King's Chapel Choir on Sunday mornings. Present-day musical endeavors build on a foundation strongly established in the past. The American premiere of Handel's *Messiah,* for example, took place at King's Chapel in 1786. The Handel and Haydn Society, formed in 1815, made its American debut there as well.

As one might expect, countless weddings and funerals have been held at King's Chapel over the centuries. When A. Bronson Alcott and Abigail May—best remembered as the parents of author Louisa May Alcott—came to Boston, they chose to hold their wedding at King's Chapel. Bronson, a sincere utopian and impractical visionary, noted the event in his *Journal* entry of May 23, 1830: "Agreeably to preceding expectation, I was this day married by Rev'd. Mr. Greenwood, at King's Chapel. Passed the evening at Col. May's [Joseph May, father of the bride], and came to Mrs. Newell's, my place of board, with my friend, Miss May, after the civilities of the evening." And that, as they say, was that!

Among the many historic funerals here was that of patriot and physician General Joseph Warren, who was killed at the Battle of Bunker Hill on June 17, 1775. Since British troops won the battle and held the hill, Warren's body—interred on the battle site—was sadly inaccessible to his fellow colonists. Once General Washington forced the British to evacuate Boston on March 17, 1776, a group of friends and family rowed over to Charlestown to exhume Warren. His decomposed body was apparently identified by Paul Revere, who recognized two artificial teeth he had fastened into his friend's mouth with silver wire (this is credited as the first documented instance of dental forensics identification). Since King's Chapel was inextricably linked with royalty and British sympathizers, the rector, Rev. Dr. Henry Caner and perhaps half of the church's pewholders had already fled for Halifax (Caner slyly taking the church's precious communion silver with him). Though King's Chapel was officially closed until 1777, it was briefly reopened to accommodate the beloved Dr. Warren's formal memorial service.

King's Chapel still honors dozens of men and women with memorials. Thirty-five commemorative plaques are displayed on walls and floor surfaces, and an obelisk dedicated to the slain Frenchman Saint Sauveur, is on display in the front courtyard. There are people buried in the chapel, too, in vaulted tombs within a large basement chamber scattered with boxes, files, old furniture, maintenance supplies, and heating pipes. The crypt, which was closed to future interment by an 1890 city act, includes twenty sealed family tombs, plus a common "Strangers' Tomb."

More than forty thousand people a year now visit King's Chapel, a popular and lovely stop on the Freedom Trail. But clearly, King's Chapel harbors a lot more of interest and import than immediately meets the eye.

THE ESSENTIALS

Address: King's Chapel, corner of Tremont and School streets, Boston. King's Chapel Parish House, 64 Beacon Street, Boston, MA 02108. **Telephone:** Parish House, (617) 227-2155; King's Chapel, (617) 523-1749. **Website:** www.kings-chapel.org. **Visitor Information:** Morning prayer and sermon every Sunday, 11:00 A.M., followed by special guided tour, with Holy Communion the first Sunday of the month. Services also on Wednesdays, 12:15 P.M., with Holy Communion on the third Wednesday. Concerts each Tuesday, 12:15 P.M. Open to the public daily, Memorial Day through Veteran's Day, 10:00 A.M. to 4:00 P.M., and on weekends the remainder of the year. Self-guided tours always available; special guided tours may be arranged with advance notice. Free; donations encouraged. Main floor is partially accessible by wheelchair; no accessible restrooms. King's Chapel and King's Chapel Burying Ground are stops on the Freedom Trail (see Chapter 10).

13 The Old North Church

GRANTED, the building popularly known as the Old North Church will be forever remembered for its association with patriot Paul Revere and his daring "midnight ride" of April 1775. Revere, that ride, and the church were all memorialized and immortalized by Henry Wadsworth Longfellow in his narrative poem of 1861, "Paul Revere's Ride."

Still, the Old North, located on the Freedom Trail in Boston's North End, has many other less widely touted claims to fame—claims that continually draw in curious visitors from around the world. The 1723 Georgian-style brick building, with its lofty white spire and grand peal of eight angelic bells, is renowned as Boston's oldest standing house of worship and an architectural treasure. Moreover, the structure's rich history includes British generals, benevolent pirates, toppling steeples, seminal Sunday schools, community outreach programs, and a wealth of art, architecture, and artifacts from Anglican, British, and American history.

The Old North's long and wide-ranging story was partly the result of the fact that, unlike so many other historic churches, it was never burned down, torn down, or converted to condominiums. Most significant, of course, is that the Old North always was and still is an active Episcopal Church; it was fifty-two years old when the warning lanterns were placed in the steeple, and—save for three stormy years during America's War for Independence—has been in continuous operation as a church since opening its doors in 1723.

So while it's true that none of the Old North staff expect visitors to come in knowing much more about the church than the Revere legend, at least the popular patriot has enticed visitors in.

Long before the Old North was constructed, the Puritan town of Boston had two major centers. One was around the main wharf and the Town House on the site of today's Old State House, and the other was the North End, Boston's first real neighborhood. Because this community was surrounded by water and wharves, the North End's inhabitants included many wealthy English families, merchants, and middle-class tradespeople. And because most early Bostonians were Puritans, most of the churches and meetinghouses created were also Puritan, though they later evolved into Congregational churches. Other Bostonians, however—including government and military officials—belonged to the Church of England and attended services in the Anglican King's Chapel.

By 1722, the Anglican congregation had outgrown the King's Chapel

The exceptionally tall box pews in the Old North Church were once purchased and decorated by individual families; during colder months, they were invariably outfitted with footwarmers.

building and a site for a second Boston church was sought in the bustling North End. The land the congregation purchased was part of Nathaniel Henchman's pasture in the old Mill Field. It seemed ideal, surrounded as it was by busy wharves, shops, spacious homes, gardens, inns, taverns, cattle pastures, a windmill, and even a burying ground on Copp's Hill. Moreover, the Reverend Dr. Timothy Cutler, a Harvard graduate and Yale's second rector (president), seemed the perfect person to get the new church started.

The Old North Church was established as Christ Church in the City of Boston, which remains its official name. For the past two centuries, however, its popular name has prevailed. According to local custom, the oldest church in the North End was generally called "Old North." Though that title presumably belonged to several other buildings before Christ Church, one in particular causes confusion to this day. The Old North Meeting House, across from Paul Revere's home on North Square, was the church served by the famous Puritan preachers Increase and Cotton Mather. That church was burned by the British for firewood in 1776.

Though there was no architect per se of Christ Church/Old North, the inspiration for its 1723 design is presumed to be Sir Christopher Wren's early-eighteenth-century London churches. (Old North appears to be a close copy of Saint Andrews by the Wardrobe, near Blackfriars station). A man named William Price did accompany Cutler to London, quite possibly to attend Christopher Wren's funeral, in February 1723. Whatever the reason, Price was one of the men who oversaw the twenty-two-year struggle to build the simple yet magnificent Georgian structure called Christ Church, with its high, vaulted ceiling and New England touches.

While panes for the tall sash windows were imported from England, most of the building materials were domestic. Wood was shipped from York, Maine (then part of Massachusetts), from the same forests that provided masts for the Royal Navy. Red bricks, laid in an English bond pattern, came from Medford kilns. Master builders Thomas Tippin and Thomas Bennett did the interior woodwork, while master mason Ebenezer Clough, along with James Varney, executed the brick- and stonework. All in all, 513,654 Medford bricks were used in the main building, laid two feet thick in the church walls and three feet in the bell tower. Clough, Varney, Tippin, and Bennett were aided in the construction process by laborers whose wages included free beer, a common practice at the time.

The Old North's cornerstone was laid April 15, 1723. When Dr. Cutler preached the first sermon on December 29 of the same year, the church was hardly completed. Rough-hewn temporary floors and pews filled the main floor. Most of the church's distinctive features—from the brass chandeliers and cherubim-decorated organ to the 197-foot spire and peal of bells—would be added during the next two decades and beyond.

- The exceptionally tall box pews, for example, were purchased and decorated by individual families in early days. In 1806, these were replaced by more compact slip pews, then returned to their original box form during the major reconstruction of 1912. Though originally heated by foot warmers, those pews were later warmed by stoves; not until 1861 was the first furnace installed in the building.
- The two ornate brass chandeliers above the center aisle, gifts of an admiring English sea captain named William Maxwell, were first lit on Christmas Day 1724. Each is topped by a dove of peace.
- Old North boasted the first organ built in the colonies. A tracker-action organ with cow-bone keys, rebuilt in 1992, sits in the upstairs gallery in a 1759 organ case. Decorating the gallery are four trumpeting cherubim donated by Captain Thomas James Gruchy of the privateer *Queen of Hungary* in 1746; the angels had been on their way to a Roman Catholic convent in Canada when Gruchy plucked them as booty from a passing French vessel. (The captain's pirating activities were widespread; widespread, too, were suspicions that a tunnel led from his house on Salem and Charter streets down to the wharves, enabling his smuggling to continue, unseen by local authorities.)

Though the modern-day exterior of Old North Church is said to be much like its eighteenth-century form, the interior has changed with various ages and fashions. Major restorations occurred in 1806 and 1912. During the 1912 reworking, which was guided by colonial revival principles popular at the time, the interior of the church was painted white, replacing a much more vibrant color scheme. Meanwhile, the pulpit periodically drifted from the left to the right to the center front, and, as mentioned above, the pews were changed from box style, to slip, then back to box.

Additional buildings and courtyards have been annexed or improved over the years as well. A series of peaceful gardens, including the 1934 Washington Memorial Garden, are still maintained by the Beacon Hill Garden Club. The 1713 Ebenezer Clough House, now used for meetings, social gatherings, and classes, was saved from demolition and acquired by the church in 1958. Clough was the first residential developer in Boston, who built houses here on spec. A second Clough structure once stood in the area now used as the lower courtyard; in the eighteenth century, that house was owned by Benjamin Franklin and inhabited by Franklin's sisters. The structure that houses the bookstore and gift shop was built as a chapel for Waldensians—pre-Reformation Italian Protestants—in 1918. (The latter fact surprises many who assume that the North End's Italian population has always been exclusively Roman Catholic.)

The steeple of Old North is one of Boston's most famous landmarks. The two lanterns hung there in 1775, warning colonists across the river of the soldiers' approach, guaranteed its place in history, but plenty of other great stories are associated with the well-known spire.

Hoisted in August of 1740, the steeple was a late addition to the church. On top of the 197-foot structure was placed a seven-foot weather vane fashioned by Shem Drowne, who also created the famous grasshopper above Faneuil Hall. Rather than a grasshopper, incidentally, the Old North vane features a pot of flowers.

Though the original weather vane remains in place, the steeple has been repaired several times and replaced twice. During the Great Gale of October 9, 1804, and during Hurricane Carol of August 31, 1954, the wooden steeple was toppled off its square brick tower. The 1806 replacement—often attributed, without evidence, to Charles Bulfinch—was fifteen feet shorter than the original. When the 1806 steeple blew off in 1954, it was replaced with a faithful copy of the 1740 original.

The bells in the steeple—heralded as the oldest bells in the Western Hemisphere—were imported from England by Old North's first pastor, Timothy Cutler, in 1744. That same peal of eight magnificent bells still rings from the Old North belfry. A fifteen-year-old neighborhood boy named Paul Revere was part of the first guild of bell ringers at the church, in 1750.

Only seven years later, a most bizarre event occurred above the belfry. Contemporary accounts reported that a local eccentric named John Childs "flew" from the top of the steeple three separate times, once firing a loaded pistol midflight. Some illustrations show him wearing Leonardo-type wings, while other versions of the story claim Childs constructed a sizable umbrella with a small opening at the apex, a prototype of the parachute. Whatever Childs's methodology—and it remains a wonderful mystery— the town fathers finally ordered him to cease and desist; the spectacle, after all, caused people to take off from their labors.

The next major event at the steeple was the night of April 18, 1775, an event still memorialized, celebrated, and reenacted at the Old North's annual Lantern Ceremony. The essence of the tale: Paul Revere and upwards of forty other couriers were dispatched from Boston to Lexington and Concord, to warn colonists that "the British were coming" to seize a cache of colonial military stores hidden in the countryside. (In all likelihood, their cries were probably "The regulars are out!" since colonist and soldier alike were all British citizens at the time.) A crucial part of their message was to report the method of attack; would the regulars approach Concord by land, first marching the long route down Boston Neck to Roxbury, or by sea, launching their boats into the Charles River from the foot of Boston Common, then rowing upstream to Cambridge? If Revere and his colleagues were captured before delivering their message, the lanterns in the steeple of Old North would still be able to alert Charlestown citizens to the danger. There was, in sum, an elaborate system of riders and signals.

After secretly meeting with his friend Paul Revere—and receiving his final instructions—the Old North's twenty-three-year-old sexton Robert Newman sneaked out of an upstairs window of his house near the church. He moved quickly and quietly, since soldiers were quartered in his home and regulars patrolled the street. As Revere prepared to start his journey (which began by traveling in a rowboat to Charlestown), Newman crept up to the steeple and quickly flashed two lights across the bay. Once finished, he raced downstairs, climbed out the sash window to the right of the sanctuary, and eventually clambered back into his bedroom. Though he was arrested the next day for generally suspicious behavior, he was released due to lack of evidence; the soldiers lodging in Newman's home agreed that he'd gone up to bed early and never left the house.

The exposed wooden window in the front of Old North today—decorated with a replica signal lantern—is the window through which Newman escaped. Though long ago bricked over and used as a display alcove for a bust of George Washington, this window was rediscovered during restoration work in 1989.

Two more characters in this curious drama deserve mention here, since they're often left out of the tale. One was John Pulling, a member of the vestry at Old North, who may well have delivered the message to young Newman to hang the two lanterns. (Some even argue it was Pulling himself who took the lanterns to the steeple.) Another was Old North's rector, Mather Byles, Jr., who "left the employ" of Old North Church the morning after the lanterns were hung. Byles, of course, was a Tory, making him *persona non grata* in this great Patriot stew. Like other Tory clergymen, Byles eventually left Boston for the safe haven of British-owned New Brunswick.

When Dr. Cutler preached the first sermon at Old North in 1723, he carefully chose words from the prophet Isaiah: "My house shall be called a house of prayer for all people." Throughout the following centuries, Old North has attracted quite a variety of worshippers and visitors, despite the tension and turmoil that openness sometimes caused.

One of the great ironies of history, for example, is that Old North served both sides during the War for Independence. British general William Gage watched the Battle of Bunker Hill from the Old North steeple—the same one from which the two signal lanterns had been hung. Major John Pitcairn, who led the British expedition to Lexington and Concord, was buried in the crypt below the church following his death at Bunker Hill.

Similarly, Old North's neighborhood has been home to a wide variety of people over the years. At the turn of the last century, the neighborhood around the church was largely comprised of Irish, Italian, and Jewish immigrants. By midcentury, Boston's North End was associated almost exclusively with its Italian population—not to mention a stunning array of quality ethnic restaurants and bakeries. Since the 1980s, the area has become increasingly gentrified, attracting young urban professionals and empty nesters drawn to the area's waterfront, proximity to the financial district, and luxury condominiums. As a result, though the North End is still chock-full of Italian restaurants, the Italian population accounts for only 30 to 40 percent of the total.

The church itself continues to maintain a reverent focus on both the dead and the living. The basement of Old North is an historic graveyard, with some 1,100 people buried in thirty-seven sealed tombs. Meanwhile, an active columbarium in an adjacent basement chamber can accommodate the cremated remains of about 720 others.

The living are represented in Old North's growing congregation, which includes many of the North End's new young professionals. In addition, the church offers music programs, daily interpretation for visitors, a bookstore and gift shop, and a new archive room. The newly invigorated Old North Foundation of Boston, Inc., now manages the church as a historic site and offers a variety of interpretive programs for more than five thousand visitors per year, from scurrying schoolchildren and fall-foliage bus tourists to scholars and world leaders.

> Listen, my children, and you shall hear
> Of the midnight ride of Paul Revere. . . .
> One if by land, and two, if by sea,
> And I on the opposite shore will be,
> Ready to ride and spread the alarm
> Through every Middlesex village and farm. . . .

And what of Paul Revere? Are visitors to Old North disheartened when they learn that Henry Wadsworth Longfellow's 1861 poem, memorized by American schoolchildren for generations, is filled with factual errors—and that Paul Revere was neither the lone rider nor the mythical hero they'd always imagined? Not really, since truth is often far more interesting than fiction.

Longfellow, it turns out, was trying to rally the Union cause at the start of America's Civil War. The poet used the cries for freedom in the American Revolution to inspire Union men to take up arms in 1861—just as their grandfathers had in 1775. (This time, of course, freedom meant abolishing Southern slavery rather than overthrowing British sovereignty.) By singling out Revere, Longfellow showed how one heroic man *could* make a difference in similarly perilous times.

Moreover, Longfellow—along with Revere, his patriot colleagues, and the two lanterns of April 18, 1775—helped make the Old North Church a symbol of revolutionary freedom for our nation—a symbol that endures, and inspires, to this day.

THE ESSENTIALS

Address: 193 Salem Street, North End, Boston, MA 02113. **Telephone:** (617) 523-6676; gift shop, (617) 523-4848. **Website:** www.oldnorth.com. **Visitor Information:** Open daily 9:00 A.M. to 5:00 P.M., November to June; 9:00 A.M. to 6:00 P.M., July to October; closed Thanksgiving and Christmas Day. Donation requested. Episcopal services, Sunday at 9:00 and 11:00 A.M. Behind-the-scenes tours given daily July and August; includes Clough House, Bell Ringers' Chamber, and crypts; call to book group tours. "Paul Revere Tonight": one-man show with David Connor, Thursdays and Fridays, July to October; call for schedule. Docent talks given regularly; call for details or to arrange tour group visits. Main floor of church is wheelchair accessible. No restroom facilities.

The Old North Church is a stop on the Freedom Trail (see Chapter 10).

14 Trinity Church

ARCHITECTURALLY SPEAKING, its credentials are impeccable. Designed by renowned Boston architect Henry Hobson Richardson in the late nineteenth century, the building is still recognized as a masterpiece of Boston ecclesiastical architecture. Moreover, it's often said to be Richardson's personal best—and among the greatest works of architecture, either secular or religious, in the United States. (Richardsonian Romanesque, named for H.H.R., was the first American architectural style widely imitated throughout the United States and Europe.)

Its name is Trinity Church. And for those familiar with the ever-changing Boston skyline, the vision of Trinity is a constantly warm, yet wondrous, sight.

Today, the rustic Romanesque structure and its magnificent tower are reflected on the glass-sheathed John Hancock tower by day, then illuminated by the play of the lights of Copley Square by night. During the winter holidays in particular, the lights seem to take on an ethereal glow. Entering the church's Victorian interior is described by some as a religious experience as well. Barrel vaults and a massive central tower lift toward the heavens, flanked by bold murals, stained-glass windows, and bas-reliefs depicting an encyclopedic array of Christian saints and biblical stories.

To those who know the church intimately, however, such architectural glory is just a part of the Trinity experience. The ministers of this nationally renowned "preaching church" have provided spiritual guidance and inspiration for more than two centuries. Trinity's long line of influential Episcopalian preachers has included Samuel Parker, Alexander Mann, Theodore Parker Ferris, and the inimitable Phillips Brooks.

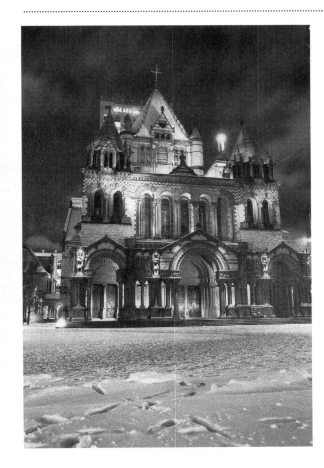

Trinity Church, the architectural masterpiece of H. H. Richardson, is vibrant throughout the year, including the festive Christmas holiday season.

Giving—and meeting the needs of those beyond its doorstep—has also been a part of the Trinity tradition. Since the church was founded, for example, serving immigrants has remained a priority: In the 1800s, Trinity sponsored a mission church in Boston's old West End and an industrial school for new immigrants. Today, immigrant services include academic tutoring, English as a Second Language, a fellowship for native Nigerians, and cross-cultural exchanges and education programs. The parish also gives more than $250,000 in partnership grants each year, offers mental health services to those in need, and sponsors a program that combines summer school and summer camp experiences for at-risk youth entering seventh grade in Boston's public schools.

But understanding how this building and congregation came together requires us to look back, heeding the Reverend Phillips Brooks's words of a century ago: "A parish, which for years has filled a place and done a work like ours in Boston, cannot forget its past."

Since the original Boston settlers of 1630 were Puritans, so too were the town's first religious meetinghouses. Still, as early as 1688, King's Chapel was built to accommodate members of the Church of England. Christ

Church, later known as Old North, became Boston's second Anglican parish in 1723. A decade later, the congregation at King's Chapel agreed that yet a third house of worship was needed in the rapidly growing port town. The decision to create Trinity Church was formalized in 1733, in a meeting at Luke Verdy's Tavern. Curiously, the spot chosen for the church was the site of another popular tavern—the Pleiades, or Seven Star Inn— at Summer and Hawley streets, near the present Filene's department store.

Bustling, commercial downtown Summer Street may seem an odd location for a house of worship today, but it made sense in 1733. At the time, the avenue was lined with large orchards, splendid mansions, bountiful gardens, and cow-filled pastures. The first Trinity Church, completed in 1735, was a wooden, barnlike box with neither steeple, tower, nor porch. The interior was somewhat more elegant, with Corinthian columns and a few fine paintings. Among Trinity's first parishioners was the wealthy merchant Peter Faneuil, the patron of Faneuil Hall. General George Washington became one of the church's most distinguished visitors, in 1789.

During the American Revolution—when churches associated with Tory sentiments were viewed as enemy outposts by many colonists—Trinity was the only Anglican church that remained open in Boston. Christ Church closed in 1775, and the ministers of both King's Chapel and Trinity fled north to Halifax during the British evacuation of 1776. But Trinity's assistant minister, Samuel Parker, kept the parish doors open, wisely agreeing to delete prayers for the British king from the church's liturgy. He also endorsed the patriot cause.

By 1828, a second, larger Trinity Church was built on the same Summer Street site. The "great, gloomy old thing," as Phillips Brooks fondly remembered it, was a massive stone building that succumbed to the Great Fire of 1872. Brooks had been Trinity's rector for three years when the building burned, along with much of downtown Boston. As he fled the flames, Brooks managed to save some of Trinity's books and robes.

According to one popular urban legend (which Trinity staff cannot, in good faith, confirm), Brooks made another "save" that day—one with an amusing twist. It seems that Boston jeweler Mr. Shreve, owner of the still-extant firm of Shreve, Crump & Low, met Brooks on the street during the Great Fire. He was afraid that his exclusive store's jewels and precious metals would be destroyed. Brooks, being a large man, offered to fill his oversize coat with Shreve's goods. He stuffed the coat, ran out to safety in the street—and was immediately arrested for being a looter!

Though the second Trinity Church was lost, the congregation remained together. Temporary services were held in an MIT lecture hall, where the New England Building stands today. Moreover, even before the fire broke out, the hardworking, wealthy, growing congregation had agreed to build another church in the newly landfilled area of town known as Back Bay. The reasons for the move were simple: In only three years of preaching in Boston, the charismatic Brooks had attracted significantly larger crowds to Trinity services. In addition, the Summer Street location had become less appealing (the street was now crowded with shops and businesses) while the Back Bay was rapidly developing into *the* new residential neighborhood in Boston.

Trinity Church was not the only cultural institution seeking greener pastures in Victorian Boston. No sooner had acres of Needham gravel been hauled in to fill the Back Bay's marshes and mudflats than many of Boston's cultural and religious institutions set up new homes on the new land. In the broad open area known as Art Square—renamed for Boston artist John Singleton Copley in 1883—those buildings included a short-lived Peace Jubilee Coliseum, the original Museum of Fine Arts, and the *New* Old South Church. Between 1877 and 1895, however, Boston's two greatest architectural masterpieces added the crowning touches to Copley Square: H. H. Richardson's Trinity Church and Charles F. McKim's Boston Public Library.

The magnificence of the Copley Square Trinity Church has always been credited to the architect, Louisiana-born Henry Hobson Richardson (1838–1886). Still, the splendid church that stands there today resulted from a variety of forces and factors—including the social and religious beliefs of Phillip Brooks; the wisdom of Brooks's closest friend, Robert Treat Paine; the talents of people like stained-glass artists John La Farge, Margaret Redmond, and Edward Burne-Jones, sculptor Augustus Saint-Gaudens, designer William Morris, and architects Stanford White and Charles F. McKim; the beneficence of countless parish members; and the exigencies of a mushy foundation.

In 1872, six firms were invited to submit designs for the new church. Of those six, Richard Morris Hunt was the most prestigious, but Richardson was selected. Though the building committee included several of Richardson's pals from exclusive Harvard clubs, it was talent and concept—not the old-boy network—that won him the Trinity job. (The plans were submitted in a blind competition.)

Despite the popularity of Gothic styling in American churches of the day, Richardson's plans were Romanesque and eclectic. A onetime student of the École des Beaux Arts in Paris, Richardson borrowed many of his design ideas from the churches of the eleventh-century French Aquitaine, but he added a distinctly American touch. The heavy building was made largely from light Dedham granite and red Longmeadow sandstone, playfully mixing colors as well as textures. To Richardson, this styling was rugged, rustic, and individualistic, like the American character itself. To Brooks, the "Richardsonian Romanesque" style was far preferable to Gothic design; while the latter emphasized the unworldly nature of God, the former reflected the visceral, tangible immediacy of the God on whom he preached.

Richardson's original contract called for a $200,000 building. By the time Trinity opened in 1877, the bill had reached an estimated half million dollars, some $7,200 of which was Richardson's salary. Theological, musical, political, physical, and financial considerations were all incorporated into the final church design—a happy marriage of art and exigency. For example, three exquisite stained-glass windows by John La Farge, considered priceless today, grace the back of the nave. Richardson once considered a rose window for that space but decided it would be too Gothic.

The architect's original design also called for a cathedral-style ceiling for the church interior. That was altered to hanging barrel vaults, which provided better acoustics for preaching as well as for choral and organ music. According to the church's current musical director and organist, Brian Jones, "Trinity has a big sound, and it's relatively resonant for an American church." In general, says Jones, Americans like "carpeting, curtains, and cushions," which tend to deaden sound. Trinity is thankfully sparse in all three.

Richardson's plan suggested that the church be filled with numbered pews, which were traditionally purchased for use by wealthy parish families. Phillips Brooks, however, threatened to quit unless free galleries were added for "the people." The galleries were added, the people came, and Brooks stayed. Eventually, in the 1940s, the practice of selling private pews was abandoned altogether. (It's interesting to note that when Trinity opened its doors, there was no pulpit; Brooks preached from a podium on the center steps—yet another way to achieve immediacy with his congregants.)

The tall central tower of Trinity, modeled after the cathedral in Salamanca, Spain, proved another change from Richardson's design; it's substantially shorter due to sheer physical necessity. The current tower, with a height of 107 feet, weighs approximately 12.5 million pounds. Richardson's original plans would have made the tower taller and heavier, which some eighteenth-century engineers assumed would have sunk the whole structure.

Because it was built on landfill—as was the whole Back Bay—Trinity was constructed on a foundation of four massive granite pyramids with thirty-five-square-foot bases. Below the foundations of the church and its adjoining parish house, a subterranean safety net of 4,502 wooden piles was laid. Since those piles must be kept saturated to retain their strength, the water table and piles have been monitored continually throughout Trinity's history. (Contrary to popular legend, a rowboat is not used to check the water levels of the pilings below the church; that task is done by a state-of-the-art water-pumping system.) Though it was feared that the piles were rotting in the mid-1930s, they remained intact. It was not until the construction of the adjacent John Hancock Tower in the early 1970s, in fact, that Trinity's foundation was seriously threatened. Trinity sued the Hancock company for $4 million in damages in 1975, explaining that the work had actually twisted the church, cracking parts of its foundation, walls, and some precious stained glass, as well as damaging a La Farge mural. When the case was finally settled in 1987, Trinity received $11.6 million—the damage award plus twelve years of accumulated interest. The funds received were used to make immediate (and partial) repairs and to create an endowment for building care and maintenance.

Another major change from the original Trinity was the addition of a magnificent marble altar, bronze candlesticks, gilded bas-reliefs, and a suspended hand-carved cross, all of which have graced the chancel since 1938. For doctrinal reasons, Phillips Brooks thought a simple communion table and his own pulpit were sufficient for his church of 1,500 seats and his standing-room-only Sunday crowds; the chancel was not refurbished until forty-five years after his death.

In his free time, bachelor Brooks—who carried three hundred pounds on his six-foot-four-inch frame—loved fast horses, fishing, billiards, and food. In the pulpit, he loved God, art and literature, dramatic language, and moving mountains. When Brooks preached, everyone listened—young and old, female and male, poor and rich. Listening wasn't always easy, though, since Brooks spoke so rapidly. Contemporaries even timed him, estimating that he delivered 213 words per minute at full speed.

Brooks died in 1893, two years after his election as Episcopal bishop of Massachusetts. His original pulpit was replaced by the Robert Treat Paine Memorial pulpit in 1916, which remains today. Nevertheless, the rector was remembered at Trinity in a variety of ways, some of them controversial. Twenty years after the building was completed, architect Hugh Shepley added a front porch and towers to Trinity. No one objected to the subjects of nine of the large statues on the porch—they were heroes of Jewish and Christian history like Moses, Abraham, and saints Matthew, Mark, Luke, and John. Not everyone was appreciative, however, when in 1925 Brooks's image was added as the de facto tenth "saint."

In 1909, a sculpture of Brooks by Augustus Saint-Gaudens was placed on the Boylston Street side of Trinity Church. On a positive note, Brooks was depicted facing outward rather than inward at the church—symbolically significant since Trinity has a remarkable history of community outreach. On the negative side, of course, is the fact that Brooks has been accused of attracting more attention than the gentleman standing behind him. The gentleman is Jesus Christ.

A bust of Brooks inside Trinity Church was sculpted by Daniel Chester French, whose seated Lincoln graces the Lincoln Memorial in Washington, D.C. The connection is appropriate, since Brooks delivered a eulogy for President Lincoln's 1865 funeral procession. (The progressive Brooks supported the antislavery movement before the Civil War and remained an advocate for African-Americans—including black priests in the Episcopal Church—in the postwar years.)

In some ways, the Reverend Phillips Brooks was a hard act to follow. His immediate successor at Trinity, the Reverend E. Winchester Donald, is reported to have said, "Someone must leap into the gulf. Why not I?" Fortunately for the congregation he did take that leap, and several succeeding generations of rectors and parishioners have as well. Today, Trinity continues to contribute mightily to the Greater Boston and Episcopal communities.

The Trinity choir, for example, grew from a quartet to a chorus of men and boys at the turn of the century. Today the church has three adult choirs, two children's choirs, a music exploration program for young children, and a handbell choir. There are free lunchtime organ concerts every Friday from early fall through late spring, and musical preludes at Sunday services. The cathedralesque sound of the organ, refurbished in the early 1960s, is partly due to the fact that the three-keyboard console runs two organs, offering a stunning "stereo" sound. This sound is evident on several Trinity recordings, including *Sounds of Trinity* and the popular Christmas collection, *Candlelight Carols*. (The church has a historical connection to holiday music as well: Phillips Brooks penned the lyrics to "O Little Town of Bethlehem," and John H. Hopkins, an assistant minister at Trinity from 1831 to 1832, wrote "We Three Kings of Orient Are.")

It's no surprise that amid all this vibrant energy other parts of the church's life remain vital too. By the turn of the twenty-first century, Trinity was clearly experiencing a Renaissance of sorts in program areas, supporting a host of classes, lectures, retreats, and service projects. In the post–September 11 world, the church also became a forum for exploring and building bridges between different religious communities. The early phases of an ambitious building restoration and renovation project are under way, with updates available on the church's award-winning website. And in a day and age when attendance at mainline churches across the nation is going down, parish growth and development at Trinity have moved steadily upward.

How can this unusual surge be explained? Partly by the influx of young professionals into the Boston area, as well as the Trinity staff that helps make the people and the programs all work. In the words of a former staff member, the growth can also be explained as that winning combination of "great location, great building, great city, great music! Trinity Church is very dignified. But it's also very accessible." The Pulitzer Prize–winning author David McCullough "summed it up beautifully, when he noted that" Trinity Church "isn't the work of an architect. This is the work of a civilization."

THE ESSENTIALS

Address: 206 Clarendon Street, Copley Square, Boston, MA 02116, facing the McKim building of the Boston Public Library on Boylston Street. **Telephone:** (617) 536-0944. **Website:** www.trinitychurchboston.org. **Visitor Information:** Church and parish house open daily 8:00 A.M. to 6:00 P.M., except when church is used for special services or functions. Trinity Bookshop open Monday through Saturday, 9:00 A.M. to 6:00 P.M.; Sunday, 10:00 A.M. to 6:00 P.M. (longer hours in November and December). Weekly organ concerts September through June, Fridays at 12:10 P.M. Self-guided tours available with award-winning map; guided tours available three to four times daily (hours vary); modest charge; group tours by arrangement. Sunday worship services at 7:45 A.M., 9:00 A.M., 11:15 A.M., and 6:00 P.M. See website or call for seasonal changes, daily worship schedule, special events, tours, seasonal services, classes, lectures, etc. Limited wheelchair accessibility; call or visit website for details.

15 The Granary Burying Ground

IN 1816, a bell was hung in the tower at King's Chapel. It was a wonderfully resonant bell, the largest ever cast in the family foundry of Paul Revere. Two years later, that same bell tolled as the eighty-three-year-old Revere joined many of his prestigious Revolutionary-era colleagues in a final reunion. John Hancock, James Otis, Sam Adams, Robert Treat Paine, the family of Ben Franklin, and the five victims of the Boston Massacre, of course, were already dead. But in 1818 Revere joined them all, ready to spend eternity in a somewhat soggy little plot of land off Tremont Street.

That soggy little plot was a hallowed place, and was better known as the venerable Granary Burying Ground. And the old patriot's funeral cortege was among the last to terminate there, since the two-acre graveyard had already been considered full decades before Revere's interment. But the end of in-town burials in no way signaled the end of pedestrian traffic through the Granary.

Quite the contrary, in fact.

Today the colonial-era Granary Burying Ground, located next to the Park Street Church on the Freedom Trail, attracts hundreds, if not thousands, of visitors daily during the busy summer months. Curious onlookers come to see the 2,345 grave markers still standing—or tilting, as the case may be—and to ponder the dozens of underground crypts said to lie below. Many of the curious headstones are decorated with intricate examples of the American folk art of funerary stone carving: cryptic verse and deathly images of skulls and crossbones, Grim Reapers, winged cherubs, and urns. Various organizations offer periodic tours, and explanatory plaques guide guests through the graveyard's history. That history includes the burying ground's most famous residents: Paul Revere and his colonial cohorts, three signers of the Declaration of Independence, nine governors of Massachusetts, and a woman some call the real "Mother Goose."

The Granary Burying Ground on Tremont Street is a virtual Who's Who of colonial Boston history.

When the Puritans of the Massachusetts Bay Colony arrived to settle Boston in 1630, life was tenuous at best. The town's first burying ground (known popularly today as King's Chapel Burying Ground) was nearly full thirty years after its opening. In 1659 and 1660, two new burying grounds were opened, one at Copp's Hill in the North End and the second on the edge of Boston Common.

Modern visitors may find it hard to imagine that this third Boston burial ground, now known as the Granary, was once part of Boston Common. Secluded behind an iron fence and neo-Egyptian granite gates, and shielded from the busy strip of Tremont Street between Park and Beacon, today's tree-shaded Granary Burying Ground is surrounded by tall buildings on three sides. Immediately blocking the graveyard from the Common, moreover, is the graceful Park Street Church and the two-way traffic of Park Street. During the seventeenth and much of the eighteenth century, however, none of these barriers or paved byways existed. Boston Common, opened for the common use of local citizens and grazing cows in 1634, stretched well beyond today's forty-eight acres. Modern Tremont and Park streets were but primitive pathways to and through the Common, and the Park Street Church was not built until 1809.

During those early years, the buildings of the Common formed the graveyard's neighborhood. Since the Common was public ground, it was used for everything from pasture and public gallows to public buildings. During the Granary Burying Ground's first century, its neighbors included an almshouse for the poor, a bridewell (prison) for criminals and the insane, and a workhouse for the dissolute and indigent. The graveyard itself was also periodically rented out for grazing bulls, cows, or pigs.

Before the Park Street Church was built, a long wooden building occupied that land. From 1737 until the American Revolution, that building was used to store grain that was sold cheaply to the poor. In 1796, the famous eyesore was removed to Commercial Point in Dorchester and converted into a hotel. Though the granary itself is long gone, the name Granary for the burying ground remained.

The two acres borrowed from the Common for that burial ground (also known, during various eras, as the New, the South, the Central, and the Middle Burying Place) were fed by underground springs and plagued by poor drainage and spongy soil; the constant moisture, combined with the New England weather, decomposed bodies quickly.

Despite the convenient rate of decay, the graveyard was evidently full to the brim by 1738—when John Chambers and other local gravediggers complained that they were forced to bury the dead four deep. Despite that unholy glut and an increasingly sickening stench, bodies were interred one upon another in the Granary Burying Ground for another 141 years. Not until 1879 did the board of health close the downtown graveyard for good. By then, perhaps as many as 5,000 anonymous souls rested below (some estimates place the number as high as 12,000).

The crowded, difficult conditions reinforced a number of burial practices that twenty-first-century men and women find unusual at best. Family members and friends, for example, were used to sharing or reusing existing tombs. The seventeenth-century diarist Samuel Sewall noted that his family tomb at the Granary had some forty occupants even before the American Revolution began.

The case of the Sullivan-Bellingham tomb, however, was not a family matter. In 1782, Judge James Sullivan expropriated the tomb in which Governor Richard Bellingham had lain since 1672. Custom dictated that if a family died out or could no longer care for its tomb, Boston selectmen could offer the space to whoever would provide needed repairs. When Judge Sullivan entered Bellingham's tomb, he found the late governor's remains floating in the water-soaked vault. Undaunted by the mess, Sullivan cleaned up the premises, became governor himself, and died in 1808. The Tomb of the Two Governors still bears the names of both Bellingham and Sullivan.

In another custom unusual by modern standards, the earliest burials at the Granary rarely included coffins. The dead were merely wrapped in a pall or linen cloth, with perhaps some lime thrown in on top. Lime is a caustic substance with many uses, including curing hides and treating sewage—both of which would have proved useful in a primitive graveyard.

While wealthier families often bought the tombs or vaults that extend around the periphery of the graveyard, other men and women placed slate gravestones in the site's central section. The oldest stone is the 1667 marker of John Wakefield, though his was hardly the first body interred. (Some of the earliest markers, fashioned from wood, are long gone.)

Originally, these chiseled slate markers were randomly placed about the graveyard's center, presumably over the bodies they commemorated; sometimes the markers were assembled together in family plots. The markers generally included a headstone and a footstone—making each gravesite resemble a bed—and were placed facing east so that the dead could face the rising sun on Judgment Day. The inscription on the headstone was directed away from the body, presumably to prevent readers from standing on top of the deceased.

Beginning around 1830, the Granary Burying Ground's grave markers were shuffled two or three times, ending up in the neat rows we find today. Needless to say, the interred were not shuffled along with them, inspiring Oliver Wendell Holmes to remark, "Epitaphs were never famous for truth, but the old reproach of 'Here lies' never had such a wholesale illustration as in these outraged burial places, where the stone does lie above and the bones do not lie beneath."

Though many sources suggest this straightening was necessitated by new lawn-mowing devices, historian Blanche Linden disagrees. Linden explains that the symmetrical stone lineup began as part of a general beautification of the site during the 1830s, which included the laying of paths and planting of trees and shrubs. Such renovations were in turn inspired by the early-nineteenth-century development of Beacon Hill into a "dense, elite residential and cultural area" and by the lavish new rural garden cemetery that had opened in Cambridge in 1831—Mount Auburn.

Throughout the centuries, the Granary Burying Ground remained an accessible, though sometimes underappreciated, outdoor museum of history and folk art. The headstones alone provide a telling glimpse of early

America's changing views of life, death, and eternity. During the Puritans' first century in Boston, for example, life was especially harsh, and their view of death was bleak. Hence death's heads, winged skulls, crossbones, and soul effigies were often carved into these slate stones by talented local artisans. Linden finds the area to the right of the imposing Franklin family obelisk particularly rich in early iconography, including the stern skulls carved on the graves of Deborah Cobham, Lydia Green, Jonathan Belcher, and Sally May.

As Boston life became easier and Puritan ways faded, the stonecutters' symbols started to emphasize spiritual regeneration over physical decay. Cherub faces and harvest scenes appear on later stones, while urns and willows—classical Greek and Roman motifs—emerged during the "Republican era" that followed the Revolution.

The Granary's greatest renown comes from its harboring the remains of more famous colonial-era heroes than any other Boston burying ground. Countless guides and guidebooks relate tales of elaborate funeral corteges, crowds of thousands, bold oratory, and general pomp and circumstance that accompanied the funerals of men like Sam Adams, John Hancock, James Otis, and Boston Massacre victim Crispus Attucks. When Paul Revere died in 1818, he became one of the last of these colonial heroes to join the historic downtown graveyard. The robust Revere's death came so much later than the deaths of other patriots that he missed inclusion in his family plot and almost missed burial in the star-studded Granary altogether.

Equally interesting are the tales of who, or what, is not in the Granary, or *might* not be there, as the case may be. Ben Franklin is not there, for example. Although the Granary's twenty-one-foot Franklin obelisk memorializes his family interred below, Franklin himself is buried in Philadelphia. Peter Faneuil, the benefactor of Faneuil Hall, is there, but the original inscription on his tomb has been changed; it used to read "P. Funel," but was "corrected" in later years.

"Mother Goose" may be in the Granary, but her gravestone is nowhere to be seen. Boston's Mother Goose was Elizabeth Foster (1665–1757), the second wife of Isaac Goose, also known as Vergoose. Elizabeth told stories to her six children and ten stepchildren (or, in other versions of the legend, to her grandchildren). These tales were supposedly collected and published in 1719 by her son-in-law Thomas Fleet as *Songs for the Nursery or Mother Goose's Melodies for Children*. No one knows if Elizabeth was *the* storyteller of nursery rhyme fame, since there is no extant copy of Fleet's volume and since serious contenders for the Mother Goose title predated her in France and perhaps England as well. Despite all that, the grave marker of Mary Goose, Isaac's first wife, is often mistakenly claimed as Mother Goose's own.

The great orator Wendell Phillips (d. 1884) was once in the burying ground, next to his father, Boston mayor John Phillips. But when Wendell's widow, Ann Terry Greene, died two years later, his body was moved to her gravesite in Milton. Another migratory corpse was General Joseph Warren, who began eternity in the common grave where he died at Bunker Hill. Warren's body was exhumed, then spent 1776 to 1825 in the Minot family tomb at the Granary Burying Ground. Exhumed again, the body was brought to a Warren family tomb under St. Paul's Church on Tremont Street, then to a family vault at Forest Hills Cemetery in Jamaica Plain in 1856.

Legend has it that the remains of John Hancock may not be all there, since his hand was severed by grave robbers the night after he was interred in 1793; others suggest that when his tomb lay open during some nineteenth-century construction on a nearby wall, someone made off with Governor Hancock altogether.

All of these stories of exhumation, alteration, and grave robbing indicate that American concepts of death and burial have significantly altered over the centuries. Not until the 1830s and 1840s, in fact—with the advent of rural garden cemeteries like Mount Auburn in Cambridge and Forest Hills in Jamaica Plain (then part of old Roxbury)—did Americans begin thinking of cemeteries as places to remember and visit the departed rather than just dispose of the dead.

The Granary began to respond to these changes in attitudes as the nineteenth century progressed, though most of its burying days were done by then. It was after 1830, for instance, that the gravestones were neatly re-aligned, numerous trees and winding paths were added, a new iron fence was built, and a bold granite Egyptian gateway was constructed at the entrance. (The latter is generally credited to Solomon Willard, designer of the Bunker Hill Monument, though historian Blanche Linden believes it was instead designed by Isaiah Rogers.)

The Granary Burying Ground experienced no major changes or concerted overhauls in the twentieth century—none, that is, until a burst of enthusiasm and funds erupted in the 1980s and 1990s. Today, the old graveyard is clearly recovering from those long years of constant use and little maintenance. Thanks to the Boston Parks Department's 1985 Historic Burying Grounds Initiative, as well as contributions from a variety of funds, trusts, historical societies, organizations, companies, and families, more than $4 million has already been spent on preserving Boston's sixteen historic burying grounds. At the Granary, the ongoing work has included gravestone conservation and stabilization, memorial cleaning, tomb reconstruction, landscaping, tree pruning, path reconstruction, a new pathway system, fence repair, and ornamental ironwork, as well as the development of a wheelchair-accessible entrance and a new, museum-quality signage system. Stones continue to be repaired and reset, inventories taken, historic tours designed, and master plans for restoration developed (the first was in 1986 and the second in 1998).

The old Revere bell at King's Chapel still tolls, by the way. Hopefully, with such ambitious restoration projects under way, that bell will never have to toll the end of the Granary Burying Ground—one of Boston's great historic treasures.

THE ESSENTIALS

Address: 83–115 Tremont Street, between Park and Beacon streets, Boston. **Telephone:** Boston Common Visitor Center, (617) 426-3115; Freedom Trail Foundation, (617) 227-8800; Boston Park Rangers, (617) 635-7383; Boston Common Ranger Station, (617) 635-7412; mayor's 24-hour hotline, (617) 635-4500. **Website:** www.cityofboston.gov; go to Calendar section for current events. **Visitor Information:** Open during daylight hours, 365 days a year. Free. Call for information about changing seasonal tour schedules. Wheelchair-accessible entrance at Tremont Place, around the corner, off Beacon Street; access throughout graveyard much better since path improvements; main Tremont Street entrance includes four steps.

The Granary Burying Ground is a stop on the Freedom Trail (see Chapter 10), the Boston Women's Heritage Trail (see Chapter 36), and the Literary Trail of Greater Boston.

16 Mount Auburn Cemetery

IN 1962, President John F. Kennedy complimented that year's Nobel Prize winners with the following observation: "I think this is the most extraordinary collection of talent, of human knowledge, that has ever been gathered together at the White House, with the possible exception of when Thomas Jefferson dined alone." If you take Kennedy's quote, and replace "the White House" with "any American cemetery," you've got a perfect description of Mount Auburn Cemetery. Although neither Kennedy nor Jefferson is buried there, the 94,000 *other* resident souls—reposing amid one of New England's prettiest landscapes—constitute quite stunning company.

Interred and memorialized in varied spots around Mount Auburn's 175 acres of rolling hills and winding pathways are dozens of historical movers and shakers known throughout the world: Christian Science founder Mary Baker Eddy, poet Henry Wadsworth Longfellow, actor Edwin Booth, architects R. Buckminster Fuller and Charles Bulfinch, painter Winslow Homer, and social reformers Julia Ward Howe and Dorothea Dix are but a few who come to mind.

There are also multitudes of celebrities whose Boston-area legacies may be better known than their names, including the founders of Babson College, Star Market, Mount Auburn Hospital, Hood Milk, the Gardner Museum, the Massachusetts Society for the Prevention of Cruelty to Animals, and the John Birch Society. The individuals who invented overnight delivery service, the elevator, and the "Gibson Girl" are all buried at Mount Auburn, too, as is the woman who may have inspired "Mary Had a Little Lamb."

It's an impressive roster, indeed, and quite fitting for a site that has now been designated a National Historic Landmark. Still, Mount Auburn Cemetery has always been more than a beautifully maintained who's who of the rich and famous. Unlike its aristocratic European counterparts, the cemetery began as, and remains to this day, a democratic burial ground, open to people of all social levels, religions, races, and political persuasions. Observing the gravestones and memorials of everyday people—with their changing art, architecture, and inscriptions—provides visitors with a fascinating, firsthand glimpse of American social history.

Inspired by Père Lachaise Cemetery in Paris, Mount Auburn was America's first rural garden cemetery; the Egyptian revival entrance gate was built from wood in 1832, then rebuilt with durable Quincy granite a decade later.

Furthermore, Mount Auburn has been a center of horticultural experimentation and creative landscape design since its founding in 1831. As such, it has continually attracted nature lovers, landscapers, horticulturists, gardeners, historians, photographers, and other artists, and has proved a popular oasis for migratory birds and avid bird-watchers.

Mount Auburn is probably best known as the first rural garden cemetery in the United States. For the two centuries before it was founded, life in Boston may have been hard, but death was even worse. The Puritans who first settled New England were an apocalyptic lot who warned of fiery postmortem fates in their sermons and disposed of their dead accordingly. The bodies of Boston's dead were buried in urban graveyards that quickly became overcrowded. Their slate headstones were often decorated with such cheerful designs as a skeletal death's head or the Grim Reaper. Many church lots were ill-kept, foul-smelling dens of decay, and blamed as a cause for epidemics. Burial "in perpetuity" was not yet in vogue—meaning new bodies were often buried on top of old ones, sometimes marked and sometimes not. City graveyards often had distinctive pockmarks, since thin wooden caskets crumbled with age, causing the earth above to collapse into the interred remains.

The historian Blanche Linden, author of *Silent City on a Hill: Landscapes of Memory and Boston's Mount Auburn Cemetery* and other treatises on historic graveyards, tells of a spine-tingling, though not unusual, incident: a nineteenth-century Bostonian passing by Tremont Street's old

Granary Burying Ground apparently gazed into James Otis's open tomb and observed how the tree roots wound through the famous patriot's skull! The deceased clearly had neither privilege nor privacy.

By the early 1800s, however, romantic new attitudes about death and the afterlife were coming into fashion. Instead of focusing on eternal damnation, many began to think of death as an ethereal repose. In gravestone art, ominous skulls gave way to cherubs, willows, and urns. The concept of a perpetual resting place for human remains—a pleasant, marked, permanent home for a single body, or for loving companions—also emerged.

Meanwhile, philanthropist-merchant George Brimmer had purchased Stone's Woods on the rural outskirts of Boston, an ample chunk of woodland in Watertown and Cambridge. (Though Mount Auburn is often associated with Cambridge, only 11 of its 175 acres are actually in that city; the bulk of land is in Watertown.) Harvard students often strolled and studied there and had nicknamed the spot "Sweet Auburn" from a reference in Oliver Goldsmith's popular poem "The Deserted Village." Brimmer wanted to save the land from development, and he eventually sold it to the Garden and Cemetery Committee of the Massachusetts Horticultural Society. That committee included Dr. Jacob Bigelow, a physician, botanist, and Harvard professor who helped found the Massachusetts Institute of Technology and popularized the word *technology*. It also included Henry A. S. Dearborn, a retired army general, civil engineer, and the first president of the Massachusetts Horticultural Society.

Bigelow and Dearborn wanted to create a garden cemetery—a spacious, peaceful, rolling, "natural" park embellished with flowers, trees, and ponds where the dead could rest intact and the living could wander, ponder, and pray. The landscape design was inspired by British pleasure parks and the Parisian estate–turned–cemetery called Père Lachaise. Initially, the committee sold a hundred burial plot subscriptions at sixty dollars each to interested citizens. Then, with the necessary funds in hand, they purchased Brimmer's seventy-two acres for $6,000 in 1831. Those acres became Mount Auburn Cemetery, and a revolutionary new era in American graveyards had begun.

Mount Auburn quickly became the "in" place for burial and visits, both nationally and internationally. Moreover, the popularity of this and other rural cemeteries that followed proved a major inspiration to the parks movement of the mid- and late 1800s (see Part 6). As Mount Auburn grew in fame and size—with twelve land purchases from 1835 to 1944—its commitment to being a garden remained steadfast. By the late twentieth century, only a handful of hearty oaks remained from the original woods; around them, however, Mount Auburn horticulturists continually planted native trees and shrubs, interspersed with many non-native experiments. Hills were leveled, topography periodically changed, and plantings altered from era to era. Marshlands were filled in or sometimes reshaped to create the cemetery's major bodies of water: Halcyon Lake, Auburn Lake, Consecration Dell Pond, and Willow Pond.

Buildings were also added as funds allowed. The Egyptian Revival entrance gate came first, built on a budget in wood in 1832, then rebuilt with durable Quincy granite a decade later. The nondenominational Gothic

Revival Bigelow Chapel and a circular, Norman-style observation tower named for President George Washington came next.

The initial statuary purchased for the cemetery—presumably the first of many projected art acquisitions—comprised four majestic statues of American heroes, which stood in Bigelow Chapel. When plans changed, the four were moved first to the cemetery's administration building and then, as space was needed, to Harvard University. (John Adams and John Winthrop now stand in Annenberg [dining] Hall of Harvard's Memorial Hall, James Otis in Sanders Theater, and Joseph Story, a U.S. Supreme Court justice and Mount Auburn's first president, in Langdell Hall at the Harvard Law School.)

Everyone has a favorite monument at Mount Auburn. Some like the neo-Egyptian symbols, which became popular in America not long after Napoleon's 1798 invasion of Egypt and the deciphering of the Rosetta stone. At the cemetery are many such examples, from the great fifteen-foot sphinx, dedicated to the preservation of the Union and the ending of slavery, to countless obelisks.

On the nineteenth-century monuments, classical symbolism predominates, with mausoleums, cenotaphs, and miniature temples galore. Staff guides, who give periodic walking tours of Mount Auburn, will gladly point out many popular symbols of the time: ascending angels, urns (representing the soul), flames (eternity), doves (the holy spirit), winged hourglasses (time flies), oak or ivy (everlasting), and sheaves of wheat (fulfilled life), to name but a few. Though sentimental Greek-inspired, full-figure sculptures appear in many places, incidentally, Madonnas and crucifixes do not. Both the anti-Catholic sentiment in Boston in the mid-nineteenth century and the insistence of many in the Roman Catholic hierarchy that their own be buried in consecrated church grounds ensured this result.

Around some family plots today you'll find ornate cast-iron gates and fences, granite staircases, and curbings. These are vestiges of the extravagance of the mid-nineteenth century at Mount Auburn; as the popularity of the cemetery grew, so did the popularity of elaborate memorial decorations. Plots acquired hedges, ivy-draped fences, and even curbs. Cast-iron "lawn furniture" was placed on some plots, while fountains were added to cemetery lakes, sometimes surrounded by exotic palms and warm-weather flora. The latter, incapable of surviving harsh New England winters, were protected from the cold in "half-hardy" greenhouses.

After the Civil War, the popularity of such clutter diminished. By the end of the century, cemetery officials had removed many such difficult-to-maintain embellishments. Private plot gardeners were banned, and "perpetual care" contracts with the cemetery began. Mount Auburn Cemetery began to return once again to a policy promoting more modest, natural beauty.

Mount Auburn was a haven for birds even in the nineteenth century. In the late Victorian period, avian enthusiasts were known to blast birds eagerly from treetops with their guns, then bring them home for study and identification. Although bird-watchers pulled such stunts in other nearby locations, like Fresh Pond, no such hunting took place on Mount Auburn grounds. Fortunately for the birds, one Ludlow Griscom pioneered a different method of avian study in the late 1920s, chronicling the flights of his feathered friends using binoculars and notepads rather than firearms. Griscom, who frequented Mount Auburn, is buried near one of the best bird-watching areas in the cemetery, the deep, mysterious, wooded spot called Consecration Dell.

Other good areas to observe the wealth of migrating land birds that pass through Mount Auburn are Auburn Lake and Washington Tower—older, more settled sections of the grounds, where the trees are taller and the growth wilder. More than 220 species of birds have been seen at Mount Auburn, including 36 species of wood warblers. Prime viewing times are spring days, from early morning until 11:00 A.M.

Mount Auburn Cemetery is also a world-renowned arboretum. The well-maintained and plentiful collection of trees, shrubs, and flowers creates an urban forest, thoughtfully planted and spaced for landscape appeal rather than scientific order. Under the guidance of resident experts, the cemetery grounds sparkle with a varied selection of predictable and unexpected colors, textures, and scents, from plants both native and exotic. Among the more than five thousand trees (many labeled for easy identification) are maples, oaks, and beeches, as well as flowering shrubs and trees like crabapples, magnolias, azaleas, and mimosas. Flowers—including snowdrops, daffodils, lilacs, and roses—also bloom at Mount Auburn from March to August.

The single most tenacious urban legend associated with Mount Auburn Cemetery concerns Mary Baker Eddy, founder of the Christian Science Church, whose beautiful pillared temple is the centerpiece of Halcyon Lake. Historian Blanche Linden assures us that the story is "totally lore," though based on a shred of truth. That shred: When the religious leader-writer died in 1910, her body was placed in a receiving tomb while her memorial was under construction. To avoid foul play—vandals, body snatchers, and the like—a watchman was assigned there, and a phone hooked up by the temple for use should an emergency arise. The legend grew, of course, that Eddy had ordered the phone so that she could check in from Eternity. No, she didn't call. And yes, the telephone is long gone.

Today, visitors can hear enlightening and engaging stories (though perhaps not the above-mentioned "phone home" tale!) from tours sponsored by Friends of Mount Auburn Cemetery, a membership organization founded in 1986 to promote the appreciation and preservation of Mount Auburn. The Friends publish a wonderfully readable newsletter, *Sweet Auburn*, and offer lectures, tours, and walks on varied aspects of Mount Auburn's unique history, horticulture, art, architecture, and ornithology. A variety of their special interest tours—highlighting the grave sites of artists, poets, African-Americans, physicians, horticulturalists, and others—are now available to visitors in pamphlet form. In addition, three beautifully produced audio tours are available for purchase or rental, and interpretive panels can be found in various locales throughout the grounds.

One popular tour offered by the Friends of Mount Auburn Cemetery includes the cemetery's famous women—women such as historian Hannah

Adams, Franklin Delano Roosevelt's secretary Missy LeHand, Mount Auburn Hospital founder Emily Parsons, cooking authority Fannie Farmer, former slave Harriet Jacobs, reformer Dorothea Dix, reformer and poet Julia Ward Howe, poet Amy Lowell, art collector Isabella Stewart Gardner, and Josephine Saint Pierre Ruffin, an early activist for black and women's rights.

People wishing to set up eternal residence in Mount Auburn today have more innovative options than in the past. Room for casket burial still exists, and Mount Auburn's staff continues to lay out new interment space. Admittedly, these spaces have become more limited as the years have passed, but new memorial choices that do not detract from the spacious, historic landscape have been developed. Mount Auburn's trustees have made clear their commitment to preserve and enhance the cemetery's horticultural character.

For those who wish to be cremated, on the other hand, there is still plenty of room. Space is available either in a niche in the Story Chapel columbarium or in the ground. The cemetery also runs its own modern crematory behind Bigelow Chapel. It performed more than nine hundred cremations in 2002, mostly for interment elsewhere. In New England, according to the Cremation Association of North America, cremations are performed on approximately 30 percent of the deceased. (The national average is 27 percent, though numbers vary dramatically from region to region.)

Pax vobiscum.

THE ESSENTIALS

Address: 580 Mount Auburn Street, Cambridge, MA 02138; on the Watertown-Cambridge line. **Telephone:** (617) 547-7105. **Website:** www.mountauburn.org. **Visitor Information:** Gates open daily, 8:00 A.M. to 7:00 P.M., May through September; 8:00 A.M. to 5:00 P.M., rest of year. Business office open Monday through Friday 8:30 A.M. to 4:30 P.M., Saturday 8:30 A.M. to 12:30 P.M. Admission free. Brochures, maps, audio tours, program schedules, and other information available at information center near entrance. Audio tours only available 8:30 A.M. to 2:00 p.m. Open for "passive recreation" only; no bicycling, picnicking, skateboarding, jogging, skating, or Rollerblading. No dogs unless kept inside cars. Grounds, restrooms, and office are all wheelchair accessible.

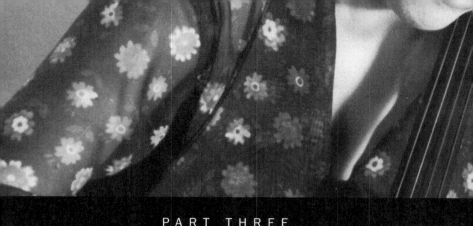

PART THREE

The Athens of America

ARTS AND ENTERTAINMENT IN BOSTON

ONE OF the most cherished epithets ever bestowed on Boston is "the Athens of America." Though most would agree the appellation was eventually well deserved, it took the town centuries to earn it. Ancient Athens, of course, was known as a center of early democracy and a wellspring of art, theater, poetry, literature, and fine-tuned athletes.

Puritan Boston may have been an efficient, self-disciplined, hardworking machine, but a center of culture and the arts it was not. Musical instruments, including organs, were long forbidden in Puritan meetinghouses. Theater presentations were strictly prohibited, since, according to the Massachusetts legislature of 1750, stage plays "tended to increase immorality, impiety and contempt of religion." Museums were essentially an unknown entity, at least until the success of Charles Willson Peale's museum in Philadelphia, begun in 1785. And artists were initially employed primarily for more practical purposes, like building furniture and carving tombstones.

By the first decades of the 1800s, however, all that began to change and Boston began to grow. The founding of the Boston Athenaeum in 1807 heralded the beginning of one of Boston's finest libraries. Moreover, the Athenaeum's patronage of the arts and artists helped lay the foundation for the Museum of Fine Arts, Boston, first opened in 1876. As Bostonians became devotees of the arts, they brought back countless treasures from their travels abroad. The collections at the MFA, the Isabella Stewart Gardner Museum, and the Art Museums at Harvard College all profited and prospered from these sojourns.

Meanwhile, the world of music took a giant step forward with the creation of the Boston Music Hall in 1852, touted as the city's first real concert hall. When philanthropist Henry Lee Higginson founded the Boston Symphony Orchestra in 1881, he rented the Music Hall as a performance space. Twenty years later, Higginson built his orchestra a more permanent home—Symphony Hall. Over in Cambridge, Harvard College fostered cultural growth on a variety of similar fronts. One of the city's favorite concert stages, Sanders Theater, was built as part of Harvard's Memorial Hall in 1876. In addition to the aforementioned Art Museums, Harvard established and nurtured on-campus museums throughout the nineteenth and twentieth centuries, in fields as diverse as botany, geology, mineralogy, comparative zoology, archeology, and ethnology.

Legitimate theaters began to emerge in Boston in the decade after the Revolution, then flourished for much of the nineteenth century. By the turn of the twentieth century, a building boom was in full swing. The stages most closely associated with the downtown theater district today—the Colonial, the Shubert, and the Wilbur—were all opened between 1900 and

1914. Fast on the heels of live theater entertainment came motion pictures and the early movie palaces; one of Boston's best live performance venues, the Wang Center for the Performing Arts, began as a movie house called the Metropolitan Theater in 1925.

It's interesting to note that aside from those downtown theaters, much of the art and cultural life that flowered in nineteenth- and twentieth-century Boston depended on landfill and reclaimed land. Symphony Hall, for example, was built on the wild frontiers of Huntington Avenue. The Museum of Fine Arts, Boston, first opened in the former marshland of Copley Square, then moved to the former marshland of the Fenway in 1909. The Fenway also hosted other centers of arts and entertainment in the early 1900s: the Gardner Museum, originally known as Fenway Court, opened in 1903, and Fenway Park, the home of Boston's indigenous baseball team, the Red Sox, celebrated its opening day in 1912.

One final note: I included the history of Park Street Station in this section because (a) there was nowhere else to put it, (b) public transit is a good way to access all these sites, and (c) the Park Street subway stop is, after all, an entertaining place.

17 The Museum of Fine Arts, Boston

SOME PEOPLE still think that an art museum is a building filled with paintings, paintings, and more paintings. And to some extent, that vision is true. Boston's Museum of Fine Arts (MFA), for example—one of the city's oldest and most revered cultural institutions—does have a world-class collection of oil paintings. But since first opening to the public on July 4, 1876, this "jewel of Boston museums" has been much more than that.

Today, the MFA's array of more than 360,000 objects is divided among eight curatorial departments and ranges from tiny painted shards of pottery, Greek vases, Indian fertility goddesses, and Peruvian tapestries to the silverwork of Paul Revere, the contents of ancient Egyptian tombs, and exquisite furniture from American and European history. Given those diverse collections, the MFA could be considered a repository of memory through vision; objects do speak to those who are willing to listen.

Oil paintings, of course, "speak" as well. And the museum's impressive collection is clearly multilingual. Nineteenth-century French painters are represented in legion force, and works include Vincent Van Gogh's *Postman Roulin*, Auguste Renoir's *Bal de Bougival*, Paul Gauguin's *D'ou venons nous? Que sommes nous? D'ou allons nous?*, and thirty-eight works by Claude Monet—one of the largest collection of Monet paintings outside France. Well-known paintings by Mary Cassatt and Georgia O'Keefe are here, too, as well as gems by Gentile Bellini, Pablo Picasso, El Greco, and Winslow Homer.

Bostonians are particularly proud of the paintings of American Revolutionary patriots in the MFA collections, which portray local heroes and represent local artists of international renown. The best known of these are Gilbert Stuart's unfinished portraits of Martha and George Washington—the latter being the 1796 rendering reproduced on our dollar bill. Other colonial men and women depicted include John Hancock, Paul Revere, Mercy Otis Warren, and Joseph Warren, all painted by John Singleton Copley, as well as Stuart's oil of Rachel Walker, Mrs. Paul Revere.

Still, the tale of Boston's proudest museum—located on the outbound reaches of Huntington Avenue—is more than a mere delineation of its vast and varied art treasures. The MFA's story began a little more than a hundred years after colonial Bostonians helped incite the American Revolution. In the early nineteenth century, Boston's principal repository of fine art was not a museum at all. The Boston Athenaeum, a private club incorporated in 1807 and located on Beacon Street since 1849, acted as a combined library and art gallery for the rapidly growing city. By the 1860s, however, the skylighted top floor of the Athenaeum was overflowing with art. Its members decided to focus on the Athenaeum's role as a scholarly society and research library and to find other quarters for its art.

At the same time that an Athenaeum committee was seeking alternative gallery space, Boston was creating a new neighborhood by filling in its Back Bay. Once a foul-smelling section of milldam mudflats, the "new" Back Bay soon became a haven for institutions of culture, learning, and religion. By the turn of the twentieth century, the streets around Copley Square boasted such illustrious structures as Trinity Church, the Boston Public Library, and the New Old South Church.

Years of effort by the well-connected Fine Arts Committee of the Boston Athenaeum finally paid off in 1870. On February 4 of that year, an act of the Massachusetts legislature established the Trustees of the Museum of Fine Arts, who were instructed to build a city art museum. They were awarded a 91,000-square-foot lot in Art Square (renamed Copley Square in 1883). As it turned out, this land grant was essentially the beginning and end of substantial city support for the Museum of Fine Arts. Instead, private citizens built the MFA and filled it with collections. Contributions to the $230,268 construction project ranged from modest gifts of thirty-five cents to the $25,000 donated by Mrs. T. Bigelow Lawrence, the wealthy widow of an Athenaeum benefactor. (Curiously, Mrs. Bigelow's interest was largely in creating a space to display her late husband's medieval armor; though the armor never made it to the MFA—it was lost in the Great Fire of 1872—Mrs. Bigelow's funding did.)

The museum's first home, an ornate Ruskinian Gothic structure at the corner of Dartmouth and Saint James streets, was designed by John H. Sturgis and Charles Brigham. The extravagant red-brick and terra-cotta building, with depictions of the "Genius of Art" and "Art and Industry" adorning the exterior, was opened to the public for America's centennial, July 4, 1876. Its first exhibits were largely composed of works loaned by the Athenaeum, including the Stuart portraits of George and Martha Washington and Thomas Crawford's marble statue *Orpheus and Cerberus*. There were also hundreds of plaster casts—sculptural copies molded from antiquities' greatest hits.

Despite an opening-day moral controversy, solved by masking the private parts of "explicit" classical casts with fig leaves, the museum proved a success. With a paid staff of six in 1876—compared with 860 in 2003—the MFA welcomed thousands of guests. In 1877, annual visitation was 158,446. By 1895, that number had grown to 301,315. (Today, visitation averages over a million per year.)

By the turn of the twentieth century, only twenty-four years after the MFA first opened its doors, the vast array of incoming art collections had outgrown the museum's Copley Square home. Despite additions to the building in 1879 and 1890, a move to larger quarters was essential. A site was finally chosen in Boston's newest frontier, a dirty, marshy area known as the Fenway, which had been transformed in the 1880s to an "arboreous state" by the work of landscape architect Frederick Law Olmsted. As had happened earlier in the Back Bay, distinguished cultural institutions—such as the Isabella Stewart Gardner Museum, Symphony Hall, and the Massachusetts Historical Society—began building in this newly attractive rural outpost of the congested Hub.

Guy Lowell was chosen to design the new fine arts museum in 1907, as-

Renowned as the "jewel of Boston museums," the Museum of Fine Arts, Boston, is also exceptionally accessible to those with special needs.

sisted by R. Clipston Sturgis, Edmund M. Wheelwright, and D. Despra-delle. Working with more than 500,000 square feet of land, Lowell and associates created much of the massive granite neoclassical building we know as the MFA today. The Huntington Avenue facade—with its Ionic temple portico and two flanking wings—was designed as the main entrance, partly as a convenience to visitors whose streetcars stopped in front. The Huntington Avenue doorway was overshadowed as the museum's main entry after I. M. Pei's modern West Wing was added in 1981. (Economic constraints closed the Huntington entrance altogether in 1990, though incoming director Malcolm Rogers reopened them in 1995 as a gesture of goodwill and outreach to the community.) In the MFA's newest incarnation—as part of phase one in a comprehensive master site plan designed by Foster and Partners of London—the museum's two main entrances will be the Huntington doors on the south and the Fenway doors on the north, both leading to a central axis at the heart of the building (see details below).

By the time the museum's Fenway home opened in 1909, the cost for building, land, improvements, moving, and installation was a staggering $2,887,968.75. The move from Copley Square to the Fenway, however, was surprisingly uneventful. Two horse-drawn carriages made repeated trips between the sites to transport the collections. No guards were hired to protect the art, and nothing of value was broken or damaged in the process.

Almost immediately the 1909 building was expanded. Between 1911 and 1915, the Evans Wing was added, increasing exhibit space by 40 percent. That wing was funded by a single gift from Mrs. Robert Dawson Evans, whose husband, a rubber and copper-mining magnate, had died when thrown from a horse in 1907. Between 1928 and 1998, other additions included the Decorative Arts Wing; the George Robert White Wing; the modern West Wing (which encompassed the White Wing and housed the museum shop, three restaurants, Remis Auditorium, education offices, and modern art galleries); Tenshin-en, the Japanese "Garden of the Heart of Heaven"; and the bookstore addition, with views into the Calderwood Courtyard.

Beginning in 2004—and taking an estimated five years to complete—the MFA will enter the first phase of an ambitious $425 million expansion that will enhance its accessibility. Reinstating the organizational clarity originated by architect Lowell in 1907, the new master site plan will again bring symmetry and logic to the layout and design of this twenty-first-century museum. Among the highlights of phase one: an expanded information center dominating the central axis of the building, accessed by the aforementioned entrances on the north (Fenway) and south (Huntington); a glass and steel "jewel box" connecting the information center with the new East Courtyard (part of the glazed "crystal spine" that will eventually run the full length of the site from east to west, enclosing two grand courtyards); a three-story East Wing showcasing Art of the Americas and Contemporary Art; new educational facilities; a state-of-the-art theater; and conservation and research studios.

"The new MFA will be an architectural landmark of international significance," explains Malcolm Rogers, Ann and Graham Gund Director of the MFA. "It will raise the profile of both the Museum and Boston, and contribute to the prominence of the city as a cultural mecca and as a destination for increasing numbers of visitors from around the globe."

Cyrus Dallin's equestrian sculpture *Appeal to the Great Spirit*, which has essentially become the symbol of the MFA, was placed in front of the Huntington entrance in 1913. The fourth of four Dallin statues depicting the attitude of Native Americans toward the intruding Europeans, this work was purchased for the museum by public subscription. Though the Native American rider is clearly from the Plains, Dallin created the work in the Boston suburb of Arlington Heights.

Over the decades, a great number of families have contacted museum offices, explaining how it was their horse, their relative, or their close friend who was the model for Dallin's landmark sculpture. The MFA has an ample file of these claims, some or all of which may be true, depending on how many different models posed for *Appeal to the Great Spirit*. It was, and still is, quite common for sculptors to use several models in the course of creating one statue.

Another piece of art that is considered part of the fabric of the MFA is the array of murals, moldings, enrichments, painted decorations, and bas-reliefs that decorate the great rotunda. The entire area, including skylights and columns, was built and then completely rebuilt at great cost to accommodate the artistic schemes of John Singer Sargent. From 1917 to 1925, Sargent executed the work, primarily in London, though occasionally from his Newbury Street studio. His models for the demigoddesses above the library entrance were three touring Ziegfeld Follies chorus girls, who were performing at Boston's Colonial Theatre at the time. (Between 1997 and 1999, MFA conservators undertook a full-scale preservation and restoration project that returned Sargent's murals to their original splendor).

While commissioned artists like Dallin and Sargent were compensated for their labors—and while art purchases were periodically made—the Museum of Fine Arts has always needed loans and gifts to fill its galleries. Though the nucleus of the 1876 exhibit was Athenaeum artwork collected over the previous fifty years, this was augmented by art borrowed from individuals and the city of Boston. Paintings composed a portion of these early loans, as did plaster casts, pottery, porcelains, textiles, embroideries, tapestries, and other decorative arts objects.

For its first fifteen years, the museum depended primarily on such loans. Gifts were a second source of art, followed by outright museum purchases afforded by "special funds." J. M. W. Turner's painting *Slave Ship*, of a flaming vessel, for example, was a loan from Miss Alice Hooper; it was purchased by the MFA in 1899 from the painting's subsequent owner. Stuart's unfinished Washington portraits were loaned to the museum for more than a century before finally being purchased from the Athenaeum in 1980. Wealthy donors and the bequests of art patrons provided many of these gifts and special funds.

The museum also was blessed by the contributions of globetrotting Bostonians, who helped create priceless collections during the MFA's formative years. According to the late historian Walter Muir Whitehill, whose definitive two-volume history of the museum was published in 1970, Edward Perry Warren was one of several friends of the MFA who proved to be "the right collector in the right place at the right time." Warren's particular expertise was classical art, which both he and John Marshall purchased in travels across Europe in the 1890s. Their acquisitions formed the foundation of the museum's Art of the Ancient World displays.

Similar turn-of-the-century expeditions formed the basis of other museum collections. In the 1880s, for example, Edward Morse, Ernest Fenollosa, William Sturgis Bigelow, and Dr. Charles D. Weld brought a wealth of Japanese artwork to Boston and helped begin the department now known as Art of Asia, Oceania, and Africa. During the first decades of the twentieth century, archaeologist George Reisner helped fill Boston's art museum with more Egyptian Old Kingdom treasures than were found anywhere outside Cairo, through a series of excavations cosponsored by the MFA and Harvard University.

Though many of the museum's finest holdings were acquired with deliberate thought and meticulous research, others were discovered with strokes of fate. For instance, the MFA contains a replica of the subterranean burial room of Egyptian queen Hetep-heres; the original was literally stumbled upon in 1925 when an expedition photographer's tripod leg sank into the ground, uncovering a secret staircase to the tomb.

In another serendipitous discovery, an original Gentile Bellini painting of a doge of Venice (doges were the tiny republic's chief magistrates) was found by a Boston woman while cleaning her attic in 1937. Assuming it was a cheap imitation, she donated it to Morgan Memorial Goodwill Industries. Luckily, that charitable organization brought it to the MFA, which verified the painting's authenticity and worth.

One of the museum's treasures is the diminutive gold and ivory statue of a Minoan snake goddess. Though the details are hazy, the statuette reportedly arrived in a cigar box carried by a Cretan peasant who was traveling from Piraeus to Boston in 1913. A Greek-speaking Bostonian on the same vessel saw the artwork, which was broken into hundreds of tiny slivers and fragments, and directed the peasant to the MFA. The gracious Mrs. F. Scott Fitz, mother of a museum trustee, donated the appropriate funds for the purchase and painstaking reconstruction of the goddess by the MFA staff. (The authenticity of the snake goddess, incidentally, has been debated and the statuette scientifically tested; the results remain inconclusive.)

As the MFA's collections grew, departments gradually formed, each with its own specialty and curatorial staff. Today, the museum has eight: Art of the Americas; Art of Europe; Contemporary Art; Art of Asia, Oceania, and Africa; Art of the Ancient World; Prints, Drawings, and Photographs; Textiles and Fashion Arts; and Musical Instruments.

Though each department has its highlights, those interested in Boston history will take particular pleasure in the Art of the Americas. A series of fully furnished period rooms recreate eighteenth- and nineteenth-century New England parlors, from the dark, rustic charm of the 1704 Brown-Pearl House of West Boxford to the opulent, hand-polished luxury of heiress Elizabeth West's rooms at her 1801 estate, Oak Hill. (As of this writing, the period rooms have been removed and are being conserved for the opening of the new American wing). Of equal interest is the display of the Swan Collection, which includes the only complete set of eighteenth-century French royal furniture in the United States. The exhibit is engaging not only because it displays possessions of the Swans (a preeminent Boston family with some wonderful skeletons in its historic closet), but also because it combines furniture with masterpiece paintings, silver, ceramics, andirons, textiles, and other objects of daily life. Such cross-pollination of exhibit materials is an exciting new direction of the MFA in general.

Among a multitude of acquisitions relevant to Boston history are some of the museum's best-known pieces. The silver Liberty Bowl, created by Paul Revere and commissioned in 1768 by the Sons of Liberty, commemorates the brave resistance of the Massachusetts legislature to British tyranny. The unfinished Stuart portraits of George and Martha are eminently popular but not always present. Since 1980, the first first couple have been jointly owned by the MFA and the National Portrait Gallery in Washington, in an arrangement that allows them to rotate between the institutions every three (or so) years.

Since its earliest decades, the MFA has been concerned with educating Bostonians about art, and with making its collections accessible to as many people as possible. As early as 1877, a "School of Drawing and Painting" was run within the old museum; a more structured entity, today's Museum School, became a part of the museum in 1901. In 1907, docents—or non-staff teachers—began offering museum visitors information on the collections; some claim that the MFA was the first to use such guides, though other museums quickly followed suit. Various efforts to reach all social and economic classes were periodically launched—including free daily access, free concerts, and even a storyteller who freely interpreted art for "slum children" from 1911 to 1919. Though much of this was apparently done in earnest, the notion persisted for decades that the MFA was a haven only for the white and the wealthy.

Today's museum staff has made an even greater effort to mold the prestigious institution into a user-friendly facility. The museum education department oversees and sponsors programs for the community, schools, and the public, offering art classes, scholarships, "artful adventures," parent-child programs, hands-on activities for youngsters, concerts, and films. More brochures are being written and more labeling is appearing everywhere, in both special exhibitions and permanent collections. Interpretation and guided tours, by volunteer gallery instructors and members of the volunteer MFA Associates, are available several times a day. The museum's accessibility to the disabled is comprehensive—arguably the best in Boston.

"The museum is committed to providing the community with a wide range of learning opportunities that enhance their experiences with the MFA's collection," says Susan Longhenry, Alfond Director of Museum Learning and Public Programs. "From family programs in the galleries to the use of technology, we hope to sustain and expand our diverse audience by introducing new ways of looking at art."

THE ESSENTIALS

Address: 465 Huntington Avenue (Avenue of the Arts), Boston, MA 02115. **Telephone:** (617) 267-9300. **Website:** www.mfa.org. **Visitor Information:** Open seven days a week: Monday, Tuesday, Saturday, and Sunday, 10:00 A.M. to 4:45 P.M., Wednesday through Friday, 10:00 A.M. to 9:45 p.m. General admission fee includes two visits in a 30-day period but does not include Gund Gallery exhibitions; fees reduced Thursday and Friday evenings after 5:00 P.M.; general admission by voluntary contribution every Wednesday, 4:00 to 9:45 p.m. Closed New Year's Day, Patriot's Day, Independence Day, Thanksgiving, and Christmas Day. Free daily tours, both of the entire museum and specific collections, begin at the information desk; call for details and times. Visitor guides in seven languages. Excellent, exceptionally well conceived wheelchair access throughout building, including exhibits, restrooms, elevators, and gift shop.

18 The Isabella Stewart Gardner Museum

IT'S SURROUNDED by a wrought-iron fence and a stark brick exterior—hardly the stuff that would inspire passing drivers to stop and stare. From the outside, neighboring institutions along the Fenway—like Emmanuel College, Simmons College, and various buildings of the Museum of Fine Arts, Boston—look far more impressive. But once inside the luxurious neo-Venetian palace of art treasures, quirky antiquities, and floral extravagance known as the Isabella Stewart Gardner Museum, visitors inevitably become enchanted.

Historian Henry Adams once described the Gardner, which opened in 1903, as "peace, repose or dream, rather like opium." Decades later, architect I. M. Pei would characterize the museum as "an oasis of calm and beauty." Actress Katharine Hepburn added a most important footnote to these rather ethereal analyses: "It's great fun," she insisted of the curious Fenway palace, "and it's a fascinating creature that it's all about."

That "creature," of course, was Mrs. Isabella Stewart Gardner, known to posterity as the founder and creator of the Gardner Museum and to her peers as Boston's *most* improper Bostonian. Gardner was a patron of the arts and a flamboyant social leader in a conservative Victorian age. She was also a learned collector, a world traveler, a multilinguist, a music lover, an accomplished social dancer, and the alternately beloved and belittled talk of the town.

Contemporary accounts suggest that Belle, as Isabella was called, had a certain individualistic spirit and energy, even in her earliest years. Her home was New York City. Her father was a Stewart, boasting a family lineage that traced back to the Stewarts of twelfth-century Scotland. Their money came from Irish linen, Pennsylvania iron, and well-invested inheritances.

In later years, her character was alternately described as "charming," "flirtatious," "whimsical," and "imperious." Morris Carter—the director of the museum from 1924 to 1955, and Mrs. Gardner's biographer in 1925—described her as "a fascinating, frail, delicate little creature, delightful to everybody, but determined to lead her own life." Today, being a strong, free-thinking woman is almost acceptable. A century ago, it was essentially scandalous.

Belle met her future husband's family through a connection with a childhood friend. The Gardners of Boston had money from sailing ships, railroads, and investments. They also had a son they called Jack, presumably to avoid confusing him with his father, the senior John L. Gardner. Belle and John L. Gardner, Jr., courted and fell in love, then married when she was nineteen. The couple eventually moved into one of the Gardner family homes at 152 Beacon Street, soon expanding it into 150 Beacon as well.

The beautifully flowered central courtyard of the Isabella Stewart Gardner Museum is a seventy-nine-foot-tall glass-roofed atrium with changing floral exhibits.

If the new "Mrs. Jack" was initially unpopular with the female socialites of Boston, it was perhaps partly because a New Yorker had married a tall, dark, and rich eligible Boston bachelor. She was also a good dancer, and an avid, educated listener—both of which were terribly attractive to men, married and single. Despite the petty jealousies that ensued, Mrs. Gardner did have many female friends.

Though she was born in 1840, a year after the invention of the camera, the best pictures of Isabella Stewart Gardner are in paintings and sketches, including ten scattered throughout the museum. Mrs. Gardner's favorite was the life-size John Singer Sargent painting in the Gothic Room; it depicts Belle as many of her early friends remember her—small, slender, and rather plain-looking, with her distinctive string of pearls wrapped around her waist. If Belle was plain, however, she was not self-conscious about it; moreover, her contemporaries continually marveled at the beauty of both her voice and her complexion.

Why Mrs. Jack began traveling and collecting artwork and finally built a home for her treasures is a complex question. As a teenager, she had confided to a friend her childhood dream of creating a palace for the people. The death of her two-year-old son, Jackie, in 1865 probably provided the impetus for making that dream become reality. The loss of her only child put Belle in a deep depression, a so-called nervous breakdown that left her bedridden for months. As an antidote, Jack took his wife on extended visits to foreign lands. The "therapy" worked then, as it would with later family crises. Belle loved many cultures and countries, though the exquisite ornamentation and Renaissance artwork of Venice took center stage in her heart.

Meanwhile, Mrs. Jack had become friends with many members of Boston's cultural elite, who sustained her interest in art. Among them were Henry James, Henry Adams, James McNeill Whistler, John Singer Sargent, art history professor Charles Eliot Norton of Harvard, and the soon-to-be-famous art critic Bernard Berenson. Belle helped support young Berenson when he graduated from Harvard in 1887. He traveled to Europe and purchased art for her there, writing her with descriptions and prices, then awaiting her response. Among the paintings he acquired for her were several Rembrandts, two Botticellis, two Raphaels, a Rubens, a Degas, and a Titian, all of which are displayed at the museum today. Because of the predilections of both Berenson and Belle, most of these purchases were Italian Renaissance painters. The Gardner collection as a whole is strongest in Italian Renaissance, seventeenth-century Dutch, and nineteenth-century American works.

The deaths of loved ones continued to haunt Belle's life; several of Jack's relatives passed on early, as did Belle's three siblings, her father, and, quite unexpectedly, Jack himself. With no husband, no heirs, and a heightened sense of her own mortality, Mrs. Jack plunged headlong into buying and building. She had ample financial resources for this pursuit: she inherited $1.6 million after her father's death in 1892 and received another $2.3 million when Jack died in 1898. These funds may seem inadequate for establishing a major art collection today; at the time, however, Mrs. Gardner purchased many museum items for as little as five or ten dollars. Other works were comparatively expensive but still affordable: she bought Titian's painting *The Rape of Europa*—a priceless piece now displayed in the Titian Room—for $100,000. Today it's considered one of the most important Italian Renaissance paintings in America.

It was inevitable that the collection would eventually outgrow the Gardner house on Beacon Street. Jack and Belle had actually discussed building a museum to display Belle's accumulating treasures years before Jack's death. Though Belle had wanted a site in their Beacon Street home, Jack pushed for a spot in the Fens, a once-marshy area that had recently been reclaimed and that Jack predicted would become "the new Back Bay."

Jack was wrong; the Fenway area never did become as prestigious as the Back Bay. Nevertheless, Mrs. Gardner began furiously building on the wide-open Fens site shortly after her husband's death, selecting Willard T. Sears as architect. Since construction was hidden behind a high brick wall, since Mrs. Gardner would not talk to reporters, and since many of her workmen spoke only Italian, myths about "Belle's folly" were favorite fodder for gossips and tabloids around the world. "WEIRD WALL SHUTS MRS. 'JACK' GARDNER PALACE IN FROM THE WORLD: Whim of a Woman!" cried a headline in one June 19, 1901, edition of the *Boston Herald*.

Behind that "weird wall," Mrs. Jack was building her own eclectic version of a Venetian palazzo. While the interior design was based on Belle's interpretation of an ornate fifteenth-century Italian palace turned inside out, the exterior resembled a simpler northern Italian villa. Because of the soft, moist land below, pilings were sunk beneath the heavy stone walls. The center courtyard, however, originally had no pilings. Hence, it sank; you can still see that the lower stairs were added to the original top steps of all four entrances.

As Fenway Court took shape, Belle occasionally bolted off to Italy to buy staircases, balustrades, lace, furniture, ironwork, and other materials. She also changed her plans in the middle of the building process—to the chagrin of her workers, who would sometimes characterize her as whimsical, mad, or egomaniacal. In fact, the periodic changes were relatively minor; in the same era, Frank Lloyd Wright, who tore down walls he had just erected, would be dubbed a genius.

Isabella Stewart Gardner's eccentricity—and her unwillingness to spoil a good story by telling the truth—spawned many urban legends in her time, some of which contained kernels of truth. Although she did not walk her pet lions on Beacon Street, as in one favorite tale, she did pet a toothless old lion and escort it around a traveling zoo that was located on the Boylston Street side of Boston Common in 1897. She did collect exotic trees for her grounds and courtyard, but she did not, as legend had it, greet guests while perched in mimosa trees. She did not have multitudinous affairs with men, although she had many male admirers. Scholars think that if she ever did have such a liaison, it was with author F. Marion Crawford, with whom she spent considerable time in the early 1880s. Belle's husband was apparently tolerant of whatever did, or did not, transpire.

And no, she did not dismantle an extant Venetian palace and bring it back, stone by stone, to build her museum. No Venetian prince would ever have built as Mrs. Jack did; though Fenway Court used many Venetian palace parts, those parts were often chronologically, regionally, and archeologically unrelated.

Contrary to popular gossip, there's no evidence that Belle liked to lie naked on a bear rug in front of Titian's *Rape of Europa;* moreover, she was never the puppet of Bernard Berenson, and actually rejected many of his recommendations for art acquisitions. She did, however, attend a concert at Symphony Hall wearing a headband that read "Oh, You Red Sox."

In her construction methods, her art and artifact acquisitions, and the way she arranged them all, Mrs. Gardner followed no rules. She did what she pleased, and even engraved the motto "C'est Mon Plaisir" over the main entrance to Fenway Court (today, the museum's exit).

Inside, Mrs. Gardner's dream is both a visitor's delight and a conservator's nightmare. The museum's collections include 290 paintings, 280 pieces of sculpture, 60 drawings, 130 prints, 460 pieces of furniture, 240 ceramic and glass objects, an archive of more than 6,000 letters, and a library of 2,300 volumes focused on the museum collection. The collections are spread throughout the building—four floors comprising thirty-one rooms, chambers, and hallways. Paintings are often placed back to back by an open window, with viewing chairs planted on either side. Antique tables, chairs, and glorious clutter occasionally obstruct the view of other artwork. Rare medieval choir stalls, statues, and art objects are open to public affection, unprotected by pedestals, glass cases, or rope barriers. Precious textiles are placed under or draped over objects as if they were common tablecloths. Enormous medieval tapestries hang free from the walls. Many paintings are hung directly across the room from bright, broad windows overlooking the beautifully flowered central courtyard—a glass-roofed atrium that is seventy-nine feet tall.

One favorite, and typically eclectic, museum area is known as the Spanish Cloister. The featured painting is the huge *El Jaleo* (1882), a vision of a Spanish dancer by American artist John Singer Sargent. The cloister—so named for its architectural design as a covered passage on the side of a courtyard—also includes Mexican wall tiles, Boston-made floor tiles, a French medieval portal, three Roman sarcophagi, and Egyptian wood carvings.

The Gardner Museum was first opened to visitors, as Fenway Court, on January 1, 1903. (The dazzling invitation-only celebration featured doughnuts, champagne, and a concert played by fifty members of the Boston Symphony Orchestra.) Mrs. Gardner made her personal living quarters on the fourth floor of the building—in spaces now used for storage and administrative offices. During her lifetime, she opened her museum to the public for two weeks each spring and fall, limiting tickets to two hundred per day. Her fee was one dollar, a sum that she thought would make the public appreciate the visit more.

While Belle was alive, her museum changed constantly. For example, the current Spanish Cloister and the Tapestry Room above it—where concerts are now held from September through May—were originally one huge two-story music room until Mrs. Gardner altered it in 1914. She also loved regular changes of the floral displays throughout the courtyard and on the surrounding grounds. The seasonal plantings continue to this day, facilitated by the acquisition of seven greenhouses for the museum site in the 1970s. Among popular favorites are the courtyard's rare orchids and its tumbling nasturtiums, which grow from the second story down, sometimes reaching twenty-five or thirty feet in length.

In her will, Mrs. Gardner specified that the museum, its contents, and their general arrangement should remain the same as they were in her last year of life, which turned out to be 1924. If the rules were broken, she stipulated, the museum would see its end—with its treasures auctioned off in Paris and the proceeds given to Harvard.

Therefore, the Gardner now features the same works of art displayed in the same places decade after decade; objects disappear only occasionally for rest, travel, or in-house conservation. Although such sameness is unusual for a major museum, many visitors find the Gardner a comfortable, familiar "home"—as well as a place where new discoveries can always be made. Some changes have taken place since Mrs. Gardner's death, necessitated by the changing demands time places on any institution. A two-story administrative wing was added in 1932—exempt from the will's conditions, since it was outside the original home and museum. A small gift shop and a café were added in 1972 and 1978 as a service to visitors. The greenhouses were additions of the 1970s, and the installation of a climate-control system throughout the museum was an ongoing project of the 1990s. In 1992, the new Special Exhibitions Gallery was opened in the 1932 annex, allowing the museum to present significant traveling exhibitions and to showcase the contemporary works of visiting artists-in-residence. Created by Anne Hawley, Norma Jean Calderwood, director, and by Pieranna Cavalchini, curator of contemporary art, the residency program continues Mrs. Gardner's legacy of support for contemporary artists of the day.

Today, the Gardner Museum invites four to six contemporary artists per year—including painters, photographers, sculptors, composers, installation and performance artists, storytellers, and writers—to live, contemplate, and create at the museum. The idea is to have these artists draw inspiration from the museum's intimate installations, architectural beauty, musical and horticultural riches, and archival histories to inspire creative thinking, artistic exploration, and ideas for new work. Visual and performance artists often present new works inspired by their residencies at the museum.

Other changes result from the ongoing conservation of Gardner treasures, a scientific and artistic process made more difficult by the museum's setup, which often subjects the works to excess light, heat, humidity, air pollution, and the wear and tear brought on by thousands of friendly visitors. A dedicated staff of professional conservators works daily in the annex, painstakingly making repairs to antique tapestries and other pieces, repairs that often take years to complete. Incidentally, virtually all the Gardner's conservation work is done in-house, with the notable exception of work on paintings.

Reparations can't be made, however, for the greatest heartbreak of Gardner Museum history: the robbery of March 18, 1990, that resulted in the loss of thirteen objects, including priceless paintings by Vermeer, Rembrandt, and Manet. Two thieves disguised as police officers talked their way past college-age security guards, dismantled the Gardner's alarm system, and then made what was touted as the "biggest art heist in history." The objects taken were estimated by some to have a value of $200 million, and a million-dollar reward was offered for information leading to the recovery of the stolen art. Nothing, alas, has ever been found.

Despite the years, periodic problems, and that singular tragedy, Isabella Stewart Gardner's dream of creating a "palace for the people" remains very real today. Classical musical concerts, a part of the Gardner heritage for decades, are still held in the Tapestry Room, on weekends from September through May. Meanwhile, the Gardner staff is working to revitalize their existing educational programs to reach more youngsters than ever, while developing a new lecture series and the above-mentioned artist-in-residence program.

Ongoing evening and daytime lectures, led by renowned art historians, curators, and visiting artists and scholars, highlight specific aspects of the museum's preeminent permanent collection and founder, as well as special exhibitions, performances, and programs. Evening lectures and a growing number of evening programs provide a rare, highly atmospheric, and memorable forum for visitors to experience the beauty of the Gardner Museum at night. Through all these activities and events, the Gardner staff is working to recreate the kind of flourishing intellectual and cultural center that Isabella Gardner established at the turn of the century. What more appropriate place than in Belle's Venetian palace?

THE ESSENTIALS

Address: 280 The Fenway, Boston; offices at 2 Palace Road, Boston 02115. **Telephone:** (617) 566-1401; concert information line, (617) 734-1359. **Website:** www.gardnermuseum.org. **Visitor Information:** Open 11:00 A.M. to 5:00 P.M., Tuesday through Sunday; open some holidays; call for details. Moderate admission fee; extra charge for concerts and lectures. Tours Friday at 2:30 P.M. Wheelchair accessible; staff assistance required for use of elevator to second and third floors.

19 Harvard University Museums and Memorial Hall

YOU DON'T have to be a student to reap the many benefits of Harvard University. America's oldest institution of higher learning—founded in 1636—has six museums open to the public on its Cambridge campus. The tickets are modestly priced, even free on Saturday or Sunday mornings (varying with the museum). Exhibits range from stunning blown-glass flowers to triceratops skulls, and from Monet's *Charing Cross Bridge* to Native American totem poles. The museums themselves vary in style from Victorian "cram-'n'-jam" setups to spacious, climate-controlled, interactive rooms with theatrical lighting and sound. Equally appealing is geographic convenience: the three Harvard University Art Museums, the Harvard Museum of Natural History, the Peabody Museum of Archeology and Ethnology, and the Semitic Museum—as well as Harvard's architectural marvel, Memorial Hall—can all be found within a few short blocks of one another.

The Harvard University Art Museums are at or near the corner of Broadway and Quincy streets, a five-minute walk from Harvard Square. Combined, these three museums house a world-class art collection featuring 160,000 objects from East and West and from ancient to modern times. One ticket admits you to all three.

The Fogg Art Museum, founded in 1891, is the eldest. In its early days, the Fogg primarily housed art reproductions. Since 1927—when it moved into the familiar Georgian red-brick building at 32 Quincy Street—the museum has become a treasure-house of European and North American originals and has served as a vital source for art education.

The Fogg's Calderwood Courtyard is a grand, two-story adaptation of the sixteenth-century Church of the Madonna de San Biagio at Montepulciano, Italy. Surrounding this centerpiece are galleries and halls that con-

Memorial Hall,
Harvard University's
Victorian Gothic
"secular cathedral,"
has literally played
hosts to cabbages
and kings.

tain masterpieces by Giotto, Fra Angelico, Rembrandt, Ingres, Renoir, Rodin, Whistler, Picasso, and Rothko. Some twenty new exhibitions are developed each year at the Fogg and its two sister museums, complementing their stellar permanent collections.

The Busch-Reisinger Museum, which occupied nearby Adolphus Busch Hall from 1921 to 1987, is now located in the new Werner Otto Hall; its entrance is on the second floor of the Fogg. The only museum in America devoted to Germanic art, the Busch-Reisinger was developed by early benefactors including Kaiser Wilhelm II and Adolphus Busch, the St. Louis beer magnate. Founded in 1901, the museum was housed in a Harvard gymnasium before the more ornate Busch Hall was built. Anti-German sentiments prevented the new building from opening until 1921 and closed it entirely during World War II.

Longtime curator Charles Kuhn expanded the Busch-Reisinger's collections between 1931 and 1968, acquiring expressionist works by Klee, Munch, and Kandinsky, as well as Max Beckmann's startling *Self Portrait in Tuxedo* and the *Actors* triptych, two of the gallery's most riveting pieces.

The sleek, striped Arthur M. Sackler Museum, at 485 Broadway, is a relatively recent addition to Harvard's Art Museums. Dedicated in 1985, the spacious Sackler highlights ancient Asian, Islamic, and later Indian art. Rare Persian and Indian miniatures, Japanese prints and ceramics, Greek vases, ancient Chinese jades, and Buddhas are among the beautifully displayed collections. A museum shop is on the main floor; the main shop is at the Fogg.

The Harvard Museum of Natural History and the Peabody Museum of Archaeology and Ethnology share one building, with entrances on 26 Oxford Street and 11 Divinity Avenue. As with the Art Museums, a single ticket admits one to both. Although they double as tourist attractions, their stellar collections were acquired for use as in-house teaching tools—a purpose they still ably serve to this day.

The Harvard Museum of Natural History (HMNH) presents the collections of the Museum of Comparative Zoology, the Mineralogical Museum, and the Herbaria to the public. With 21 million specimens covering 4.5 billion years, the HMNH can obviously display only a fraction of their collections at any given time. (The advantage here is the ability to mount temporary exhibits that reveal never-before-seen treasures.)

The most popular exhibit at any of these museums is undoubtedly the display of glass flowers. Formally known as the Ware Collection of Glass Models of Plants and created by artists Leopold Blaschka and his son, Rudolph between 1887 and 1936, the three thousand exquisitely blown and hand-shaped flowers are unique. Apparently only the Blashkas had the patience, or the expertise, to create every pistil, stamen, petal, and stem of 850 plant species in such intricate detail.

Nearby are the collections of the Museum of Comparative Zoology. Begun in 1859, this Victorian-era wonderland of halls and chambers is packed with fossils, skeletons, and stuffed creatures of every size and shape. The largest figures include skeletons of the giant sea serpent kronosaurus, the "Harvard Mastodon" (a historic skeleton from Hackettstown, New Jersey, presented to Harvard in 1846), and the first type specimen of the dinosaur triceratops ever described by science. Smaller items include two golden Chinese pheasants given to George Washington by the Marquis de Lafayette, which, after they died, were driven by stagecoach to Charles Willson Peale's museum in Philadelphia and stuffed with pepper as a preservative. (Peale's museum was touted as the first popular museum in America. When it closed in 1850, half its collections were purchased by showman P. T. Barnum, and the other half went to the Boston Society of Natural History. In 1913, portions of the latter collection—including the Washington pheasants—were acquired by Harvard.)

While many of the display rooms at the MCZ have been colorfully and creatively modernized in recent years, the Mineralogical galleries still have a decidedly nostalgic feel. Though most of the display cabinets are flat-topped wood-and-glass Victorian-era cases, they've been spruced up with pastel paints and matching rugs. The venerable "Geological Museum" was established in 1784, and its impressive geological collection—including gems, minerals, ores, and meteorites—is the oldest and largest in the United States. One of its first curators was John Webster, who was hanged in 1849 for the murder of another faculty member in the macabre George Parkman Case.

The esteemed Peabody Museum of Archeology and Ethnology was founded in 1866. Its ground-floor Hall of the North American Indian was reopened in 1990 following a ten-year multimillion dollar renovation. Today it's a colorful, interactive exhibit highlighting ten Native American cultures and five hundred artifacts, from a fearsome Crow warbonnet to delicately woven baskets (see Chapter 40).

The Peabody includes two additional floors of exhibits. While the gallery dedicated to Oceania has old-fashioned decor and presentation, the artifacts themselves are interesting—though more to curious academics than casual museumgoer. In stark contrast is the newly redesigned third floor, which opened in December 1992 with the long-term exhibit "Encounters with the Americas." The "hook" of this new hall is the Columbian Quincentennial of 1492. Rather than praise or damn Columbus and the "Age of Discovery," the exhibit uses 1492 as a dividing line from which to observe five specific South and Central American cultures, past and present. The question of how five centuries of encounters between East and West forged a complex cultural mosaic in the New World is explored through a variety of beautifully presented objects, from huge plaster casts of classic Mayan monuments to modern displays chronicling the plight of the Amazonian tropical forest.

Two galleries on the third floor and two on the first feature changing exhibits that highlight the Peabody's exceptional collections. They include the Lewis and Clark collection of Native American artifacts, as well as a photographic gallery offering two to four exhibits a year culled from the half million images in the Peabody's photographic archives.

The Semitic Museum, founded in 1889, is Harvard University's museum of ancient Near Eastern archaeology, located in the classical-style building at 6 Divinity Avenue. Its collections include more than 40,000 artifacts, most from museum-sponsored excavations in Israel, Egypt, Jordan, Syria, Iraq, and Tunisia. Exhibits drawn from these collections are devoted to the art, archaeology, languages, and cultures of the ancient Near East. Some of their displays—like "The Houses of Ancient Israel: Domestic, Royal, Divine," which features a full-scale replica of a two-story Iron Age village house—do stay up for long periods. The small museum's activities include such gallery exhibits as well as an active outreach program with docent-led tours and teacher workshops.

Although it's not technically a museum, no tour of the area would be complete without a visit to Harvard's Memorial Hall. New England novelist Jane Langton clearly spent time in the engaging old structure, then used it as the setting for her chilling 1978 mystery, *The Memorial Hall Murder.*

> The building rose above him like a cliff face, mass piled upon mass, ten thousand of brick laid upon ten thousand. It was ugly, majestically ugly. Augustly, monumentally ugly. It was a red-brick Notre Dame, a bastard Chartres, punctured with stained-glass windows, ribboned around with lofty sentiments in Latin, finialed with metallic crests and pennants, knobbed with the heads of orators . . .
>   . . . The colossal edifice contained a theater and a great hall and a memo-

rial transept and a lecture room and radio station and a lot of small offices and classrooms, but now in its gloomy grandeur it was a mausoleum as well. When it had been erected in the 1870s it had been intended as a half-secular, half-sacred memorial to young graduates who had died in the Union cause in the Civil War. Now it was an actual coffin.

All things considered, Memorial Hall—Harvard's own 1874 Victorian Gothic "secular cathedral"—was an ideal location for Langton's fictional murder. To this day, it is filled with memorials to the dead, endless Latin inscriptions, marble busts, dark wooden walls, and cavernous chambers. Overhead hovers a series of catwalks, gargoyles, medieval-looking stained glass, chandeliers, and vaulted ceilings.

But there's much more to its story than that. Since its grand opening more than a century ago, Harvard's very adaptable hall has catered not only to murder mystery writers, but quite literally to cabbages and kings. The building's best-known chamber is Sanders Theater, an intimate hybrid of theater and lecture hall that has hosted everything from Elizabethan drama to Gilbert and Sullivan, the Boston Symphony Orchestra to Pete Seeger, Prince Charles to Jesse Jackson, Igor Stravinsky to John Cage, and Social Analysis 10 to Foreign Cultures 48. Across the hallway from Sanders is Annenberg (formerly Alumni) Hall, also known as the Great Hall, which served as a major Harvard dining area until 1926 and returned to that function late in 1995. In the intervening years, it was used sporadically for rehearsals, registrations, final exams, blood drives, book sales, dances, and receptions.

Dividing the two—much like the transept of a cathedral separating the choir (Sanders) from the nave (Annenberg)—is the memorial transept itself, lined with the names of the dead and lit by two stained-glass windows. Although it serves today primarily as an intermission vestibule and a convenient passageway for Harvard students on cross-campus jaunts, this section is the least understood and perhaps the least appreciated of the building's three major chambers; yet it's the transept itself that best reflects why Memorial Hall was created in the wake of the American Civil War.

Hundreds of young Harvard students and graduates had marched off to battle in the bloody War Between the States. By the war's end in 1865, a committee of fifty Harvard alumni was actively planning a structure to honor those who had died for the Union cause. The two-acre site they chose was a wide-open playing field nicknamed the "Delta," which Harvard had acquired in 1816. To rationalize using such a large lot, the new structure would have to fill other needs of the college as well as serving as a memorial; it was proposed that the building contain an academic theater for literary festivals, a dining hall large enough to serve commencement dinners, and dozens of meeting rooms and classrooms.

Two Harvard graduates, William Robert Ware (class of 1852) and Henry Van Brunt (1854), won the design competition for Memorial Hall. The architects modeled Sanders Theater after Oxford University's Sheldonian Theater, then combined elements from London's Westminster Hall and the dining halls at Cambridge and Oxford universities for the rest of the building. The final structure was more than twice its original planned length and cost more than twice the initial budget of $150,000. Of the $390,000 finally spent, an astounding $368,980 was contributed by alumni.

Thanks to the recent replacement of a long-missing tower and extensive renovations completed by 1995, Memorial Hall's exterior looks much as it did in Ware and Van Brunt's day. (Memorial Hall had a sawed-off look for forty-four years since the last tower was destroyed in a 1956 fire and never replaced. The new tower was painstakingly constructed to replicate the 1878 design, which itself replaced the 1874 design rather than the design of the clock tower sizzled in 1956; the $4 million project was finished in February 2000.) What Memorial Hall does not look like, however, is any other Harvard building.

Its architects designed the structure in the Ruskinian Gothic, or High Victorian Gothic, style. Popular in England in the 1860s, such Gothic revival buildings typically have animated silhouettes, massive and assertive shapes, an overflow of finely crafted details, and, most distinctively, a multitude of colors. In Memorial Hall's case, the predominant red brick is interspersed with stripes of black tar-dipped brick and buff sandstone. A similar polychrome motif stretches to the roof, which has been likened to both "streaky bacon" and a Navajo blanket.

Although Memorial Hall resembles a cathedral in many ways, both in design and in decorative touches, architect Van Brunt denied throughout his lifetime that the structure was meant to be churchlike in any way.

Less than four years after the cornerstone was laid in 1870, Memorial Hall opened its doors to Harvard's festive June commencement activities. Sanders Theater (named for benefactor Charles Sanders, class of 1802) would not be complete until 1875 and the tower not set in place until 1877, but the sparkling new dining hall and memorial vestibule were dedicated and opened on June 23, 1874.

The vestibule is literally and figuratively the heart of Memorial Hall. Twenty-eight white marble tablets solemnly list the names of 136 Harvard graduates and students who died in the Civil War and the battles in which they fell—including Gettysburg, Antietam, and Fredericksburg. That those listed were all Union men is a long-standing controversy: some sixty-four slain Harvard Confederates remain unnamed to this day. Among those memorialized is Paul Joseph Revere, grandson of the famed Paul Revere, and an 1860 medical school graduate called Benjamin Franklin Peirce—whose name may have inspired the full name of the "Hawkeye" character on the beloved television series *M*A*S*H*.

The vestibule has other pop-culture connections as well: it was there that Jane Langton's fictitious victim fell prey to a fatal bomb blast in *The Memorial Hall Murder*, and it was there that actor Christopher Reeve pondered the memorial wall tablets while playing Southern Civil War veteran Basil Ransom in the 1984 film version of Henry James's *The Bostonians*.

The sixty-foot-tall vestibule's ecclesiastic feel—and its popular name, Memorial Transept—comes primarily from the two gorgeous stained-glass rose windows that dominate its north and south entrances; each one spans an impressive 708 square feet. Though the aura is sacred, the messages are quite secular. The refurbished north window, originally designed by Donald MacDonald in the late nineteenth century, lists all the virtues in Latin, explained Louise Ambler, a Fogg Museum curator who was active in the restoration. "If you read the Latin . . . carefully," she added, "you'll see that one word is meaningless. It was reassembled incorrectly during the repair!"

The south window was donated in 1898 by Martin Brimmer, class of 1849. The window's designer, Sarah Wyman Whitman, was affectionately dubbed "our wild woman of stained glass" by architect Peter Riley, who helped coordinate Memorial Hall's restorations of the late 1980s. Whitman included some 35,000 pieces of glass in this work, some sandwiched six layers deep, in order to create certain color effects. The north window, by contrast, contains a mere 7,800 segments.

The rest of Memorial Hall's veritable museum of nineteenth-century American stained glass graces the high walls of cavernous Annenberg Hall. When the 165-foot-long, 9,000-square-foot dining hall was completed in 1874, all eighteen of its windows were filled with plain white glass. Between 1879 and 1902, however, seventeen of those spaces were filled with stained glass, primarily donated by alumni classes and designed by well-known artists like Whitman, John La Farge, Frederic Crowninshield, and the Tiffany Glass Company.

The windows portray scenes of war, peace, bravery, morality, and enlightenment. The historic personages depicted on them are hardly Harvardians, though most were learned "soldiers" of some sort. Generally standing in pairs, with a scene or inscription below, the characters are as diverse as Pericles, Leonardo, Shakespeare, Charlemagne, Christopher Columbus, and Joseph Warren. (The last was a local fellow and a beloved patriot who died at the Revolutionary War Battle of Bunker Hill.)

A break from that standard posed pattern—and one of Memorial Hall's most moving pieces—is the famous Battle Window, designed by John La Farge and donated by the class of 1860. Twelve members of that class died in the Civil War, including Robert Gould Shaw, who led the black all-volunteer 54th Regiment commemorated in bas-relief on Boston Common (see Chapter 34).

Above these stained-glass scenes is the Hall's great hammerbeam trussed ceiling, inspired by the medieval halls at the colleges of Oxford and Cambridge in England. Down below is a gallery of marble busts and rippling oil paintings depicting soldiers, statesmen, and Harvard sons of the Civil War era.

The rest of Annenberg Hall is a vast open space that was once filled with long dining tables and hungry Harvard students—a use it lost for seven decades then resumed in the fall of 1995. (Today, dining services typically serve some 3,400 meals there each day of the academic year.) In his 1907 work *The American Scene*, Henry James commented on the curious irony of the space's dining use, calling Memorial Hall "the great bristling brick Valhalla . . . that house of honor and hospitality which . . . dispenses . . . laurels to the dead and dinner to the living." Following its retirement as a dining hall in 1926, Annenberg Hall's use was limited. Like the rest of Memorial Hall, it was frequently rented by non-Harvard individuals and organizations, which helped the building pay for its own upkeep.

Thanks to a $12 million grant from the Walter H. Annenberg Foundation, the old Great Hall (renamed for Annenberg's late son, Roger, class of 1962) and the rest of the building underwent major renovations during the 1990s. The basement area of Memorial Hall, for example—for years the home of WHRB radio plus a flurry of little classrooms and offices—now houses a Harvard "common," or informal student center, named for and financed by Katherine Bogdanovich Loker, who gave $7 million to the project. The popular Loker Commons now provides a variety of student services, including computer labs; copy, fax, and ATM services; an electronic board displaying student activities, events, and announcements; a performance area; and several informal eateries.

Renovations were also made on Sanders Theater, the other half of Memorial Hall, which has always been a strange sort of place as performing stages go. It has no real marquee. There is no greenroom, performer waiting room, or backstage area immediately adjacent to the stage. There are no individual seats in the audience—just rows of cushioned wooden pewlike benches. Still, Sanders Theater, named for the alumnus who bequeathed $56,000 for its completion, has long been extolled as a magical, surprisingly intimate theater with excellent sight lines. With 1,166 seats, it remains Harvard's largest theater, roughly comparable in size to Berklee Performance Center and Jordan Hall in Boston.

Even though it was created for literary festivals and academic lectures, which still take place there, Sanders has seen it all. In recent years, classical and acoustic music groups of all sizes have shown a particular fondness for the space. Professional performing ensembles such as the Boston Philharmonic, Christmas Revels, and Boston Baroque are regularly seen there. Folk legend Pete Seeger even wrote in a 1974 letter to the newspaper *Harvard Today*, "Sanders Theatre is one of the greatest auditoriums in the country. . . . The very reverberations which make it difficult for lecturers and some music make it ideal for singers. It's like singing in a bathtub."

While modern halls are too often sterile, Sanders has character in abundance. Above the stage is an enormous inscribed panel heralded as the "queen" of Harvard's Latin inscriptions by historian Mason Hammond. The panel chronicles the 1636 founding of Harvard College "in wooded and uncultivated places." Down below, stage left and right, are marble statues of Josiah Quincy—the Boston mayor and Harvard president—and colonial-era orator James Otis. The marble Otis, like the statues of John Winthrop and John Adams that guard the inner entrance at Annenberg Hall, was moved to Memorial Hall from Mount Auburn Cemetery in 1936. A John La Farge stained-glass portrait of the Greek goddess Athena, posed in a classic mourning motif, looks down from the balcony. Below La Farge's masterpiece are what some consider the best seats in Sanders, by the way: the C, D, and E sections of the mezzanine.

Memorial Hall and its unusual chambers are wonderful places to settle in for a show or special event. (Alas, visitation is restricted to Sanders and Annenberg outside of such events). But if you're thinking of renting out any part of the hall, be forewarned of one unusual restriction: no helium balloons are allowed. Once trapped in Memorial Hall's High Gothic trusses, they may never escape, even if deflated. Legend has it that tiny bits of colored rubber still rest in the eaves up yonder.

THE ESSENTIALS

Harvard University Art Museums

Address: 485 Broadway and 32 Quincy streets, adjacent to Harvard Yard, Cambridge, MA 02138. **Telephone:** (617) 495-9400. **Website:** www.artmuseums.harvard.edu. **Visitor Information:** Open 10:00 A.M. to 5:00 P.M., Monday through Saturday; 1:00 to 5:00 P.M., Sunday. Closed all national holidays. Admission fee; one ticket gives access to all three Art Museums. Free Saturday, 10:00 A.M. to noon, and every day after 4:30 P.M. General tours offered at each of the three museums; call for times and details. Wheelchair access to the Fogg and Busch-Reisinger is on Prescott Street at the entrance to the Fine Arts Library; entrance to the Sackler is wheelchair accessible. Accessible bathrooms available in all three museums; for questions call (617) 495-4040.

The Harvard Hot Ticket offers visitors admission to all six Harvard museums—the Sackler, Busch-Reisinger, Fogg, Natural History, Peabody, and Semitic museums—for a single modest price. Available at all participating museums except the Semitic and in the Harvard Collections Store, Holyoke Center, Harvard Square.

Harvard Museum of Natural History

Address: On the Harvard University campus at 26 Oxford Street, Cambridge, MA 02138. **Telephone:** (617) 495-3045. **Website:** www.hmnh.harvard.edu. **Visitor Information:** Open seven days a week, 9:00 A.M. to 5:00 P.M. Admission fee charged; includes entrance to Peabody Museum. Free of charge Sundays 9:00 A.M. to 12:00 noon, and from 3:00 to 5:00 P.M. Wednesdays, September through May. Closed Thanksgiving, Christmas Eve, Christmas Day, and New Year's Day. Special events, lecture series, travel programs, and other educational activities throughout the year. Museum shop open museum hours. No regularly scheduled tours, though special group tours can be arranged for a fee. Wheelchair accessible, including bathrooms.

Peabody Museum of Archaeology and Ethnology

Address: On the Harvard University campus: 11 Divinity Avenue, Cambridge, MA 02138. **Telephone:** Reception desk and information, (617) 496-1027. **Website:** www.peabody .harvard.edu. **Visitor Information:** Open seven days a week, 9:00 A.M. to 5:00 P.M. Admission fee charged; includes entrance to Harvard Museum of Natural History. Free of charge Sundays 9:00 A.M. to 12:00 noon, and from 3:00 to 5:00 P.M. Wednesdays, September through May. Closed Thanksgiving, Christmas Eve, Christmas Day, and New Year's Day. Teacher workshops, interactive programs for children, classes and special events for families, and public lectures are offered; call (617) 495-2341 or (617) 496-5402. Call ahead to arrange wheelchair access.

Harvard Semitic Museum

Address: On the Harvard University campus: 6 Divinity Avenue, Cambridge, MA 02138. **Telephone:** (617) 495-4631. **Website:** www.fas.harvard.edu/~semitic. **Visitor Information:** Open weekdays, 10:00 A.M. to 4:00 P.M., Sundays, 1:00 to 4:00 P.M. Closed Saturdays and holiday weekends. Free. Tours must be scheduled; call for information. No wheelchair access.

Memorial Hall
Address: 45 Quincy Street, Cambridge, MA 02138. Located at the junction of Kirkland, Quincy, Cambridge, and Oxford streets on the Harvard University campus. **Telephone:** Director's office, (617) 496-4595; Harvard University box office and recorded information on events, (617) 496-2222. **Website:** www.fas.harvard.edu/~memhall. **Visitor Information:** Memorial Hall Transept and director's office open Monday through Friday, 10:00 A.M. to 6:00 P.M. Free. Sanders Theater open to the public for specified public events only; Annenberg Hall is a private dining facility and not available for viewing. Ground floor and basement of Memorial Hall, as well as restrooms, are wheelchair accessible. Tours available as listed through Harvard's Holyoke Information Center (617-495-1573) and Admissions Office (617-495-1551); free. Extensive information, history, and imagery on Memorial Hall available on the above-listed website.

20 Symphony Hall

ANY "living legend" that's more than a century old and still going strong must be doing something right. And such is the case with the beloved Boston landmark known as Symphony Hall. The simple, stark, shoebox-like building—home to the Boston Symphony Orchestra and the Boston Pops—has dominated the busy intersection of Huntington and Massachusetts avenues since the turn of the twentieth century. And though its dull neoindustrial exterior has been the subject of endless jokes, the structure's overall design has made Symphony Hall one of the most acoustically perfect performance spaces in the world. Such acoustic excellence is quite appropriate, of course, given that the building has been full of music since the first symphony concert was held there on October 15, 1900.

Symphony Hall was the brainchild of Civil War veteran, philanthropist, and amateur musician Henry Lee Higginson (1834–1919). Though born in New York, Higginson was of old New England stock rooted in nine generations of Massachusetts soil. A dropout from Harvard College (bad eyes) and professional music (in his own words, "no talent"), Higginson harbored a youthful notion that the wonderful orchestras he had heard while travelling in Vienna should be replicated in Boston. And since no one else was creating such an orchestra, Higginson did.

In 1881, he founded the Boston Symphony Orchestra (which he also sustained for years thereafter). By 1893, the fabulously wealthy Higginson had persuaded some friends to help him buy a parcel of land on the outer reaches of Huntington Avenue, where they could create a permanent home for the orchestra. They came, they built—and their conquest remains an internationally renowned center for music to this day. Founder Higginson is commemorated in both an enormous John Singer Sargent painting at the Massachusetts Avenue entrance and a bust by Bela Pratt in the Hatch Memorial Room, the building's original entrance foyer. Though Higginson was a colonel when honorably discharged from the Union army, he preferred to use his former title, Major. (Besides, his older cousin, the abolitionist, writer, and war veteran Thomas Wentworth Higginson, had already adopted the "Colonel Higginson" moniker). During service in the Civil War, Henry Lee Higginson survived three saber cuts and two pistol shots; still, the scar on his right cheek—apparent in both pieces of art—was incurred during a private scuffle over a horse.

When Higginson began plans to build a home for the BSO, he believed that the orchestra's old residence—the 1852 Music Hall, located on Hamilton Place, where the Orpheum Theatre stands today—was going to be demolished. Hence, he would call his building the new Boston Music Hall. As it turned out, the old Music Hall was not demolished as planned, but Higginson made the discovery too late to warn his builders. As a result, the railings along the new building's marble staircases are decorated with BMH medallions, and the exterior lacks any prominent sign identifying it as Symphony Hall, unless you count the small I.D. plaque added by the Bicentennial Commission in 1976. Apparently, a few interior fixtures actually were stamped with the words "Symphony Hall" in the early building—the metal toilet paper holders in the restrooms. When those fixtures were removed during a later building renovation, some three hundred symphony fans bid to take the precious powder room souvenirs home.

The architect of choice was Charles Follen McKim of the acclaimed New York architectural firm of McKim, Mead, and White. Charles McKim's original drawings for Symphony Hall's exterior had much more "frosting" than the somewhat Georgian, very basic red-brick and limestone-trim exterior we see today. His other major works—including the Boston Public Library, the gates and fence at Harvard Yard, and New York's Pennsylvania Station—all had their share of intricate ornamentation. During Symphony Hall's construction, however, the funds simply ran out, and the McKim trimmings were never added.

Moreover, the building's main entrance on Massachusetts Avenue looks less impressive than the architect ever imagined. McKim actually designed the structure's lavish front doors to open onto Huntington Avenue. Unfortunately, Huntington was widened during the 1930s, forcing the primary entrance to be switched to the Massachusetts Avenue side. Although the exterior Huntington Avenue doors have remained shut since then, the gorgeous main marble staircases with the BMH medallions can still be seen inside.

Symphony Hall's main auditorium, known simply as the Hall, is about a quarter of the size of an average football field. Overall, the motif is simplicity, with touches of gold and crimson on surfaces of wood, brass, and leather. The aisles, once covered with terrazzo tile, now have industrial-strength red runners; lovely plush carpets would have absorbed too much sound and been harder to maintain. The wall areas are decorated with a flat pattern of panels and statues, which *Boston Globe* architecture critic Robert Campbell once compared to "a Robert Adam wallpaper; it is like a light pencil sketch of a room rather than a heavy oil."

The chairs are turn-of-the-twentieth-century originals, and they're kept in good condition by the basement repair shop. Though these seats' firm wooden frames and thin leather padding have always elicited some complaints about comfort, their acoustic qualities are superior. On the arms of more than 550 of them are gold plaques that have been purchased by patrons for up to $10,000 each; such endowed seats became a new tradition during the orchestra's 1980–81 centennial campaign. The practice of endowing seats hearkens back to the first years of Symphony Hall, when seats were "auctioned off" to socialite bidders; these men and women would add their bid price to the cost of a twenty-four-concert season ticket. Patrons who "bought" seats were given first priority on those spots the following season—which began the tradition of passing down seats within a family. Who bought what seats, incidentally, made great news in the society pages of all the Boston papers of the day.

The most elaborate ornamentation in the Hall is on the gold-leafed proscenium, which bears the name Beethoven on the top. Though eight other cartouches spread out from Beethoven's name, they are conspicuously blank. Beethoven—acknowledged as the father of orchestral music—was apparently an uncontroversial choice for commemoration; since agreement could not be reached on whom else to include, the remaining frames were left empty.

Several other fascinating features are scattered about the large hall:

- The four small chandeliers in the Hall have 71 bulbs each, and the fifth one in the middle has 110. Any of the twenty-five-watt bulbs that burn out are replaced when the chandeliers are lowered from the ceiling hydraulically, which happens twice a year.
- A clock was added at center stage in 1942, though it's often concealed by a small set of doors. The clock's raison d'être is that since 1942 the BSO has been unionized, which means that every minute counts.
- If you see a piano on the stage floor, it's likely to be a Steinway (visiting artists, however, are always permitted to rent or bring another brand if they don't want to use the "house piano").
- The sixteen statues of mythical and real-life heroes in the balcony nooks may look like marble, but they're really plaster with a marbleized finish. The scantily clad figures created a scandal in the eyes of certain proper Bostonian ladies when the Hall first opened. (Wealthy art patron Isabella Stewart Gardner was one of the few Symphonygoers who understood the uses of nudity in art and approved of the statuary.) Though plaster casts seem an odd choice today, in the nineteenth and early twentieth centuries they were all the rage. These sixteen were executed by Pietro Caproni, a talented Italian immigrant who set up shop in Roxbury and was considered a master at casting fine plaster copies from Old World originals.
- Patrons in floor row Q are actually sitting on one of Symphony Hall's three elevators. That particular elevator is a hydraulic lift used to stow away all the seats as well as the slanting orchestra-level floor during the Christmas and the Pops seasons, when food and drink are served on café tables on the floor. Once the risers and 1,492 leather-covered seats are removed, the upwardly sloping back half of the Hall is taken away in sections, assuring that foodstuffs don't slip off the 288 tables hauled in for the festivities. (The tables themselves won't slip—they're

bolted to the floor.) The physical transformation takes about eight hours; the floor removal alone involves 160 trips on the elevator.

- From 1930 until 1942 the atmosphere during Pops concerts was downright frivolous; the stage was decorated to look like an outdoor garden, replete with green and gold decor and lovely latticework. The deadly Cocoanut Grove fire of 1942—a downtown Boston blaze that claimed 490 victims—put an end to that decor; Symphony Hall decided the festive greenery was a potential fire hazard.

- Symphony Hall has always had an organ. Even if patrons don't hear it, they certainly see it, since the back of Symphony's stage is dominated by a facade of the Hall's original forty-eight organ pipes (more than 4,500 other pipes lurk behind that facade, added in 1949). Symphony Hall's original American Classic–style organ, installed in 1900, was the work of George Hutchings. In 1949, parts of the Hutchings instrument were incorporated into the fine new instrument built for the Hall by the Aeolian-Skinner Organ Company, America's leading organ builder of the mid-twentieth century. It was inspected during construction by a variety of experts including the Nobel Prize–winning physician, organist, and Bach authority, Albert Schweitzer. When the new organ made its Symphony Hall debut on November 14, 1950, the concert was a benefit for the Albert Schweitzer Hospital, located in what was then called French Equatorial Africa. 1950 was a perfect "birth" year for the instrument, since it marked the fiftieth year of Symphony Hall and the two hundredth anniversary of the death of J. S. Bach, considered the greatest of all composers for organ. At the time of the new organ's installation, Symphony Hall's organist was the world-famous E. Power Biggs. (In January 2003, a $3 million renovation by Foley-Baker, Inc., of Connecticut was begun on the famed but worn organ. Among that firm's recent projects have been the renovation of Aeolian-Skinner organs in Boston's Trinity Church and The First Church of Christ, Scientist.)

For fans of all kinds of music, Symphony Hall has proven to be a stellar listening room for more than a century. Internationally known BSO conductors, like the late Serge Koussevitsky, Seiji Ozawa, and the current music director designate James Levine, have led the full orchestra through scores of classical treasures; stars like the late Arthur Fiedler, composer John Williams (of Hollywood film–score fame), and now, Keith Lockhart have conducted the Boston Pops in its lighter musical fare, featuring guest vocalists from the worlds of pop, rock, Broadway, and jazz. (Thanks to John Williams, film impresario Steven Spielberg recorded soundtracks for both *Schindler's List* and *Saving Private Ryan* in Symphony Hall with the BSO.)

Meanwhile, successful hall rentals have ranged from the rocking folkabilly of Nanci Griffith to the a cappella gospel of Sweet Honey in the Rock, and from the topical folk tunes of Joan Baez to the sultry jazz of Cassandra Wilson. Barbershop quartets once sang there on Sunday afternoons. Automobile and powerboat shows were standard fare for many a year. Anna Pavlova danced there with the Ballet Russe. Even plays were performed there from time to time. (In 1971, Dame Judith Anderson appeared as

Symphony Hall,
home to the Boston
Symphony Orchestra
and the Boston Pops,
has been filled
with music since
October 15, 1900.

Hamlet on the Symphony Hall stage, and twenty years earlier, Agnes Moorhead, Charles Laughton, Cedric Hardwicke, and Charles Boyer read from Shaw's *Don Juan in Hell* on the same boards.) Finally, of course, come the "regulars"—like the Handl & Haydn Society, who have performed there since 1900, and the Celebrity Series (originating as the Aaron Richmond Concerts but now called the Fleet Celebrity Series), which has been produced at Symphony Hall since 1938.

One of the keys to the Hall's tremendous success with all kinds of acts and audiences is its unusually good sight lines. Unlike many venues with larger balcony overhangs, Symphony Hall has only six seats with views blocked by support columns (and those, according to the management, are only "slightly obstructed"). The total seating capacity is 2,625, reduced to 2,371 during Pops concerts.

A major Symphony Hall appeal, of course, is the acoustic excellence— the origins of which take us back again to the late 1890s. Acoustics was more a matter of luck than science before the turn of the century. Hence, when noted Harvard physics professor Wallace Clement Sabine reluctantly agreed to take on the challenge of making Symphony Hall the perfect spot for orchestral music, he became one of the first to apply scientific principles to an artistic problem. Charles McKim had planned to shape the Hall like a rounded Greek theater; Sabine replaced that design with a simple shoebox shape. The resulting box-within-a-box design—with hallways and offices all around the Hall—created an airspace sound buffer, keeping out noise from the busy surrounding streets.

Just how good are the acoustics? According to a 1981 article by Robert Campbell, acoustical scientist Leo Beranek set out to discover the finest concert hall in the world in the 1960s; he eventually considered fifty-four halls in sixteen countries. After polling numerous conductors, performers, and music critics—who rated the halls on an elaborate scale—Beranek concluded that Boston's Symphony Hall was number one.

It's not simply a matter of McKim's shoebox-in-a-box design, however. Multiple layers of brick, tile, steel, and plaster were used when Symphony Hall was built. Though these measures were intended to protect against fire—making Symphony Hall the first major structure in Boston built with fireproofing in mind—the layers also helped insulate the Hall from outside street noise. Inside the Hall, furnishings also continue to contribute to these near-perfect acoustics. There are no lush carpets, drapes, or billowy-cushioned seats to absorb the sound; oak floors, leather seat covers, and plaster walls provide a more neutral background. The stage is built with its floor, ceiling, and walls all sloped outward in the shape of a giant truncated "horn." And the baffled ceilings lack domes and arches that could turn sound around or jam it up in a corner. Moreover, there are just enough nooks and statues to avoid broad, flat, bounce-the-sound surfaces.

The acoustics, incidentally, are calibrated for a full house of patrons. So during rehearsals and auditions, when the sound might reverberate and echo unduly, a huge burlap curtain is hung from ceiling hooks directly above row F to stifle the excess vibrations. You can see those hooks up near the hanging mikes. Those microphones are used for recording, radio or television broadcasts, and for other performers who rent the Hall—never for orchestral performances. Insiders tell us, incidentally, that the sound is best when there are at least 1,000 in the audience.

Though the Hall is the heart of the Symphony Hall structure, interesting items exist all around the building. Plaques and tributes are found throughout the hallways, listing various benefactors over the past century. A hallway plaque on the Massachusetts Avenue side is a memorial to eight musicians "who were drowned, still playing, as the *Titanic* went down, April 15, 1912." None, it seems, was in any way connected to the BSO. Isabella Stewart Gardner just wanted it displayed there, and her clout made it happen.

The Cohen Wing, an adjacent building annexed in 1980–81, was once the home of a bowling alley and two ballrooms. The building, renovated in 1990, houses several Symphony offices, conference and function rooms, the switchboard, a handsome display of the prized ancient instrument collection, and the enlarged Symphony Shop. The multitude of ever-changing chambers in the original building still contains offices, greenrooms, locker rooms, workshops, libraries, conference rooms, storage areas, practice booths, and lounges.

Other relatively new additions to the building include a handicapped-accessible restroom and a patron lounge named in honor of Leo Beranek, a longtime Symphony supporter, former chairman of the board of trustees—and the man who "proved" Boston's Symphony Hall was acoustic perfection!

THE ESSENTIALS

Address: 301 Massachusetts Avenue, Boston, MA 02115. **Telephone:** Symphony Hall main number, (617) 266-1492; SymphonyCharge ticket sales, (617) 266-1200 or (888) 266-1200; recorded concert information, (617) 266-2378. **Websites:** www.bso.org and www.bostonsymphonyhall.org. **Visitor Information:** Administrative offices open Monday through Friday, 9:00 A.M. to 5:00 P.M. Building open other hours for concerts and events. Tours available by advance arrangement; call for information. Wheelchair ramp and accessible bathroom available at west entrance, in the Cohen Wing.

21 The Colonial Theatre

THE HANDSOME, intimate Colonial Theatre is not only one of the most popular stages in town but also the oldest continuously operating legitimate theater in Boston. As such, it has seen a sizable slice of stage history. Today, it hosts theater pieces that run from intimate dramas like *The Graduate, Driving Miss Daisy,* and *Children of a Lesser God* to elaborate musicals such as *Mamma Mia!, Les Miserables,* Disney's *Beauty and the Beast, Hairspray,* and *The Producers.*

On its opening night of December 20, 1900, however, the Colonial staged a very different kind of spectacle—a high-tech Biblical blockbuster.

"Nothing So Beautiful, Pictorially and Mechanically, Ever Seen Before on a Boston Stage," proclaimed a *Boston Globe* subheadline about the opening of *Ben Hur.* The hyperbolic comment may well have been true. In the heroic melodrama's most widely touted scene, the lush Colonial stage was bursting with period props and tunic-clad actors backed by an enormous panorama of the Roman Coliseum. Meanwhile, four hydraulic lifts elevated a dozen frisky horses from their basement "stable." Hitched to ornate Roman chariots, the steeds galloped across the stage for the show's climactic chariot race—prevented from plunging into the audience by an ingenious treadmill built into the stage boards.

While memories of that turn-of-the-century production have since faded away, the beloved Colonial has not.

That the Colonial Theatre has flourished for more than a century is due in part to the beauty of its classically inspired building. Historian Douglas Shand Tucci called it "as sumptuous and elegant as any of the productions its proscenium has disclosed." Part of its endurance is surely due to its charming intimacy, superior sight lines, and excellent acoustics—the latter thanks to Thomas A. Edison, whom the Colonial's management hired to improve the sound in the theater's early years.

"It is said that no work of construction in the city of Boston for a long time has aroused so much interest among builders and capitalists as that on the Colonial," read a *Boston Globe* analysis of February 14, 1900. The location was Boylston Street across from the historic Boston Common, originally the site of the Boston Public Library. (Once the library was moved to its present home in Copley Square, its old Boylston Street structure was leveled, allowing the Colonial to slowly emerge in its place.)

The sight must have been a fascinating one for curious Bostonians. Workmen could be seen below ground level, driving yards of hydraulic tubing into the earth—tubes that would later hook up to those four famous rear-stage elevators. Above ground, enormous mounds of dirt were eventually replaced by a ten-story building. Though relatively plain on the outside, it would soon be filled with fine, functional business offices and one gem of a theater.

Funds for the $1.5 million venture came from the estate of Frederick L. Ames, an industrial entrepreneur and enlightened philanthropist who had died in 1893. The architect was Clarence H. Blackall, whose design credits

Boston's Colonial Theatre was the stage where actors like Danny Kaye, Jane Fonda, and Barbara Streisand got their first breaks and first major critical recognition.

eventually included the Wilbur and Metropolitan (today's Wang) theaters, the Kenmore and Braemore hotels, the Little Building, and Tremont Temple Baptist Church. Credited as the first architect to make a building entirely framed in steel, Blackall also founded the Boston Architect's Collaborative.

Though the Ames family chose to call their theater the Colonial, the lavish interior work executed by Blackall and his colleagues was hardly colonial in style. Instead, classical motifs filled room after room, inspiring one Boston critic to gush in 1900, "It glitters like a Venetian jewel box . . . with examples of the art of Pompeii, Florence, Rome and Italy employed!"

Visitors to the theater entered through the seventy-foot-long box office vestibule lined with Italian marble walls and frescoes; the floor was a magnificent crescent-design mosaic of 40,000 tiles. While reviewers likened this spacious, simple entrance hall to Pompeii, the adjoining foyer was compared to a lavishly ornate Louvre gallery. The luxurious ladies' lounge, in turn, was "suggestive of the throne room of the Fontainebleau Palace near Paris."

If the allusions were exotic, so too was Blackall's Colonial. The theater has actually changed very little in its more than one hundred years, thanks in part to an ambitious $750,000 restoration in 1960 and a lavish $2 million "face-lift" from 1992 to 1995. (The latter—spearheaded and largely funded by Colonial CEO Jon B. Platt—included rebuilding the stage, refurbishing the fly loft, repainting the ceiling, expanding restroom space and wheelchair access, and regilding portions of the auditorium using some 50,000 sheets of gold leaf.) As a result of all this painstaking work, the Colonial's "Louvre-style" foyer still features giant plate mirrors, ceiling paintings, cupids, bucolic landscapes, bronze staircases, gilt ornamentation, and intricately carved wood designs, the latter by John Evans and Company. Such visual ebullience—with its fruits, cupids, palms and lutes—continues in the fan-shaped auditorium. There, two wraparound balconies, three chandeliers, imposing columns, pearl-necklace lights, and a grandiose dome frieze threaten to distract the viewer from the stage. Painter Herman Schladermundt created the ceiling's allegorical male figures representing Tradition, Truth, and Inspiration, as well as the female figures in the adjoining circles—Epic Poetry, History, Tragedy, and Comic/Pastoral Verse.

Even the expansive backstage areas at the Colonial are a story wonderland. More than three dozen dressing and chorus rooms are spread out over long hallways and endless flights of stairs. The tiny, cluttered prop room is a veritable museum of theatrical glossies, autographs, buttons, posters, graffiti, and other memorabilia. The hovering fly floor—the loft far above the stage from which scenery is lowered and raised—is strung with so many lines of heavy hemp that it looks like a reunion of clipper ships. The stage basement has been so sawed, reshuffled, and rebuilt to accommodate the trapdoors and distinctive underbelly mechanics needed for different productions that it resembles an oversize shanty from Tobacco Road.

"Blackall had a great intellectual capacity," explained writer and historian Bettina A. Norton. "He was attuned to the business community and aware of multipurpose uses of buildings. He thought of the theater audience—of layout, sight lines, comfort and circulation patterns—along with using fine materials. Blackall was also an excellent architectural journalist. In fact, he probably wrote many of the newspaper reviews that ran on the Colonial when it opened!"

If the architectural splendor of the Colonial Theatre set it apart from other Boston theaters before and since, so did its use. Some theaters were built to accommodate other kinds of entertainment—vaudeville, motion pictures, opera, or exhibitions—as well as plays. But, though the ten-story Colonial Building did contain rooms for business offices, the sumptuous space at its core was constructed for "legitimate theater," pure and simple; moreover, its layout and seating capacity of close to 1,700 made it ideal for both musical and dramatic productions.

Legendary Boston drama critic Elliot Norton fondly remembered his earliest visits to the Colonial from 1910 through the early 1920s. "While I was still in school I saw some of the musicals. Then, of course, came Ziegfeld's revues. Revues had no plot—just songs, dances, and sketches, all held together by the music and the same performers. They were enormously ornate, elaborate, and beautiful. His shows cost $100,000, maybe $150,000, and they advertised they had the most beautiful girls in the world. There were 'ponies'—small girls who danced. And 'showgirls'—tall ones who just paraded. I remember the highest paid showgirl was named Gladys Glad."

The Ziegfeld revues the young Norton and his peers saw at the Colonial featured many legendary talents in the history of music and comedy. Fred and Adele Astaire, W. C. Fields, Fanny Brice, Will Rogers, Bob Hope, Eddie Cantor, and Ed Wynn all performed there, as Flo Ziegfeld sculpted his annual *Follies* into final form before taking each show and its performers to New York.

From the 1920s through the 1970s, in fact, Boston—like Philadelphia and New Haven—was well known as a "tryout town," where producers and directors polished and perfected Broadway-bound plays, using the Hub's sophisticated audiences as a barometer of their successes. The Colonial hosted an ample share of these previews. *Porgy and Bess,* for example, celebrated its world premiere at the Colonial in 1935. "The original production was sung from end to end," recalled Elliot Norton. "It was an opera. All the drama critics loved it, and all the music critics hated it. Later on, it became a success when they introduced spoken dialogue instead of sung dialogue. It has since been restaged as a fully sung opera."

Richard Rodgers and Oscar Hammerstein opened a musical called *Away We Go!* at the Colonial in 1943. In Boston, Rodgers and Hammerstein revised the show and successfully revitalized its slow-starting second act. The production later became a hit under the name of the song that opened Act II—*Oklahoma!* Another Rodgers and Hammerstein favorite, *Carousel,* began in Boston's Colonial as well.

The enormous oval onyx table located in the Colonial's sumptuous ladies lounge was often used for such revisions, incidentally. When the great German director Max Reinhardt directed Thornton Wilder's *The Merchant of Yonkers* at the Colonial in 1938, for example, Wilder did an immediate rewrite in the lounge. (Wilder's Boston rewrite failed, and the play was turned into a comedy called *The Matchmaker;* under a new director, it starred Ruth Gordon and again opened at the Colonial. Unfortunately, only the third and final version of the play will be remembered—the musical comedy *Hello, Dolly!*) In the book *Boston's Colonial Theatre: Celebrating a Century of Theatrical Vision,* author Tobie S. Stein recalls another famous incident on the ladies' lounge table: During the Blizzard of 1978, choreographer Bob Fosse wanted to demonstrate a new tap routine for the opening of *Dancin'.* Since the stage was being used at the time, he hopped onto the table to show his fancy footwork, accidentally chipping the green top in the process (and thereby leaving an "autograph"). Stein also notes that Katharine Hepburn liked the table so much, "she threatened to steal it."

The famed table, incidentally, was actually gone from the Colonial for many years. It disappeared when the theater changed owners in 1981; the departing Jujamcyn Corporation apparently walked off with the piece of furniture, along with much of the Colonial's archival material. Having great nostalgia for the historic piece, Jon B. Platt negotiated its return from Jujamcyn in 1995 during the pre-Broadway tryout of Carol Burnett in *Moon over Buffalo.*

Some well-known actors and actresses—including Danny Kaye, Jane Fonda, and Barbra Streisand—got their first real breaks and their first major critical recognition at the Colonial. An impressive number of internationally renowned stage and film stars have performed there as well, including Ethel Barrymore, Ethel Merman, Henry Fonda, Paul Robeson, Helen Hayes, Ethel Waters, James Earl Jones, Julie Harris, Katharine Hepburn, Kathleen Turner, Quentin Tarantino, Lauren Bacall, Kelsey Grammer, Richard Chamberlin, and Marisa Tomei. Still, fame never guaranteed artistic or commercial success, or even an easy run. When English star Nicol Williamson opened in Hamlet at the Colonial in 1969, for example, he threw a fit and walked offstage, disgusted by what he considered to be the mediocrity of his own performance.

Williamson's was but a minor eruption compared to the day when Edward Albee's *Who's Afraid of Virginia Woolf?* came to town in 1963. Albee was ordered to cut some allegedly obscene words from his original script. When the playwright complied, drama critic Kevin Kelly chided him in the *Boston Globe.* After Albee replied with an explanation of his actions, an illegal censorship pact between certain city officials (the so-called city censors) and local theater management was exposed, and the American Civil Liberties Union took action. It was the beginning of the end of stage censorship in the city, which had made "banned in Boston" an international joke.

The Colonial's long life has seen several major owners, under whom a multitude of management teams and lessees have operated with surprising continuity. The Ames family of New York, who built the theater, maintained it from 1900 until the Great Depression. The Depression—plus the success of early films, radio, and other factors—drastically reduced the number of legitimate theaters in America, from an estimated four thousand in 1900 to some four hundred in 1932. The Colonial was saved from possible demolition when purchased by the Shubert Organization in 1934. (The Shuberts saved many such theaters across America during the Depression, buying out what others could no longer maintain.)

As a result, the Colonial became one of seven Boston stages owned by the New York–based entertainment empire from 1934 through 1956. Antitrust legislation forced the Shuberts to break up their Boston theater monopoly, however, and the Jujamcyn Corporation purchased the building and maintained it from 1957 to 1981. (Under Jujamcyn, extensive renovations were made while Boston waned as regular tryout town.) From 1981 to 1999, the theater was owned by realtor Martin S. Berman and Sons. In 1990, Jon B. Platt, owner of American Artists, acquired the lease and made another round of major renovations. By August 1998, SFX Entertainment had purchased Platt's company, taking ownership of the Charles Playhouse and the leases of the Colonial and Wilbur theaters. Platt served as president, then chairman of SFX Theatricals Boston. On March 1, 2000, the *New York Times* reported that Clear Channel Communications would acquire SFX Entertainment. The Colonial Theatre is currently leased to the Boylston Street Theatre Corporation, a Clear Channel Entertainment company. (Since early 2000 the Colonial Building and its theater have been owned by Bryce Tinmouth.)

The mid- and late 1980s were not the best of times for Boston theater in general. For one thing, pre-Broadway tryouts had clearly shifted to other American cities, including New York itself. Still, while the theater district suffered some ominous dark periods, that decade and the one that followed had their bright points. The 1980 production of the musical *Annie*, for example, became the Colonial's longest running show ever—only to be outdone by the twenty-two-week run of *Joseph and the Amazing Technicolor Dreamcoat* in 1996. The Colonial also hosted the premiere of two award-winning musicals: *La Cage Aux Folles* in 1983 and Tommy Tune's *Grand Hotel* in 1989. In 1988, *Cabaret* became the production with the highest weekly gross in Colonial history. That record was subsequently broken by *Man of La Mancha* in 1992, then by *Fosse* in 2000 and by *Mamma Mia!* in 2001. In 2003, *The Producers* smashed all those previous records!

If you are planning to attend a performance at the Colonial, be prepared to pay significantly more than turn-of-the-twentieth-century Bostonians did for tickets. During opening week in 1900, the Colonial's best orchestra seats sold for $2.00. By 1925, these seats averaged $3.30. Top tickets for the 1992–93 productions of *Evita*, *The Secret Garden*, and *Guys and Dolls* went for $55.00. By 2003, the best seats for *Hairspray* and for *The Producers* (which won more Tony Awards than any show in history) were selling for $97.00. Unsold seats on the day of performance, however, are often available for half price at the Bostix booths in Quincy Market and Copley Square—as are tickets for most Boston shows.

One final note of trivia on that two-dollars-a-seat debut show of 1900: When *Ben-Hur* opened at the Colonial, its stars included William Farnum and William S. Hart, both of whom went on to later fame as cowboys in the silent movies. Farnum's brother Dustin costarred as well, and one of his avid fans later named her infant son after him. Yes, it was Dustin Hoffman's mom.

THE ESSENTIALS

Addresses: 106 Boylston Street, Boston, MA 02116. Broadway in Boston/Clear Channel Entertainment, 100 Boylston Street, Suite 950, Boston, MA 02116. **Telephone:** (617) 426-9366. **Website:** www.broadwayinboston.com/html/theatres/colonial. **Visitor Information:** General box office hours, Monday through Saturday 10:00 A.M. to 6:00 P.M.; closed Sunday. When there is a production at the theater, box office hours are Monday, 10:00 A.M. to 6:00 P.M., Tuesday through Saturday, 10:00 A.M. to a half hour past evening curtain; Sunday, 12:00 noon to a half hour past evening curtain. No tours. Main Boylston Street entrance is flat and wheelchair accessible, as is ladies' lounge; unisex wheelchair-accessible restroom; reduced ticket prices available on wheelchair spaces in orchestra; call in advance to arrange specifics.

22 The Shubert Theater

ASK BOSTON theatergoers about the character of downtown stages and they're bound to respond with a variety of strong opinions. Some will rave that the Wang is the biggest, the Charles is the funkiest, or the Colonial is the coziest in town. Others reminisce that the finest theater ever conceived and constructed in the city was the old Opera House (sadly, it was razed in 1957 to make way for Northeastern University dormitories).

Still, close to the hearts of many Bostonians—and located in the heart of Boston's theater district on Tremont Street—is a living monument to the history of the twentieth-century American stage. The grand old Shubert Theater, built in 1910, was once one of seven Boston theaters owned or operated by New York–based Shubert brothers, one of the most powerful theater families in U.S. history. Over the years—and especially during the decades when Boston served as a major pre-Broadway tryout town—the Shubert hosted a variety of theater greats, from Richard Burton, Maurice Evans, and Sir John Gielgud to Angela Lansbury, Gertrude Lawrence, and Julie Andrews. Today, due to antitrust legislation of the 1950s, the active Shubert is the only Boston theater the Shubert organization still owns. But it's a gem of a remnant, thanks largely to a $1.4 million refurbishing in 1980 and a mammoth $6 million renovation in 1996, which returned the old structure to the gleam of its heyday while adding twenty-first-century conveniences.

Since 1996, the Shubert has been managed and operated by the non-profit Wang Center for the Performing Arts, which signed a forty-year lease on the theater with the Shubert organization. As a result, the Shubert has become a perfect complement to the Wang, conveniently located directly across the street: while the Wang is booked with larger Broadway-style touring companies, the Shubert now specializes in smaller-scale productions from Boston's not-for-profit arts organizations, such as Boston Lyric Opera, World Music, and the FleetBoston Celebrity Series dance events.

"If the Wang Theater is the grand dame of Boston theaters," explains Wang president and CEO Josiah Spaulding, Jr., "then the Shubert is the little princess."

Back on opening night on January 24, 1910, some critics raved more about the city's newest playhouse than about the notable production of Shakespeare's *The Taming of the Shrew*. "NEW PLAYHOUSE CHARMS THRONGS: Shubert Theatre Opening Made Brilliant Event" read the *Boston Globe* headlines. In smaller print was a postscript about the performance: "Sothern and Marlowe Seen in 'Taming of the Shrew.'" The *Globe* critic acknowledged his—and the crowd's—overriding interest in the new building, designed by architect Thomas M. James. He was even willing to ignore that the plush backs to the chairs had not yet arrived, since the glorious Shubert had wide, comfortable seats, great sight lines, an unusually wide and deep orchestra pit, a beautiful, picturesque lobby, an ornate marble entranceway, a speedy coat-check system, a spacious foyer, near-perfect acoustics, and a chandelier copied from those at the Petit Trianon at Versailles.

Contemporary theatergoers, accustomed to more spacious foyers, pits, and lobbies, might not agree with that generous assessment. Nevertheless, the charm of such old theaters remains, according to Elliot Norton, the dean of Boston theater critics. "They were created for audiences of a previous time," he explained in a 1993 interview. "But they have a warmth and an elegance that makes them something special. When you go in you feel this is going to be a special event. You're going to be lifted out of the street world and into an exotic world. Another kind of world. A place in which you live in another way." (Norton died in 2003 at the age of one hundred; an icon of the twentieth century, he had reviewed some 6,000 performances over a forty-eight-year career.)

Catherine and David Shubert must have noticed the entrepreneurial genius of their sons Lee, Sam, and Jacob J. (J.J.) quite early in the game. As kids, the Shubert boys sold papers in the streets. As young adults, they began working in—and eventually operated—theaters in their hometown of Syracuse, New York. Though the family had begun in poverty—one sister reportedly died of malnutrition—the three sons went on to become America's leading theatrical producers and managers, powerful businessmen who eventually leased or owned theaters in almost every major city in the United States and held a virtual monopoly on the world of the legitimate theater.

Lee, born in 1871, was the eldest. Next year came Sam, "boyish in appearance and short in stature," who was known among colleagues as "Peanut." J.J., who later became a major presence in the Shubert's Boston holdings, arrived in 1880. By 1900, the brothers had hit Manhattan, buying, selling, and producing their way to the top. They effectively battled the all-powerful entertainment syndicate of Klaw and Erlanger. They brilliantly booked the finest talent available in the world—paying Sarah Bern-

Boston's Shubert Theater was built and owned by the New York–based Shuberts, one of the most powerful theater families in U.S. history.

hardt in gold, for example, to make her first American appearances. In their heyday in 1927, the Brothers Shubert owned or operated 110 theaters across the United States and booked productions into 1,000 others. Until 1956, they controlled all seven of Boston's legitimate theaters.

What part brother Sam could have played in building the Shubert Theater empire is mere conjecture now. Sam was the first to arrive in New York City, pulling Lee behind him. Only after Sam's death in 1905 did J.J. join Lee in the Manhattan business. Sam was twenty-nine when he was killed in a fiery Pennsylvania train crash. Newspapers across the nation reported the train's explosion, Sam's rescue through the flaming window, and his death a day and a half later.

Though we know that Sam was considered a shrewd businessman, many photos and accounts of him also portray "Peanut" as a sensitive artist, a devoted brother, and a passionate theatrical impresario. When Lee and J.J. built their Boston Theater in 1910—completing construction in less than five months—it was named the "The Sam S. Shubert Theater" in their brother's memory. Sam's picture was hung in the foyer (it still hangs in the theater, though it's no longer in a public space). In fact, Lee and J.J. sent framed photos of Sam to all their theaters—and charged the theaters ten dollars for each. Throughout their lives, Lee and J.J. ran the growing Shubert empire together with utmost skill, all the while maintaining a fierce sibling rivalry. After Sam's death, they rarely saw each other, communicating primarily through messengers.

Except for the Shubert's facade, which underwent a few alterations because of the widening of Tremont Street in 1926, much of the theater still looks like it did when it opened in 1910. There have, of course, been a few changes, mostly related to modern convenience and monetary considerations. Restrooms, bars, and coatrooms have been reshuffled and former doorways have been blocked off. The old standing-room space at the back of the orchestra section is gone, replaced by spaces for patrons using wheelchairs as well as conventional seats. The addition of three more rows in the *front* of the orchestra in 1980 led to the reduction of the orchestra pit—though that pit was expanded in the 1996 renovation, alongside a brand-new stage. The antiquated Shubert cooling system—a fan blowing over a bin of block ice—is long gone, replaced by updated electrical, mechanical, and heating and cooling systems.

Backstage, the sets are often bigger than in the old days. The set-up time is much longer than when house carpenters used to build the sets. Longtime house workers explain that the Shubert's backstage quarters are too cramped for some of the bigger modern musicals. Among the various chambers, halls, offices, and storage areas in that backstage area are fourteen small dressing rooms, plus a large wardrobe center.

Acoustics and amplification are also far different than the early days of legitimate theater—at the Shubert as well as most other large stages. For centuries, actors depended on good lungs, vocal training, and fine acoustical design to ensure that their words reached their audience. In recent years, however, microphones have been added for what theatrical oldtimers refer to as "acoustic crutches." Today, mike transmitters are generally fastened under clothing and on the actors' backs, while tiny microphones are frequently lodged in their hair, right above the forehead; in some productions, like *Rent*, the actors have sported visible Madonna-style mikes.

It's surely no surprise that an even more drastic change has come in the price of theater tickets. In 1925 a seat at the Shubert cost $3.30. Local motion picture "palaces" at the time charged seventy cents for admission; you could stay there all day, catching three or four films for the price of one. Both theater and film prices had increased more than 800 percent by 1993, when a balcony ticket for a popular musical like *A Chorus Line* at the Shubert cost $30.00. By 2003, top prices at the Shubert ranged from $25.00 to over $100.00, depending on the production.

As the twentieth century progressed, theater became a big business in America, the Shuberts became a big name in theater, and New York City became the production center of note. Since Manhattan's opening night critics and crowds were known to be ruthless, producers often sought educated tryout towns to smooth out their productions before opening on Broadway. For decades—until tryouts became too costly to mount and other cities promised better deals—Boston was a major pre-Broadway stop. According to Elliot Norton, a typical pattern for a new play might have been three days in New Haven, two weeks in Boston, then off to Manhattan. During the trial period, actors could be switched, lines or whole plays rewritten, and songs composed or deleted.

Among the major stars and productions Norton remembered passing through the Boston Shubert were Mary Martin and Ezio Pinza in Rodgers and Hammerstein's *South Pacific* ("Everybody loved the show," Norton explained, noting that many Bostonians hated one song that had an antiracist theme—"We were pretty racist here at that time."); Richard Burton and Julie Andrews in *Camelot* ("She was charming and he was very exciting."); Burton's first appearance in America, in a small role in *The Lady's Not for Burning* (1950); John Gielgud's first and grandest Boston performance in *Hamlet* (1936); Laurence Olivier in *The Entertainer* (1958); Maurice Evans's first U.S. performances as Romeo to Katharine Cornell's Juliet (1935); and Burton's controversial 1964 *Hamlet,* directed by Gielgud and performed in rehearsal clothes. ("[Burton] admitted he used to play forty different characters in the course of one production . . . and people still weren't paying any attention to him; at any rate, many of them weren't—Liz Taylor was in the audience!").

Among the audience favorites at the Shubert—from a box office perspective—were the 1925 production of *Rose Marie,* which ran for twenty-nine weeks, and *Evita* and *Cats,* which each had twenty-one-week runs in the early 1980s. When the Shubert reopened under Wang management in 1996, its first production was Jonathan Larsen's Tony Award– and Pulitzer Prize–winning *Rent,* which premiered its first national tour in Boston; the musical ran for twenty-nine weeks.

Needless to say, Boston audiences didn't enjoy every New York tryout. When Angela Lansbury opened at the Shubert with *Mame* in 1966, and when *Dreamgirls* premiered there in 1981, it's reported that producers could not even give tickets away before opening night. So much for audience prescience!

Incidentally, though Boston audiences were often willing to watch the kinks worked out in shows, the so-called Boston city censors posed a unique problem for many theatrical productions from 1907 through the mid-1960s. They censored "risqué" lines, lyrics, outfits, and scenes in a dubious practice that brought the phrase "banned in Boston" worldwide notoriety.

One of Elliot Norton's favorite anecdotes about pre-Broadway tryouts at the Shubert involved that "enormously exciting, brilliant" play of 1951 called *The King and I.* During the brief Boston run, apparently, Rodgers and Hammerstein decided they needed three more songs to round out the show, including one that would fit Gertrude Lawrence's limited vocal range. Hammerstein found a discarded love song originally penned for *South Pacific* and wrote new lyrics to suit the tale of Anna and the King of Siam. The song, "Getting to Know You," wasn't sung for opening night in Boston, but it was well integrated into *The King and I* by the time it left the Shubert. It became Lawrence's signature tune.

Critic Norton estimated that American legitimate theater was at its finest from roughly 1930 to as late as 1975. During those decades, however, a variety of phenomena chipped slowly away at theater audiences. Increasing theater ticket prices, as well as "talkies," radio, television, VCRs, and rock concerts took their toll, as did the decline of good plays, good theater writers, the value of a dollar, and U.S. education.

The Shubert monopoly also eroded during these years, most dramatically after 1956 antitrust legislation. In Boston, the Shuberts held on to Sam's namesake, letting their other six houses go. The Copley, Plymouth, and Majestic theaters became movie houses; the Boston Opera House was sold to Northeastern and demolished; and the Wilbur and Colonial theaters yielded to other ownership or management.

Lee Shubert died in 1953, and J.J. in 1963. J.J.'s son John was intended to run the organization, but he suffered a fatal heart attack on a train a year before his father passed on. Today, Phillip J. Smith and Gerald Schoenfeld are the president and chairman, respectively, of the Shubert Organization and the Shubert Foundation. Shubert owns or operates seventeen theaters in New York and three others across the country.

Some longtime Shubert employees openly admitted that they respected their new bosses more than they did the old. (J.J. Shubert in particular seems to have been unpopular, while "down-to-earth" Lee was clearly their favorite; since 1996 the point has been moot, since the theater has been run by the Wang organization.) During the decades when they ran their own kingdom, of course, the Shuberts were bound to be hated for their power, fortune, and monopoly over American theaters. They were also feared because they were known to try to censor critics who wrote unfavorable reviews of their productions. Elliot Norton remembered discovering that he was on the Shubert's "hit list" as early as a year after he started reviewing, in 1934. The Schubert's tactics for taming Norton were direct: they tried to have him fired by his editors, with no success; they also banned him from their theaters—but the critic just went out and bought his own tickets.

On the positive side, the Shuberts helped break up the early Klaw and Erlanger theater monopoly. Equally important, critics agree, was that the Shuberts single-handedly helped pull American theater through the rough Depression years by purchasing and producing in many theaters that might otherwise have been demolished. Without their work, American legitimate theater—and theater houses—might have disappeared in the 1930s, and Boston would be much the poorer today.

THE ESSENTIALS

Address: 265 Tremont Street, Boston, MA 02116. Located in the heart of Boston's theater district. **Telephone:** (617) 482-9393. **Website:** www.wangcenter.org. **Visitor Information:** Box office hours, Monday through Saturday, 10:00 A.M. to 6:00 P.M. Tickets also available by phone at (800) 447-7400 or online. Main Tremont Street entrance, orchestra seats, and restrooms are wheelchair accessible; there is no elevator to upper levels.

23 Fenway Park

ONE OF the most apt descriptions of Boston's favorite ball field is also the most succinct. "Fenway Park is a lyric little bandbox of a ballpark," noted novelist John Updike. "Everything is painted green and seems in curiously sharp focus, like the inside of an old-fashioned peeping-type Easter egg."

Calling the park small and somewhat antiquated is an endearment, of course, not an insult. First opened in 1912—and now the oldest major league ballpark in the United States—Fenway is both a remnant and a reminder of golden baseball days gone by. In the early years of the twentieth century, it was among the nation's largest ballparks. Today, it's the smallest—and the last single-deck stadium in the major leagues.

Unlike most other fields, Fenway Park was never razed or replaced—though the threat of demolition did seem real for a spell at the turn of the twenty-first century. Instead, Boston's beloved ballpark has worked to balance old and new—growing and changing with the times while keeping most of its cozy, intimate charms intact. To this day, those distinctive charms include live organ music, a hand-operated scoreboard, honest-to-goodness live bluegrass, and a looming left-field wall known to generations of fans as the Green Monster.

It may not be the original "Field of Dreams," but Fenway's flock of avid fans thinks it's about as close as you can get.

Since its birth in 1912, Fenway Park has played home to more than the landlord Red Sox. Boston's other major league baseball team, the National League's Boston Braves, used Fenway Park in the 1914 World Series, when their own Braves Field was under construction. (The Braves abandoned the city for Milwaukee after 1952 and eventually landed in Atlanta.)

Throughout its history, the park has also been used on occasion for such diverse fare as revival meetings, concerts (including the 1973 Newport Jazz Festival and the 2003 Bruce Springsteen performances), memorial services (for the World War I armistice and for slugger Ted Williams), basketball exhibitions (the Boston Celtics and the Harlem Globetrotters), soccer games (the Boston Beacons) and football games. Three pro football teams, in fact, called Fenway home for several years at a stretch: the Boston Redskins, now in Washington, D.C.; the Boston Yanks, now the Indianapolis Colts; and the Boston Patriots, now the New England Patriots of Foxborough, Massachusetts. The park is still used for amateur baseball games, and it hosts the extremely successful new "Fenway Magic" events, which include opening the ballpark and field to fans on Father's Day and Halloween.

But the reason Fenway Park was built—and the reason it stands today—was to accommodate Boston's long-standing love affair with the Red Sox. The Sox were founded in 1901 and were quickly recognized as an important franchise in the newly formed American League. Originally known as the Americans, they ran through a variety of nicknames—including the Pilgrims, the Puritans, and even the Plymouth Rocks—before deciding on Red Sox in 1907. (The name was descriptive of the outfits the team wore at home games starting in 1908—white uniforms with fire-engine red stockings.) The Red Sox's first field was the old Huntington Avenue Grounds, now part of Northeastern University. That old-fashioned, multipurpose space had a capacity of 10,000 to 14,000; the larger numbers came when fans stood on the field during the game, a popular practice in the early days of baseball.

Fenway Park itself was the project of John I. Taylor (1875–1938), an early Red Sox owner and son of *Boston Globe* publisher General Charles H. Taylor. John Taylor was also involved in the Fenway Realty Company, a group developing the reclaimed marshland area known as the Fenway.

The plot Taylor purchased for the team's new home was a strangely skewed piece of land in that once-marshy Fenway area, tightly lodged between existing streets and conveniently located near the Boston trolley line. The park Taylor built there struck a balance between old-fashioned wooden ballparks and their more modern concrete-and-steel counterparts. Though today's visitors are impressed by the park's politely indus-

First opened in 1912, Fenway Park is the oldest major-league ballpark in the United States.

trial red-brick exterior, the decorative mosaics and diamond designs on the outer walls, and the tons of concrete that underpin the rambling interior, fans in 1912 were most astonished by another innovation—eighteen whizzing turnstiles that made entry and egress a simple operation.

No one knows for sure whether the park's legendary asymmetrical interior angles were dictated by the adjacent streets or the shape of the lot or were simply the way the field was placed. The result, in any case, was a field bordered by seventeen facets and barriers—and governed by numerous regulations as to how many bases a hitter takes when his ball ricochets off this or that wall, pole, screen, scoreboard, or bevel.

Two Fenway quirks in particular have become part of Red Sox lore. Before 1934, a ten-foot hill along the left-field wall served as a viewing spot for fans and a warning to players that the back wall was imminent. The fans were rarely in danger of being hit by a ball, incidentally: until 1920, homers of any sort—over the left-field wall or anywhere else—were relatively rare, since the old rag "dead ball" was still in use. The hill's greatest historic moments came with the career of outfielder Duffy Lewis, who played for the Sox from 1910 to 1917. Lewis became famous for successfully scampering up and down the left-field embankment to make spectacular catches; the incline was named Duffy's Cliff in his honor. Since that cliff proved an exasperating stumbling block to scores of unknowing outfielders, however, it was removed during park renovations of 1934. Today, a gravel track provides players the warning that The Wall is near.

During that same modernization of 1934, the park's original wooden left-field wall was replaced by a significantly larger, thirty-seven-foot-high concrete-and-tin barrier. The wall became popularly known as the Green Monster—and has proven to be the nemesis and obsession of sluggers ever since. Hit a high fly ball over the top, for example, and you've scored one of the shortest home runs in any major league ballpark. If you hit the wall instead, a line drive that might have been a homer anywhere else could end up a single or a double. (In 2003, 274 Green Monster seats were added atop that left-field wall, providing a unique view and an exciting experience for fans.)

John Taylor named his park Fenway—"It's in the Fenway, isn't it?" was his laconic explanation—and officially opened it on April 20, 1912. Though Fenway's debut and the Red Sox's eleven-inning, 7–6 victory over the New York Highlanders (Yankees) were major news, Boston's newspapers failed to give the story much space on the front page. Writers were too busy reporting the sinking of the *Titanic* that week.

After Taylor sold the park, also in 1912, the Red Sox and Fenway Park eventually fell into disarray. Among the park's many problems was owner Harry Frazee, who bought Fenway in 1917. The high-powered entertainment mogul has long been accused of siphoning off Fenway's profits to support his floundering entertainment business, including a new musical called *No, No, Nanette*. Among the worst of Frazee's follies was trading Babe Ruth to the New York Yankees in January 1920—for $100,000 and a $300,000 mortgage on Fenway Park. The Sox won the World Series in 1912, 1915, 1916, and 1918, but never again after Ruth's trade; legend says that "the curse of the Bambino" remains on Fenway Park to this day, apparently unbroken by exorcism rites offered by comedian "Father Guido Sarducci," a.k.a. Don Novello, in 1992.

Though this Frazee tale is one of the most popular anecdotes in Red Sox history, its accuracy has now come into question. Recent research by sports historians Glenn Stout and Richard Johnson—delineated in delightful detail in their book, *Red Sox Century*—suggests that Frazee was demonized for his sins perhaps more than is justified. Frazee, it seems, did not have a series of theatrical failures and was not badly strapped for cash at the time. His trade of Ruth in particular was partly a power play against American League president Ban Johnson and partly a reaction to Ruth's increasingly tiring shenanigans on and off the ball field. (In 1919 there was also a legitimate question as to how good—and how consistent—a player Ruth could ever become; the Bambino actually had trouble hitting in Fenway Park, which helps explain why only eleven of his eventual forty-nine home runs for the Red Sox were belted at home games.)

Whatever the reasons, Frazee's mistakes, player trades, and cavalier attitude won him a slew of enemies, especially among Boston fans. If that weren't destructive enough for Red Sox morale, a major fire illuminated and eliminated Fenway's wooden left-field bleachers in 1926. Then came the Great Depression.

Curiously, it was in the midst of that Depression, in 1933, when Fenway Park's fortunes took a turn for the better. Four days after his thirtieth birthday brought him an inheritance of $7 million or more, Thomas A. Yawkey, the "Savior of the Sox," bought the ball club and the park. By 1934, Yawkey had already begun rebuilding the team and renovating Fenway at a cost of 2 million Depression dollars.

Yawkey's physical improvements resulted in much the same park we see today. Concrete bleachers replaced the old wooden ones; the grandstand was enlarged and seating increased; the facade was sandblasted; Duffy's Cliff was leveled and the Green Monster built; a larger scoreboard with traffic light–style signals plus American and National League scores was featured; and the entire park was painted its distinctive shade of green.

Yawkey officially reopened his "new" Fenway Park on April 17, 1934. The park began serving beer for the first time in 1934 as well—a tradition that continues to this day, often in conjunction with that historic hot dog, the Fenway Frank. According to Dick Johnson, curator of the Sports Museum of New England, "Thomas Yawkey did for sports in this city what Henry Lee Higginson did for music." (Higginson was the founder and patron of the Boston Symphony Orchestra in 1881 and the man who financed the building of the orchestra's permanent home, Symphony Hall, in 1900.)

Though the much-respected and loved Yawkey died in 1976, his memory and name live on in Fenway. Among the memorials was the renaming of Jersey Street, where the park's facade is located; since 1977 it has been called Yawkey Way. His widow, Jean Yawkey, remained general partner and president of the Red Sox until her death in 1992 and was the first woman elected to the board of directors of Cooperstown's National Baseball Hall of Fame and Museum. Another tribute to the Yawkeys is covertly ensconced on the hand-operated scoreboard; descending between the R and the P on that board are the initials of Thomas and Jean Yawkey, written in Morse code.

The sixty-eight-year Yawkey era came to a final close, incidentally, when a new ownership group led by John W. Henry, Tom Werner, and the team president/CEO Larry Lucchino took control of the team prior to the 2002 season.

The peculiar logistics, size, and shape of Fenway Park have been blamed for altering the course of ballgames since Fenway history began. The short distance to the Green Monster—an "official" 310—can increase homers, for example. Before a 1975–76 renovation, The Wall also gave Red Sox outfielders a definite home-field advantage; old pros like Carl "Yaz" Yastrzemski had mastered the art of altering their catching stances depending on whether the ball ricocheted off the bouncy cement at the bottom or the deadening metal above. The park's angular corners and smaller-than-average foul areas—not to mention the glaring afternoon sun, whipping wind, and occasional pigeons colliding with balls—have also altered the course of plays and even games over the decades. As a result, baseball scores are apt to change mercurially in Fenway.

On the other hand, the players have sometimes changed the park as well. Charismatic Sox slugger Ted Williams, for instance, is credited with moving the bullpen from the right-field corner to the front of the right-field bleachers after his rookie 1939 season. Williams was a powerful left-handed batter, and the club wanted to make the most of his hits. The area where Williams could slam his homers free and clear after the bullpen move was dubbed Williamsburg—Boston's counterpart of Yankee Stadium's Ruthville. The last time Ted Williams visited Fenway Park, by the way, was the 1999 All-Star game. The eighty-year-old Williams (whose named graces the newest tunnel to Boston's Logan Airport) was driven to the mound in a golf cart and wildly lauded and applauded by fans and colleagues alike. "There was a baseball love-in on the mound," read the Associated Press review the following day, "the stars of the night and the stars of the century swamping Ted Williams, gazing at him in awe, reaching over each other to shake his hand."

Various renovations have changed the park since Williams's day. Large ads once posted across The Wall were painted over in 1947 to improve ball visibility, though various logos and ads have reappeared there since 1998. During the 1975–76 park renovations, The Wall was modernized and recreated in fiberglass. Fenway Park's longtime official charity, the Jimmy Fund of the Dana-Farber Cancer Institute, benefited from that particular wall change: green sheet metal from the old facade was clipped into snapshot-size rectangles, mounted on wood, and sold to fans in a fundraiser for cancer research. In 1976, safety padding was added to the outfield walls, plastic red and blue seats appeared in the stands, and the club's first huge electronic message board was installed above center field. That board was replaced by a color "videoboard" in 1987–88.

Skyview seating was added on either side of the press box in 1946. That press box was replaced in 1989 by the 600 Club, a plush, glass-enclosed section of 610 stadium seats; in 2002, the 600 Club was in turn replaced by the .406 Club, named in honor of Ted Williams's historic 1941 batting average. (A new broadcast booth and press box were installed on top of the club section.) With the advent of new Sox ownership in 2002, even more seating and dining options were added. Two rows of dugout seats were installed on either side of home plate, then extended past each dugout for 2003. Old standing-room slots were converted to new seats, a new back row of roof box seats was added above the first and third base lines in the form of stationary barstools, and Fenway's first front-row handicapped seats made their debut. A new dining area was added behind center field, and on game afternoons, Red Sox management began to essentially annex Yawkey Way as an outdoor ballpark concourse. By putting turnstiles, concessions, picnic tables, and varied amusements on Yawkey Way, they literally took the festivities to the streets.

"The new owners of Fenway Park have done a good job at being stewards of tradition," explains sports historian Dick Johnson. "They are utilizing the park much more, and adding seats, glamour, and pizzazz. But they're managing to keep the old and maintaining the intimate confines, while adding new twists. The more Fenway has changed, the more it's stayed the same."

Well, in *most* ways, anyway.

One final change at Fenway has been the price of tickets. On opening day in 1912, bleacher seats cost twenty-five cents and "pavilion" seats half a dollar. In 1993, the price of bleacher seats was seven dollars, reserved grandstand seats ten dollars, and box seats ranged from fourteen to eighteen dollars. By 2003, the price range from bleacher to box was twenty to seventy dollars. But, as legions of longtime fans—from comic Frankie Fontaine and Mrs. Calvin Coolidge to former Speaker of the House Tip O'Neill and novelist Stephen King—would surely testify, it's a small price to pay for the Fenway Park experience.

THE ESSENTIALS

Address: 4 Yawkey Way, Kenmore Square, Boston, MA 02215. **Telephone:** Ticket office, (877) RED-SOX9; administrative offices, (617) 267-9440; tours, (617) 236-6666. **Websites:** www.redsox.com; www.sportsmuseum.org. **Visitor Information:** See Red Sox website for game times, dates, and ticket information. Tours are available year-round, Monday through Sunday, 9:00 A.M. to 4:00 P.M.; admission fee. Fenway Park has 109 wheelchair spaces, along with at least 109 companion seats; there are a total of 76 other handicap locations, which include seating for the vision impaired and ambulatory seating for those in need of easier access and larger seats.

24 Park Street Station

ITS ADMIRERS see it as a wondrous gem lodged in the center of Boston—
"the epitome of Beantown," "the hub of the Hub," and "the melting pot of
the whole system." Its detractors view it as just another downtown dungeon—a necessary byway for zipping from here to there.

Most people probably don't think about Park Street Station at all. They
just use it, take it for granted, count on its being there day after day and
decade after decade. On an average weekday, an astonishing 91,000 people enter, exit, or make trolley transfers at Park Street Station, using 5,265
cars on 2,579 trains.

What they're missing, however, is a sense of this subway stop's historic
significance. First opened in 1897, Park Street was one of the four original
stations in the Tremont Street Subway, the first subway in the United
States. Since 1964, both the station and its headhouses have been honored
with National Historic Landmark and National Historic Civil Engineering
Landmark status.

Park Street Station was also the nucleus of a system that grew from a
half-mile downtown strip to one serving 175 cities and towns in the
Greater Boston area. Though the system itself has changed and grown over
the last century—and has been known by a variety of names (the El, the
MTA, the MBTA, and the T)—Park Street Station has remained as one of
four junction points at its center. Park Street trolleys can transport riders
in, around, and far away from Boston's downtown in a matter of minutes.
On its top level are Green Line cars, which travel west to Boston College
and Brookline and north to East Cambridge. From the platform down
below run Red Line trains, which go north to Cambridge and Somerville
and south to Boston neighborhoods like Dorchester and Mattapan, and to
suburban Quincy and Braintree.

Given all those accomplishments, it's certainly no surprise that Park
Street Station and the surrounding system have been heralded in sonnet,
song, film, and legend. The nineteenth-century sage Oliver Wendell
Holmes was one of the first to wax poetic about the Hub's first subway, in
"The Broomstick Train." A. J. Deutsch penned an eerie science-fiction tale
about a Cambridge-bound train disappearing into thin air in a 1950 story
called "A Subway Named Mobius." The Kingston Trio had a smash hit in
1959 with "The MTA," a song about a man named Charlie who got trapped
on Boston's underground by the addition of a five-cent "exit fare." Both
Joanne Woodward and Robert Urich have performed in Park Street Station, during respective filmings of the movie *See How They Run*, and the
television series *Spenser for Hire*.

In 1972, then–Boston College professor Brian Cudahy wrote an entire
book, *Change at Park Street Under*, about the history of Boston's subway
system and its trains. In 1979, there was even a short-lived television com-

Park Street was one of the original underground stations of America's first subway system. Much of that history is alluded to in this mosaic mural by Lilli Ann Rosenberg.

edy series called *Park Street Under,* whose main claim to fame was inspiring yet another Boston-based sitcom, the long-running *Cheers.*

That a simple downtown subway stop should prove so uplifting is quite logical to George Sanborn, reference librarian of the State Transportation Library. "Whenever you think about Boston, sooner or later you get back to Park Street. Whenever you talk about Boston, Park Street eventually enters the conversation. There's no other place like it. Many of the other stations are—well—sterile, bland. But Park is fascinating. It has a distinctive ambiance. There's that mosaic mural by Lilli Ann Rosenberg, a pictorial representation of Boston through the ages, as it revolved around Park Street. And there are the people who use it every day—the mainstream of humanity.

"London has its Trafalgar Square; New York has Times Square. But you mention Boston, and you think of Park Street. And no matter what goes through Park Street, whatever changes are made at Park Street, it always remains Park Street."

In the early days, Boston had no need for an underground rapid-transit system. When legs wouldn't do, horses, cows, and tethered carts were enough to transport colonial people and their colonial possessions around the town's narrow, winding streets and alleys. Little by little, however, the scale of Boston life began to change. In 1800, only one in thirteen Americans lived in cities; by 1895, that number had increased to one in three. In Boston and other urban centers, congestion and overcrowding became serious problems, and improving public transportation a major issue.

As a result, Boston introduced its first horsecars in 1852. For two decades, these horse-drawn streetcars provided both reasonable transportation and a good source of revenue, through the sale of fares, inside advertising cards, and horse manure. In the 1870s, however, horsecars were dealt a double blow. A virulent equine influenza, the "Great Epizootic," spread throughout horsecar stables in the eastern states in 1872, disabling or destroying great numbers of animals. Moreover, inventors were beginning to experiment with alternative power sources for streetcars, including steam, compressed air, naphtha, mechanical legs, cables, and even giant clock springs.

It was not until 1888, when engineer Frank Sprague equipped the streetcars of Richmond, Virginia, with electric motors, that urban mass transit really arrived. One year later, Boston's West End Street Railway—one of the largest horsecar companies in America—went electric. The remaining horsecars were slowly phased out; the last one ran in Boston on Christmas Eve, 1900.

As the 1890s unfolded, Boston's new electric trolleys proved so successful that they created even greater problems. The city streets became crammed with tracks, wires, feeds, posts, crossings, and junctions that offended the eye and periodically immobilized the town. One observer noted that between five and six-thirty P.M., a man could walk down Tremont Street from Scollay Square (near today's Government Center Station) to Boylston Street on the roofs of streetcars without ever touching the ground. Tremont itself was four lanes wide—three of which were covered by trolley tracks. (Brooklyn, New York, had a similar trolley glut—so much that their baseball team was called the Brooklyn Trolley Dodgers, a name that was later shortened.)

Politicians and citizens alike argued about the most logical solution to the surfeit of electrified surface trolleys. The two strongest factions agreed that public transport must be taken off the streets: one group insisted on elevated tracks, while the other espoused the "European transit system" —subterranean trolley tunnels—which had already proven successful in Glasgow, Paris, London, and Budapest. After prolonged debate, the subway idea prevailed, although elevated streetcar tracks were added on Boston's periphery beginning as early as 1901.

The corner of Tremont and Park streets was a logical starting point for the initial leg of America's first subway. The area was part of Boston Common, a place Bostonians had used for cow grazing, military drills, public meetings, hangings, and other festivities since 1634. A variety of buildings had graced that broad corner in times past, including a granary, a workhouse, and the still-standing Park Street Church.

Nevertheless, when the Boston Transit Commission was created in 1894 to plan the subway, and when chief engineer Howard A. Carson began construction on March 28, 1895, tempers ran high. Some people worried the digging project would tie up traffic. Others feared damage to the Common, inspiring Mayor Nathan Matthews to remark that Boston's eleventh commandment seemed to be "Thou shalt not touch the Common."

Despite public fears, the commandment was disobeyed for almost three years, as laborers dug up clay, gravel, and sand along the Common's Tremont Street edge, from the Park Street intersection to the far corner of the Public Garden. Working with teams of a hundred workers doing ten-hour shifts, the crews hauled out tons of dirt using steam-driven carts on overhead trestles and then dumping the unwanted soil on the end of the Common where the baseball field exists today.

In spite of inaccurate or nonexistent utilities maps, beds of quicksand, and accidental explosions—like the one at the corner of Boylston and Tremont that killed nine workers—work went on. Work went on, too, though some one thousand colonial cadavers were inadvertently exhumed; the bodies were reinterred in the northwest corner of the Common's burying ground, facing the Colonial Theatre on Boylston Street.

Work went on, and persistence won out: the first leg of the Tremont Street Subway was ready to open on September 1, 1897. The total cost of that first subway line was $4,404,958.25, substantially under the original estimate of $5 million. Of that expense, $350,000 was for Park Street Station itself. The subterranean streetcar stop was constructed using steel beams, brick, and concrete masonry. Though the steelwork on the roof was left exposed, the walls were lined with white porcelain brick or tile, and the supporting steel columns were encased in concrete and painted white.

The original station was on the level of the modern-day Green Line; the Red Line's "Park Street Under" was not added below until 1912. In a space about half the size of today's upper-level station there were four tracks, two island platforms, two loop tracks for return cars, plus a space for disabled or extra cars. Stairs with patent safety treads led up to four headhouses on the street level, two of which are still in use today.

Those boxlike headhouses were designed by Edmund Wheelwright of the architectural firm Wheelwright and Haven. The kiosks' walls were made from granite brought in from Deer Island, Maine. Their roofs were glass, and the exterior details were neoclassical, featuring decorative dentils and pilasters, high, brass-screened windows, and—in 1897—no doors in the doorways.

Wheelwright's careful design was not appreciated by contemporary critics and the press, who complained that the entrance cubes looked like mausoleums.

Those critics had nothing but good to say about the opening day of the subway, however. In the wee hours of September 1, 1897, crowds began to assemble at both the Boylston and Park Street stations. Back in the western suburb of Allston, where the car would begin its journey, an overflow crowd of 175 jammed into the 50-person streetcar. By the end of the day, 100,000 riders would make the same trip.

Conductor Gilman T. Trufant and motorman James Reed—both West End Railway veterans—guided car number 1752, an open-bench four-wheel trolley, on the inaugural run. "All aboard for Park Street!" was the cry as the trolley traveled on preexisting surface tracks from the Allston car barns, across the River Street Bridge to Pearl Street in Cambridge, then across the Harvard Bridge, toward an incline that began at the Public Garden. Swinging off Boylston Street, the car descended underground, arriving at the Park Street platform at 6:02 A.M. to cheers and waving flags.

That first strip of Boston subway was only six tenths of a mile. But little by little, the subway expanded—extending throughout downtown, over to

Cambridge, out to South Boston and East Boston, and beyond. Sometimes it grew under ground and sometimes above ground, on the elevated lines built outside the busy city center. (The elevated lines were much cheaper to construct than their underground counterparts but were considered too great an obstruction and too much of an eyesore to place in congested downtown areas.) The fares grew too—from five cents in 1897 to $1.25 in 2004. Incidentally, the first subway riders paid their fares with tickets; coins were used later, starting in 1915. Of the payment methods in use today, tokens were introduced in 1951. The T pass, allowing for a month of subway rides, was first used in 1974, and the Boston Passport, allowing for either three or seven days of unlimited public transportation travel, in 1989. (The Boston Visitors Pass is now available in one-, three-, and seven-day denominations.) Most recently, the T has instituted automated fare collection (AFC) equipment in the subway system and onboard buses, introduced Smart Cards, and installed a wide-area network to support AFC as well as various communications and control functions.

The Boston Elevated Railway Company, which opened in 1894 and built and operated most of "the El," was a private stockholder corporation that took control of the pioneering West End Street Railway in 1922. In 1947, the whole system was transferred to a public agency created by the Massachusetts State Legislature—the Metropolitan Transit Authority. The MTA, which served fourteen cities and towns, was replaced in 1964 by a larger transit provider, the Massachusetts Bay Transportation Authority. Complete consolidation of mass transit under one provider finally occurred when the MBTA acquired the Middlesex and Boston Street Railway in 1972. The MBTA, which still exists today, expanded their service district to 79 communities, and finally to today's astonishing number: 175 cities and towns.

Under the MBTA, Boston's four historic "streetcar lines" were labeled with the color codes we know today. The original Boylston-Tremont trolley subway became the Green Line (the green honored Boston's Emerald Necklace of parks, which the line intersected). The Cambridge–Dorchester line, begun in 1912, became the Red Line (Harvard's school color was crimson); the 1901 Main Line El became the Orange; and the 1904 East Boston line was Blue. Since each of the four lines was developed at different times by different groups, the equipment was never made interchangeable. Hence, the complex history of subway and elevated rapid-transit vehicles in Boston—from the earliest trolleys to sophisticated World War II–era Pullman PCCs, Boeing SLRVs, Kinki-Sharyo Type 7s, and Type 8 Breda low-floor trolleys—has four different versions: one for each line. Each line has its own idiom as well. People still throw around terms like *trains, cars, streetcars,* and *trolley cars* to refer to all sorts of different vehicles. Technically, however, Green Line cars are called light rail vehicles, and they're run by operators; Red Line cars are heavy rail vehicles, also called trains, and are run by motorpersons.

What all the T's vehicles do have in common is 600 volts of direct current, provided today by the local utility company NStar. For decades, however, Boston's subway system had its own power plants and generated its own electricity; during the Great Northeast Blackout of November 1965, the MBTA kept running while the New York City subways stopped dead in their tracks. The T's generating plants were eventually deemed expensive and impractical and were phased out between 1977 and 1981. (The MBTA does maintain the ability to generate traction power electricity in emergencies; their own turbine generators were fired up on December 31, 1999 as a Y2K precaution and again on August 14, 2003, when the Great Blackout of 2003 resulted in the loss of electrical power to much of the northeast—though not, as it turned out, to Boston.)

Another major change of the past three decades has involved personnel, both at Park Street and throughout the entire MBTA. Women are on the job everywhere now—making up roughly a quarter of all T staff. During the subway's first seven decades, its personnel were essentially all male. Not just any men, mind you. As far back as 1901, the company outlined strict standards for its employees: "Our conductors must be presentable, for the very appearance of some men gives offense quickly in a cultured community. These men must have all their fingers and thumbs, and now-a-days must have all their toes. . . . [They also need] a reasonable number of either real or artificial teeth."

Park Street Station itself has changed and improved since 1897. The Red Line platform was added in 1912, and the Green Line's track-and-platform space was enlarged twice. Two of Park's original four street-level headhouses are gone, and newer additions—such as elevators, escalators, computerized systems, and a little-known concourse to the Orange Line—have made the station a bit more modern. All of the vendors that used to crowd the Green Line platform have disappeared, leaving the platforms free for their most important components: token booths, an information booth, and people.

The whole MBTA system doesn't operate out of Park Street as it once did, nor does the station act as "Emergency Backup for Central Control" from a spartan chamber hidden behind the long mural; those systems are now based on the top floor of 45 High Street. The aforementioned mural, however, a 1978 mosaic by Lilli Ann Rosenberg, is still located on the Green Line level near the entrance. It's a creative and colorful collage that incorporates ceramic and found objects—like railroad spikes, horseshoes, hammers, and wheels—in a fanciful city scene filled with tidbits about Boston and its famed subway system. The only artwork on the Red Line below are praying hands, set in the arches above the track, executed by Ralph Helmick, the artist who created the Arthur Fiedler bust on the Charles River Esplanade.

Today, Park Street bears few signs of the crises it has endured in past decades. There were, for example, the racial tensions, the damage from the 1975 fire, and the old, unreliable equipment that led to constant breakdowns and delays. There were also ongoing financial shortages, which caused the T to shut down entirely on December 6, 1980, for a period of twenty-six hours, and a major renovation of the station in the late 1970s that proved architecturally controversial at best.

Fortunately, better equipment and more dependable streetcars have arrived since then. A $6–7 million renovation executed in 1992 and 1993—

as well as ongoing improvements to this day—has given the station a cleaner, brighter environment, improved signage, some historical commentary, and better wheelchair access to platforms. Most recently, the MBTA has installed a network to support automated fare collection and various communications and control functions, as well as a system-wide radio to upgrade communications for operations, safety, and security. Another improvement has been a more lyrical one. "There was a joke among the guys in the mid-1970s," explained one MBTA official. "We said, 'If we can't provide them service, we'll give them music to soothe their nerves!'" Hence, the official policy of inviting musicians to play in Park Street Station—and eventually throughout the T—began. Many of the varied folk, rock, jazz, and classical musicians who have played the crowds at Park Street over the years agree that subway gigs are fine experiences. It's true that noise and constantly changing audiences are inherent problems, and that street-corner shows attract higher contributions than their subway counterparts. "But it's great training in winning over an audience," mused one longtime performer. "Plus you can work out new music. Who's going to know if you play the same song all day?" (And yes, though it's been almost half a century since it was a hit tune, there are still folkies who occasionally belt out the classic strains of "Charlie and the MTA.")

Meanwhile, with sweet melodies in the background, the constant crush of humanity continues to swarm in and out of Park Street Station, day after day. And the same old questions are asked of T personnel with clocklike regularity.

"How do I get to Harvard?"

"How do I get to Fenway Park?"

"How do I get to the MFA?"

"How do you get to the other side?"

"Excuse me, but where's 'Cheers'?"

THE ESSENTIALS

Address: Corner of Park and Tremont streets, on Boston Common, Boston, MA. Varied MBTA offices at 10 Park Plaza, Boston, MA 02116. **Telephone:** MBTA customer service and travel information, (617) 222-3200. **Website:** www.mbta.com. **Visitor Information:** Park Street Station, and subway lines in general, open from approximately 5:15 A.M. to 12:30 A.M. daily. Modest fee. No scheduled tours. Green Line trolleys are wheelchair accessible; Red Line accessible via elevator in kiosk at Tremont and Winter streets, plus raised platforms at Park Street Under that allow patrons to wheel directly onto trains. Call Office for Transportation Access (OTA) for current information on accessibility: (617) 222-5976, or (617) 222-1542. No public restrooms.

Additional sources for those interested in subway, trolley, and train history: www.mbta .com; go to Inside the T, T at a Glance, History; also, the Boston Street Railway Association, P.O. Box 181037, Boston, MA 02118; Seashore Trolley Museum, 195 Log Cabin Road, Box A, Kennebunkport, ME 04046 (phone 207-967-2800; www.trolley-museum .org).

PART FOUR

Athens Two

LITERARY BOSTON

THE CULTURAL awakening of Boston that began in the second quarter of the nineteenth century continued through the time of the American Civil War. That flowering involved not only the arts and entertainment world but the literary world as well. It was two of Boston's nineteenth-century literary lights, in fact, that gave Boston its nicknames "the Athens of America" and "the Hub of the Universe." William Tudor, a founder and the first editor of the *North American Review* and an original Athenaeum member, is credited with making the first comparison to Athens, in a letter of 1819. Oliver Wendell Holmes called Boston "the hub of the solar system" in his 1858 work *The Autocrat of the Breakfast Table,* and later generations expanded that phrase to include a much larger chunk of the heavens.

To make books and literature available to Bostonians, libraries were needed. In the first half of the nineteenth century, the area's prime book repositories were Harvard College and the Boston Athenaeum. Books were therefore within the reach of only a relative few. By 1854, however, the Boston Public Library opened its doors, making waves as the first free municipal library in America. Creating new books and literature also required that there be book publishers. And though publishers had existed in Boston long before, it was the firm of Ticknor & Fields, lodged at the Old Corner Bookstore, that revolutionized Boston and American publishing in the mid-nineteenth century.

Jamie Fields in particular drew the area's finest authors to the Old Corner Bookstore building. The shop's location at the corner of Washington and School streets became known as "Parnassus Corner," yet another reference to the era's classical cultural inspirations and aspirations. The road that led from Washington Street to the new State House on Beacon Hill became the regular haunt of numerous literary luminaries, from Harriet Beecher Stowe, Louisa May Alcott, and Margaret Fuller to Henry Wadsworth Longfellow, Ralph Waldo Emerson, and Charles Dickens. Nearer to the State House, on Beacon Street, was the Athenaeum, where many read, researched, and assembled. At the intersection of Beacon, Tremont, and School streets were two of Boston's finest hotels, the Tremont House and the Parker House. The latter became the festive center of the literary "Saturday Club" during the second half of the nineteenth century.

Downtown theaters were also a part of the nineteenth-century literary world. Stages like the Tremont Theater (now Tremont Temple Baptist Church), the old Music Hall (now the Orpheum Theatre), and the long-gone Boston Museum and Howard Athenaeum were popular sites for presenting plays and musical events to Boston audiences; but literary readings by poets and authors—as well as inspired orations by reformers like William Lloyd Garrison and Frederick Douglass—were just as likely to draw large crowds. A perfect microcosm of the intermingling of arts and other aspects of culture that occurred during this period was the Boston Museum, which opened on Tremont and Bromfield streets in 1841. Concerts, plays, and lectures were offered in its upstairs performance space, while the first floor housed a museum that included both paintings and stuffed animal specimens.

Many of the writers, poets, and philosophers associated with the flowering of nineteenth-century Boston actually lived outside the city. Henry David Thoreau and other transcendentalists preferred a pastoral existence, viewing city life as a "menacing artifact." Little towns like Concord—and, in Thoreau's case, a tiny house by Concord's Walden Pond—were sometimes deemed more appropriate homes. Still, plenty of the literati stayed right in the Hub, often in stylish enclaves like the Back Bay, Beacon Hill, and the Hill's private, cobblestoned block known as Louisburg Square. In-town locations, after all, made "Athens" all the more accessible.

In 1999, incidentally, I was honored with the assignment of helping to create an actual literary trail for the Greater Boston area—a literary counterpart to our Freedom, Women's Heritage, and Black Heritage trails. Sponsored by the nonprofit Boston History Collaborative and Houghton Mifflin, my book *Literary Trail of Greater Boston: A Tour of Sites in Boston, Cambridge, and Concord* was published in 2000. It's an excellent addition to the following chapters of *Boston Sites and Insights* for those who want to pursue the theme of literary Boston even further.

25 The Boston Athenaeum

FEMINIST JOURNALIST Margaret Fuller studied here, and so did philosopher Ralph Waldo Emerson. Statesman Daniel Webster happily whiled away the hours in these chambers, as did essayists, authors, and poets like Oliver Wendell Holmes, Lydia Maria Child, Amy Lowell, and Henry Wadsworth Longfellow. Filmmaker Ken Burns sifted through antique photographs and Confederate imprints, assembling materials for his television documentary series *The Civil War*. Here, too, amid a sea of library stacks and shoulder-to-shoulder neoclassical busts, historian Doris Kearns Goodwin wrote *The Fitzgeralds and the Kennedys* and historian David McCullough researched his biography of Harry S. Truman.

Few proper Bostonians would be surprised to hear that the place where these nineteenth- and twentieth-century movers and shakers all hunkered down was the Boston Athenaeum. What's more surprising to some is that the Athenaeum, renowned as Boston's oldest existing library and first real art museum, has served scholars and ordinary folk alike in its two centuries of existence. Though this Beacon Hill institution is a membership library, qualified scholars are invited to use the research facilities for free, and nonmembers are welcome to visit the art gallery and to join free weekly tours. Those tours, incidentally, won *Boston* magazine's 1989 award for "Best Out-of-Body Experience"—a citation that still perplexes and amuses Athenaeum staff.

The Athenaeum began in 1805, when fourteen Boston gentlemen formed the Anthology Society, their own literary and dining club, to edit the *Monthly Anthology and Boston Review*. Within its first year, the society set an even more ambitious goal: to create an institution with "a reading room, a library, a museum and a laboratory" for its members. They opened to subscribers in 1806 and incorporated as the Boston Athenaeum on February 17, 1807.

Why *Athenaeum*? Defined as "an institution or society for the promotion of literary and/or scientific learning," the term also evokes the classical Greek word *athenaion,* a temple dedicated to the goddess Athena, where poets read their works aloud. Some Anthology Society members were certainly familiar with the Athenaeum and Lyceum of Liverpool, England, as well.

While simultaneously working on other projects, such as creating the *North American Review* in 1811 (a periodical still published today), the Athenaeum's founders went about finding a home for the books and artwork they had begun to collect. After housing the collection briefly in Scollay's buildings on Congress and Tremont streets, members bought the Rufus Amory House, next to King's Chapel Burying Ground, in 1809. In 1822, when that space proved too small, they moved to a new home on

Pearl Street, made from two separate houses combined by architect Solomon Willard.

Once collections overflowed yet again, the Athenaeum's present structure was built at 10½ Beacon Street, opening to great fanfare in July 1849. Its Italianate, neo-Palladian style was chosen by Edward Clarke Cabot, who won the Athenaeum's design competition.

In many ways, Cabot's Athenaeum looked much as it does today: a dignified exterior of rosy sandstone, with Corinthian pilasters defining tall, arched window bays and a central entrance. Inside, long, high-ceilinged rooms are filled with little balconies, alcoves, and nooks and are packed with eclectic, easily accessible collections of books. To this day, 75 percent of the 600,000 volumes remain on open stacks.

Unlike the modern Athenaeum, the 1849 building had only three floors —two for art galleries and a third for books. To no one's surprise, the collections continued to exceed available space. Sometimes this was dealt with in a small way; in 1888, for example, the entrance foyer's monumental Sumner staircase was sacrificed to make room for new stacks. Other times, physical expansion came in a big way. During 1913–14, Henry Forbes Bigelow choreographed a total renovation and fireproofing of the Athenaeum, adding two more floors to Cabot's original building (resulting in today's five-story structure). In the 1990s, plans were drawn for yet another renovation, this time to address climate control, lack of space for books and programs, and an out-of-date building infrastructure.

Between 1999 and 2002, most of the Athenaeum staff—and all of its books—relocated to temporary quarters in the Drydock area of South Boston while 10½ Beacon Street underwent a mammoth $30 million modernization. During that three-year period, the interior of the Athenaeum was virtually demolished and a modern climate-control system installed. Space next door, at 14 Beacon Street, was purchased or leased for use as the Norma Jean Calderwood Art Gallery, the new Children's Library, expanded book storage space, and a state-of-the-art conservation lab. (The Art Department was also relocated to the top level of Pilgrim Hall, at 14 Beacon.) A long first-floor chamber was returned to its nineteenth-century gran-deur. And a Special Collections reading room and study carrels for scholars were added to the Reference Department, which itself was moved to the second floor. By the summer of 2002, books and personnel were all shuttled back to Beacon Street—with great fanfare and a great sigh of relief.

In the beginning, the Athenaeum tried to be all things to all people. Its art gallery accumulated and exhibited treasures by American artists such as Gilbert Stuart, John Singer Sargent, Washington Allston, Chester Harding, Thomas Crawford, and John Frazee. It also supplied studio space, moral support, and financial backing for working artists. Meanwhile, its library became one of the five largest in America. With 50,000 volumes by 1851, its collection equaled that of the Library of Congress.

Later in the nineteenth century, the Athenaeum's role changed. The Boston Public Library opened in 1854, and in 1872 the Athenaeum helped to establish the Boston Museum of Fine Arts (which opened four years

Created as Boston's finest library and first art museum, the Boston Athenaeum is still a wonderful place to read, browse, research, and attend art openings and special events.

later), lending it many of its first exhibits. No longer inspired to be *the* library and *the* art museum of Boston, the institution gradually committed itself to more limited, and more specialized, acquisitions and goals. In particular, the printed word took precedence over art.

Nevertheless, artwork—including spectacularly fine or wonderfully curious nineteenth-century paintings and sculptures—is still displayed throughout the building. A first-floor gallery with changing exhibits is a favorite attraction for visitors.

The paintings and sculpture on view—gently crammed into every available wall, pedestal, and corner—are primarily the work of American nineteenth-century artists. Artwork connected to Athenaeum history has also deliberately been kept, making the place look like "a big family house." Among the more extraordinary pieces in the library's possession are several paintings by Gilbert Stuart; Giovanni Panini's *Interior of St. Peter's, Rome;* and Gregorio Lazzarini's *The Golden Age.* Among the pieces most requested in duplicate form—for display, research, or publication outside the Athenaeum—are Jean Antoine Houdon's busts of Washington, Lafayette, and Franklin; Chester Harding's painting of Daniel Webster; and Allan Crite's painting *Harriet and Leon.* (Crite is a pioneering twentieth-century African-American artist and art historian based in the Boston area.)

As the Athenaeum reduced its role as art museum over the decades, it sold many works of art. Perhaps the most regrettable loss was Thomas Crawford's marble statue *Orpheus and Cerberus*, which was loaned to Boston's Museum of Fine Arts in 1872. A century later, in 1975, the statue was purchased by private individuals and donated to the MFA, where it's still on prominent display. The MFA and the Smithsonian Institution jointly acquired Gilbert Stuart's unfinished portraits of George and Martha Washington from the Athenaeum in 1980 in a $4.9 million sale that stipulated that the first "first couple" be shared by the Museum and the Smithsonian's National Portrait Gallery. (The "sharing" process is simple: generally around three years in Boston, followed by three years in Washington, ad infinitum.)

Not all of the nonbook objects at the Athenaeum can be classified as art. Among the stranger items in its special collections are a breastplate and sword from the battlefield at Waterloo, and shoes purportedly owned by President McKinley's wife. The Athenaeum's more scholarly highlights include a superb group of Confederate states imprints, eighteenth- and nineteenth-century Boston newspapers, and one of the finest groupings of nineteenth-century prints in the nation. (An engaging and beautifully printed book, *Boston Lithography, 1825–80,* assembled by staff members Sally Pierce and Catharina Slautterback and based on historic lithographs housed in the Charles E. Mason Jr. Print Room, is among the Athenaeum's stellar publications.)

The Athenaeum's present emphasis on reading and research is readily apparent—if only because books are lodged in every conceivable cranny of the building. The first floor, redesigned to accommodate functions for the public, features a reception area, circulation desk, lecture and concert hall, art gallery, and children's library. It also includes a large, comfortable newspaper-reading room, as well as members' room and seminar room. The second floor—with its chandeliers, well-trod Oriental rugs, and polished old tables—is home for the Reference Department, Print Room, and the Special Collections reading room and study carrels. Technical services now dominate the third floor, and administrative offices fill much of the fourth. One of the building's most fascinating spaces is the fifth, uppermost level—a peaceful, cathedral-like reading room reserved for members only.

When Athenaeum members come there to read, they're sometimes seeking books that plenty of other libraries have—and sometimes books that are nowhere else to be found. Obscure, out-of-print titles are, after all, an Athenaeum specialty. Some of the books are in fragile condition, but most remain in unusually usable shape, thanks largely to the Athenaeum's conservation department.

Among the most prestigious volumes are those from George Washington's library, purchased from Mount Vernon in 1848; the Schoolcraft Collection of books in Native American languages; and volumes from the King's Chapel theological collections. Among the most surprising resources—especially to those who view the Athenaeum solely as a serious research library—is one of the finest collections of detective fiction in the country.

The most infamous book is certainly the autobiography of an executed nineteenth-century highwayman, which, following his request, was bound in his own skin. Once on display, the autobiography has been tactfully tucked away from the public eye. The library has 600,000 volumes in all, a number increasing at the rate of 5,000 per year. In 1998, some 19,467 of those volumes were circulated to various readers. When not in use by members, the books are accessed by an online catalog called Athena or borrowed through hundreds of other institutions, both private and public, via a growing number of computerized interlibrary loan networks. Though about three quarters of their books are still cataloged on the Athenaeum's peculiar in-house Cutter classification system, all acquisitions since 1978 use the modern Library of Congress method. (Most recently, electronic records for the Athenaeum's collection of prints and photographs have been developed through the efforts of the Electronic Scriptorium, a group of digitally savvy monks from West Virginia.)

In its earliest years, the Athenaeum was essentially a gentlemen's reading room for wealthy white Bostonians. The resulting nineteenth-century biases were reflected in the book classification system developed by Athenaeum librarian Charles Ammi Cutter. According to Stephen Nonack, the head of Reader Services, "It's an alpha-numeric system that is logical and user-friendly. But 'Class D' lumps together books on education, the poor, women, and slavery."

It was not long, however, before demographic changes in Athenaeum membership began to take place. In the 1820s, when women were often excluded from colleges and private libraries, writer Hannah Adams was allowed to study here. Granted, the woman renowned as America's first full-time professional female author was locked in the library at lunchtime to pursue her studies "in modesty." But she did get in, and she was awarded permanent free access by 1827.

Once Adams got her foot in the door, others followed. In 1856, the Athenaeum became the first library in America to hire a female staff member. The nineteenth-century African-American sculptor Edmonia Lewis was among the artists supported by the institution, as was Gilbert Stuart's daughter Jane. A higher percentage of paintings and sculpture of and by women was accumulated—and is still displayed at the Athenaeum—than by most other historic buildings in Boston.

Despite these inroads by women, and despite many of its members' being ardent abolitionists and reformers, conservatism remained a strong force at the Athenaeum; when member Lydia Maria Child wrote "An Appeal in Favor of the Class of Americans Called Africans"—an immediatist tract that angered gradualists in abolitionism—she found her privileges mysteriously revoked.

Today, the Athenaeum remains a curious mix of conservative and liberal, of old and new. "A lot of people still think this is an old gentleman's club," muses Ann Wadsworth of the Athenaeum's Research Department. "Actually, there are still a few old gentlemen here who think that!" Alongside them, and heartily welcomed by the Athenaeum, are those not accommodated in the past. In 1850, one might have been shocked to find a woman wandering through the first floor art gallery with her baby stroller, preschoolers enjoying story time, or a well-attended lecture on Native American, black, or gay and lesbian history. But today they're all a matter of course. Members can no longer smoke in the library as they once did, but they can still bring in well-behaved dogs. Increased access and outreach are also evident in newly developing programs with the Boston public schools, fellowship programs for private and public school teachers, and resource assistance to select day-care centers, administered through the Children's Library.

And, yes, the tradition of afternoon tea is still maintained one afternoon a week. Indeed, the best of the nineteenth century remains alive and well at 10½ Beacon.

THE ESSENTIALS

Address: 10 1/2 Beacon Street, Boston, MA 02108. **Telephone:** (617) 227-0270; fax (617) 227-5266. **Website:** www.bostonathenaeum.org. **Visitor Information:** Building open 9:00 A.M. to 5:30 P.M., Monday through Friday, year-round; open 9:00 A.M. to 4:00 P.M. Saturdays, September through May. Closed all major national holidays plus Patriot's Day and Bunker Hill Day. Free guided art and architecture tours Tuesdays and Thursdays, 3:00 P.M.; advance reservations required through Circulation Department (x279). All main floors are wheelchair accessible; elevators available to all floors; accessible restroom on first floor.

The Athenaeum is a site on the Literary Trail of Greater Boston; information at www.littrail.org.

26 The Old Corner Bookstore Building

IT'S BEEN more than a century since the editor of New York's *Home Journal* observed that, with a little exaggeration, all of Boston could be said to pass through the Old Corner in a day. That's a bit far-fetched, of course. Still, anyone versed in Boston's literary history knows that the quaint brick building at the corner of School and Washington streets—affectionately known to generations as the Old Corner Bookstore—has been a mecca for avid readers, illustrious men and women of letters, and other curious Bostonians since the mid-nineteenth century.

Between 1845 and 1865 in particular, when the shop was run by the prestigious publishing team of Ticknor & Fields, the guests on any given day might range from Norwegian violinist Ole Bull or popular American actresses Charlotte Cushman and Fanny Kemble to authors like Harriet Beecher Stowe, Henry David Thoreau, and Nathaniel Hawthorne. The British novelist Charles Dickens passed frequently through the shop's portals, as did local literary heroes such as Oliver Wendell Holmes, Henry Wadsworth Longfellow, and Ralph Waldo Emerson.

When you add to this group a broad array of doctors and lawyers, ministers and midwives, artists and professors, abolitionists and librarians, and just plain people, it becomes clear why the intersection of School and Washington sometimes looked a bit like Grand Central Station. What's more, it was nicknamed "Parnassus Corner" after the sacred Greek mount where the Muses and Apollo once held forth. If Boston was "the Hub of the Universe," the bookstore was arguably the cultural "hub of the Hub," at least during the tenure of William D. Ticknor and James T. Fields.

But the history of the Old Corner Bookstore neither started nor ended with Ticknor and Fields. During the last two decades of the twentieth century, for example, the Old Corner housed bookstores focusing on Boston and New England themes and served as a downtown presence for the *Boston Globe*. The building itself—a site on the Freedom Trail, the Literary Trail, and the Boston Women's Heritage Trail—is owned and managed by Historic Boston Incorporated, a nonprofit group that saved the old bookstore structure from demolition in 1960 and continues to assist preservation efforts for other Boston landmarks. (Historic Boston's offices occupy part of the building, along with various other professional offices, shops, and a restaurant.)

In 1999, Historic Boston commissioned a comprehensive historic struc-

Internationally acclaimed nineteenth-century publishers Ticknor & Fields put the Old Corner Bookstore on the literary map of America.

tures report, aided by a matching grant from the Massachusetts Historical Commission's Preservation Projects Fund. The report described the architectural history of the buildings there, outlined standards and criteria for future changes to them, and established a detailed time line of the various uses of this site as a commercial center for almost three centuries. The report noted that, in addition to its significance to Boston's literary heritage, the Old Corner was a case study in the evolution of historic preservation practices. (In the 1990s, Historic Boston used nineteenth-century photographic evidence to begin restoring the building exterior to its actual historic appearance—rather than the conjectural ones that preceded.)

All of which simply shows that history was indeed made—and continues to be made—at the hallowed Old Corner Bookstore building.

The corner on which the Old Corner Bookstore sits is considered a prime downtown location. Oddly enough, that was also true in 1630, the year Boston was settled by the Massachusetts Bay Company. Many of the first colonists constructed crude homes near the freshwater spring that bubbled up where Spring Lane is found today. Boston's first church, market, and townhouse (the last term meant a public building, not a private family condo, at the time) were all built within two blocks of the future site of the Old Corner Bookstore.

A prominent East Anglican Puritan named Isaac Johnson was the original owner of the bookstore site and several surrounding acres. But Johnson and his equally prominent wife, Lady Arbella Fiennes, failed to survive the severe Boston winter. Anne Hutchinson, her husband, William, and their children, who arrived in Boston on September 18, 1634, subsequently built a home on the half-acre corner lot that Johnson had once owned. The spot was clearly at the heart of the village, where "the street leading to Roxbury" met "the lane leading to the Common." The prestige of the area was also evidenced by the Hutchinsons' immediate neighbor: Governor John Winthrop lived across the street, a circumstance that Mrs. Hutchinson would soon learn to regret.

Hutchinson became a popular, powerful woman, respected as a midwife and as the spouse of an established merchant. She was also a brilliant thinker and a leader of the controversial Antinomian sect, which took issue with prevailing Puritan thought. Hutchinson argued that both men and women could find true spirituality in the personal and the mystical—thereby challenging the Puritan establishment's academic foundations, their religious disciplines, and the authenticity of their "learned clergy." She also attracted more and more ardent female followers to the prayer meetings in her home. Such mysticism and feminism combined as a formidable affront to the eminently rational, all-male Puritan hierarchy.

As a result, Winthrop and his colleagues were incensed. In 1637, the General Court of Massachusetts banished Hutchinson for heresy. Like most religious refugees of the time, she fled to Rhode Island, along with her family and several friends. After her husband died, Hutchinson and her fourteen children moved to Long Island, where they were killed in 1643 by Siwanoy Indians who were quarreling with the area's Dutch settlers.

Two years after Hutchinson's death, Governor Winthrop waxed philo-

sophical about women like her, whom he thought suffered from excess in-
tellect—from too much reading, writing, and thinking; such a woman
would have had a less troubled life, wrote Winthrop in his journal, "if she
had attended to her household affairs and such things as belong to women,
and not gone out of her way and calling to meddle in such things as are
proper for men, whose minds are stronger."

Following the Hutchinsons' forced departure, their house was passed
through a variety of owners. An apothecary named Dr. Thomas Crease
bought the home in 1708, then lost it in the Great Fire of October 2, 1711,
which swept away hundreds of downtown shops and residences. By 1718,
however, the apparently well-to-do Crease had built a solid brick structure
in its stead. Though the interior has been altered over the centuries, the
building's massing and much of its original fabric remain visible today.

Like many of his contemporaries, Crease built his progressive English-
style townhouse with a shop on the ground floor and his residence above.
The structure had stately sides of rose red brick and a sloping gambrel
roof. On the School Street side, string courses of brick were laid as decorative bands dividing the building's three stories. Squared blocks of Connecticut sandstone, known as quoins, added both visual flair and an air of
importance to the exterior corners. Today the building remains one of
Boston's oldest brick structures, as well as a rare surviving example of eighteenth-century brick, gambrel-roofed domestic architecture.

For a hundred years after Dr. Crease built his dream house, a series of
pharmacists and physicians lived upstairs while selling their wares on the
busy street level below. In 1817, ownership fell to Dr. Samuel Clarke, father
of the celebrated liberal thinker and Unitarian minister at King's Chapel,
the Reverend James Freeman Clarke.

During this period, little changed at the Old Corner building except the
address. When Crease bought the property in 1707, the intersecting streets
were known as "the main street leading to Roxbury" and Schoolhouse Lane
(Boston Latin School had been lodged up the street since 1645). In 1708, a
town committee officially named them School Street and Cornhill. Though
School Street has maintained its 1708 designation, Cornhill became Washington Street in 1824. After Washington Street was lengthened in 1875, the
Old Corner building became number 283. Its address remains 283 Washington to this day, though the current tenants use One School Street as the
address for their store.

The biggest changes to the structure at School and Washington came in
1828, when young Timothy Harrington Carter obtained a lease from the
building owner, George Brimmer. Carter was a former bookseller's apprentice from Lancaster, Massachusetts, who harbored ambitious ideas
about the future of book publishing. He envisioned the old Crease house as
an ideal location for the world of books and spent seven thousand dollars
to alter the aging pharmacy and private residence into a modern commercial space.

Carter added projecting, small-paned windows to the ground floor, giving the shop what's been called a "Dickensian London touch." He also re-
bricked that first story and lowered the floor three to four steps to street
level. On the School Street side, where Thomas Crease once had a garden,

Carter added a brick extension to his structure, creating the area where a restaurant resides today. The corner apothecary was transformed into a bookshop, and the extension housed seven printing presses, first run by Canadian horses and later by steam.

Carter set himself up as a silent partner, with his brother Richard Carter and Charles Hendee as booksellers (a fourteen-year-old youngster named James T. Fields, from Portsmouth, New Hampshire, was hired as an apprentice not long thereafter). The Old Corner Bookstore was officially born, with Carter & Hendee as the first of ten firms of booksellers and publishers to be housed there over the next seventy-five years.

In 1833, Carter & Hendee were replaced by Allen & Ticknor. When John Allen left that company in 1836, William D. Ticknor continued his book business alone. The consistent thread through these three original firms was one building—the Old Corner Bookstore—and one apprentice, the bright, witty, charming, versatile, and ambitious Jamie Fields.

While carefully and cheerfully scrutinizing his employers, other publishers and booksellers, artists, authors, and the book-browsing public, Fields developed a vision of the Old Corner as a magnet for the authors who were then creating the first body of truly American literature. Many of these writers, including Hawthorne, Thoreau, Emerson, Longfellow, and Whittier, lived in New England. Ticknor came to believe in Fields's vision. In 1842 he made Fields a junior partner, and by 1845 the firm was officially known as Ticknor & Fields.

Before promoting Fields, Ticknor had a shop that was solid but nondescript, with no real specialty or personality. As did many booksellers of the day, he also published works now and then—generally at the authors' risk and expense. But with the ideas, personality, and push of Fields and the financial backing of investor John Reed, Jr., Ticknor & Fields eventually ushered in a whole new era of Boston book publishing.

Fields wanted to publish and sell fine American and English literature, and his tactics were brilliant. At that time, authors were neither bound by legal contracts to a single publisher nor protected from later "pirate" editions of their work. Hence, there was little sense of loyalty or obligation between author and publisher. It was also customary for authors to be paid in a standard lump sum for their manuscripts. To lure authors and secure exclusive American publishing rights, Fields formulated the royalty system, which gave authors both the standard manuscript sum and 10 percent of retail sales. He also secured ownership of prestigious magazines like the *North American Review* and the fledgling *Atlantic Monthly,* for which his writers became the literary backbone.

Fields was a master of promotion, as epitomized by the lucrative American lecture tour he organized and publicized for Charles Dickens in 1867–68. He was also a huckster who planted publicity in periodicals, "bought" reviewers, wrote his own glowing reviews under false names, and fabricated accolades for his stars. Equally important, he became the friend, protector, literary counselor, and guardian of his flock of writers. While the more solitary Ticknor occupied a counting room at the back of the shop's book-lined sales floor, Fields held court in a cozy rear nook behind a green curtain. There, explains William S. Tryon in his 1963 book *Parnassus Cor-*

ner, Jamie Fields blossomed. "In what appeared to be hopeless confusion he wrote his letters, read his manuscripts, and entertained his friends. Amid whispered consultations, endless talk and bright anecdotes, jokes and shouts of laughter, Fields was creating something new in the literary and business world of America."

While Fields gained everlasting renown as the man who put the Old Corner Bookstore on the literary map of America, some of his peers have been less heralded by history. His wife, Annie Adams Fields, for example, helped consolidate Ticknor & Fields's literary relations by hosting salons for authors in the Fields home on Charles Street. She also supported the work of many women writers of her time, in part by bringing together luminaries like Willa Cather and Sarah Orne Jewett.

Meanwhile, tenants who worked in other parts of the Old Corner building attracted nineteenth-century patrons as well. Bookbinder George Gould, printer Isaac Butts, boot maker Isaac Waitt, and the toy-vending Calender family had shops in the corner complex for years. So did the famous Boston hairdresser, William Dudley, and Mrs. Abner Haven, whose popular, packed coffee room was known by contemporaries for serving "perfect toast," thick lemon pie, and "an exhilarating boiled coffee suspected of brandy infusion."

By the turn of the twentieth century, much had changed at the Old Corner Bookstore building. After William Ticknor died in 1864, Jamie Fields assumed sole ownership and moved the business to more spacious quarters on Tremont Street. The firm's descendants later merged with the Riverside Press, established by Henry Houghton in 1852, which evolved into Houghton Mifflin and Company. (In 1979, that company restored the Ticknor & Fields imprint as a tribute to its predecessor.)

The last booksellers to inhabit the corner building departed in 1903, though they used the name Old Corner Bookstore for their new, larger space on Bromfield Street. On Christmas Eve of 1979, that Old Corner Bookstore—then owned by Doubleday Books—closed its Bromfield Street doors and the business, a victim of competition from huge bookstore chains.

In the decades after 1903, the building at the corner of School and Washington went through a variety of incarnations, from haberdashery to photo supply store. By 1960, the nearly unrecognizable, deteriorated structure hosted a pizza parlor and was plastered with billboards advertising "15 cents, Sliced Crispy Pizza" and the Boston Five Cents Savings Bank. Meanwhile, urban renewal was taking its toll on Boston. Certain developers viewed the Old Corner Bookstore building as worthless—and in a prime space for a downtown parking garage.

In response to the threat of demolition, a public-spirited group of Bostonians—including Athenaeum director Walter Muir Whitehill and John Codman, Chairman of the Beacon Hill Architectural Commission—organized the nonprofit organization Historic Boston Incorporated. With encouragement from the City of Boston, generous contributions of some $100,000 from dozens of private donors throughout the country, and a bank loan, HBI took the title to the Old Corner building on December 30, 1960. The cost was $275,000 for the entire L-shaped complex, which included both the expanded 1829 bookstore building and the attached Andrew Cunningham House (ca. 1722) at 277 Washington.

Historic Boston's goal was to prove that small, historic, commercial buildings did not have to be turned into museums that were exempt from city taxes and that such structures could indeed contribute to the city's tax base without sacrificing their historic uses and appearances. Hence, between 1960 and 1985, hundreds of thousands of dollars were used restoring the building's exterior to its mid-nineteenth-century look and modernizing its interior to accommodate contemporary needs for retail sales and office spaces. In the beginning, Historic Boston needed help to make this possible.

In 1965, the *Boston Globe* provided the answer. It lent Historic Boston money to repay its bank loan and agreed to restore the corner building in exchange for a long-term lease. For two decades, the *Globe* used the ground floor for in-town classified advertising offices, which were located amid a minimuseum of the bookstore's history. *Globe*-owned companies like the Globe Pequot Press and the Globe Corner Bookstore became tenants (both, incidentally, are now long gone from that site). The *Boston Globe* set up its own store space there in 1997 and continued to lease office space in the upper floors. The *Globe* also chose to provide some of their space to nonprofit philanthropic agencies like the Freedom Trail Foundation and the Boston Adult Literacy Fund.

As downtown commercial real estate values soared in the mid-1980s, the Old Corner building's value also increased. As result, it became the oil well, the nest egg, the endowment, and the home of Historic Boston Incorporated—supporting preservation projects in all parts of the city and providing a source of credibility for a charitable institution engaged in business transactions to preserve Boston's cultural heritage.

Today, hundreds of folks still bustle and browse through the old brick building at the corner of School and Washington. It's ironic that probably few of them know they're in a structure that needed saving less than five decades ago and is now dedicated to saving others. How many realize, moreover, that they're standing on a spot that was once home to radical Puritans, revolutionary publishers, crispy sliced pizza . . . and a potential parking garage!

THE ESSENTIALS

Address: The Old Corner Bookstore building is on the corner of School and Washington streets, Boston. Historic Boston Incorporated, 3 School Street, Boston, MA 02108. **Telephone:** Historic Boston Incorporated, (617) 227-4679. **Website:** www.historicboston.org. **Visitor Information:** Varied hours for businesses on ground floor of the building. No interior tours, though the building is included as a stop on several historic walking trails (see below). Some ground-floor shops are wheelchair accessible. No public restrooms.

The Old Corner Bookstore building is a stop on the Freedom Trail (see Chapter 10), the Literary Trail of Greater Boston, and the Boston Women's Heritage Trail (see Chapter 36).

27 The Boston Public Library

"BEAUTY AND THE BEAST" aren't only in fairy tales. They're also affectionate nicknames for that massive duet of buildings in bustling Copley Square officially known as the Boston Public Library. "Beauty," of course, is the McKim building, an elegant 1895 structure with an ornate facade inspired by the Italian Renaissance and a magnificent interior decorated by some of the country's leading artists. "The Beast" is the library's mammoth, modern, unadorned 1972 addition designed by architect Philip Johnson. One longtime library administrator offered an insider's perspective on this curious architectural non sequitur: "McKim's is the 'palace,' while Johnson built the addition to be a workable library—a fusion of a good architect and a librarian. And we're blessed to have both buildings."

Indeed, it's true. While the old McKim building resonates with marble staircases, majestic columns, vaulting arches, and artistic treasures, the modern Johnson structure sparkles with wide open spaces, wheelchair accessibility, functional design, and optimal light and ventilation. All things considered, an odd couple with conveniently compatible traits.

But architecture isn't everything—especially to an institution that's busy welcoming two million visitors a year. When it first opened its doors in 1854, the Boston Public Library was already the talk of the town. Though often touted as "America's first free public library," it was, more precisely, the first *major* free municipal library in the country. Still, it was and continues to be a quiet innovator. During the twentieth century, the BPL pioneered in circulating paperback books and offering services for elders. During the nineteenth century, it was the first public library to allow patrons to borrow materials, the first to issue an annual report of library trustees, and the first in the nation to develop branch libraries.

A major cultural and educational center for Boston since the turn of the twentieth century and a National Historic Landmark since 1973, the BPL currently sponsors five thousand free lectures, concerts, films, exhibits, and programs every year. It's one of only two public libraries qualified to belong to the Association of Research Libraries. Moreover, it's home to more than six million books, ninety special collections, and two million archival items, which include such diverse artifacts as a gold medal awarded to George Washington, the first book printed in the United States, and the memorabilia of comic Fred Allen—all kept in various chambers, nooks, and cases scattered about the two buildings. (Many of the archival images can now be viewed—and fine reproductions purchased—at www.bpl.org/store.)

Meanwhile, a tearoom, a full-service restaurant, and an efficient new connector between the McKim and Johnson buildings now grace the two-acre site as part of the McKim's $65 million restoration and renovation campaign. Hence, visitors can enjoy a unique dining experience in a spot

The old McKim building is resonant of nineteeth-century Boston, with marble stair-cases, vaulting arches, and artistic treasures.

that's a bibliophile's dream—sharing luncheon or high tea with a splendid view of the McKim's Italianate courtyard or sipping an espresso and nibbling on a fine salad in a space that was originally the library's map room.

In the 1840s, when the idea of a free public library in Boston began to take shape, the area already had two large book repositories—the Harvard College library, open to Harvard students and faculty, and the privately run Boston Athenaeum. Every proper nineteenth-century Bostonian had an Athenaeum card, it seems, since it was deemed as important a status symbol in Victorian Boston as a season subscription to the Boston Symphony or a family plot at Mount Auburn Cemetery.

So why did certain Brahmins and their colleagues—including such diverse characters as Athenaeum trustee George Ticknor and a quirky, controversial French visitor known worldwide as Monsieur Alexandre the Ventriloquist—want a free library, too? Part of their rationale was reactive: Boston was being flooded by new waves of immigrants, many of whom were illiterate; it was assumed that a public library would help provide the education needed for these new arrivals to become responsible, law-abiding, job-holding Bostonians. A second motive was more idealistic—the desire to create a cultural center accessible to all, where knowledge could be disseminated without charge. Such a concept was fully in keeping with Boston's long-standing status as a hub for progressive thought and action. The motto "Free to All," is still visible on the keystone of the McKim building's central arch, above Minerva's helmeted head.

The city was finally persuaded to found this much-discussed public library in 1852; in 1854, its doors opened on Mason Street, one block off the

Tremont Street side of Boston Common, though a move to larger quarters on Boylston was necessitated only four years later. In 1895, the very mobile Boston Public Library made one more move, to a Copley Square lot donated by the state. (Its former Boylston Street site was used for a zoo, which was in turn supplanted by the Colonial Theatre.)

The architect Charles Follen McKim, of the New York architectural firm McKim, Mead, and White, was commissioned to build the Copley Square "palace" for $1,165,000. In the end, he spent more than two and a half times that amount. The results were then—and still are today—appropriately lavish.

Built on pilings driven through slippery blue clay to the bedrock beneath, McKim's structure was a magnificent jewel. The granite Italian Renaissance revival facade, replete with chiseled dolphins, laurel wreaths, medallions, and lofty windows, took inspiration from three magnificent models: Bibliothèque Sainte-Geneviève in Paris, Tempio Malatestiano in Rimini, and, somewhat less glamorously, the Marshall Field Wholesale Store in Chicago. The entrance was guarded by Art and Science in the form of two heroic female figures sculpted by Bela Pratt. Three huge bronze doors in the vestibule, depicting Music and Poetry, Knowledge and Wisdom, and Truth and Romance, were designed by Daniel Chester French.

Inside, the vaulted Roman entrance hall was tiled with colorful mosaics with the names of famous Boston men embedded in the mosaic domes above. The noble stairway, crafted from yellow Sienna marble veined in black, was guarded by marble lions. The main reading room upstairs, called Bates Hall after a major library benefactor, was designed like a cavernous Roman bath, filled with oak tables and bookcases, and lavishly decorated with Italian Renaissance embellishments. (Benefactor Joshua Bates, who grew up in poverty, had taught himself to read in the back rooms of Boston's bookstores; as an adult and a senior partner in a major London banking firm, Bates delighted in creating his longtime dream, a grand reading room that would be open to the public, free of charge.) All of these figures, flourishes, and decorative motifs remain intact to this day.

Suffice it to say that from room to room and hallway to hallway, the majesty and the cost of the Copley Square palace kept escalating—escalating, that is, until the money ran out. As a result, longtime research supervisor Joseph O'Neil once explained, the rear of the McKim was much more "pedestrian" than the front.

Charles McKim spared no expense for the artists he employed to decorate the library's walls, halls, and galleries. The Parisian painter Puvis de Chavannes, for example, created the series of murals that top the Grand Staircase, including a main panel titled *The Muses of Inspiration Welcoming the Spirit of Light*. The imagery was Greek and the attitude typically Victorian. The crowd of hovering, gift-giving Muses were depicted as girls, while the object of their adoration, Enlightenment, was shown (in a decidedly unenlightened fashion) as a nude boy. The aging de Chavannes didn't come to Boston, incidentally, but made his murals in his Paris studio then shipped them stateside. As with all the other murals in the library, his works were painted on canvas then permanently adhered to the walls with white lead.

John Singer Sargent is also represented on the library's walls. Though best known for his portraits of the nineteenth century's rich and famous, Sargent decorated the gallery above de Chavannes's with an unusual series on the history of religion. Sargent created quite a stir in Boston when he depicted Judaism as a wounded, suffering being in contrast to the triumphant pose of Christianity. He also created a stir when he died unexpectedly in 1925. His central panel, *The Sermon on the Mount,* had not yet been painted. To this day, that middle space has been left blank, though we have a sense of Sargent's intended imagery, based on his rough sketches, or cartoons, which are displayed in a chamber off the Wiggin Print Gallery.

Other conspicuously blank walls in the McKim are found in the archways and the Boylston Street end of Bates Hall. The London-based painter James McNeill Whistler was supposed to paint the framed horizontal panel at the hall's end, but that contract fell through. John La Farge, a painter and stained-glass artist, was then offered the commission, but he declined it—and no other artist was ever hired. Given the difficulty of altering a National Historic Landmark today, the space will probably remain blank forever.

To no one's surprise, virtually all the engraved names, statues, and busts throughout the McKim are tributes to men. One important exception is in Bates Hall, where feminist Lucy Stone and physician Elizabeth Blackwell are among those commemorated with busts. Another exception, in a backhanded sort of way, is the ceiling mural in the Elliott Room. Joseph O'Neil used to enjoy explaining that each of the winged female figures in the *Triumph of Time* mural was modeled after a Boston debutante of the day. "See that lantern jaw?" he'd ask as he pointed to one angel. "I bet she's a Saltonstall!"

A more recent acquisition, now on display in the lobby of the BPL's Johnson Building, is a 1980 mural by Ellen Lanyon called *Notable Women of Boston.* The ambitious work spans almost four centuries and commemorates nine Boston women: Anne Hutchinson (1591–1643), Phillis Wheatley (1753–1784), Sister Ann Alexis (1805–1875), Lucy Stone (1818–1893), Mary Baker Eddy (1821–1910), Ellen Richards (1842–1911), Mary Morton Kehew (1859–1918), Anne Sullivan (1866–1936), and Melnea Cass (1896–1978).

The library's Venetian-inspired, open-air courtyard is a favorite green oasis for the city-worn and study-weary. Since the year 2000, the central fountain has again been graced with a famous piece of art once associated with the Boston Public Library but curiously absent for more than a century—Frederic MacMonnies's *Bacchante with Infant Faun.*

When the statue was installed in 1896, an immediate furor arose; it was allegedly immoral (Bacchante was naked, and maybe even a strumpet) and promoted intemperance (the statue represented a celebrant of riotous intoxication). National and local periodicals weighed in with their opinions, some serious and others more tongue-in-cheek. In the latter category was the *Boston Globe,* which recommended that McKim replace

Bacchante with "a nice moral statue—of a Sunday school teacher, say." Eventually, the Puritan ethic won out and *Bacchante* was banned in Boston. McKim donated the statue to the Metropolitan Museum of Art in New York, while the Museum of Fine Arts, Boston, retained a bronze replica. As for the BPL's central fountain, it remained conspicuously sans statue. In 1993, as part of the BPL's late-twentieth-century restoration project, a bronze recasting of the MFA's *Bacchante* was made. The recast statue was installed seven years later, in accordance with McKim's original design. (The whole McKim building courtyard was renovated as well, with new landscaping, painting, fountain restoration, cleaning and repairing of the masonry, and the addition of handicap accessibility.)

It's curious that *Bacchante* was banished while the seal of the BPL—featuring two beautiful nude boys with a shield, an open book, a batch of dolphins, and laurel—survived, albeit amid another uproar. Some speculate that the seal, or its most prominent version above the McKim's central outdoor archway, may simply have been too hard to remove.

The most unusual artwork in the McKim building may well be the intricately composed miniature dioramas created by Louise Stimson (1890–1981). Stimson was born in Brooklyn Heights, New York, but spent forty years as an artist in Concord, Massachusetts. She created almost fifty historical dioramas from the 1940s to the 1960s. The project reportedly began as a way to amuse Stimson's older sister, who was bedridden most of her life. Fortunately, many of the final products—including *The London of Charles Dickens, Alice in Wonderland, Arabian Nights,* and *Printmakers at Work*—were donated to the library. Each three-dimensional scene, fabricated from cardboard, paper, and other accessible household sundries, is a "living picture" representing an episode from a famous book or imagining the creation process of well-known art prints. As you move from one scene to the next, you'll find—in Alice's Wonderland words—that Stimson's dioramas get "curiouser and curiouser." They are arguably the best conversation pieces in the library. (When this book went to press, the dioramas were still out for restoration; check the BPL's website for news of their return.)

The art and architectural glories of the Boston Public Library are appropriately matched by its seemingly infinite resources. The library's 6 million volumes—with 250,000 new books added each year—rest on some sixty-five miles of bookshelves. Each floor of stacks is one acre in size and holds nearly a million pounds of books on more than 22,000 shelves. Meanwhile, the library stores nearly 10 million patents, 3 million government documents, 120,000 musical scores, 8,500 sixteen-millimeter films, 400,000 archival drawings, 75,000 prints, drawings, and watercolors, 350,000 maps, 400 online databases, and 4.5 million units of microfilm—making the BPL the largest pubic research library in New England.

Appreciating certain Boston Public Library attractions, however, requires some special inside knowledge. For example, some staff members love the archives of old architectural drawings and bridge plans stowed in the Johnson building's upper floors. Others delight in the architectural wonders of the Johnson addition, constructed for $24 million in 1972: its curious "hanging floors," innovative indoor "bridges," and sturdy beams, all allowing optimum open space and flexibility and better service for the public. (Today, the Johnson building serves as the general library, enabling the McKim Building to house research collections.)

Others are thrilled by the changes brought on by new library technologies, such as audiovisuals and the widespread use of microcomputers. The BPL offers many computers for public use—visitors easily take advantage of the wireless technology offered in the main library and all its branches. Moreover, the Johnson building's Access Center offers sophisticated services for those with special needs, including speech-automated software and machines that translate Braille.

It's perhaps surprising that so-called antiquated technologies have held their own at the BPL as well. An old pneumatic tube system, for instance, which takes book request slips to and from the stacks, is as practical in the twenty-first century as the day the library opened. Research books themselves travel from the stacks to the circulation desk via a conveyor belt built in the 1950s (some believe the old "miniature railway" system the conveyor belt replaced functioned far better).

Today, though it bears the city's name, the Boston Public Library is open to all residents of the state. Moreover, neighborhoods are serviced by its twenty-six smaller branch libraries and the downtown Kirstein Business Library. In its ongoing efforts to reach the widest possible audience, special facilities have been developed in the Johnson building to accommodate children, young adults, non-English-speaking people, senior citizens, and the physically handicapped. Some forty-five languages are represented in the mezzanine-level foreign language section. More than a hundred copies of the classic Boston children's book *Make Way for Ducklings* are on hand, including one in Braille.

It's a far cry from the nineteenth century, when no such amenities existed. Kids, in particular, were *persona non grata* at the original BPL. Old rule books explain that in 1854 no one under the age of sixteen was welcome. By 1896 the age minimum was lowered to twelve. The 1896 book also warned that "all annoying and disagreeable behavior, such as hawking, spitting on the floor, humming, whistling, whispering, is strictly prohibited."

Come to think of it, not a bad idea at all.

THE ESSENTIALS

Address: 700 Boylston Street, Copley Square, Boston, MA 02117. **Telephone:** (617) 536-5400. **Website:** www.bpl.org. **Visitor Information:** Open 9:00 A.M. to 9:00 P.M., Monday through Thursday; 9:00 A.M. to 5:00 P.M., Friday and Saturday; closed Sundays and all legal holidays. Free hour-long tours of the BPL given Mondays at 2:30 P.M., Tuesdays and Thursdays at 6:00 P.M., and Fridays and Saturdays at 11:00 A.M.; call to confirm. Johnson building completely wheelchair accessible; McKim accessible with assistance; all restrooms accessible.

Two new restaurants, operated by Sebastians Café and Catering, are available to patrons: Novel features a luncheon buffet and afternoon tea; open Monday through Friday, 11:30 A.M. to 4:30 P.M.; and Sebastians Map Room Café offers breakfast, lunch, and snacks; open 9:00 A.M. to 5:00 P.M., Monday through Saturday; for lunch reservations call (617) 385-5660.

The Boston Public Library is a stop on the Literary Trail of Greater Boston and the Boston Women's Heritage Trail (see Chapter 36). Details at www.lit-trail.org and www .bwht.org.

28 The Parker House

THE FAMED Parker House is arguably the grand dame of Boston hotels and *the* downtown hotel of choice for historic-minded Bostonians. And it's not simply because it's the only Boston lodging set directly on the Freedom Trail. Just mention its name and a century and a half of rich and varied history comes to mind. Moreover, it's a compelling, contemporary, full-service hotel that has meticulously maintained its nineteenth-century charms and sense of history.

Located at the junction of Tremont and School streets, the Parker House—now part of the international family of Omni Hotels—is the oldest of Boston's elegant inns, as well as the longest continuously operating hotel in America. One of its great claims to fame is as the nineteenth-century meeting place of the Saturday Club, a monthly gathering of literary giants such as Ralph Waldo Emerson, Nathaniel Hawthorne, and Henry Wadsworth Longfellow. The Parker House is also celebrated for its contributions to American cuisine—most notably, the fluffy Parker House roll, invented in Parker kitchens by a nineteenth-century German baker named Ward, and Boston cream pie, now the official dessert of the state of Massachusetts.

First opened by Harvey D. Parker in 1855, the historic hotel has had more than its share of famous patrons over the decades. Mayor James Michael Curley, Senator John Fitzgerald Kennedy, art patron Isabella Stewart Gardner, and baseball greats Ted Williams and Babe Ruth regularly dined there. Authors Charles Dickens and Willa Cather each lived there for a time; actress Charlotte Cushman and one of Jimmy Hoffa's lieutenants *died* there. Other prestigious lodgers have ranged from Sarah Bernhardt, Joan Crawford, Elizabeth Cady Stanton, and Ulysses S. Grant to John Wilkes Booth, William "Hopalong Cassidy" Boyd, Adam "Batman" West, and Kelsey Grammer. Malcolm X once worked there as a busboy, and Ho Chi Minh was employed as a baker. As if all that weren't impressive enough, that nineteenth-century man of letters Oliver Wendell Holmes even penned some light verse about the place. Which is all meant to suggest that the Parker House has enough history and charm to last a lifetime.

In colonial Boston, there were no hotels in the contemporary sense of the word. Instead, local taverns and inns provided rest stops for weary travelers—colonial males, for the most part, whose major interest seems to have been the quaffing of multitudinous pints of colonial beer.

As these precursors to the modern hotel developed beyond simple tap-rooms, however, they began to call themselves "houses." One of the most luxurious of these lodging and dining houses, built on the edge of Beacon Hill in 1828, was the Tremont (no relation to the Boston hotel that now bears that name). Over the next twenty years, competitors emerged around Boston—including the American House, the Shawmut, the Adams, and the handsome Revere House.

In 1825, a twenty-year-old farm boy named Harvey D. Parker arrived in Boston Harbor on a packet from Maine. With less than a dollar in his satchel, Parker immediately sought employment. His first job, as a care-taker for a horse and cow, brought him eight dollars a month. A subse-quent vocation as coachman for a Watertown woman provided even higher earnings.

Whenever Parker and the coach were in Boston, the young man ate his noonday meal at John E. Hunt's dark cellar café at 4 Court Square. He be-came so enamored of the café that in 1832 he purchased it for $432. After renaming it Parker's Restaurant, he began to attract a regular clientele of lawyers, newsmen, and businessmen, who appreciated Parker's combina-tion of excellent food and perfect service. In 1847, Parker chose John F. Mills as a partner. And by 1854, he was ready to embark on a grander en-terprise.

Parker wanted to build a new, first-class hotel and restaurant, and he wanted to build it a stone's throw from the successful Tremont House. The site Parker purchased on April 22, 1854, was on School Street, just south-east of the Tremont-Beacon junction where the Tremont House stood. Parker's lot already had a lodging of sorts—a decrepit boardinghouse known as the Boylston Hotel, which had once been the fine 1704 mansion of John Mico. Parker razed the old structure and built in its stead a glori-ous five-story, marble-fronted hotel he initially called Parker's. (After a se-ries of negotiations and sales over the next two decades, Parker eventually owned the bulk of the land bordered by Tremont, School, and Bosworth streets and Chapman Place.)

Despite the nearby competitor, the location was ideal. Once a narrow lane flanked by wooden homes, barns, livery stables, gardens, orchards, small shops, churches, and the famous Boston Latin School, School Street had already developed into a classy, much-traveled thoroughfare by the mid-nineteenth century. Next door to Parker's was the granite Horticul-tural Hall (on the former site of Boston Latin, America's first public school), which Parker purchased and demolished in 1860 to create his lofty east wing. (The Massachusetts Horticultural Society subsequently moved Horticultural Hall twice; the second site, facing Symphony Hall, became its permanent home in 1901.) Across School Street was King's Chapel; next to it, a French Empire–style City Hall would be built in 1865. At the other end of School Street was the 1829 Old Corner Bookstore, a magnet for poets, authors, and philosophers. And just a brief walk up School and Bea-con streets was the seat of state government. That Parker's became situated on the "hot line" between the State House and City Hall was a fortuitous accident, perhaps—but it ensured regular governmental clientele for more than a century.

The excellence that came to be associated with Parker's in-house restaurants was no accident at all. In a day when a good Boston cook could be hired for $8 per week, or $416 a year, Parker paid a gourmet French chef named Sanzian the astonishing annual salary of $5,000. The investment paid off; Sanzian's versatile menu drew continual accolades and large crowds. In another innovation, Parker implemented the "European Plan," which separated charges for food and lodging, allowing guests more flexibility. Moreover, though most hotels of the era had fixed dining hours, Parker made food available at any time during the day or evening. Added to his business acumen was Parker's attitude. He was the ultimate host, lavishing personal attention on every detail.

On May 31, 1884, after guiding his hotel and restaurants to world renown, Parker died. The Maine farm boy who had arrived in Boston with less than a dollar in 1825 had a net worth of $1,272,546.94 when he drew his last breath. His hotel's fame is documented in the *King's Handbook* of 1885, which described Parker's as one of the finest restaurants in the United States, with "a central location, sumptuous equipment, and ancient prestige." Gentlemen, the book explained, were provided a great dining room and fine basement billiard room; ladies had their own café; politi-

The historic Omni Parker House, the "grande dame of Boston Hotels," was home to the Saturday Club and the Parker House roll.

cians and businessmen were provided a rendezvous; and the 260 well-designed guest rooms ranged from one to five dollars a night, with luxury suites at eight to twelve dollars.

Fine food, superior service, fair prices, elegant surroundings, and an ideal location all brought the Parker House a clientele that included poets, philosophers, politicians, and performers. Many nineteenth-century actors were familiar with the neighborhood before the hotel was even built. The popular Tremont Theater (1828–43), which later became the Tremont Temple Baptist Church, was around the corner, and several other legitimate stages were but a few blocks away. In the nineteenth century, Parker's guests included world-class actors such as Sarah Bernhardt, Adelina Patti, Ellen Terry, Charlotte Cushman, Richard Mansfield, Henry Irving, Augustin Daly, and Edwin Booth.

One of the theater-world guests Parker rarely discussed was actor Edwin Booth's younger brother. John Wilkes Booth arrived at the hotel in April 1865, visiting Boston while his sibling performed on a downtown stage. While residing at Parker's, John Wilkes practiced his pistol aim in a cellar shooting gallery at the corner of Chapman and School streets. Eight days after departing, he assassinated President Lincoln at Ford's Theater in Washington.

In a 1992 *Boston Globe* interview, John Brehm—a retired bellman who had been a Parker House employee from 1941 to 1993—remembered another type of performer who frequented the hotel. "In the 1940s we still had 'permanent guests'—guests who lived here for months, or years, at a time. All the hotels did, until it was phased out in the decade after the war. In the '40s and '50s burlesque queens stayed here, because we were the nicest hotel in the area, and so close to Scollay Square, the Old Howard, and the Casino." (Boisterous Scollay Square and its popular, seedy burlesque theaters all disappeared in the 1960s, before and during the construction of Government Center.) "I recall one woman named Lois de Fee, who was huge—six feet four inches tall!—and walked her little Pekinese dog on a twenty-foot leash! . . . They were all good tippers." Brehm was also a bellman when powerful, charismatic politicians from Mayor James Michael Curley to Senator John Fitzgerald Kennedy paid regular visits to the hotel. According to Brehm, Curley lunched daily in the main dining room and tipped in silver dollars. Kennedy chose the Parker House to announce his candidacy for the U.S. Congress in 1946, and to host his bachelor party in 1954.

Until the construction of Boston's new city hall and Government Center in the late 1960s—which left the hotel off the new path from City Hall to the State House—political "power breakfasts" and meetings were part of the Parker fabric. So too were reporters and editors from old Newspaper Row, legal eagles from Pemberton Square courthouses, financiers from the banks near Post Office Square, students from Harvard, and traveling baseball umpires. There were even visits from Red Sox slugger Ted Williams, who was once engaged to a woman who worked in Parker's now-defunct Paul Revere Room. Many of these famous men, women, and events are depicted in the historic photos on the walls of one of the hotel's restaurants, the Last Hurrah. Other memorabilia from the Parker House's past are displayed in glass cases in the main lobby.

Of all the famous guests, the most illustrious certainly came as part of the nineteenth-century Boston men's social gathering known as the Saturday Club. Originating in the Literary Club and the Magazine Club, two private associations of the mid-1850s, the Saturday Club began as a small group of friends who held festive roundtables on the last Saturday afternoon of every month. Philosopher and preeminent transcendentalist Ralph Waldo Emerson, poet and *Atlantic Monthly* editor James Russell Lowell, and scientist Louis Agassiz were soon joined by novelist Nathaniel Hawthorne, poets John Greenleaf Whittier and Henry Wadsworth Longfellow, diplomat Charles Francis Adams, historian Francis Parkman, sage-about-town Dr. Oliver Wendell Holmes, and many others.

The Saturday Club's afternoons were taken up with poetry readings and book critiques, gossip and discussions, seven-course meals and free-flowing elixirs. Visiting British novelist Charles Dickens, who resided at the Parker House during his 1867–68 American lecture tour, joined club members for their November 30, 1867, meeting. The colorful Dickens, who died two years later, preened and practiced his animated talks in front of a large mirror that now rests in the mezzanine level hall by the Press Room. Artifacts from his stay were long kept on display in the Dickens Room. Today, that room is used for meetings and dining, but it still holds the marble fireplace mantel Dickens used. Other famous guests—from Hawthorne to Holmes, and John F. Kennedy to Martin Luther King—are likewise remembered in meeting room names along the mezzanine and lobby level.

(At the turn of the twentieth century, actor Gerald Charles Dickens—great-great-grandson of the novelist—reminisced at the Omni Parker House while appearing in a critically acclaimed one-man rendition of *A Christmas Carol* at Tremont Temple, the same place great-great-granddad played the tale to an audience that included Henry Wadsworth Longfellow and Oliver Wendell Holmes, Sr.)

Though the Parker House still maintains the nineteenth-century charms, comforts, and fine foods that Dickens and the Saturday Club enjoyed, much has changed. When Harvey Parker died in 1884, only his wife, Julia Ann Parker, survived him. His original partner, John F. Mills, had passed away, as had both of Parker's sons—one at age ten and the second, lost at sea, at age twenty-four. Per the instructions of Parker's will, the building was leased to his later partners, Edward O. Punchard and Joseph H. Beckman, who added a new wing, annex, and elaborate exterior decorations. Roxbury grocer Joseph Reed Whipple, who had worked under the supervision of John F. Mills, took over in the 1890s. Though Whipple died in 1912, the J. R. Whipple Corporation bought the hotel from the Trustees of the Parker Estate in 1925.

To the horror of many, the Whipple Corporation demolished Harvey Parker's old "marble palace" and built in its stead the "new" Parker House —essentially, the one we know today—which opened on May 12, 1927. Designed by G. Henri Desmond of Desmond & Lord, the 1927 version was arguably more beautiful than its predecessor. Built fourteen stories high, with polished Quincy granite on the exterior, it featured lush, ornamented public chambers with oak paneling, plastered ceilings, crystal chandeliers, bronze-detailed doors, and eight hundred guest rooms. Even today, the lobbies—with their dark little enclaves resembling private club rooms—retain a comforting nineteenth-century beauty.

Through the hotel's subsequent owners—Glenwood Sherrard in 1933, the beloved Dunfey family in 1968, and, most recently, Omni Hotels—the Parker House has had its ups and downs, its changes, additions, and alterations. Beginning in 1927, the old basement billiard room was converted to casual restaurants like the English Grille room, then the Last Hurrah, and now a spiffy new fitness center. The mezzanine-level lobby lounge, landing, and reading library gave way to the cozy Parker Bar. The magical rooftop terrace of 1935—closed in 1969, when taller downtown buildings outstripped its height and aerial view—now hosts special functions as the only rooftop ballroom in the city. The spirit of the Saturday Club was even rekindled in the New England Circle, private evening gatherings begun by the Dunfeys in 1974 and continuing to this day.

Bowing to modern needs for space, the 800 guest chambers of 1927 have been restructured into 551 larger, though sometimes oddly shaped, rooms and suites. Chambers that once featured four-channel radios now have multichannel color television sets and high-speed Internet access. Room furnishings, decor, utilities, and services have been upgraded and adapted to each new era, while the staff that included 600 in 1941 has shrunk to 334. The faces of Parker House waitstaff have changed, too—from mainly Irish, to predominantly African-American, to today's multicultural mix—though their attentiveness and hospitality have remained constant.

In the nineteenth century, Harvey Parker and his successors ensured the excellence of Parker's dining experience by hiring European chefs like Sanzian and Bonello and bakers like Ward. In the twentieth and twenty-first centuries, that tradition continues. Executive chef Gerry Tice is part of a long line of restaurant stars—including Joseph Ribas, Lydia Shire, Jasper White, Emeril Lagasse, and Paul O'Connell—who all directed or creatively cooked in Parker's kitchens while sharpening their culinary craft. As a result, fine food is still available at Parker's, in its restaurants or via room service, from five-thirty in the morning to ten o'clock at night (twenty-four hours a day in the case of room service).

Aromatic Parker House rolls are still served, piping hot and free of charge, to diners. (Their ingredients became public knowledge after 1933, the year Franklin and Eleanor Roosevelt requested the recipe be sent to them in Washington). Boston cream pie, which was perfected at Parker's beginning in 1871, is another "historic" specialty still popular today. So too is scrod—a term that, according to legend, was coined in the Parker kitchens. Scrod, incidentally, is not a type of fish; the word is used for cod or other white-fleshed fish that are either the youngest, freshest, or smallest of the day's catch.

Today, the Parker House still attracts a down-to-earth crowd of businesspeople, vacationing families, and conference-goers, and its restaurants continue to draw local professionals and politicians. Tourists, of course, are enamored by its gentle aura of historic import, as well as its convenient location on the Freedom Trail. And who knows how many are enticed to visit by these words from Oliver Wendell Holmes's "At the Saturday Club," written a century ago:

> Such feasts! The laughs of many a jocund hour
> That shook the mortar from King George's tower;
> Such guests! What famous names its record boasts,
> Whose owners wander in the mob of ghosts!

THE ESSENTIALS

Address: 60 School Street, Boston, MA 02108; corner of School and Tremont streets. **Telephone:** (617) 227-8600 or (800) THE-OMNI. **Website:** www.omniparkerhouse.com. **Visitor Information:** Open twenty-four hours a day, 365 days a year. Food is available through restaurant outlets from 5:30 A.M. to 10:00 P.M., or via round-the-clock room service. Call hotel for room prices. Lobby is wheelchair accessible at Tremont Street entrance; passenger elevators access most areas, though service elevator is needed to reach the ballroom; accessible guest rooms and restrooms are available.

The Omni Parker House is the first stop on the Literary Trail of Greater Boston; information at www.lit-trail.org.

29 Louisburg Square

SINCE THE mid-nineteenth century, the green garden of Louisburg Square has been a welcome surprise among the endless red bricks of Beacon Hill. One of Boston's finest residential neighborhoods, the square is neatly lodged between Pinckney and Mount Vernon streets—a shady urban oasis filled with handsome red-brick Greek revival houses facing a meticulously maintained private park and cobblestone roadway.

Lyrically lovely as it may be, Louisburg Square is not just another pretty place. For starters, this short Beacon Hill block has been home to some of Boston's finest writers. In recent decades, those residents have included Robin Cook, author of medical thrillers such as *Coma* and *Outbreak*, and Pulitzer Prize–winning poet and playwright Archibald MacLeish. A century ago, historian John Gorham Palfrey, author of *The History of New England* and owner/editor of the *North American Review*, lived at number 5. William Dean Howells, novelist and editor of the *Atlantic Monthly*, lived first at number 16, then at 4, from 1882 to 1884. Howells frequently entertained and discussed literature with novelist Henry James inside number 16, and began writing his master work, *The Rise of Silas Lapham*, while residing on the square. Editor, biographer, poet, and antiquarian M. A. (Mark Antony) DeWolfe Howe—whose many books on Boston history included *Memories of a Hostess, Letters of Charles Eliot Norton*, and the

A meticulously maintained private park and cobblestone roadway are at the center of the very exclusive and very historic Louisburg Square.

Pulitzer Prize–winning *Barrett Wendell and His Letters*—also had a home at that same number 16.

Most popularly renowned of the Louisburg literati is certainly Louisa May Alcott, who, along with her father, Bronson, lived at number 10 between 1885 and 1888. Louisa had already won fame and fortune from her writings, especially *Little Women*, which literally rescued her family from poverty. The relocation to Louisburg Square was both evidence of her success and the last of her many moves; she died in the spring of 1888, two days after her father's demise.

A second major significance of the square is its history, which in some respects goes back further than the city itself. That history may have begun with William Blackstone (or Blaxton), the first European settler in the place that became Boston. Blackstone was an eccentric Anglican clergyman who arrived on the Shawmut peninsula with Robert Gorges's expedition in 1623 and remained when the others returned home. He settled on a hill (Beacon Hill), found a freshwater spring on a spot some historians identify as modern Louisburg Square, and enjoyed a hermit's life, drinking, reading from his large library, and riding his white bull across what would later be called Boston Common.

Blackstone himself was immortalized by poet and novelist Conrad Aiken in his 1947 poem, "The Kid." Moreover, Blackstone's freshwater fountain became the source of wonderful urban legends for centuries to come. In the late nineteenth century, Dr. Edward Everett Hale said that every resident of Louisburg Square claimed to have the original Blackstone spring in his cellar. In Robert McCloskey's *Make Way for Ducklings*, however, Mr. and Mrs. Mallard pondered raising their ducklings in the Square, then abandoned the thought since "there was no water to swim in." Clearly, things had fairly well dried up by the middle of the twentieth century.

But let's return again to 1630. Governor John Winthrop and the Puritans of the Massachusetts Bay Colony had settled in nearby Charlestown but were disturbed by its impure waters. Blackstone invited Winthrop et al to share the Shawmut peninsula and partake of its potable springs. The Puritans came—and proceeded to found the town of Boston. The eccentric Blackstone soon became claustrophobic and moved to the more rural countryside. Despite the "overcrowding" that offended the hermit in 1630, the area we now know as Louisburg Square—like much of Beacon Hill—remained upland pasture for Boston's first 150 years. It eventually became part of the farmland owned by painter John Singleton Copley.

When the new state house designed by architect Charles Bulfinch was being planned on the slopes of Beacon Hill, developers saw the potential to turn the rest of the hill's rural acreage into fine residences. In 1796, a syndicate called the Mount Vernon Proprietors bought Copley's farm for $18,450. At the time, Bulfinch sketched street plans for Beacon Hill, which included a large square inspired by the elegant residential squares of London. Thirty years later, surveyor Stephen P. Fuller drew up the manicured streetscape of Louisburg Square, possibly based on Bulfinch's earlier plans. Whatever the source, the London look was still there, so much so, in fact, that when Hollywood filmmakers wanted to replicate Russell Square for their filming of William Thackeray's *Vanity Fair* in 1915 (the second of four silent films made based on that same novel), they chose Louisburg Square as their shooting location.

When the hillside square was finally developed between 1826 and 1847, it was called Louisburg (pronounced as the English "Lewis," not the French "Lou-ie"). The name allegedly commemorates a 1745 battle in which Massachusetts colonials helped capture the "impregnable" French-Canadian fortress of Louisbourg, thereby securing the Atlantic seaboard for England. (The victory's exact connection to the square is unclear. One legend says that Blackstone's grandson was killed in the battle. Others offer a more ironic interpretation: that Louisburg Square, like the French fort, was built to be impenetrable by the outside world.)

Between 1834 and 1847, a variety of housewrights built the stately row houses we see today—orderly lines of harmonious, shoulder-to-shoulder brick homes. Though each had its distinct characteristics, trends did occur, partly because the structures were often built in pairs or larger multiples. The houses at numbers 2 through 22 generally have three stories and bow fronts. The upper, odd-numbered side of the square features more flat-faced, four-story structures. Red-brick exteriors, iron fencing, stone front steps—and, in later years, shutters and gas street lamps—all added to these buildings' charms. As with most Beacon Hill residences, the homes were built fairly narrow and multileveled, with staircases connecting the floors.

In 1844, when all but a few lots had been filled, the homeowners formed the Proprietors of Louisburg Square—a prototypical civic association that functions to this day, and which includes several adjoining houses on Pinckney Street. Annual dues are used for maintenance of the private way, the partly cobbled, partly paved strips connecting Mount Vernon and Pinckney. Dues also cover the promise of two parking spaces per home, and the care of the fenced central park. From 1844 to the present day, incidentally, Louisburg Square has remained a city within a city, a privately owned property that issues its own parking tickets and tows away transgressors.

Despite plant diseases, storms, and the noxious fumes of city life, the oval park at the square's center is still lush and green, filled with grand old elms, honey locusts, rhododendron, mountain laurels, and other plants and flowers. The garden also includes two small, semiobscured Florentine marble statues, one of Athenian statesman Aristides the Just, the other of Christopher Columbus. The statues were donated by ship owner and merchant Joseph Iasigi, who lived at number 3 in the mid-nineteenth century. Suffice it to say that the statues' artistic merits and historic significance have eluded critics for decades.

Over the years, a fascinating and eclectic group of people molded Louisburg Square into a unique Beacon Hill community. And for generations they maintained its distinctive holiday traditions, from strolling carolers and handbell ringers to candlelit windows and informal open houses. Granted, purists will say that Christmas Eve street caroling began at the nearby Church of the Advent early in the nineteenth century and then spilled onto Louisburg Square and the rest of Beacon Hill. West Cedar Street residents claim to have originated the concept of the candlelit window in the 1890s. Still, all these traditions were somehow more compacted, more noted and noticeable, in the brief block of Louisburg Square. One person to notice was poet Sylvia Plath, who lived a block from Louisburg Square in 1958. Though her poems were often impassioned and angry, one of her lighter verses saluted the hill's off-key Christmas carolers and odd violet-paned windows.

Just who were the square's residents over the years? Some were Brahmins and bluebloods with recognizable family names such as Cabot and Vanderbilt. Some were students, writers, artists, judges, and other professional people. Some were celebrities who were just passing through. Singer Jenny Lind, for example, renowned in the nineteenth century as the "Swedish Nightingale," was married at number 20, in the townhouse of Samuel Gray Ward. Ward was, among other things, a founder of the Boston's prestigious Saturday Club and Union Club, and a prominent banker who raised the cash for the United States to buy Alaska from Russia. (He was not, however, the brother of Julia Ward Howe—that was a different banker, also named Samuel Ward.) Another famed guest was the future King Edward VII of England, who made merry at number 19 at an 1860 bash touted as "the grandest party in Boston in the nineteenth century."

The home belonged to Boston's Civil War–era mayor, Frederick Lincoln. The "family" that lived in Louisburg Square the longest was the Anglican convent of the Society of Saint Margaret, whose gentle, social service–oriented sisters occupied numbers 13 through 19 for more than a hundred years before leaving for Roxbury in 1990. (One section of Saint Margaret's, number 19, is now the Boston residence of U.S. senator John Kerry of Massachusetts and his wife, philanthropist Teresa Heinz Kerry.)

Today, about half of the Louisburg Square residences are single-family homes. The rest have either been split and made into condominiums, or are owner-occupied, with the owner residing in a portion of the house and renting out the rest. Economic reality has clearly caused the latter: homes that might have sold for $18,000 in the late Victorian era soared to $4 or $5 million by 2003. Hence, both purchase prices and city taxes on these sites are astronomical.

Despite its aura of impenetrability, the square has seen a bit of disruption, much like any other residential neighborhood. The first such intrusion was probably in 1850, when overzealous boys knocked off one of Columbus's fingers; barricades were periodically put up at the street's ends in the last half of the nineteenth century to prevent such transgressions. In 1962, the square was more seriously shaken when a young female resident from a reputable family fatally shot her errant boyfriend in the gory episode known as the Debutante Murder. Though Albert de Salvo never murdered anyone on Louisburg Square, the self-avowed Boston Strangler apparently cruised the area during his notorious 1962–64 spree: two of his female victims were killed only blocks away. By the 1990s, the tremors were more cosmetic than cataclysmic: when Celtics co-owner Don Gaston installed a high-tech satellite dish at his number 14 home in 1991, you'd have thought, from the accompanying uproar, he'd applied vinyl siding to his brick abode.

Despite these fusses—some petty, some real—the allure of Louisburg Square remains. What's changed since the early 1980s, however, is the profile of its residents. Skyrocketing real estate prices have ensured that mostly multimillionaires buy homes on Beacon Hill today. And while high-income residents have pretty much ensured that their historic homes remain in good condition, many of these newcomers—young, rich, and seldom home—have let the sense of community, and the beloved holiday traditions, slide away. Nevertheless, according to one longtime resident, "the Hill is still quite cohesive for a city."

With its beautifully maintained grass and trees, its prim homes, and its textures of brick and cobblestone, Louisburg Square looks much as it did a century back, save, of course, for the automobiles. Very few residential neighborhoods in Boston—or anywhere else, for that matter—can truthfully say the same.

THE ESSENTIALS

Address: Between Pinckney and Mount Vernon streets, Beacon Hill, Boston, MA. **Visitor Information:** Louisburg Square is a private roadway and residential area. Square itself accessible twenty-four hours a day, 365 days per year, free; homes are open only by personal invitation of a resident.

Several local tour groups, however, offer seasonal guided tours of Beacon Hill that include Louisburg Square; among the best are Boston by Foot, (617) 367-2345 (24-hour Hot Foot line, 617-367-3766, website www.bostonbyfoot.com) and Historic Neighborhoods, (617) 426-1885. Moderate tour fees. Louisburg Square is also part of self-guided historic tours including the Literary Trail of Greater Boston (www.lit-trail.org) and the Boston Women's Heritage Trail (www.bwht.org).

Wheelchair access often difficult, due to rough surfaces.

30 Walden Pond

EACH YEAR, more than half a million people visit Walden Pond State Reservation, a beautiful, wooded site that spans 411 acres in the suburban towns of Concord and Lincoln. Many, of course, come simply to enjoy the swimming, picnicking, hiking, fishing, boating, skating, and cross-country skiing available on the lake and in the surrounding woods. Walden Pond, after all, has served Greater Boston as a popular recreation area since the end of the Civil War. Today the area's many offerings have expanded to include ten miles of established trails, summer-season lifeguards, and a pond stocked with thousands of rainbow and brook trout, provided by the state's Fisheries and Wildlife Division.

Still, recreation is hardly the only reason to visit this bucolic retreat. Since the late nineteenth century, scholars, poets, social activists, nature lovers, and rugged individualists have taken the half-mile trek to one specific spot on a far, wooded corner of the pond. Their pilgrimage ends at the site where writer and philosopher Henry David Thoreau once lived in a rustic house—a sojourn chronicled in his 1854 classic, *Walden*. A replica of Thoreau's tiny house stands near the entrance of the reservation's parking lot, sparsely furnished with bed, desk, chair and woodstove, but purists and pilgrims insist on seeing the original location, too. Some drop commemorative stones on the cairn that Bronson Alcott and Mary Adams began there in 1872. Others stare and ponder the rough outline of the long-gone house's foundation, wondering at the life and thoughts Thoreau engaged in there between 1845 and 1847.

All of this is meant to suggest that there's a lot more at Walden Pond than initially meets the eye.

It's perhaps appropriate that Walden Pond has served as a stage for so many different types of players over the years, since it's located in a natural amphitheater. First-time visitors are often stunned by the site's dramatic bowl-like form: woods and paths descend to smooth blue-green waters, as the pond's warm, flat sandbars suddenly give way to chillier depths of up to a hundred feet. The shape is actually a "kettle hole," molded during the end of the ice age some ten thousand years ago, when an enormous chunk of ice broke off from a retreating glacier. Streams of melting water

The pond that inspired Thoreau's *Walden* has been a popular recreation area since the end of the Civil War.

gradually surrounded the glacial remnant with gravel and sand deposits, forming the steep sides of today's basin. Emerson Cliff, a wooded hillside to the left of Walden Pond's main beach, is a glacial outcropping created during that period. The hill was named for Ralph Waldo Emerson, who bought the land in 1844 for a mere eight dollars an acre, to protect the woods from timbering.

Though Native Americans passed through the area for several thousand years, leaving plenty of arrowheads, artifacts, and a network of paths still used today, it's likely that no major villages were established at Walden. The pond's waters were too still and sterile to satisfy their needs, and a large fishing village already existed in nearby Concord. Native American legends do tell of a large hill on the site where Walden Pond rests today. It's probably not a geographical error but a story dating back to the Ice Age—before the hill made of ice melted down into today's basin.

Seventeenth-century Europeans also left Walden Pond essentially unsettled. Its glacial legacy gave the Walden area dry, sandy, acidic soil, unsuitable for farming. Settlers did build a few homes within a half mile of Walden Pond—perhaps eight of them by 1800. But the land was clearly best suited for use as woodland and pasture.

The names of various sites and paths on Walden trail maps today reflect people and events from its long history. Thoreau's name lives on in a sandy cove near his house site, while his famous backyard bean field survives as a path. Wyman Meadow was a wetland owned by a local potter named Wyman, and Red Cross Beach reflects a group who gave swimming lessons there during the 1950s. In the 1840s, Irish laborers built the old Fitchburg Railroad (which still carries commuters from north central Massachusetts to Boston today); their rustic temporary huts are remembered in Shanty Town Path. Ice Fort Cove was where a nineteenth-century ice company stored blocks of Walden Pond ice awaiting shipment to India. And nearby Brister's Hill commemorates former slave Brister Freeman, one of several free black residents of the area in the early 1800s.

The origin of the name Walden itself remains a matter of conjecture. It may, as Thoreau suggested, have simply described the "walled-in" pond. Or it may have derived from Saffron Walden, England, which had many connections to Concord through the Minots and other old New England families. The pond may have been named for Walden, a mythical Native American woman who survived the traumatic transition of the site from melting glacial hill to pond. Some historians note that it could simply be a corruption of *wald* or *wold*, common Old English terms for forested areas. Finally, one Major Waldren—a trader with Native Americans in the area—may have been commemorated, albeit in a misspelled fashion, in the Walden name.

The man who made Walden famous was the multitalented, Harvard-educated Henry David Thoreau, who moved into a ten-by-fifteen-foot hand-hewn house by Walden Pond on July 4, 1845. He was twenty-eight years old when he came to Walden, and he would spend two years, two months, and two days reading, writing, walking, and thinking in spartan semisolitude.

Ironically, though history and world literature have forever linked Thoreau and Walden, it was not so in the mid-nineteenth century. Thoreau's widespread fame emerged only in the socially conscious, antimaterialist, environmentally aware decade of the 1960s, a century after Thoreau's death at the age of forty-four. In 1847, Walden's most famous citizens were Ralph Waldo Emerson and Frederic Tudor. Emerson was already a prestigious essayist and local landowner by then; it was he who gave his friend Thoreau a parcel of land on which to build a house. "Ice King" Frederic Tudor had expanded his international ice-export business to Walden in 1847, when the new Fitchburg Railroad line offered him easy access from pond to port. Thoreau actually enjoyed the fact that Walden ice might go to India; he loved the Indian philosophers and kept the *Bhagavad Gita*, the sacred Hindu text, close at hand. Close by, too, was his copy of the Greek epic poem *The Iliad*.

In his book *Walden*, Thoreau related his observations, thoughts, and encounters with nature and society, based on the journals he had kept while living at the pond. "I went to the woods because I wished to live deliberately," he explained, "to front the essential facts of life and see if I could not learn what it had to teach, and not, when I came to die, discover that I had not lived." Like his colleague Emerson, Thoreau argued that studying nature and knowing oneself were one and the same. Both believed that the Divine was located in the human soul, and that the Self, as the source of the Divine, could perceive the Divine in the rest of the world. Such thoughts were part of the nineteenth-century idealist philosophy known as transcendentalism.

Despite these philosophical contributions, Thoreau's nineteenth- and twentieth-century detractors have periodically labeled him a shiftless hermit, hippie, freeloader, fraud, or misanthrope who lived in a primitive house to save money and escape the responsibilities of working adulthood. More often than not, however, Thoreau is today admired as a pioneer of passive resistance and wilderness preservation, and an inspiration to Martin Luther King, Jr., Mahatma Gandhi, Leo Tolstoy, and environmentalist John Muir.

Far from being a hermit, lazy, or free of responsibility, Thoreau was arguably the most practical man alive. While living at Walden, he welcomed visitors, walked into town, and earned money surveying, selling vegetables to neighbors, and even lecturing. He had made improvements in his father's pencil-making business and built his own home in the woods using building skills learned with his father. Because Thoreau borrowed an ax, cut nearby pines for his frame, and bought boards from the shanty of a neighboring Irish railroad worker, he was able to construct his house for just $28.12½. (The Thoreau house replica, in the park's parking lot, was built in 1986 at a cost of $7,000.)

On many issues, Thoreau was a thinker ahead of his time. He had few class pretensions, decried corporal punishment of schoolchildren, and doubted the benefits of succumbing to the world of business and material accumulation. Moreover, if his brother John hadn't died, Thoreau might never have come to stay at Walden, nor immortalized that stay in his book. Certainly, Thoreau wanted to learn to simplify his life, appreciate nature, "live deliberately," find peace and quiet, and work on his writing career, but he also needed to recover from the loss of his beloved older brother. John had died in Henry's arms three years earlier from a freak accident, a straight-edge razor cut that led to tetanus. (Henry himself suffered from psychosomatic lockjaw afterward.)

Like Thoreau, Walden Pond, the house, and the woods have also attracted their share of misconceptions. Many people believe, for example, that the area was a wooded wilderness in Henry's day. In fact, woodsmen had collected so much lumber there by 1845 that fewer trees stood there then than do today. Massive planting efforts by the state and by concerned citizens like the group Walden Forever Wild have helped bring the shoreline back to its original splendor; still, more money and staff are always needed.

Walden Pond itself was rumored to be bottomless until the skillful surveying of civil engineer Thoreau put that idea to rest. Some suggested that Walden was fed by a huge system of underwater rivers that traveled from New Hampshire's White Mountains to Cape Cod; but Walden is so deep simply because it intersects the water table.

By 1945, the exact location of Thoreau's former house was a mystery. Roland Wells Robbins, a Thoreau enthusiast and amateur historian, excavated the old foundation and several artifacts in that year. The house itself, of course, had long since disappeared. The popular account of its fate generally goes like this: Thoreau first gave his house to Emerson, who sold it to his gardener, who moved it from the site as a home for *his* family. The gardener, however, abandoned his family and the house—the latter of which sank into the cellar hole he had dug for it. Two farmers finally bought Thoreau's house, dragged it away with oxen, and used it for grain storage. In 1868, the roof was transferred to a pigsty, and the sides became first a stable and finally scrap lumber.

True, half true, or largely apocryphal, it makes a fine tale.

The Walden Pond area had started to suffer from misuse and overuse even during Thoreau's time. The Fitchburg Railroad began rumbling through Walden Woods in 1844, leaving the abandoned shanties of railroad construction workers in its wake. Meanwhile, ice and wood from the area were regularly hauled away and sold for profit. Between 1866 and 1902, a railroad excursion park called the Picnic Grounds—a pleasure park that city dwellers came to by train—brought thousands of visitors tromping through Ice Fort Cove. Swings, bathhouses, dancing and speaking pavilions, boat rides, concession stands, a baseball diamond, and a cinder track for runners and bicyclists drew both rich and poor out to Walden. Famous speakers on popular topics like spiritualism drew crowds as large as those that gathered for church picnics and chowder parties.

By 1922, part of Walden Pond had become a park; eighty acres had been donated to the state by private landowners—an area since quintupled by several land acquisitions. Still, the abuse of Walden continued. By the 1930s, a sweltering Sunday might bring 25,000 bathers out to the pond, compared to today's 5,000 or 6,000 (they are now also limited to 1,000 bathers at a time). In 1957, the woodland behind Red Cross Beach was bulldozed to make room for an expanded swimming program. Later years brought motorcycles, alcohol abuse, cars parked randomly along the roadsides, and a general lack of control.

By 1975, when management of the park was transferred from Middlesex County to the Massachusetts Department of Environmental Management (the DEM, which in 2003 was replaced by the new Department of Conservation and Recreation, or DCR), Walden Pond had been literally loved to death, and drastic steps were required to save the area from recreational abuse and overuse. Specifically, parking and daily attendance quotas were established and vigorously enforced, dramatically reducing the number of people allowed into the park at any one time. Much of the pond's bank was restored and replanted, the buildings renovated, ugly concrete piers removed, and interpretive programs added.

The controversy over the appropriate use of Walden Pond State Reservation continues to the present day. Some groups want to ban all or some of the active recreation at Walden, for the sake of historic and natural preservation. Others—angered when told that the parking lot and park are full for the day—want full recreational access restored. Meanwhile, a continuing shortage of state funding has cut park staffs and stalled improvement plans.

Beginning in the 1980s, large condominium and office development projects in parts of the surrounding Walden Woods—efforts condoned by the town of Concord—further threatened Walden from without. As a result, a variety of preservationists began a fight to save the land made famous by Thoreau's writings. Musician Don Henley, a former member of the Eagles, founded the Walden Woods Project in 1990 and helped choreograph a variety of rallies, walks, concerts, and other fund-raisers and consciousness-raisers to protect the property from commercial development. The group's primary goal was to purchase the land and allow it to remain woodland. Among their fund-raising efforts was the publication of *Heaven Is Under Our Feet*, a book of essays by celebrities, authors, and environmentalists dedicated to preserving the lands around Walden Pond. In 1992, Henley was named the Massachusetts Historical Commission's "Man of the Year" for his ongoing efforts. By 1993, the group's success was assured: commercial development on the land had been stopped and the process of buying the woodland begun.

Through all that controversy—and, indeed, to this day—the park's interpretive staff continues to enlighten visitors to the pond's literary, historical, and natural past and present. Park interpreters are generally available to the public at the Thoreau house replica; the DCR also offers special programs throughout the year from the park office building on Route 126.

Other resources for visitors curious about Henry David Thoreau include the Thoreau Society Shop at Walden Pond. The shop, open daily year-round (with extended summer hours), is filled with Thoreau-related books and other items. The Thoreau Society, the oldest and largest organization devoted to the study of an American author, offers a full schedule of educational programs, excursions, and publications related to Thoreau's literature, lifestyle, landscapes, and legacy. One of the many roles of the society is acting as the Friends of Walden Pond, which supports visitor services, park operations, and conservation efforts at the pond.

The Walden Woods Project founded by Don Henley, in collaboration with the Thoreau Society, has established the Thoreau Institute at Walden Woods, a research facility located on the hill above Walden Pond. Meanwhile, Thoreau's original bed, desk, and chair from the Walden house are on display with other Thoreau artifacts (including his snowshoes, spyglass, and surveying tools) in the Concord Museum, at the junction of Lexington Road and the Cambridge Turnpike. Yet another replica of Thoreau's house stands outside that museum. In addition, the Special Collections at the Concord Free Public Library hold many documents associated with the author, his town, and his times.

All in all, these intertwining individuals, organizations, and facilities are a fitting tribute to the man who reminded us, "We must learn to reawaken and keep ourselves awake . . . by an infinite expectation of the dawn."

THE ESSENTIALS

Addresses: Route 126, off Route 2, Concord; reservation spans parts of Concord and Lincoln. Walden Pond State Reservation, 915 Walden Street (Route 126). Thoreau Society, 55 Old Bedford Rd., Concord, MA 01742. **Telephone:** Walden Pond State Reservation, (978) 369-3254; Thoreau Society Shop at Walden Pond, (978) 287-5477; Thoreau

Society Office and Friends of Walden Pond, (978) 369-5310; Thoreau Insititute at Walden Woods, (781) 259-4730; Concord Museum, (978) 369-9763. **Websites:** www.massparks .org; www.walden.org; www.thoreausociety.org; www.shopatwaldenpond.org; www.con-cordmuseum.org. **Visitor Information:** Open 365 days a year, 5:00 A.M. to dusk. Staff hours 8:00 A.M. to dusk. Park admission free. Parking fee required in adjacent lot. Visitors limited to 1,000 at a time. Visiting groups require prior reservation; please call. Call for details on guided walks and educational programs. No fires, camping, pets, alcoholic beverages, off-road vehicles, bicycles, motorcycles, flotation devices, or boats powered by internal combustion engines. Limited wheelchair access; special parking spaces in lot; steep ramp to main beach accessible with assistance; trails not accessible; main beach toilets accessible; wheelchair-accessible gift shop and bathrooms; phone ahead for special accommodations.

Walden Pond is the last stop on the Literary Trail of Greater Boston; information at www.lit-trail.org.

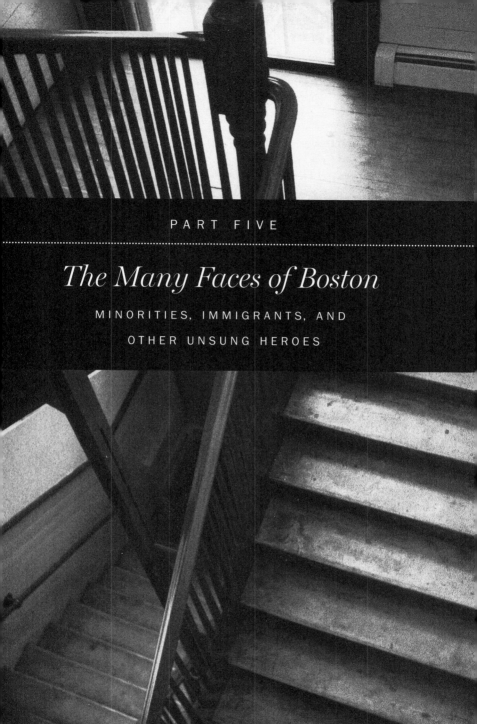

PART FIVE

The Many Faces of Boston

MINORITIES, IMMIGRANTS, AND
OTHER UNSUNG HEROES

As RECENTLY as forty years ago, most histories of Boston—and most of the city's historic walking tours—gave the distinct impression that the town was created by and for white Anglo-Saxon Protestants. A closer look suggested an even narrower vision: the Hub of the Universe consisted of a small, select group of middle- and upper-class white males, many of whom could trace their family lineages back to Boston's seventeenth century. A jocular look at the legendary "Proper Bostonian" was provided by John Collins Bossidy in a toast he delivered in 1910:

> And this is good old Boston,
> The home of the bean and the cod,
> Where the Lowells talk to the Cabots
> And the Cabots talk only to God.

Though Bossidy's rhyme was amusing, it was hardly an accurate picture of Boston history. Boston did begin as a Puritan colony, populated largely by immigrants from the British Isles. And although religious controversies and schisms erupted constantly in colonial times, they generally involved Protestants arguing with other Protestants. Native American religions were disregarded, as were the accomplishments and contributions of local tribes. Women were invisible, disenfranchised daughters, mothers, and wives—except, of course, when they became outspoken heretics or witches. African-Americans were treated as second-class citizens even after slavery was abolished in Massachusetts in 1783. And Catholics and Jews were rare indeed (when the Italian Judah Monis became the first Jew to teach at Harvard College in 1722, he converted to Christianity before teaching his first semester).

As the nineteenth century unfolded, however, the many faces of Boston became harder to hide, more difficult to disregard. Boston's African-American community fought and won battles to abolish slavery in the United States and to gain equal status in churches, public schools, and the community. Women began entering the workforce in greater numbers—inspired, in part, by the mill girls of Lowell—and started the first phase of the women's movement. Women and blacks began to emerge as writers, artists, orators, educators, reformers, and community leaders, sometimes side by side. Meanwhile, immigrants flooded into Boston as the century progressed. Irish Catholics, escaping the potato famine and British oppression, were one of the first and largest groups; they were soon followed by German Jews, French Canadians, Italians, Portuguese, Eastern European Jews, and many others. Though Hispanic and Asian immigrants were part of this move, they came in the greatest numbers in the twentieth century.

Today, more and more histories of Boston—and more of our historic walking tours—reflect the lives and contributions of Boston women, minorities, immigrants, gays and lesbians, and other formerly unsung heroes.

The development of the Black Heritage Trail in the 1960s, the Boston Women's Heritage Trail and Boston's Irish Heritage Trail in the 1990s, and various excursions from the Boston History Collaborative at the turn of the twenty-first century (the Literary Trail, Innovation Odyssey, Boston by Sea and BostonFamilyHistory.com) were sure signs of such inclusion. Even the prestigious Freedom Trail has significantly broadened its vision of Boston, in tour guide information, in interpretation and programs at the individual sites, and in National Park Service programs offered on Boston history.

It's true that discovering the stories behind the many faces of Boston still requires work and exploration. But it's well worth the extra effort.

31 The African Meeting House

THE VOICE of Frederick Douglass? Ruth Batson, the dynamic former director of Boston's Museum of Afro-American History, was known to say she'd heard the great abolitionist's voice when standing inside one of Boston's brightest historic lights, the African Meeting House.

"There's a feeling you get when you go into the Meeting House," explained Batson of the oldest standing African-American church structure in the country built primarily by black artisans. "First you have to have the knowledge that in 1806 black people created that building. So you certainly must be captured by the spirit there. Now, Frederick Douglass happens to be one of my heroes—his oratory, his courage, the way he would say things. He took great risks in explaining the problems of his people. And his voice? Well, who can say what I can or cannot hear!

"All kinds of voices were heard at the African Meeting House," Batson continued. "Children's voices. Abolitionist voices. Black voices. The voices of refugee slaves. . . . Sometimes those voices were in agreement, sometimes in opposition."

Today the old structure—restored to its simple beauty and reopened to the public late in 1987—is filled again with varied voices from Boston and beyond. The African Meeting House is a major stop on the Black Heritage Trail, a walking tour that explores the history of Boston's nineteenth-century black community. It is also a site on the Boston Women's Heritage Trail (see Chapter 36) and the Literary Trail of Greater Boston. Moreover, unlike hands-off museum relics encased in glass, this sturdy historic building enjoys a contemporary life of its own.

"The meetinghouse is a means of drawing the people of Boston together," explains former museum director Marcus Mitchell. And it's true: celebrations, lectures, concerts, workshops, exhibits, and book signings all play a part in the new African Meeting House, as they did in the old.

The African Meeting House was built in 1806, at a time when the opportunities for African-Americans to worship were dismal, despite Massachusetts's reputation as a relatively welcoming state for blacks. African slaves first arrived in Boston in 1638. Some earned status as freemen and women over the ensuing decades, and the American Revolution brought even louder cries for liberty. In 1783, slavery was declared illegal in the commonwealth. According to the first federal census of 1790, Massachusetts was the only state in the newly formed Union that recorded no slaves.

But freedom, it was soon discovered, had little to do with equality. By 1800, there were some eleven hundred free blacks living in Boston, first primarily in the North End and later in the West End and the north slope of Beacon Hill. Though blacks held a variety of jobs around the city—in-

The African Meeting House is the oldest standing black church built primarily by free blacks in the United States.

cluding a virtual monopoly on the barbering trade—they could not vote. Even worse, they did not have their own churches.

Boston blacks *were* generally allowed into the town's many white churches. But they were required to stay in the back galleries, out of sight of both preacher and white church members. Certain African-Americans avoided such indignities by worshipping in private homes. Others attended religious meetings in Faneuil Hall, offered on Tuesday and Friday afternoons (never, alas, on Sunday).

According to James and Lois Horton's book *Black Bostonians,* some proud locals tried to defy the segregated system. In the early 1800s, for instance, blacksmith James Easton and his family were forcibly thrown out of one area church after they refused to sit in the "black section." In response, Easton purchased a pew in a local white Baptist church. Their effort to block that sale having failed, some white members tarred Easton's pew. Undaunted, Easton hauled a clean carriage seat to his pew. Indignant whites removed the pew altogether. Easton's response? He and his family sat through services in the aisle.

Though creating a church specifically for black Bostonians was one obvious solution to this problem, the building of the African Meeting House wasn't simply a response to racism. The African-American community had grown and flourished. A meeting place where black self-expression could grow, where ideas could be exchanged and nurtured, was sorely needed.

When plans for the African Meeting House began to take shape, an appropriate black preacher was already available. Thomas Paul of New Hampshire had been attending religious meetings in Boston since 1789, when he was only sixteen. By 1805 he was an ordained Baptist minister. Soon after, he assembled twenty members and formed the First African Baptist Church.

Time clearly had come to build a permanent home for the church. But where? The North End, where most African-Americans lived, was too congested; the West End, on the other hand, was wide-open farmland at the time—a perfect place to build a religious meetinghouse and to attract and absorb the expanding black population.

Funds for the meetinghouse project came from both black and white supporters. Cato Gardner, an ambitious, English-illiterate native of Africa, swiftly collected $1,500—an ample portion of the final cost of $7,700. A plaque above the African Meeting House's front door still reads, "To Cato Gardner, First Promoter of This Building."

The new meetinghouse—from its red-brick outer walls to its spiraling staircases and broad pine floors—was built almost entirely by free black laborers. Since funds were limited, plans for the facade were adapted from an existing townhouse design by Boston architect Asher Benjamin. The interior layout was simple and plain, though up to date. Many of the materials, including floorboards, pulpit, and trusses, were recycled items, presumably gathered from the nearby Old West Church, which was being dismantled at the time.

Just how economically was it done? The ornate and elegant new State House, built on Beacon Hill eight years earlier, cost $133,333. The naval frigate USS *Constitution* was billed at $302,718 in 1797. The African Meeting House's total building budget of $7,700 equaled roughly what Paul Revere had been paid to lay copper on the *top* of the State House dome and the *bottom* of Old Ironsides. Small miracles can indeed be made on a shoestring.

When the Reverend Thomas Paul and his Baptist congregation moved into the African Meeting House, it was a time for revel and revolution. The revolution in question began with a whisper, not a roar. Supportive white Bostonians who were invited to attend the dedication ceremonies on December 6, 1806, were given the superior floor seats while black members sat up in the gallery. "No one would do that again," insists local historian and longtime state representative Byron Rushing, "and they shouldn't have then! But they were so confident of their control of the space that they could do it." Besides, it was probably good public relations.

From the start, the African Meeting House was more than just a church building. It was a place where blacks could find solace from segregation and prejudice and rejoice in their community, culture, and accomplishments. It was a place where they could argue over hot, divisive issues: the proposed resettlement of freed blacks in Liberia or Haiti; the effectiveness of violence versus nonviolence in antislavery protest; and separate versus integrated schools.

By 1808 the meetinghouse basement was also housing a school for black children, who were banned from attending white public schools. Archaeological evidence suggests that people may have lived there as well: a nineteenth-century trash pit, excavated in the backyard, was full of domestic debris like porcelain, glassware, and edible-animal remains—too much of it to be the result of church suppers.

The African Meeting House's most famous nineteenth-century events— "the shouts heard 'round the world"—were certainly its abolitionist meetings, which earned the building such nicknames as "the Abolition Church" and "the Black Faneuil Hall." Boston's influential white activist William Lloyd Garrison founded the New England Anti-Slavery Society in a stirring speech delivered inside the meetinghouse in 1832.

"We have met tonight in this obscure schoolhouse," Garrison began, "our numbers few and our influence limited; but mark my prediction, Faneuil Hall shall ere long echo with the principles we have set forth. We shall shake the Nation by their mighty power." Although the twelve signers of the preamble to the society's constitution were white, an estimated quarter of the seventy-two signers of the constitution itself were African-Americans.

Often banned from speaking against slavery in public places, many other eloquent white reformers—including Wendell Phillips, Charles Sumner, and Angelina Grimké—addressed their supporters within the welcoming meetinghouse as well. Black speakers such as Frederick Douglass, William Nell, and Maria Miller Stewart also shook the rafters with cries for black freedom.

Douglass and radical activist Lewis Hayden were two of the black leaders who encouraged African-American enlistment in the Union army during the Civil War. The meetinghouse became their recruiting center for the renowned 54th Regiment, and it served as the Union's celebratory send-off site as those valiant "colored" soldiers marched off to war.

Despite rumors to the contrary, the African Meeting House was never a stop on the Underground Railroad. Simply put, it was just too obvious a spot. Fugitive southern slaves *were* hidden elsewhere in Boston, as they followed the North Star of the Little Dipper (known by some, and heralded in song, as the "Drinkin' Gourd") while working their way toward the Canadian border. And many risky escapes *were* choreographed or aided by Bostonians who used the meetinghouse as their political base.

In the famous Abolition Riot, for example, brave black Boston women charged into a courtroom and bore the fugitive slaves on trial to a waiting carriage. On another occasion, Lewis Hayden stood with a torch and two kegs of gunpowder on his porch, threatening to blow his home sky high if slave-hunters tried to apprehend the fugitive hidden inside. Hayden's house on Phillips Street—another stop on the Black Heritage Trail—was indeed an Underground Railroad station.

As the nineteenth century progressed, so did the African Meeting House. Physically, the structure underwent a major face-lift in 1855, and a major renovation in the 1980s restored it to that 1855 appearance—from color schemes and window layout to gaslight fixtures and the cinder-block pattern on the wallpaper. (No known photos exist of the building's earlier appearance.)

In historical references, the building's name periodically changed, too. It was sometimes called by the names of the congregations that actively used the space, like the First African Baptist Church or the First Independent Baptist Church of the People of Color of Boston. Others referred to it by location, alternately calling it the Joy Street Church or the Belknap Street Church (after Joy Street's former name). Its most popular designations, as noted before, were the Black Faneuil Hall and the Abolition Church.

Meanwhile, the building's uses changed as well. When students moved to the Abiel Smith School in 1835, and then, twenty years later, into integrated public schools, the meetinghouse basement was no longer needed as a classroom. Other black churches were founded in Boston, and the congregation begun by the Reverend Paul eventually split. His direct heirs include today's People's Baptist and Twelfth Baptist churches, now located in the South End and Roxbury, respectively.

By 1898, the African Meeting House congregation had outgrown its headquarters and Boston's black population had largely migrated to other parts of the city. The building was sold to the Hasidic Jewish congregation called Anshei Libovitz and remained a synagogue through much of the twentieth century.

In 1964, Sue Bailey Thurman and her husband, the Reverend Dr. Howard Thurman (Martin Luther King, Jr.'s, mentor and Boston University's first black chaplain, credited as the most influential black theologian of the twentieth century) founded the Museum of Afro-American History. By 1965, the prototype for the Black Heritage Trail had been established. Seven years later, the museum was able to purchase the African Meeting House, which was designated a National Historic Landmark in 1974.

Only a year after the 1972 purchase, however, disaster struck. While struggling to solidify a dangerously rickety roof, a worker accidentally ignited a fire. The losses were massive: the meetinghouse's original pulpit and trusses and the old slate roof were destroyed, while the original pews were badly burned and damaged. (Most of those pews were put in storage, awaiting further donations to the pew restoration fund.)

Thanks to aid from the National Park Service, the Museum of Afro-American History forged ahead with the Meeting House Project in the 1980s. The building was finally refurbished and reopened to great fanfare late in 1987. Currently, a new round of improvements—in preparation for the celebration of the two hundredth anniversary of the meetinghouse in 2006—includes archeological investigations and architectural research, which will guide further restoration of the building and its original pews. Other planned improvements include full wheelchair accessibility, air conditioning on all floors, and a new heating system.

Over the years, the museum has developed a broad range of educational and public programming related to African-American history and culture. The most popular of their education programs is the Underground Railroad Overnight Adventure, which incorporates the incredible collection of

Underground Railroad homes located on the north slope of Beacon Hill. Through guided walking tours, exhibits, education programs, book signings, and a variety of special events, the museum continues to preserve and interpret the remarkable history of the African-American and white abolitionists whose steadfast and gallant commitments changed this nation. (Contact the museum directly for current program information.)

Meanwhile, the simple, stark, and proud old meetinghouse stands as a statement and an inspiration. During the festivities of 1987, museum chair Henry Hampton explained, "The reopening of the African Meeting House is more than a rededication of bricks and mortar. It is a renewal of historic purpose." Now, almost twenty years later, current executive director Beverly Morgan-Welch continues to find uplift, energy, and purpose in the building: "It is an honor to share the legacy of those who built this unassuming yet stately brick building with children and adults from around the globe. Today the museum's programs, research, collections, exhibits, and publications educate world citizens about the movement our foreparents advanced to fulfill this nation's promise of freedom and justice. Visitors depart the museum challenged by the courage and tenacity of these patriots and empowered by the dignity and industry of Americans who accomplished the extraordinary."

Extraordinary, indeed: yesterday, today, and tomorrow.

THE ESSENTIALS

Addresses: African Meeting House, 8 Smith Court (adjacent to 46 Joy Street), Beacon Hill, Boston, MA 02114. Museum of Afro-American History administrative offices, 14 Beacon Street, Suite 719, Boston, MA 02108. Boston African American National Historic Site administrative offices, 14 Beacon Street, Suite 503, Boston, MA 02108. **Telephone:** Museum of Afro-American History offices, (617) 725-0022. Museum Store and Education Department, (617) 720-2991. **Websites:** www.afroammuseum.org; www.nps .gov/boaf. **Visitor Information:** *The interior of the African Meeting House is closed for renovation, in preparation for celebration of the building's bicentennial in 2006. Visitors can view exhibits about the meetinghouse next door at the Museum of Afro-American History's Abiel Smith School.* Once work is completed, the African Meeting House will be open Monday through Sunday, 10:00 A.M. to 4:00 P.M., June through August; open Monday through Saturday, 10:00 A.M. to 4:00 P.M., September through May. Small donation requested. Tours are free. Fully wheelchair-accessible bathrooms, ground floor, and—following renovations—sanctuary.

The Museum of Afro-American History operates two adjacent historic sites on Beacon Hill, the African Meeting House and the Abiel Smith School, as well as two historic sites on Nantucket.

The African Meeting House is a stop on the Black Heritage Trail (see Chapter 35), the Boston Women's Heritage Trail (see Chapter 36), and the Literary Trail of Greater Boston.

The Black Heritage Trail® is a registered trademark of the Museum of Afro-American History.

32 The Charles Street Meeting House

EVERYONE KNOWS that you can't judge a book by its cover. But rarely is the difference between a building's interior and exterior so pronounced as in the modern-day Charles Street Meeting House.

Inside the historic structure, which has graced the corner of Mount Vernon and Charles streets for some two centuries, is a thoroughly modern complex of shops and offices, topped off by a home and office for the building's current owner, architect John Sharratt. There are sleek staircases and elevators, several ground-floor retail shops, thirty upscale, upper-level offices, and bright, boldly modern chambers punctuated by archways and large glass partitions.

On the outside, however, the simple, elegant, red-brick church building looks much the same as it did in 1807. Tastefully embellished with recessed arches, tall multipaned windows, fan-lighted doors, and a beautiful old clock tower, the structure often reminds viewers of the Old West Church on nearby Cambridge Street—which it should. Both churches were built in the early 1800s, and both designed in the Federalist style by the well-known Boston architect Asher Benjamin.

It's this exterior, of course, that suggests the years of history that have passed through the Charles Street Meeting House. When constructed in 1807, the building was designed to accommodate the word of God, not the world of commerce and industry. Between 1807 and 1980, four consecutive congregations—the Third Baptist Church, the First African Methodist Episcopal Church, the Universalist Church of America, and the Unitarian Universalist Association—called this structure home. Throughout those years, the meetinghouse also served as a community center that sheltered meetings, educational forums, and impassioned debates involving everyone from Sojourner Truth to Dr. Benjamin Spock, from the abolitionists to the Black Panthers, and from the Beacon Hill Civic Association to various gay, feminist, civil rights, peace, arts, theater, and dance groups. The groundbreaking *Gay Community News* had its first home at the Charles Street Meeting House. And so did the modest black heritage display that grew into the Museum of Afro-American History.

As Boston entered the nineteenth century, water entered the area we now know as Charles Street; during high tide, in fact, the Charles River flowed right up to the base of Beacon Hill. In 1795, however, a group of Boston developers known as the Mount Vernon Proprietors began plotting to add more land, and more buildings, to Boston proper. With the aid of a rock-hauling apparatus known as "the first gravity railroad," they began lopping off the top fifty feet of Beacon Hill, then carting the gravel down to the banks of the Charles for use as landfill.

By 1805, Charles Street was born—and appropriately named for the

Now privately owned by a Boston architect, the Charles Street Meeting House has a long history as a center of religious, cultural, political, and social life in Boston.

river it partly displaced. Only two years later, a handsome new Federalist-style church was constructed on one segment of this Charles Street landfill for the sum of $27,000. Apparently patterned after drawings from the popular copybooks of architect Asher Benjamin—which liberally integrated designs by the great Charles Bulfinch—the Charles Street Meeting House was built to accommodate the rapidly growing Boston Baptist community.

Back in 1765, there were only thirty-two Baptist churches in the area later known as New England. By 1795, that number had increased tenfold; 330 churches with 22,000 parishioners called themselves Baptist. It was the 337 members of the Third Baptist Church, recently departed from the First and Second Baptist Churches, who moved into the Charles Street Meeting House in 1807.

The structure these Baptists worshiped in presumably looked on the outside much like the building we see today. The exterior brick was laid in the stylish Flemish bond pattern, and the tall, white, wooden arches and paned windows helped make a fairly plain, square building appear unusually vertical. A beautiful balustrade with urn finials graced the porch roof, which was topped by a clock tower destined to signal time to all of Charles Street for generations to come.

Inside, a single vaulted chamber occupied most of the space. Slender Grecian columns supported the gallery around the sides and back of this auditorium, while a high wooden pulpit and draped curtains dominated the front. Dark box pews lined the wooden floors, with the organ console and pipes set in the rear.

When the church's first pastors preached there—beginning with the Reverend Caleb Blood and followed by the forty-two-year reign of the powerful Reverend Daniel Sharp—the congregation was actively engaged in the practice of baptism by immersion. Since the Charles then flowed right up to the riverside wall of the meetinghouse, where River Street runs today, baptisms may have been performed directly outside the church; other sources suggest that an inlet may have been cut so that the river flowed into the church itself, allowing baptisms to occur within its walls.

The Baptist congregation that first owned and inhabited the Charles Street Meeting House was mainly white. In an age when the best seats in the house—being the mahogany box pews on the main floor of the church—were sold to wealthy churchgoing families, poorer members were relegated to seats in the backs of distant galleries. Included in the latter group were Boston's free black families, many of whom lived on the north slope of Beacon Hill.

Timothy Gilbert (1797–1865), a white parishioner of the Charles Street church, chose to challenge such segregation. Known by his peers as "the Grandest Abolitionist," Gilbert was a cabinet and piano maker who sold his wares in the South, then used his profits to fight Southern slavery. Gilbert's home, once located at number 2 Beech Street, was a hotbed of antislavery rhetoric and a stop on the Underground Railroad. At one time as many as six fugitive slaves hid in Gilbert's home on their way to freedom at the Canadian border.

In 1835, Gilbert decided to test the segregated seating policies of New England's white churches by filling his front-row pew at the Charles Street Meeting House with black Baptist friends. Though the antislavery elements of the church were delighted, the strong proslavery segments were not. Whether Gilbert was angrily expelled after the event or left voluntarily—as one biographer cautiously put it, "to seek a more congenial atmosphere [for] his anti-slavery opinions"—is unclear. But it is clear that Gilbert and many of his abolitionist friends left the Charles Street congregation soon thereafter to form the first truly integrated church in America, the Tremont Temple Baptist Church.

Meanwhile, back at the meetinghouse, the issue of abolitionism was getting hotter and hotter. The Reverend Sharp allowed plenty of debate within the red-brick walls, and several major antislavery leaders—including Sojourner Truth, Harriet Tubman, Frederick Douglass, William Lloyd Garrison, Wendell Phillips, and Charles Sumner—found receptive audiences there.

By 1876, however, both the world and Boston's West End had changed significantly. The Civil War was over. Slavery had been abolished. Vast migrations from the South had swelled Beacon Hill's black population. And the white members of the Third Baptist Church had largely moved out to Back Bay. The white-run congregation sold their meetinghouse to the black members of the First African Methodist Episcopal Church, which maintained the sturdy brick structure for the next sixty-three years. The Charles Street AME Church, as it came to be known, proceeded to become a major community leader in black religious, social, and cultural activities. The purchase of the Charles Street property alone, bought in 1876 for $45,000, was an impressive accomplishment for a congregation of only two hundred. The National Federation of Afro-American Women was organized there in 1895 (it later merged into the National Association of Colored Women). Sarah Gorham (1832–1894), the first woman missionary sent to Africa by the AME Church, left for Sierra Leone from the Charles Street congregation in 1888. Two of the church's pastors went on to become bishops.

As the twentieth century progressed, however, the church began to falter. Maintaining the big building proved to be a financial drain, and the black community had gradually moved from Beacon Hill and the West End to the South End and Roxbury. Hence, in 1939 the building was sold to a group of religious liberals known as the Charles Street Meeting House Society. The Society sold the building nine years later to the Universalist Church of America and helped relocate the Charles Street AME congregation to the St. Ansagarius property in Roxbury, at Warren Street and Elm Hill Avenue. To this day, that large and active black community church proudly bears the name "Charles Street AME," though its address is 551 Warren.

During the Unitarian Universalist tenure at the meetinghouse, the building became a haven for a variety of local cultural, social, and political groups. Members of the gay community fondly remember the gay coffeehouse there and the seminal years of the nation's oldest gay newspaper, *Gay Community News*. African-Americans established the first displays of the American Museum of Negro History in the meetinghouse, displays that later evolved into the Museum of Afro-American History. Vibrant performances, meetings, lectures, rallies, debates, and support groups were all a part of the building's social fabric.

By the late 1970s, however, the aging building itself was in dire need of repair—much more repair than its owners could afford. No educational, religious, cultural, or charitable group could be found to buy and renovate the grand old structure. Hence, under the watchful eye of the Society for the Preservation of New England Antiquities—and just about everyone else who had ever loved or used the meetinghouse—architect John Sharratt was allowed to move in and to repair and renovate the space at a cost of more than a million dollars.

In order to save the meetinghouse, some compromises were necessary. Aside from ground-floor shoppers and visitors to the Charles Street offices, the building is not currently open to the public. Furthermore, the tall auditorium was carved up into multiple floors and smaller units, which were then rented out by Sharratt to help defray costs of renovation, exterior preservation, and high property taxes.

Although the changes were drastic, it wasn't the first time that the historic interior had been "compromised." A fire in the mid-nineteenth century had destroyed many of its original elements. Radical stylistic changes were also voluntarily imposed there in the 1850s: the floor was raised, box pews discarded for slip-style benches, and pseudo-Norman columns and arches replaced the early Grecian ones. The roof's pitch was changed, as were the windows and the pulpit. Somewhere along the line, someone had even painted the exterior brickwork brown—a murky tint that was not blasted off until the 1920s.

Moreover, even the site was not really original. In 1921, when the city decided to widen Charles Street from fifty-five to sixty-five feet, most residents were forced to clip ten feet off the fronts of their buildings. Rather than chop up the Meeting House—or, even worse, level it for a high-rise building or a parking lot—Beacon Hill residents and the Charles Street AME Church combined forces and finances to pick up the historic building and move it ten feet closer to the river. Architect Frank Bourne oversaw the stunning move, as well as subsequent changes and renovations to the structure.

Though many Bostonians are still saddened that some version of the old church interior was not preserved, no one can fail to be grateful for what is there. The principal architectural landmark of Charles Street is alive and well, its exterior restored to its splendid look of 1807. As travelers of the Black Heritage Trail know, it is a sparkling and proud chunk of history for new generations to watch, touch, and enjoy.

THE ESSENTIALS

Addresses: Charles Street Meeting House, 125 Mount Vernon Street, Boston, MA 02108; corner of Mount Vernon and Charles streets, Beacon Hill, Boston. Boston African American National Historic Site (Black Heritage Trail) offices, 14 Beacon Street, Suite 506, Boston, MA 02108. Museum of Afro-American History, administrative office, 14 Beacon Street, Suite 719, Boston, MA 02108. **Telephone:** Meeting House offices, (617) 367-7171; John Sharratt Associates, (617) 227-0094; Black Heritage Trail/Boston African American National Historic Site offices, (617) 742-5415; Museum of Afro-American History, (617) 725-0022. **Websites:** Black Heritage Trail: www.nps.gov/boaf. Meetinghouse offices: www.mh-offices.com. **Visitor Information:** Interior of building open only to shop customers or office visitors. Offices open 9:00 A.M. to 5:00 P.M., Monday through Friday. Some retail stores open weekends also. No organized tours, but building is discussed on Black Heritage Trail (see Chapter 35) tours. Ground-level retail shops are wheelchair accessible; remainder of building is difficult because of steps by front door; once inside, all floors accessible by elevator.

33 The Abiel Smith School

IT'S A plain, box-shaped building on the corner of Joy Street and Smith Court—not the sort of place that would normally stop passersby in their tracks. But the old Abiel Smith School is more than the sum of its simple

A vintage-looking blackboard and podium are among the displays at the old Abiel Smith School, opened in 1835 as the first Boston public school to educate African-American children.

exterior parts—the sturdy red bricks, gabled roof, and twenty-four-pane window sashes that have held it intact for more than 170 years.

Today the building is one of the primary artifacts of the Museum of Afro-American History. It houses permanent and rotating exhibitions, including a video object theater, computer interactive stations, and a museum store. Most every day of the year, groups of visitors stop by, from school groups and followers of the Black Heritage Trail to curious tourists from around the nation and the world.

Less immediately evident is the fact that this same structure was at the eye of a nineteenth-century storm. Opened in 1835 as the first Boston public school to educate the city's African-American children (and the first building in the United States constructed solely to house a black public school), the Abiel Smith served Boston's black community for twenty long and frequently turbulent years.

In the decades preceding the Civil War, of course, the turbulence that most often comes to mind when speaking of Boston's black history is the argument over slavery. Boston in general and Beacon Hill in particular were known as hotbeds of abolitionism and antislavery sentiment. Next door to the Smith School, for example, at the African Meeting House, fiery abolitionists like William Lloyd Garrison, Frederick Douglass, and Angelina Grimké continually entranced exuberant antislavery crowds. Radical activists like Lewis Hayden—who valiantly aided fugitive Southern slaves on their Underground Railroad route to freedom at the Canadian border—lived only a short distance away.

Though abolitionism may have received the most press, the most pressing *civil rights* issue of the time concerned segregated schools. The debate over school integration, which so divided Boston in the twentieth century, actually began at the Smith School shortly after its dedication on May 3, 1835. According to longtime state representative Byron Rushing, Boston's human library of black history, "Boycotting schools, setting up freedom schools in people's homes, the invention of the concept of 'separate but equal'—all these things seem so modern. But they all happened here." And that's where the fascinating story of the Abiel Smith School begins.

Though their attitudes may not seem praiseworthy today, many white Bostonians of the late eighteenth century were proud of their "progressive," humanistic views on Boston's black population. Blacks had been enslaved in the city since their first arrival in 1638, only eight years after the founding of the Massachusetts Bay Colony; but by 1783, in the era of American Revolutionary idealism, slavery was legally abolished in the commonwealth. In the first federal census of 1790, Massachusetts was the only state reporting no slaves.

Moreover, by 1800, Boston was home to almost 1,100 free African-Americans, making it one of the largest free black communities in North America. (Boston's total population at the time was 24,397.) Before 1800, many black men and women lived in the crowded, run-down North End. As the century progressed, however, they slowly began to migrate to the north slope of Beacon Hill.

Boston's growing black community may have been free, but it was clearly not equal. Though Boston's whites could pursue a wide variety of careers, blacks were often limited to a few vocations—as dockworkers, shipbuilders, sailors, caterers, blacksmiths, servants, caretakers, street laborers, shopkeepers, barbers, and such. Jobs with higher pay or more prestige required more schooling. And while no law prevented Boston blacks from enjoying public education, blatant prejudice and outright abuse in the white-dominated schools effectively denied black children such benefits. Widespread public indifference allowed discrimination to continue. In addition, economics played a role. Poor families couldn't afford to send a child to school if help was needed at home.

Boston's black leaders were aware that education was essential if African-American families were to improve their lot. One such leader, Prince Hall, petitioned and pleaded for a decade before the city finally approved a private school for black children. Classes began in 1798, in the home of Hall's son, Primus.

Supported by white philanthropists, and sometimes staffed by Harvard student teachers, the Primus Hall school struggled along with erratic success. Finally, in 1808, a "real" schoolroom was created in the basement of the brand-new African Meeting House. Blacks and whites together had made education for black children possible in Boston, in the only way that seemed viable at the time—the de facto establishment of segregated schools.

The school that began in the basement of the African Meeting House eventually became known as the Abiel Smith School. Who was Abiel

Smith? The details are scarce. We know he was a white philanthropist and business leader, and one of Boston's "merchant princes." (Popular lore suggests his fortune was amassed thanks, in part, to $20,000 worth of gold coins his wife and sister secreted through British lines during the American Revolution.) On more than one occasion, Smith was asked by the eloquent black teacher Prince Saunders to contribute to the school. When Smith died in 1815, he left Boston close to $5,000 worth of shares in New England turnpikes and bridges, plus U.S. Bonds, to be used "for the free instruction of colored children in reading, writing and arithmetic."

Though the records are sketchy—a problem sadly true of much black history—it seems the African Meeting House school received some of these funds soon after and was renamed the Abiel Smith School in appreciation. While the city agreed to allocate two hundred dollars per year for educating blacks—a sum that never increased, though student populations grew and two more ad hoc black schoolrooms were created in the 1820s—students still had to contribute twelve and a half cents per week to help cover costs. Every Boston school relied partly on students' fees to meet costs, but, as ever, the poorest were hit hardest.

Eventually, overcrowding and intolerable conditions in the meetinghouse basement convinced a reluctant school committee to apply Smith's legacy to building an actual schoolhouse for African-American children. Construction began on a parcel of land owned by Augustin Raillion, next to the meetinghouse. The mason may have been a man named Cushing Nichols, and the front door may have originally been on the left (as suggested by a site sketch in the 1849 *Boston Almanac*). The final cost of the building was $7,485.61 in 1834 dollars.

One year later, on May 3, 1835, the simple, two-story Abiel Smith School was dedicated, the first city-owned school building ever constructed for black Bostonians. It was not in the best section of Beacon Hill; wealthier folks lived farther up Joy Street, while the north slope housed stables and simpler lodgings. Moreover, the new school, like its predecessors, was a segregated or "race" school. Abiel Smith students were being taught the basics of reading, writing, and arithmetic, but, unlike their white counterparts, they were prohibited from instruction in advanced grammar.

The basement classroom, where the museum store sits today, initially housed a primary school. In the 1830s, primary schools taught basic skills to students aged four to seven. Shortly after it opened, this subterranean level of the Smith School was converted to an "intermediary" school, geared to older children who had not yet learned those fundamentals. Some records suggest that adult education classes may have been held here from time to time as well.

The first floor and second floors housed the grammar school, where students eight through fourteen years old gained an educational foundation for their lives. Grammar schools were organized into two departments: the first floor, which now houses permanent and rotating exhibitions, served as a "writing department"; the second floor, where the video and computer exhibits are located today, was the "reading department," where students practiced reading and recitation skills. This second-floor chamber is meant to recreate the feel of a mid-nineteenth-century schoolroom. (Students who could afford to continue their classroom education, incidentally, went on to high school at Boston Latin, where subjects included Latin and Greek.)

According to archaeologist Beth Bower, digs behind the African Meeting House have unearthed pieces of slate, slate pencils, toys, marbles, and ceramic cups—items that may well have been used at the Smith School. Beyond that, details of the school's operation and physical setup are not really clear.

What is clear, however, is that political battles and economic conditions made the Smith School fall rapidly from grace after its opening in 1835. A school committee report of 1847 decried the school's disrepair, overcrowding, and generally "deplorable" condition; special attention was called to the outhouses in its tiny backyard, accessible only "through a dark and damp cellar."

It's difficult to know today how conditions compared to other Boston schools. Contemporary reports, however, suggest that Smith School classrooms were more overcrowded, supplies more limited, teachers less educated, white headmasters more immoral, and facilities more marginal than in the dozens of white schools scattered about Boston by mid-century. Moreover, white students could easily walk to the nearest neighborhood school while blacks had to travel to the Abiel Smith from throughout the city.

Compared to the best white primary or grammar schools of the period—like the majestic three-story 1824 Phillips School on the corner of Pinckney and Anderson streets, which now houses condominiums—the black-only Smith School was indeed a third-rate facility. Still, according to Stanley Schultz's book *The Culture Factory,* the average Boston schoolroom of 1833 crammed one teacher and sixty-two students into a nineteen-by-twenty-six-foot space and was often located in one of the densest, most rundown sectors of town.

For many of Boston's African-American citizens, the all-black Abiel Smith School—though not equal to its white counterparts—was an educational solution they could live with. For others, like black activist William Cooper Nell, separate was unacceptable, and equal education for blacks was essential. In 1840, Nell began to mount a campaign that would eventually bring an end to lawful school segregation in Boston.

Some historians suggest that Nell's drive to abolish black schools and end segregation came from one particular childhood event. As an honors student in the old Smith School (when it was still housed in the basement of the African Meeting House), Nell had won the coveted Franklin Medal for scholastic achievement, along with top white students around the city. Because of his color, however, Nell was denied the prize and the special Faneuil Hall dinner honoring medal winners. Actually, Nell *was* permitted to attend the dinner—but only as a waiter!

Whatever the reason, Nell was a prime mover behind relentless petition drives and an eleven-year Smith School boycott, which helped the black school's attendance dwindle from 263 in 1840 to 50 in 1849. Meanwhile, powerful abolitionists like former senator Charles Sumner and black attorney Robert Morris added clout to Boston public school integration forces when they brought the case *Sarah C. Roberts vs. the City of Boston* to court.

The case involved a six-year-old student named Sarah Roberts, who was allegedly denied access to the five white public schools she had to pass on her way to the Smith School. Her father, printer Benjamin Roberts, sued the city for damages, testing the legality of segregated schools in Boston. In 1850, Judge Lemuel Shaw ruled against Roberts, arguing that Sarah did have access to a public school, the Abiel Smith, and that the school had in no way been proven inferior.

Though the battle was lost, the war was all but won. By 1855, aided by furor over the federal Fugitive Slave Law—which required that runaway slaves be returned to their owners—a bill to end segregation in Boston public schools passed the legislature and was signed by the governor. In the fall of that year, the Abiel Smith School was officially closed. The black children of Boston were finally free to attend the public school nearest their homes. (Despite Boston's pride as a pioneer in free education, incidentally, its school integration program came later than those in some other Bay State cities, including Salem, New Bedford, Lowell, Cambridge, and Worcester.)

The old Smith School building continued to serve the city in less earth-shaking ways. Sketchy records suggest that, though shut down for a period, the structure was periodically used as a "Primary School House" before being relegated to a city storage building sometime after 1875. Starting in 1887, veterans groups began using it as a meeting place. The first such group was Post 134 of the Grand Army of the Republic (GAR), who were veterans of the Civil War. Later veterans groups listed in city registers included "colored veterans," the American Legion, and the United Service Organization (USO). It was not until a century later, in 1987, that the USO left the building and Boston's black community regained primary use of this important historic site.

Over its many years of civil service, the Abiel Smith School has undergone several physical changes to accommodate different uses. Major upgrading, renovation, and structural reinforcing were financed by the City of Boston in 1975; the National Park Service undertook interior rehabilitation in 1988, in exchange for office space therein. (In the 1980s and 1990s, the building served as the headquarters of both the Boston African American National Historic Site and the Museum of Afro-American History.) The Smith School's most recent federally funded renovation, begun in 1998, resulted in its current incarnation as a museum space and retail store, starting in the year 2000.

Despite these cosmetic changes, the Abiel Smith School building probably looks much the same today as it did in 1835. Visitors can still see the bright brick walls, the brownstone lintels, the rows of large twelve-over-twelve sash windows, the two chimneys, and the gabled roof of the institution that first inspired then infuriated black students in the decades before the Civil War. The substance, as well as the spirit, has survived the ages.

THE ESSENTIALS

Addresses: Abiel Smith School, 46 Joy Street, at Smith Court, Beacon Hill, Boston MA, 02114. Museum of Afro-American History administrative offices, 14 Beacon Street, Suite 719, Boston, MA 02108. Boston African American National Historic Site administrative offices, 14 Beacon Street, Suite 503, Boston, MA 02108. **Telephone:** Museum of Afro-American History offices, (617) 725-0022; Museum Store and Education Department, (617) 720-2991; Boston African American National Historic Site, (617) 742-5415. **Websites:** www.afroammuseum.org. www.nps.gov/boaf. **Visitor Information:** Smith School open daily, June through August, 10:00 A.M. to 4:00 P.M.; September through May, Monday through Saturday, 10:00 A.M. to 4:00 P.M. Building wheelchair accessible. Museum of Afro-American History administrative offices open 10:00 A.M. to 4:00 P.M., Monday through Friday.

The Abiel Smith School is the last stop on the Black Heritage Trail (see Chapter 35). The Museum of Afro-American History operates two adjacent historic sites on Beacon Hill, the African Meeting House and the Abiel Smith School, as well as two historic sites on Nantucket. There are Black Heritage Trails in both locations.

The Black Heritage Trail® is a registered trademark of the Museum of Afro-American History.

34 The Shaw/54th Regiment Memorial

It sits on the high corner of Boston Common, near the intersection of Beacon and Park streets. And for some, this imposing hunk of sculpted bronze, granite, and marble simply marks a convenient byway in a busy city. On the site are long, low benches, plus the shade of two soaring nineteenth-century elms. Moreover, the bus stops out front, unloading visitors on a perfect spot to view, photograph, or protest the State House, which sits majestically across the street.

Still, the most important thing at the corner of Beacon and Park is the "imposing hunk" itself—the Shaw/54th Regiment Memorial, widely acknowledged as Boston's most outstanding piece of public art. A commemoration of the first free black regiment in the Union army, the bronze sculpture portrays Colonel Robert Gould Shaw and twenty-three black infantry volunteers. In this remarkable work, the three-dimensional figures of Colonel Shaw and his prancing steed emerge from a bas-relief background of marching men. As the monument's many visitors know, something else is quite remarkable about this statue—the temptation to touch the bronze colonel's three-dimensional saber. (Please resist the urge, since repair is costly!)

The Shaw/54th Monument, sculpted by Augustus Saint-Gaudens, is the first stop on Boston's Black Heritage Trail. As such, its tale is told daily by park rangers leading visitors on the fourteen-site black history tour. A century of books, poems, and songs also have told the story of the 54th Regiment, works by men such as Luis Emilio, Lincoln Kirstein, James Russell

Lowell, Robert Lowell, and Charles Ives. In 1989, the stirring Civil War tale of the white Bostonian Robert Gould Shaw and the brave black regiment he commanded was portrayed in the Academy Award–winning film *Glory,* directed by Edward Zwick.

Henry Lee, president of the Friends of the Public Garden and Common, explains the monument's enduring popularity. "The odd thing about the Shaw/54th is that it's both a great work of art and important piece of history. It honors the memory of Shaw and the 54th Regiment, their courage and service. But it's also a symbol of something deeper, of black and white working together for liberty and equality. It's an eternal reminder of people of both races who gave their lives together in harmony: a source of conscience to whites, a source of pride to blacks. And it's a reminder to carry on."

The first free black regiment of the Union army was formed about two years into the Civil War. Shortly after President Lincoln issued the Emancipation Proclamation in January 1863, secretary of war Edwin Stanton accepted a petition from Governor John Andrew of Massachusetts, requesting permission to form a regiment of black soldiers in Boston. By May of that year, the 54th Regiment of Massachusetts Volunteer Infantry had been created—and was actively drilling and ready to march into battle.

It was not the first black regiment in America, but it was the first Union grouping of free black volunteers—soldiers fighting to emancipate their black brothers and sisters, end slavery, and perhaps even prove their equal abilities to white Civil War soldiers. There was certainly an abolitionist sentiment supporting the 54th's formation: Boston was a hotbed of anti-slavery agitation, and the governor himself a staunch abolitionist. But those were not the only reasons. "The 54th was recruited in part because the Union was losing so badly by 1862," explains Marilyn Richardson, a historian and former curator of the Museum of Afro-American History. "Blacks had volunteered for service before then but were turned down. And, of course, there was [for over a year] a pay differential between white and black soldiers."

Black abolitionist Frederick Douglass played a major part in recruiting for the 54th. Much of that recruiting was done at the African Meeting House on Beacon Hill. Dozens of men from Boston's African-American population volunteered for the 54th, joined by hundreds of black volunteers from as far afield as Canada, the Caribbean, and Detroit. By the war's end, some 180,000 blacks had joined the Union forces, forming 10 percent of the total Union army.

Selected as the 54th Regiment's commanding officer was Robert Gould Shaw, a twenty-five-year-old Bostonian and Harvard dropout. Son of a prominent abolitionist family, Shaw already had seen action in two battles. Despite initial misgivings and his recent marriage, he agreed to lead the 54th and proceeded to train the men rigorously at Camp Meigs in Readville, near the modern-day neighborhood of Hyde Park.

The 1989 motion picture *Glory* both succeeds and fails to bring the 54th Regiment to life. On the positive side was the film's faithful outline of the regiment's story: the development of mutual respect and care between

The Shaw/54th
Regiment Memorial,
commemorating
the first free black
regiment in the Union
Army, is arguably
Boston's finest piece
of public art.

Shaw and the troops; the rampant racism in both Northern and Southern armies; the 54th's pride and military prowess; and their glorious departure march down Beacon Street on May 28, 1863, hailed by 20,000 spectators as they headed toward the Boston docks.

The grisly battle scenes, including the regiment's final assault on Fort Wagner, South Carolina, are also surprisingly true to life, thanks largely to the contemporary Civil War reenactment groups who participated. It was during the futile night siege of Fort Wagner on July 19, 1863, that Shaw and many of his men were slaughtered by Confederate troops. The soldiers in the enormous, impenetrable seaside fortress outnumbered their Union invaders two to one. Shaw's body was hurled into a mass grave along with those of his black comrades. Shaw's parents later refused efforts to extricate the colonel's body and give it a special, separate burial; they were sure their son "Rob" would have chosen to remain with his men.

One of *Glory*'s main failures, however, related to the African-American soldiers portrayed. Though the names and faces of the 54th's black soldiers—including two of Frederick Douglass's sons—were readily available, the film used fictional black characters instead. New Bedford sergeant William Carney, for example, the first African-American to win the Medal of Honor, was not represented in the film. Carney was rewarded for brave combat and for saving the regiment flag as he barely escaped death on the Fort Wagner battlefield. "To tell the story of the 54th without Sergeant Carney," claims Marilyn Richardson, "is like telling the story of the Boston Massacre without Crispus Attucks," the colonial African-American who was the first to die in that 1770 skirmish.

It's significant that both *Glory* and the 1897 bronze memorial dedicated to Shaw and the 54th leave the black soldiers anonymous while depicting Shaw clearly and well. In the case of the Shaw/54th Memorial, the renowned sculptor Augustus Saint-Gaudens claimed solid artistic reasons: he could fit only twenty-three black marching infantrymen in the final version of his intricately detailed bronze bas-relief, even though some one thousand once swelled the ranks of the 54th. In the artist's view those twenty-three black faces had to represent a broad array of physical types. (Saint-Gaudens was often seen pursuing black strangers walking in the streets near his New York City studio to persuade them to model for his head studies.)

Creating a grand memorial statue to the martyrs of the 54th Regiment was a commission granted to Saint-Gaudens but not his own idea. In 1865, some black veterans and citizens of South Carolina attempted to create a monument to Shaw near Fort Wagner itself. Though that plan failed, a group of Bostonians—including Governor John Andrew, Senator Charles Sumner, Colonel Henry Lee, and Joshua B. Smith (a former fugitive slave who once worked for the Shaw family)—began raising funds for a memorial in Boston.

"Talk about bureaucracy, and talk about taking a long time!" exclaims Henry Lee, great-grandson of the concerned Bostonian who helped raise money for the memorial. It took another nineteen years and a public subscription purse of $22,620.95 before the young sculptor Saint-Gaudens was hired to begin the project. Another delay came from the artist: the memorial project was supposed to take two years, but Saint-Gaudens took fourteen. By the time the memorial was dedicated, many of those most intimately involved were dead—or precariously close to it.

Saint-Gaudens, who began his illustrious artistic career as a cameo cutter, was hired to create a classic equestrian statue of Shaw. Shaw's family objected, however, insisting the colonel be portrayed with his men. Saint-Gaudens then faced the challenge of creating an emotionally moving, physically animated army in bronze—not to mention fusing a bas-relief sculpture of twenty-three black infantrymen around a three-dimensional figure of Shaw on horseback. As a result, the artist spent many of those fourteen years thinking about, not actually modeling, the monument.

The late Dr. Edwin Gittleman, a University of Massachusetts professor and scholar of Shaw and the 54th, admired Saint-Gaudens's mix of realism and allegory in the memorial. "There's the symbolic floating figure on top holding poppies and an olive branch—death and peace. Then there's the photographic detail. Look at the men's knapsacks, and Shaw's tunic, filled with creases and wrinkles. It suggests a civilian soldier, not the spit and polish of a professional soldier. There are also more rifles than figures you can account for—though each rifle is accurately presented. This suggests the statue should be taken figuratively, not literally. Still, the memorial is accurate in a way that's almost obsessive, when compared to the free and easy style of the film."

Saint-Gaudens's stunning sculpture was cast in bronze and set in a marble and granite terrace fashioned by celebrated architect Charles F. McKim for another $20,000. The structure was built around the two elms that still grace the monument's front porch. On Decoration Day, May 31, 1897, two hundred black Union veterans—from the 54th Regiment, the 55th Infantry, and the 5th Cavalry—triumphantly marched through Boston during a daylong gala celebration of the monument's official unveiling. A few surviving monument committeemen, like treasurer Edward Atkinson, were there. So too were illustrious speakers like the governor, the mayor of Boston, Colonel Henry Lee, and philosopher William James, who had two brothers who served as officers in the 54th.

Though contemporary accounts suggest that Booker T. Washington, founder and president of Tuskegee Institute in Alabama, gave the day's most electrifying oration, his words were not immortalized on the monument. Instead, the thoughts of white men—like poet James Russell Lowell, Harvard president Charles W. Eliot, and former governor John Andrew— had already been inscribed on the stone. The names of the 54th's white officers were also listed, but nary one black soldier was named.

That error was not rectified until 1982, when the names of the black infantrymen of the 54th killed at Fort Wagner in 1863 were added to the back of the memorial. An early-1980s campaign by the Committee to Save the Shaw/54th was the fund-raiser behind that long-overdue inscription. Eventually collecting some $200,000, the Save the Shaw Committee also helped restore the badly deteriorating memorial and provided an endowment for ongoing maintenance administered by the Friends of the Public Garden. The effort also helped to save many of Boston's other historic memorials by inspiring the city's Adopt-a-Statue program, which began in 1987.

In May 1997, the centennial celebration of the Shaw/54th Memorial was celebrated with a variety of public programs over a period of several days. Well-attended events included an encampment of African-American Civil War reenactors on the Esplanade, a reenactment of the veterans march of 1897, a screening of *Glory* at the Hatch Shell (a popular performance space on the banks of the Charles River), and scholarly symposia, from which the book *Hope and Glory* (2001) was fashioned. The principal public ceremony, attended by the Massachusetts governor William Weld and addressed by Colin Powell, occurred on May 31, the traditional Memorial Day. (Memorial, or Decoration Day, became a public holiday shortly after the end of the Civil War and was designed to honor fallen American soldiers.) As chairman of the Joint Chiefs of Staff and the nation's highest-ranking military officer, Powell spoke of standing on the shoulders of the men depicted in the statue behind him. In his subsequent foreword to the book *Hope and Glory*, Powell wrote: "To my dying day, I will also never forget that I became chairman because there were men of the Fifty-fourth,

Buffalo Soldiers, Tuskegee Airmen and others who were willing to serve and shed their blood for this country."

Visitors can learn more about the memorial today from a variety of sources. The Shaw/54th is the first of fourteen stops on the Black Heritage Trail walking tour, given by park rangers from the Boston African American National Historic Site. The free tour visits many Beacon Hill sites connected to black social and political history in Boston, including Underground Railroad stops, a gambling house, the first integrated public school, and the homes of famous citizens. The history of the monument itself is chronicled in the documentary *Return to Glory*, produced by the Museum of Afro-American History in association with WCVB-TV Boston and available at the museum store. A bust of Robert Gould Shaw, as well as his ceremonial sword, are displayed in the museum at the Abiel Smith School.

Across the street from the Shaw/54th Memorial is the State House Hall of Flags, where a detailed photographic replica of one of the 54th state flags is on display, open free to public viewing. The State House has three of the 54th's original flags—including the one Sergeant Carney saved in battle—stored in a controlled environment in the Massachusetts State Archives at Columbia Point. It is hoped that eventually these original flags, along with other state flags, will be on display again in the hall.

The finest place to view the other works of Saint-Gaudens, including numerous plaster casts for the Shaw/54th, is the Saint-Gaudens National Historic Site in Cornish, New Hampshire. (Though casts of the heads of the soldiers are on view, the plaster cast of the monument is on long-term loan to the National Gallery in Washington, D.C.) Saint Gaudens's elegant country estate is open from late May through the end of October; call (603) 675-2175 for more information.

THE ESSENTIALS

Addresses: Boston Common, at Beacon and Park streets, Boston. Boston African American National Historic Site administrative offices, 14 Beacon Street, Suite 503, Boston, MA 02108. Museum of Afro-American History administrative offices, 14 Beacon Street, Suite 719, Boston, MA 02108. **Telephone**: Boston African American National Historic Site, (617) 742-5415. Museum of Afro-American History offices, (617) 725-0022. **Websites**: www.nps.gov/boaf; www.afroammuseum.org. **Visitor Information**: Memorial accessible to the public at all times. First stop on the Black Heritage Trail (see Chapter 35). Free Black Heritage Trail tours available year-round, though schedules vary with season; call Boston African American National Historic Site for information. Monument is wheelchair accessible from Beacon Street.

35 The Black Heritage Trail

THOUGH IT'S still not as well known as the Freedom Trail, the Black Heritage Trail—a two-hour, 1.6-mile trek through nineteenth-century Boston—is one of the most extraordinary walking tours in town. Its treasures bring to life tales of secret tunnels, runaway slaves, fiery abolitionist orators, and military massacres. The trail evokes stories of early desegregation battles in Boston's public schools, the successes of former slaves, and the best gambling hoax on Beacon Hill, and includes the largest concentration of pre–Civil War black historic sites in the United States.

Moreover, it's the only U.S. trail that commemorates the development of a free African-American community with extant historic buildings—as opposed to small bronze markers reminding visitors what *used* to stand on the site.

The first aspect of the Black Heritage Trail to both confound and delight visitors is often its location. Since Boston's African-American community has been associated with areas like Roxbury, the South End, and Mattapan in recent decades, to some it's surprising to find the Black Heritage Trail meandering around Beacon Hill. But the fact is that Boston was home to one of the three largest communities of free blacks in the United States from the late eighteenth to the late nineteenth century, and during that period the north slope of Beacon Hill was an African-American neighborhood of major national significance.

Enslaved black Africans first arrived in Boston in 1638, only eight years after the founding of the town. As the century moved on, and as more and more blacks gained their freedom, a community of free blacks began to form in the North End. Prince Hall, founder of the African Lodge of Masons, was one such North Ender. He's buried in that neighborhood's Copp's Hill Burying Ground.

The American Revolution was a turning point in the emancipation process in Massachusetts. Individual blacks—such as poet Phillis Wheatley, Bunker Hill hero Peter Salem, and Crispus Attucks, a victim of the Boston Massacre—gained recognition in that period, and slavery was outlawed by the Commonwealth in 1783.

As Boston's free black community increased, it outgrew the North End neighborhood, and many black families began to move to the West End and the north slope of Beacon Hill. Throughout the nineteenth century, this Beacon Hill area grew into a tight-knit community where the battles of the day were played out: struggles to establish equal education, fight American slavery, and create independent supportive institutions by and for blacks.

Soon after Howard and Sue Bailey Thurman moved to Boston in 1953, they became interested in the area's rich African-American heritage. Howard Thurman became the first black chaplain at Boston University, and in that role provided inspiration for the young Martin Luther King, Jr. Sue Bailey Thurman helped found the American Museum of Negro History and the Negro Freedom Trails of Boston, forerunners of today's Museum of Afro-American History and the Black Heritage Trail. The latter organizations were spurred on by the events of 1963—the centennial of the Emancipation Proclamation and the year of the great March on Washington.

According to local black historian and longtime state representative Byron Rushing, "After meeting with a group of friends, doing research, and developing the idea, Sue and her daughter, Anne Chiarenza, published a poster-size map. It was called the 'Negro Freedom *Trails* of Boston,' not *trail*—because it included sites related to African-Americans on Beacon Hill, in Cambridge, in Roxbury . . . I remember it even included Symphony Hall, because of Roland Hayes, the famous American tenor. You couldn't walk it . . . unless you were a hiker!"

Meanwhile, J. Marcus Mitchell and his wife, Gaunzetta—who had moved to Boston in 1947—had a similar plan. Marcus Mitchell had helped create an artists' group called the Boston Negro Artists Association. In trying to formulate ways to celebrate the Emancipation Proclamation's centennial, Mitchell organized history and art exhibits and set up another trail that followed black art and history in Boston.

Around 1964, the Mitchells and Mrs. Thurman met. Within a relatively short time, Sue Bailey Thurman's first dream became reality. The American Museum of Negro History opened, with the Charles Street Meeting House as its home and Marcus Mitchell as curator and director. At the

In 1997, historic reenactors, shown here on Boston Common, helped celebrate the centennial of the Robert Gould Shaw/54th Regiment Memorial, a centerpiece of the Black Heritage Trail.

time, the meetinghouse was owned by the Unitarian Universalist Association. With assistance from historians at the Boston Athenaeum, the Society for the Preservation of New England Antiquities, and the Beacon Hill Civic Association, more research was done into historic African-American sites, especially in the dense Beacon Hill area.

The second dream—developing the black version of Boston's Freedom Trail—followed naturally, and the Mitchells' concept of the trail, geographically and chronologically more focused than Thurman's, began to predominate. Because Beacon Hill's history spoke volumes about abolitionism, black families, African-American neighborhoods, the struggle for freedom, political developments, and education, that area became the center.

The last major change for the trail in the late 1960s was its name. The word *Negro* had fallen out of favor, both within the black community and without, so the museum became the Museum of Afro-American History and the walking tour was called the Black Heritage Trail.

The Mitchells typed up the first trail guide in 1968. It was a small booklet that concentrated on Beacon Hill but also looped into the North End. On May 9 of that year, Marcus Mitchell led a crowd of some four hundred people on the trek. The Black Heritage Trail, in something akin to its modern incarnation, had been officially established.

Meanwhile, Henry Hampton, executive producer of the documentary *Eyes on the Prize* and honorary chair of the Museum of Afro-American History, discovered that the old African Meeting House—which had been used as a synagogue on Beacon Hill since the turn of the century—was coming up for sale. Knowing Byron Rushing's reputation as an ace fundraiser, Hampton asked him to join the cause.

Thanks to the success of those fund-raising efforts, the African Meeting House—the oldest standing black church building in America and the core of the black Beacon Hill community—was purchased in 1972 by the Museum of Afro-American History. In 1974, it became a National Historic Landmark. The structure was renovated and opened to the public in 1987.

These events had major effects on the Black Heritage Trail. The fact that the African Meeting House—the trail's major site and the only trail structure owned by the museum—was a National Historic Landmark gave the tour added prestige. That, in turn, helped attract people involved in Boston's U.S. bicentennial celebrations, as well as the National Park Service.

Hence, as part of the nation's 1976 bicentennial, the city funded a new Black Heritage Trail pamphlet. Written by Rushing, it was geographically broader than today's trail. Among the non–Beacon Hill sites included were the Copp's Hill Burying Ground in the North End and the Emancipation Group statue in Park Square. Clearly, the trail still needed fine-tuning.

When yet another version of the trail was hammered out over the next four years—thanks in part to new information culled from intense research and archeological digs—Rushing and the museum's board finally agreed on two criteria for inclusion. First, the trail would not commemorate buildings that were no longer standing. Second, the trail would include, in Rushing's words, "no 'Phillis Wheatley slept here' history. The site had to be more connected to the black community than that. That criterion eliminated the Old South Meeting House, where Phillis was once a member."

In 1980, the historic credentials of the trail were further enhanced when an act of Congress made these Beacon Hill stops the Boston African American National Historic Site. A new brochure was developed. And by 1982 the museum and the National Park Service had begun a cooperative partnership that endures to this day.

The Boston African American National Historic Site is unusual as national parks go. There are no valleys, no fields, no mountains. Moreover, the land is not owned by the federal government: eleven sites on the trail are privately owned, two are retained by the city, and one belongs to the Museum of Afro-American History.

Still, the Black Heritage Trail is an eye-opening and quite literally breathtaking trek that generally takes visitors two hours to travel, either alone or accompanied by a park service ranger. One word of caution and conscience: please respect the privately owned sites by restraining your impulses to look, or get invited, inside; except for the Smith School and the Meeting House, interior visits are not allowed.

The first stop on the trail, the **Shaw/54th Regiment Memorial**, is also its newest structure. Sculpted by Augustus Saint-Gaudens over a fourteen-year period, the compelling bas-relief—considered by many to be Boston's finest piece of public art—was dedicated in 1897. It commemorates the first black regiment recruited in the North to fight in the Civil War, and the regiment's white commander, Colonel Robert Gould Shaw. Shaw and many volunteers of the 54th were killed in their 1863 attack on Fort Wagner, South Carolina. (Their heroic Civil War tale was loosely depicted in the 1989 film *Glory;* in 1997, the memorial's centennial was celebrated in grand style, with costumed reenactors from the Civil War era, an official visit by General Colin Powell, and related events.)

George Middleton also led an all-black company of soldiers, "the Bucks of America." Middleton was an African-American jockey and horse breaker, and the war was the American Revolution. The **George Middleton House**, at 5–7 Pinckney Street, dates from 1797 and is the oldest remaining house on Beacon Hill built by an African-American.

Although the inside of the old **Phillips School** has been renovated into pricey condos, the exterior still bears a clear carving of "1824," the year this Boston schoolhouse was built. Until 1855, the Phillips, located on the corner of Anderson and Pinckney streets, was a white-only school; when educational segregation was declared illegal in 1855, the Phillips became one of the city's first integrated schools.

At 86 Pinckney is the **John J. Smith House**. Smith was a hairdresser-barber whose shop was frequently visited by black abolitionist activists, fugitive slaves, and the illustrious Charles Sumner during the turbulent antebellum period. After the Civil War, Smith was elected to the Massachusetts House of Representatives.

The **Charles Street Meeting House**, at Mount Vernon and Charles streets, played a vital role in the development of Boston's African-American culture. The structure was built in 1807 by the white Third Baptist Church of Boston. In 1835, white abolitionist Timothy Gilbert filled his front-row pew there with black Baptist friends, causing an uproar in the white establishment and leading to the founding of Tremont Temple Baptist Church, the first integrated church in America. From 1876 until 1939, the meetinghouse was home to the large black congregation of the Charles Street AME Church.

At 66 Phillips Street is the popular **Lewis and Harriet Hayden House.** Born into slavery, Lewis Hayden escaped on the Underground Railroad, resettled in Boston, and became a fervent abolitionist. The Haydens used their home as a fugitive slave station and claimed to keep kegs of explosive gunpowder in their basement to protect those fugitives. They hosted antislavery celebrities like Harriet Beecher Stowe, John Brown, and Harriet Tubman. The house has been beautifully preserved and maintained, especially by recent owners John and Mary Gier.

The stories about **Coburn's Gaming House,** at the corner of Phillips and Irving streets, are almost as wild as those about Haydens'. Some are probably even true. Coburn, a clothing dealer by vocation, hired Boston architect Asher Benjamin to design his house in 1843. Shortly thereafter, he adapted part of this structure into a private gambling center for wealthy white men. The handsome (illegal) profits were invested back into black culture—including Coburn's pocket, his church, and, according to some accounts, abolitionist causes.

The centerpiece of the Black Heritage Trail, as well as the only building on the trail owned by a black organization, is the **African Meeting House,** at 8 Smith Court. The stately yet simple brick structure was built by free black laborers in 1806 and used as an African-American church, meetinghouse, school, community center, lecture hall, and center for antislavery activities. Speakers there included a who's who of abolitionism, from William Lloyd Garrison and Frederick Douglass to Angelina Grimké and Maria Miller Stewart. Since reopening in 1987, it's been an active center for cultural events, with changing museum exhibits on the ground floor. (Renovations begun in June 2003 will limit access to the African Meeting House until completed.)

A stone's throw from the Meeting House are five **Smith Court** residences, which are considered typical homes of black Bostonians in the nineteenth century. Number 10 was built for black chimney sweep Joseph Scarlett in 1853. The enterprising Scarlett owned many pieces of real estate, including numbers 7 and 7A. The double house at number 3 was purchased by James Scott, a black clothing dealer, and rented for five years to William Nell, America's first published black historian.

The final stop on the trail, at Smith Court and Joy Street, is the **Abiel Smith School** (1835), the first building in the United States constructed for the soul purpose of housing a black public school. When public school segregation was outlawed in 1855, the Smith School was closed. It later served as a city storage area and as a post for several veterans' groups, including black veterans of the Civil War. Thanks to federally funded renovations in the 1990s, the Smith School opened as a museum space for the first time in February 2000. It now houses the Afro-American History Museum's first permanent exhibitions and a new museum store.

Over some forty years of its existence, the Black Heritage Trail has clearly changed for the better. In 1997, the Shaw/54th Memorial was heralded across the nation for a century of inspiration. The Smith School and the African Meeting House have been restored and have enjoyed a marked increase in public awareness. Both the Boston African American National Historic Site and the Museum of Afro-American History continue to develop educational programs for public schools in and around Boston, as well as year-round programs for the general public. (The National Park Service, for example, has partnered with the Freedom Trail Foundation for their Resisting for Justice program, which uses role-playing to involve Boston public school students in the history of the 1773 Boston Tea Party and the 1851 rescue of fugitive slave Shadrach Minkins.)

In the eyes of Ken Heidelberg, longtime site manager of the Boston African American National Historic Site, the greatest joys of the trail are still in visitors' reactions. "I hear it again and again," he reports. "Things like, 'I didn't know that!' 'Why isn't that in the history books?' 'You mean *all* of that *happened?*'"

THE ESSENTIALS

Addresses: Trail begins at Shaw/54th Memorial, at the corner of Beacon and Park streets, directly across from Massachusetts State House, and extends across north slope of Beacon Hill, Boston. Boston African American National Historic Site administrative offices, 14 Beacon Street, Suite 503, Boston, MA 02108. Museum of Afro-American History administrative offices, 14 Beacon Street, Suite 721, Boston, MA 02108. **Telephone:** Boston African American National Historic Site, (617) 742-5415; Museum of Afro-American History offices, (617) 725-0022. **Websites:** Black Heritage Trail and Boston African American National Historical Site: www.nps.gov/boaf, click on In-Depth; Museum of Afro-American History: www.afroammuseum.org. **Visitor Information:** Tours of the Black Heritage Trail begin at the Robert Gould Shaw/54th Regiment Memorial. Free. Group size limited to 30. From Memorial Day though Labor Day (summer season), guided tours leave daily at 10:00 A.M., noon, and 2:00 P.M. (Call at least 24 hours in advance for groups of 10 or more). Labor Day to Memorial Day (winter season), Monday through Saturday only, at 10:00 A.M., noon, and 2:00 P.M.; winter-season tours conducted by reservation only.

Free self-guided tour brochures available through National Park Service office, (617) 742-5415, or on websites (see above). Trail extremely difficult to navigate by wheelchair due to slope, bumpy sidewalks, and erratic curb cuts on Beacon Hill.

The Black Heritage Trail® is a registered trademark of the Museum of Afro-American History.

36 The Boston Women's Heritage Trail

IN SOME ways, the Boston Women's Heritage Trail is a lot like its older cousins, the Freedom Trail and the Black Heritage Trail. All three are downtown walking tours that lead visitors past venerable old Boston sites, educating and entertaining guests with colorful stories about the city's rich history. All three evoke Boston-based heroes—dead ones, for the most part. Like the Freedom Trail, the Boston Women's Heritage Trail—which made its debut in May 1990—takes visitors to the Paul Revere House, the Granary Burying Ground, the Old South Meeting House, and Faneuil Hall. Like the Black Heritage Trail, it includes sites on Beacon Hill, such as the African Meeting House and the Lewis and Harriet Hayden House, both nineteenth-century centers for abolitionist activity.

If all the Boston Women's Heritage Trail did was highlight some of the sites of its kindred treks, it would still be an important educational tool. But the scope and goals of this unique historic tour—which includes five different neighborhood walks and 102 separate sites—are far grander and far more focused than that. One glance at the opening quote of the trail's guidebook (an essential tool, since the trail is not guided by national park rangers nor marked by a painted line) provides a hint as to what's to come:

"We should have every path laid open to woman as freely as to man."

—MARGARET FULLER

Unfathomable as it may seem, women's "paths" were, for the most part, unheralded, unmarked, and unchronicled until fairly recent times. Back in 1776, the outspoken Abigail Adams implored of her husband John, "Remember the ladies, and be more generous and favorable to them than your ancestors!" As it turned out, neither John nor the generations of men that followed did much to commemorate women's accomplishments—even in Boston, the acknowledged "Cradle of Liberty."

But the Boston Women's Heritage Trail has helped change all that. When visitors pass sites they recognize from other tours, the tales they encounter have a decidedly different twist. At the Revere House, for example, people learn about Rachel Revere, who held the family and business together while her husband embroiled himself in politics and industry. The Granary Burying Ground stop focuses on Ben Franklin's mother and Boston's storytelling "Mother Goose" rather than John Hancock, Sam Adams, and the men slain in the Boston Massacre. The Old South Meeting House is heralded as the church of poet Phillis Wheatley, not the rallying place of raucous Boston Tea Party–goers. Faneuil Hall becomes the stage where an Omaha named Suzette LaFlesche spoke out against America's cruel Indian reservation system in 1879, and where working women founded the Women's Trade Union League and the Massachusetts Nurses Association.

The statue of free-thinking Anne Hutchinson and her daughter, on the grounds of the Massachusetts State House, was one of the first public memorials to famous women in Boston.

But the Boston Women's Heritage Trail offers far more than just a new perspective on familiar old places. It's likely that a majority of the historic landmarks on the trail are not covered in most downtown walking tours at all. These range from the Telephone Exchange on Harrison Avenue, where eight thousand female employees waged a successful strike in 1919, to the onetime Byron Street offices of the Women's International League for Peace and Freedom, whose members included activist Florence Luscomb and Emily Greene Balch, the second American woman to earn the Nobel Peace Prize.

"We borrowed more from the Black Heritage Trail than the Freedom Trail," explained Meg Campbell, who originated the women's trail idea in 1988. Although the accomplishments of wealthy white Boston men have been documented everywhere, the contributions of African-Americans, Asian Americans, Hispanics, Native Americans, and women from a variety of socioeconomic backgrounds have often gone unrecognized. "The idea of this trail," finished Campbell, "is to make some of those people visible."

The idea of creating a trail to commemorate women's accomplishments in Boston first occurred to Campbell in the mid-1980s. At the time, she was a senior research analyst at the State House, and her children were attending Boston public schools. Campbell's concern began when she noticed children touring the State House; she became acutely aware of the paucity of positive female images available to children in and around the building. Inside, she saw only one woman represented—in a statue of an anonymous nurse comforting a wounded soldier. Outside were the only public sculptures of women in the entire city: Anne Hutchinson and Mary Dyer, two seventeenth-century women who were respectively banished and hanged for their outspoken and "unorthodox" views on faith. "There were no images of women of power in the seat of power in Massachusetts," observed Campbell. "So I wondered, What is the message here for children?"

In February 1988, Campbell went to work for District A superintendent Diana Lam as a Boston public school writing specialist. School administrator Isabel Mendes had already been encouraging the idea of doing something special in the schools for Women's History Month, celebrated in March every year. The group agreed to do something different and new, perhaps even pursue a grant. But the clincher came when Campbell announced, "I have this idea I've kind of been saving, but let's all do it. In the spirit of community." The Boston Women's Heritage Trail was born, semi-officially.

Other visions of a women's history trail had been proposed before in Boston. In 1984, for instance, author Mary Maynard and her daughter Mary-Lou included a "Women's Freedom Trail" in their book, the useful and whimsical *Hassle-Free Boston: A Manual for Women*. As far back as 1978, Maynard had written about stops on such a trail in her columns for *Equal Times*, the now-defunct women's newspaper. But the trail we know and walk today was a product of the Boston public schools. Building a walking tour that visitors and students alike could travel, using statues, markers and other public art to commemorate historic women with Boston connections, was part of a broader plan to incorporate the contributions of women of all classes, races, careers, and historic periods into the public school curriculum. In a way, developing that part of the curriculum—especially in the very formative grades four through eight—was the "inside" goal; the trail was more a vehicle or catalyst than an end in itself.

With the help of a grant from the U.S. Department of Education, Boston students and teachers helped research and identify the accomplishments of local women, voted for their favorite historical figures, participated in related activities, and, in short, helped create the Boston Women's Heritage Trail. In July 1989, educator Patricia C. Morris was hired as project director. Under her watchful eye, methodology and goals began to change and evolve. Though the grant specified that six elementary and middle schools would find and identify twelve women and make twelve plaques in their honor, the numbers and interest grew. In the end, some seventeen schools, forty-two teachers, and approximately a thousand children were involved, representing every neighborhood in Boston. Women and men from local schools, colleges, historic sites, arts organizations, museums, the National Park Service, and the City of Boston also contributed to the effort.

"Resident historian" Polly Kaufman—a theoretically retired Boston educator who was simultaneously teaching at the University of Massachusetts and writing her most recent women's history book—was hired to write the trail booklet. As Kaufman listened to and absorbed all the information given her by various sources, a major problem emerged: many more women's names were uncovered than ever imagined. Moreover, the researchers discovered that many of the accomplishments of women were done by groups—"ladies" clubs, unions, societies, and other organizations. The result was a nomination list of 123 women, many with organizational affiliations. Participating Boston students were then asked to vote for their ten favorite women. Though many tended to choose women from their own neighborhoods, the highest number of votes went to Revolutionary-era African-American poet Phillis Wheatley.

The first, quite modest version of the trail guide was published for the Boston Women's Heritage Trail's grand opening on May 30, 1990. The gala events included a parade of more than two hundred students and teachers, who marched with banners, cheers, and the occasional period costume from the Old South Meeting House to the State House.

The current and expanded edition of the guidebook—rewritten by Bonnie Hurd Smith with the assistance of Polly Kaufman, Mary Smoyer, and several board members, and published in 1999—features more than one hundred women and forty related organizations. It has stops at 102 sites, refers to multitudes of others, and deals with four full centuries of female life in Boston. In the latter respect, the Boston Women's Heritage Trail is much more ambitious than its kindred walking tours: the Freedom Trail includes sixteen stops, all of which are tied to the American Revolutionary and early national period; the Black Heritage Trail has fourteen sites, neatly and logically focused on the Beacon Hill community in the nineteenth century.

Fortunately, the lengthy Boston Women's Heritage Trail is divided into five easier walks; each features twelve to thirty-five sites, has a loosely defined central theme, and can be covered in two hours or less. When guided walking tours are given—primarily during Women's History Month and the summer tourist season—most of the guides limit their walks to select downtown stops, much as is done on "short form" Freedom Trail tours.

The Downtown Walk, with twenty-four sites, illustrates "The Search for Equal Rights." Women who spoke out against slavery, for women's suffrage, for Native American rights, and for rights for the mentally ill are all included, featuring some familiar names like Lucy Stone, Dorothea Dix, Elizabeth Foster Vergoose (Boston's "Mother Goose"), Helen Keller, and Mary Baker Eddy, the founder of the Church of Christ, Scientist. The starting point is the gold-domed State House, where statues of that inspirational duo of strong colonial women—Anne Hutchinson and Mary Dyer—remind us how and why the Boston Women's Heritage Trail was first conceived.

The North End Walk presents "A Diversity of Cultures." It spans twelve sites and tells of the variety of ethnic groups that have lived in Boston's oldest neighborhood. It ranges from Rachel Walker Revere and the Revolutionary period to various Irish, Jewish, and Italian women and their civic groups, which emerged along with the influx of nineteenth- and twentieth-century immigrants. Honorees include Pauline Agassiz Shaw, founder of America's first trade school; internationally known nineteenth-century actress Charlotte Cushman; and Clementina Poto Langone, who continually aided twentieth-century Italian immigrants and the unemployed.

The Beacon Hill Walk features "Writers, Artists, and Activists" and seventeen different sites. Its highlights include the studio of sculptor Anne Whitney, the last Boston home of Louisa May Alcott, and the Underground Railroad site through which Ellen Craft escaped from slavery. Many of these sites focus on women's efforts throughout the nineteenth and twentieth centuries to bring peace to the world and freedom to its diverse peoples: on Byron Street is the old headquarters of the Massachusetts Women's International League for Peace and Freedom; the African Meeting House, off Joy Street, was a center for abolitionist and feminist thinkers like Maria Stewart; Julia Ward Howe, whose many accomplishments included initiating the idea of Mother's Day as a day to demonstrate for peace, once lived on Chestnut Street.

The South Cove/Chinatown Walk is arguably the most interesting, if only because it includes so many sites rarely visited by most Bostonians. Fourteen stops tell of "Women's Action for Economic and Social Justice" and include tales of educational reform, women's unions, women in a Catholic religious community, telephone operators, and garment workers. Two favorite stops on this walk are the site of the old Denison House on Tyler Street, where Amelia Earhart did social work in the late 1920s, and the corner of Beach and Tyler streets, where Phillis Wheatley first landed from a slave ship in 1761, debarking on a long-gone wharf. Other interesting tales include that of the pioneering Chinese restaurateur Ruby Foo, as well as those of the eight thousand women who successfully waged the Telephone Operators' Strike of 1919. Another site, at 15 West Street, shows where Elizabeth Peabody, "the grandmother of the American kindergarten," once ran her bookshop, a hotbed of nineteenth-century transcendentalist and feminist thought.

The final, and most recently developed, of the five tours is the **Back Bay Walk**, which honors "Educators, Artists, and Social Reformers," and connects the Chinatown Walk with the Beacon Hill Walk with a loop through the Back Bay. Among the fascinating women discovered along this route are composer Amy Beach, art patron and collector Isabella Stewart Gardner, black community leader Muriel Snowden, and Harriet Hemenway, cofounder of the Massachusetts Audubon Society. Historic organizations of, by, and for women encountered en route include the Women's Educational and Industrial Union, the nation's first YWCA, the Massachusetts Woman Suffrage Association, and the Junior League of Boston.

Unlike the Freedom and Black Heritage trails, the Boston Women's Heritage Trail includes the former locations of buildings that have since been destroyed; many of its sites are empty lots or simple markers that tell what once was there. And though the women's trail, like the other tours, focuses on deceased heroes, the women who molded this particular historic walking tour made one notable exception: Rose Kennedy's birthplace was included on the North End trail though the Kennedy matriarch was still alive—having reaching her one hundredth birthday!—when the Boston Women's Heritage Trail made its debut. (Mrs. Kennedy passed away in 1995; her funeral, like her christening, was held at St. Stephen's Church on Hanover Street in the North End.)

Today, the Boston Women's Heritage Trail is led by a volunteer board of twenty women who represent a wide array of interests and skills. Board members include a number of educators and administrators from the Boston public school system—who continue to bring women's history into Boston classrooms in innovative ways—balanced by artists, writers, activists, and intellectuals from area universities, museums, city government, the National Park Service, historic sites, libraries, and beyond. Thanks to the board and its consultants, the trail continues to develop school curricula, present slide shows, workshops, and lectures, lead guided tours on request, and offer visitors a fact-filled website. And though it's still one of the newest kids on the historic-tour block, the Boston Women's Heritage Trail has already inspired, encouraged, or sponsored the development of other women's history trails in New England. They run the gamut from minitrails of Boston's neighborhoods created by students and their teachers, and a collaborative trail with the Museum of Fine Arts, Boston, to full-blown tours in Salem, Massachusetts, Portland, Maine, and Boston's South Shore, all developed by professional writers, journalists, and historians.

In part due to the broad reach of the trail and the activism of its board members, Boston's other major walking trails and tour organizations—including the Freedom Trail, the Black Heritage Trail, city park rangers, the National Park Service, the Boston History Collaborative, and Boston by Foot—have all added more women's stories to their walks and talks. Should they ever forget, these organizations and sites are sometimes politely reminded of their omissions—as in 1996, when a group of Charlestown fifth-graders marched on the Bunker Hill Monument, chanting "Two, four, six, eight/We're here to set the story straight." (The Freedom Trail site had neglected to include mention of Sarah Josepha Hale in its brochure and signage; editor Hale had organized a glorified bake sale in 1830, which financed the completion of the famed Bunker Hill obelisk.)

Times have changed quite a bit since the day when Meg Campbell found only two public statues of women—one of whom was hanged and the other banished—for children to view in Boston. Case in point: the name of Amy Beach is now carved on the Hatch Shell on the Esplanade along with those of eighty-seven male musicians; a bust of feminist editor and suffragist Lucy Stone is now displayed in Faneuil Hall; a group of women who influenced state politics are commemorated in the *"Hear Us"* installation inside the State House; the mural *Nine Notable Women* hangs in the Boston Public Library; and the first women to join the all-male statuary of Commonwealth Avenue Mall—Abigail Adams, Lucy Stone, and Phillis Wheatley—are commemorated in the new Boston Women's Memorial, already one of the most popular destinations in town.

"The Trail is a wonderful, ever-changing project," muses Mary Smoyer, longtime president of the BWHT. "People call and e-mail from all over— we even did a tour for a group from Australia once—and they're always so positive about the trail. They want to know more, and to tell us about their 'special woman.' Boston is such a great walking city, and walking in these women's footsteps continues to inspire and excite us all."

THE ESSENTIALS

Address: Trail includes 102 sites in five Boston neighborhoods: Downtown, North End, Beacon Hill, South Cove/Chinatown, and Back Bay. Boston Women's Heritage Trail, c/o Mary Smoyer, 22 Holbrook Street, Boston, MA 02130. **Telephone:** Guidebooks and general information available from Mary Smoyer, Boston Women's Heritage Trail, (617) 522-2872. **Website:** www.bwht.org. **Visitor Information:** Self-guided tour possible anytime; guidebooks available via mail (see above), or at Boston Common Visitors Center, Boston National Park Service Headquarters (15 State Street), Old South Meeting House, Old State House, and other historic site and bookstores. Guided tours available by appointment for a moderate fee; call (617) 522-2872.

Much of tour, which passes exteriors of sites, is wheelchair accessible via curb cuts and sidewalks; some minor rerouting needed; Beacon Hill segment is very difficult for wheelchairs due to hills and bumpy sidewalks; Faneuil Hall Marketplace area also has bumpy surfaces.

37 Hanover Street

HANOVER STREET is best known today as the heart of Boston's Italian North End—home to dozens of quality Italian restaurants and cafés, interesting and unusual shops, and joyous summer street festivals. What's less immediately apparent to the casual visitor is the rich history that predates this neighborhood's most recent identity. For Hanover is not only the heart of the Italian North End—it's also the heart of one of Boston's oldest neighborhoods.

The North End began as a center for maritime commerce and colonial housing in the seventeenth century, home to many middle- and upper-class residents of English descent who attended Puritan meetinghouses or Anglican churches. After the departure of a multitude of wealthy Tories following the American Revolution, the area became a center for craftspeople, tradespeople, and various shipping and mercantile enterprises. Then, throughout the nineteenth century, the North End welcomed a variety of foreign-born settlers, including large numbers of Irish Catholics, Eastern European Jews, and Italian Catholics. It was not until the early twentieth century that Italian-Americans became the dominant North End group.

Hanover Street itself is one of Boston's oldest public roads. As such, its buildings have included Revolutionary-era churches, colonial taverns, late Victorian casinos, and seedy sailors' delights. Among the street's most famous historic residents have been the Reverend Cotton Mather, Benjamin Franklin, colonial patriot Dr. Joseph Warren, nineteenth-century actress Charlotte Cushman, clan matriarch Rose Fitzgerald Kennedy, and merchant Eben D. Jordan, founder of the local department store Jordan Marsh. Jordan's first small dry-goods store, begun when he was nineteen, once stood at 168 Hanover. (Young Rowland Hussey Macy opened his first store in the North End during that same period; perhaps ironically, in the 1990s, the mighty Macy's bought out Jordan Marsh.) The road also boasts one of Boston's most infamous ghosts—poor Peter Rugg, whose spectral horse and carriage keep mysteriously passing by his Hanover Street home, from whence they disappeared in the 1770s.

Exactly when Hanover Street was laid out is not certain. What is clear is that from the earliest days of Boston's settlement—certainly from the 1630s or 1640s—it led up from the sea, bisected the North End, and terminated at what eventually became known as Tremont Street. During colonial times, Hanover was interrupted by a creek that ran from Boston's Town Cove to Mill Pond—an area outlined today by Blackstone Street. (A short bridge enabled colonists to cross the creek and continue on Hanover toward Tremont.) During the 1950s and 1960s, that southwestern section of Hanover was again interrupted, first by the construction of the highway known as the Central Artery, then by the building of Government Center, which simultaneously obliterated its old terminus at Scollay Square on Tremont Street. As if that weren't enough, beginning in the 1990s, Boston's Big Dig brought yet another seemingly endless upheaval and interruption. Incidentally, though many people assume that Hanover ends at Mother Anna's Restaurant (211 Hanover) and the artery, a small, inconspicuous sector remains on the other side of the highway, passing near Haymarket and the Union Oyster House.

Twentieth- and twenty-first-century construction projects were not the only activities to change the face of Hanover Street, of course. Many of the street's oldest buildings were lost either to fires—the worst being in 1676, 1679, 1690, 1692, 1775, and 1835—or to a road-widening project after the Civil War.

One of Hanover Street's earliest epithets was "the Way to the Winnisimet [Chelsea] Ferry." The ferry did indeed land at the foot of Hanover, near the site where USS *Constitution* was completed in 1797 and a U.S. Coast Guard base is located today. In 1708, when all of Boston's byways were given official names, modern Hanover was given three separate designations: from the ferry to Bennett Street was called North Street (not to be confused with the North Street now found in the North End), from Bennett to Blackstone it was Middle Street, and from there to "the Sign of the Orange Tree," a colonial tavern that boasted Boston's first hackney coach stand, it was Hanover. In 1824, all three sections were united as Hanover, after the British royal family.

Retaining the name Hanover was an unusual act for 1824. In the years following the Revolution, many Boston streets were renamed in honor of the new commonwealth and the new nation. King became State Street; Queen became Court; and Cornhill was renamed for General George Washington. Still, Hanover wasn't alone in the North End. The names of a variety of other nearby roads—including Fleet Street, Sun Court, and Prince Street—hark back to Old England and the monarchy to this day.

During summer months, lively street *festas*—Roman Catholic religious festivals honoring patron saints, like St. Anthony—draw neighbors and throngs of delighted visitors to Hanover Street and Boston's North End.

Throughout the seventeenth and eighteenth centuries, the North End was a favored residence of Boston's elite English settlers, as well as of hard-working tradespeople. The much-despised British governor Sir Edmund Andros (1637–1714) and the much-beloved patriot Dr. Joseph Warren (1741–1775) both had homes on the section of Hanover near present-day Government Center. Increase and Cotton Mather, pastors of the Old North Meeting House on North Square and outspoken religious leaders, also lived on Hanover, near Bennett Street. (The Old North Meeting House, known as "the church of the Mathers," was pulled down for firewood during the Revolution; it's often confused with the Old North Church of Paul Revere fame, which still stands on Salem Street.) At Union and Hanover, not far from the current home of the Bell in Hand Tavern, was the Blue Ball, where Josiah Franklin resided and dipped candles for a living. As might be expected, his son Ben was frequently seen darting in and out.

Hanover Street was as well known for its churches as for its numerous taverns. Its most famous church was built in 1712, when the Old North Meeting House on North Square was becoming overcrowded. "Seventeen substantial mechanics" founded the New North Meeting House at 401 Hanover Street. Built in 1714 and enlarged in 1730, the New North was redesigned by the architect Charles Bulfinch from 1802 to 1804, making it the only Boston Bulfinch church still standing. The chandeliers inside were replicas of those in the new State House, which had also been designed by Bulfinch only a few years before.

The church was originally Congregational, reflecting the area's Puritan roots. Though many guidebooks explain that Paul Revere and his family were among its members, there is no historic evidence to substantiate the claim. (In 1804, however, a bell cast by Revere was hung in its belfry; Revere copper was also used on the small dome.) In 1813, the church became Unitarian—as did many Congregational Churches of the time—and remained so until 1849. Francis Parkman, father of the famous historian, was the minister during that period. By 1850, the North End was populated largely by Irish immigrants, followed by an influx of Portuguese and Italian settlers. The New North Meeting House eventually became a Roman Catholic house of worship as St. Stephen's Church. Among that church's well-known members was Rose Fitzgerald Kennedy (1890–1995), who attended St. Stephen's as a child. The daughter of Boston mayor John ("Honey Fitz") Fitzgerald who later earned her own international fame as matriarch of the Kennedy clan, Mrs. Kennedy lived to the age of 104; both her christening and her funeral were held at St. Stephens.

St. Stephen's Church has undergone a variety of changes over the years. In 1870, the entire building was moved back twelve feet to accommodate the widening of Hanover Street. Two major fires occurred, in 1897 and 1929. By 1964, there was talk of tearing down the very worn old building. Fortunately, Richard Cardinal Cushing became involved and helped raise funds to restore the historic structure to its original Bulfinch appearance. The Boston Society of Architects gave its Award for Historic Preservation to the cardinal in 1970, honoring the fine restoration work on this Hanover Street landmark.

While many of the North End's Irish Catholic citizens attended St. Stephen's, other immigrant groups adapted or constructed their own houses of worship as well. The growing Italian presence of the late nineteenth and early twentieth centuries was reflected in the church and "Peace Garden" at the corner of Hanover and Prince Streets. Built in 1873 and beautifully restored in 1988, St. Leonard's was the first Italian Roman Catholic church established in New England, and the first founded by Italian immigrants in Boston. (Another religious "first" on Hanover Street is not readily apparent today. The North End Community Health Center, at 332 Hanover, was the site of the wooden First Universalist Church, where Reverend John Murray, "the father of Universalism," preached from 1793 until 1815.)

Meanwhile, across the street from St. Stephen's is the broad, tree-shaded Paul Revere Mall, created in 1933 as an urban renewal project. Built along the lines of a *prado*—a park where people congregate in a typical small Italian village—the mall had two purposes: one was to create space to reduce the risk of fire to nearby historic churches; a second was to design a welcome open place in an overly congested neighborhood. Today, the mall is a favorite resting place for mothers and fathers with baby carriages, playful kids, neighborhood seniors, and Freedom Trail hikers. The majestic equestrian statue of Paul Revere at its center was modeled by Cyrus Dallin in 1885 though not cast and put in place until 1940, when the project finally found financing through the George Robert White Fund. Earlier in this century, the mall was filled with old buildings, including a men's hotel called the Webster House. At that time, Hanover was still paved with stones and lined with streetcar tracks that stretched from the ferry landing to Scollay Square.

Clubs, casinos, pawnshops, and flophouses filled the Hanover Street section near Scollay Square up until the 1950s and early 1960s. Save for that long-gone sailors' district and the paved-over roads, longtime residents agree, Hanover has actually looked much the same throughout this century. "Years ago no one had bathtubs or toilets in their homes," explained longtime resident Frank Gulla, who was born on Hanover Street in 1923, "and they packed more people into the living spaces. I do miss seeing the horse and wagons all loading down by Blackstone Street. Horse and wagons also delivered ice, oil, and coal. But most of the buildings haven't changed much—except that everything now is an Italian restaurant!"

In fact, more than two dozen sit-down Italian restaurants can be found on Hanover Street on any given year (though their names and owners do periodically change), arguably the largest number on any street in the city. These range from simple pastry and coffee shops like Mike's and the Modern, to popular restaurants like Bricco, the Daily Catch, Caffe Paradiso, Giacomo's, and Mother Anna's (the latter is credited as the oldest Italian restaurant in the North End). One of the most enjoyable and entertaining ways to experience Hanover Street's and the North End's culinary delights and distinctive cuisine, incidentally, is by taking Michele Topor's award-winning North End Market Tour, which treats guests to three and a half hours of shops, markets, food and wine tastings, cultural commentary, and lore.

Like its restaurants, Hanover Street's summer festivals draw both locals and guests from around the world. The popular weekend galas are Roman Catholic religious festivals honoring various patron saints, like St. Jude, St. Agrippina, and St. Anthony. Organized by religious societies—descendants of villagers from Italian towns holding devotion to a particular patron saint—these outdoor *festas* usually take place from mid-June through late August and feature plentiful food, colorful lights, waving banners, and joyous processions. (Despite the numerous festivals and Italian restaurants, today only some 30 to 40 percent of the North End's residential population is actually Italian; increasing gentrification since the 1980s has resulted in skyrocketing prices and a proliferation of young urban professionals and empty nesters living there, especially in the revitalized waterfront area.)

In other ways Hanover Street is like any other busy Boston street. Though less than a half mile in length, it boasts churches, banks, pharmacies, dry cleaners, and convenience stores. There are shops where you can purchase cookware, tobacco, cold cuts, insurance, flowers, shoes, booze, and airline tickets. There are places to fix your teeth, curl your hair, straighten your back, tickle your funny bone, frame your art, mail your letters, and put out your fire. (There was once a place to embalm your dead as well, but Langone's Funeral Home, lodged for decades at 383 Hanover, is now gone. Undoubtedly, Langone's most famous customers were immigrants Nicola Sacco and Bartolomeo Vanzetti, apparent victims of the political unrest, Red-baiting, and xenophobia that followed the First World War. After their electrocution on August 23, 1927, the pair were embalmed at Langone's, from whence a huge funeral cortege stretched down Hanover Street; the wake drew some 100,000 mourners and the procession an estimated 50,000 marchers.)

Today, it's summer *festas*, groups of friends, and camera-toting tourists that are most likely to pack the roadway. Meanwhile, many of the old four- and five-story buildings that line the street combine business on the ground floor with residential apartments in the upper stories.

One result of this plethora of activity is important to visitors: there is nowhere—*nowhere*—to park. Fortunately, there are parking lots on nearby Atlantic Avenue and Commercial Street; on the other side of the Central Artery (Big Dig) Project are the Government Center garage and a new parking facility at the Haymarket/Orange Line T station. Though no subways travel to the North End, that Haymarket T stop, located on the truncated sector of old Hanover Street, is not far away. The experience of visiting Boston's oldest and one of its most delightfully Old World neighborhoods is well worth the walk.

One footnote to Hanover Street is far from a footnote in world history. Near the far end of Hanover, where the Artery-truncated section of the old road meets Union and then Congress streets, is Carmen Park. Since its dedication in October 1995, the monument there—six riveting steel-and-glass towers representing the six million Jews who died at the hand of the Nazis—has deeply touched millions of visitors. Designed by San Francisco architect Stanley Saitowitz, the New England Holocaust Memorial's columns are etched with six million numbers, in random order, to symbolize the tattoos branded on Jews when they arrived at the six major death camps—Auschwitz-Birkenau, Chelmno, Sobibor, Treblinka, Majdanek, and Belzec. The memorial's placement on the site is particularly meaningful, since it straddles the red line of Boston's Freedom Trail and touches on segments of the old North End and West End, neighborhoods where Jewish immigrants found freedom and opportunity in the nineteenth and early twentieth centuries.

THE ESSENTIALS

Address: North End, Boston. **Telephone:** see special interest numbers below, in Visitor Information. **Websites:** www.northendweb.com; www.northendboston.com; www.bostonfamilyhistory.com/neigh_nend.html. **Visitor Information:** North End festivals are celebrated almost every weekend from June through late August; for more information, contact the Mayor's Office of Special Events and Tourism at (617) 635-3911 or visit www.northendboston.com.

Parts of the North End are on both the Freedom Trail and Boston Women's Heritage Trail tours (see Chapters 10 and 36 for details; or visit www.thefreedomtrail.org and www.bwht.org). A variety of other tours include the North End, or specifically focus on the area; among the best: Michele Topor's North End Market Tours (617-523-6032; www.northendmarkettours.com); the North End Secret Tour (www.northendboston.com);

Boston by Foot's North End tour (617-367-2345; 24-hour Hot Foot Line 617-367-3766; www.bostonbyfoot.com); fees are charged for these tours.

38 The Old Quincy School

HIDDEN AWAY on a quiet road in the Chinatown neighborhood of Boston is an old brick building that's not really the kind of structure that would immediately catch the eye. The simple, stark exterior is faded red brick, punctuated by large, multipaned sash windows. Two old flagpoles protrude from the front, and a statue of Confucius stands guard near the glassed entranceway. Aside from the inscription "QUINCY SCHOOL 1847" —set high on the structure's facade and virtually illegible today—you'd never guess the old building was a landmark of Boston educational history. But indeed it is.

During its 129 years as a public grammar school, the Quincy School at 90 Tyler Street was an educational melting pot for generations of immigrants who moved into Boston's South Cove. Those immigrants included the Asian-Americans who have molded Chinatown's character over the past six decades, as well as the English, Irish, Italians, Syrians, Jews, Lebanese, Greeks, Russians, and other immigrant groups who preceded them.

Moreover, the Quincy School—named for Josiah Quincy, Boston's second mayor and one of three Josiah Quincys elected mayor of the Hub—was a pioneer in nineteenth-century education. Begun as "the Experiment" of educational innovators such as Horace Mann, the Quincy was hailed as America's first school with graded classrooms and the first to provide a separate seat for each student. Though its years as part of the Boston public school system ended in 1976, the building continues to educate today, as a home to Chinese-American community associations and their related cultural activities.

During colonial times, the neighborhoods that later surrounded the Quincy School—Chinatown and Bay Village, as well as the area now occupied by the Tufts–New England Medical Center—were generally under water. In their place was a section of Boston Harbor known as South Cove, an area of spacious tidewater flats filled with wharves and still-houses.

By the early nineteenth century, however, landfill fever had begun to infect local developers. Railroads were rapidly becoming the transportation of choice, and new land was needed for tracks and terminals. The first encroachment of land into the South Cove occurred in 1804, when the Front Street Corporation filled in what's now Harrison Avenue. Then, in 1833, the South Cove Associates began a landfill project that all but obliterated the cove in six years. Gravel from the nearby communities of Dorchester and Roxbury was hauled in, and fifty-five acres of new land, plus three miles of new streets, emerged. Among the area's earliest landmarks was the United States Hotel, at Lincoln and Beach streets, which enjoyed brief renown as America's largest hotel. The rest of the area was consumed, to a large degree, by railroads.

Boston's Chinese community did not begin to take shape in the South Cove area until later in the nineteenth century. Some Chinese men and women had come to Boston earlier, in the wake of the American Revolution or as a result of the China Trade; increased knowledge of America's new frontiers and opportunities was enticing to a hearty few. But it was the completion of the transcontinental railroad in 1869 that led to the first major Chinese settlements in Boston. Initially attracted by work on the cross-country tracks, Chinese laborers moved east in search of employment once the railroads were complete. By 1875, the core of a Chinese community had been established in a huddle of tents on Ping On Alley. The community was doomed to remain small, insular, and predominantly male for a time by the Chinese Exclusion Act of 1882, which barred Chinese immigrants from entering the United States.

Immediately following World War II, partly as a result of the repeal of the Chinese Exclusion Act in 1943, the Boston Chinese community began to grow and to include more women and children. It was not until the 1960s, however, that the liberalization of immigration laws under President Kennedy finally enabled the development of the large Chinatown we know today to take place.

The unprecedented influx of immigrants from other foreign nations beginning in the mid-nineteenth century prompted a major change in the Massachusetts public school systems. Due in part to that immigration, Boston's population grew from 43,000 to 178,000 between 1820 and 1860. Overcrowding and an unusually heterogeneous population were among the results.

Many members of Boston's elite reacted to the increased immigrant population with a sort of benevolent xenophobia. They feared that increasing numbers of immigrant children on the streets would lead to truancy, vagrancy, and a threat to public safety; if those newcomers could be safely ensconced in schools, they reasoned, everyone would be better off. Hence, Massachusetts enacted the nation's first statewide compulsory school attendance law in 1852.

The Quincy School was erected on Tyler Street in 1848 to relieve overcrowding at two of Boston's other grammar schools, the Brimmer and the Winthrop. But under the guidance of educational innovators like Horace Mann, Samuel Gridley Howe, and George B. Emerson, the new Quincy School took a decidedly modern turn. First, it was agreed that the school, established on September 6, 1847, would be housed in a four-story building with twelve classrooms and a large assembly hall. That multiunit plan was deemed more economical than creating a series of one-room schoolhouses, as was customary at the time (the average Boston schoolroom of 1833 was a nineteen-by-twenty-six-foot chamber, with one teacher and sixty-two students of varying ages and abilities). In fact, it cost $6,000 to operate the entire Quincy School during its first year. (Today, more than $10,000 per year is spent for a single Boston public school student.) Secondly, since the building was large enough to accommodate six hundred students, the children were separated by age and attainment. Prussian model schools had shown that the "factory system" of education—in essence, using a division of labor and pushing the "product" through a step-by-step, year-by-year assembly line—was highly efficient. And so it was.

The Quincy School's designers added other innovations as well. When the building was dedicated as a boys' grammar school on June 26, 1848, it became the first Boston schoolhouse with a separate room for each teacher and class. It was the first to provide each pupil with his own desk; long common benches had been the rule prior to that time. It was the first school to end the cumbersome system of two equally ranked headmasters, and to replace it with a headmaster and submaster. This meant more uniformity in schooling; teachers no longer had to cope with two masters' divergent ideas on books and curriculum. It also featured a larger proportion of female teachers than ever before employed in a public school for boys. By 1860, the new methods inaugurated by the Quincy had been copied by all of Boston's primary and grammar schools.

Under the leadership of headmaster John Dudley Philbrick (1818–1886), who later became superintendent of the Boston public schools and

Winding wooden staircases in Chinatown's Old Quincy School, where generations of immigrants were educated and assimilated.

a national authority on education, the Quincy School flourished. From 404 boys in 1847, its enrollment grew to 562 students in 1848 and 662 in 1849. Philbrick added many creative changes. The *Ohles Biographical Dictionary of American Educators* summarized the headmaster's special appeal in one telling sentence: "He drastically reduced punishment by whipping, and added drawing and music to the curriculum."

The nationalities represented in the student body—and in the surrounding South Cove neighborhood—changed dramatically over the years. According to the old Quincy School's enrollment books, during the first decades after 1847 the students were boys, primarily eight to fourteen years of age, with English and Irish surnames. Among the school's nineteenth-century graduates were movers and shakers from many of Boston's oldest, most respected families—names like William B. Peabody, Samuel B. Capen, Joseph A. Sprague, Henry Lyman Shaw, Granville B. Putnam, Edward C. Burrage, and William Lloyd Garrison, Jr.

By the last quarter of the century, however, growing lists of Murphys and O'Briens were sharing classrooms with boys named Jacobs, Liebman, Abramoff, D'Amico, Pacino, Apostoles, Alexanian, Sarkisian, and Assad. By 1921, Boston had a population of close to 800,000 people. More than a third were foreign born, while another third had at least one parent who was foreign born.

During the day, this international array of neighborhood children attended the Quincy School. By night, their parents often went to the Quincy for evening classes designed for working adult immigrants. Adults in the 1920s studied books like *A Little Book for Immigrants in Boston*, which gave the following suggestions:

> Learn English well. Use good words. Pronounce them clearly. Copy the language of your teacher and of educated people . . . Teach your children to be neat, industrious and polite. Give your wife a nice dress and let her have some recreation outdoors . . . Make friends with Americans. If some are rude and arrogant, do not mind them.

The Quincy evolved from a boys' grammar school to a coed facility serving students in kindergarten through sixth grade during the first quarter of the twentieth century; still, as late as the 1940s boys and girls had separate play areas. Where the wheelchair ramp now enters the glass front door of the building was an old fire escape, plus a small playground where schoolboys enjoyed stickball, handball, and other games. Throughout the 1940s and 1950s, Syrians composed one of the largest ethnic groups in the school. Meanwhile, there was a rapidly growing number of Chinese students studying alongside an international mix of Greeks, Italians, Jews, African-Americans, Russians, Lithuanians, Lebanese, and even some white Anglo-Saxon Protestants.

"All the teachers were Caucasian when I was a student there in the 1950s," recalls Richard Chin, executive director of the South Cove YMCA. "As children, we were taught not to trust the rest of the world. But the teachers there were different—they were loving, trusting, and wonderful to the Chinese kids."

Today, the *new* Quincy School—opened two blocks away from the old building in 1976—includes Asian-American teachers and regular education in Chinese holidays and culture (it also offered bilingual education for many years, though "immersion" was reintroduced to this and other Boston schools in 2003). In the early cold war era, however, no one wanted to appear "un-American" by accommodating the needs of foreign-born students. Hence, no "non-American" cultural education was offered in the old Quincy School (or any of the other Boston public schools), and children were taught English the "old-fashioned" way—sink or swim. In one teacher's classes during 1947, for example, students read books like *The Three Bears* into a microphone; if the reader made a pronunciation mistake, fellow students raised their hands in "cooperative objection." The beloved Mary Dowd's first grade classes at the old Quincy—which spanned the years 1949 to 1976—effectively used repetition and pictures rather than mikes.

In spite, and perhaps because, of those methods, the Chinese students of the old Quincy School overcame language barriers and other obstacles. "Success stories happened all the time," remembered longtime teacher Bill Muello. "Most of them went on to Boston Latin School, which required both passing an exam and getting written recommendations."

Despite its years of educational excellence, the old Quincy School building has faced the threat of demolition many times during its history. The first came on December 17, 1858, when a fire destroyed the "model" school. It was rebuilt a year later and lasted until 1938, when the Great Hurricane of that year destroyed the school's fourth-floor auditorium and roof. The fourth floor was eliminated when the school was repaired, and the building survived as a three-story structure. Since the auditorium was gone, students did their physical exercises next to their desks and assemblies were held in the downstairs hallway.

Though the building underwent a $64,000 renovation in 1939, a 1944 report to the Boston School Committee argued that the aging Quincy School should be closed. It didn't happen. In 1962 and 1965, the Sargent report on Boston Schools and a similar Harvard Study recommended immediate demolition of the famous, but decrepit, old school. Again, the school remained open.

In the late 1950s and early 1960s, the Quincy School's enrollment—as well as housing stock in the surrounding Chinatown neighborhood—was badly hurt by the building of the Central Artery, followed by the construction of an entrance to the Massachusetts Turnpike. The expansion of the Tufts–New England Medical Center in the 1960s and 1970s only exacerbated the problem. In the meantime, the school's utility systems became obsolete, the bathrooms decayed, and the roof leaked. Still, the school's administration, teachers, and students carried on in academically superior style through June 1976.

In that year, a new Quincy School complex was opened a short walk away, at 885 Washington Street. The massive, award-winning building is a modern, multiethnic elementary school filled with computers, bright colors, wide-open classrooms, a rooftop playground, and achieving students. Meanwhile, Mayor Kevin White sold the old Quincy building to the Chinese Consolidated Benevolent Association, representing the Chinatown community, for a token price of one dollar.

Today, 90 Tyler Street is a bustling community center, housing the offices of the Chinese Consolidated Benevolent Association of New England (the CCBA) and the Chung Wa Academy. Dedicated to education, the preservation of Chinese culture, and community service, the CCBA also provides affordable housing through projects it has constructed and continues to manage. Number 90 Tyler has also been an interim home for the Acorn Child Care Center operated by the Boston Chinese Neighborhood Council, as well as a facility for adult ESL (English as a Second Language) programs, varied cultural programs for youngsters and senior citizens, a choir that performs internationally, and general assistance programs for community residents. Special and seasonal programs are also operated from the vintage building—from summer school classes, summer day care, and summer lunch programs to legal and tax assistance provided by university students and community volunteers, a Ping-Pong club, and special events. Over the years, those events have included ambassadorial visits, exhibitions, Asian book festivals, recitals, cultural festivals, and meetings held by diverse community organizations.

It's appropriate that the old Quincy School building is used by service organizations that educate and help immigrants and the community, and that an image of Confucius—the revered fifth-century teacher, sage, and moralist—welcomes them at the door. Because even in its declining years as a public school, the building at 90 Tyler Street was a safe home away from home for generations of youngsters. That tradition continues today, in a new, vibrant, and unexpected form.

THE ESSENTIALS

Address: 90 Tyler Street, Chinatown, Boston, MA 02111. **Telephone:** Chinese Consolidated Benevolent Association of New England, (617) 542-2574, (617) 542-2578. **Websites:** Related sites for local Chinese culture—www.roc-taiwan.org/boston/event; http://yerkes.mit.edu/mbta/Chinatown/chsne.html. **Visitor Information:** Building open for business 9:00 A.M. to 5:00 P.M., Monday through Friday. Special events, meetings, and classes are also held during the evenings and on weekends. First floor and restroom wheelchair accessible via ramp; other areas inaccessible due to long staircases.

39 The Vilna Shul

LIKE THOSE of so many of Beacon Hill's oldest structures, the walls of the Vilna Shul have a story to tell. But this particular building is a bit different from all the other quaint, red-brick homes nestled in the narrow back roads of historic Beacon Hill. Its tales are not of Puritan preachers or Revolutionary War heroes, abolitionists or freed slaves, or even of State House politicians or picketing protesters. Instead, the Vilna Shul, at 18 Phillips

Street, is a lone survivor from an altogether different era of Boston history—the time when thousands of impoverished and persecuted Eastern European Jews immigrated to America.

Although the city of Boston was founded in 1630, the city was without a significant, stable Jewish population until the 1840s. In many ways, that was by design. The city's founding Puritans revered the Hebrew language, history, and culture, and even welcomed an Italian Jew, Judah Monis, to Harvard College as a student and teacher of Hebrew and Old Testament studies in 1722. But they saw the actual practice of the Jewish faith as a threat to the purity, homogeneity, and success of their community. Indeed, religious dissenters of all sorts—including Quakers, American Indians, Roman Catholics, and witches—were often deported, banished, forcibly converted, or hanged. The first Jew to appear in the recorded history of Boston came face to face with this philosophy. Solomon Franco (or Frankel) arrived in 1649 but didn't stay long. A legal dispute with Major General Edward Gibbons, to whom Franco had brought cargo, ended with orders for Franco to vacate twelve days later.

While most seventeenth- and eighteenth-century Jewish immigrants settled in other, less hostile parts of the United States, some did come to

The Vilna Shul on Beacon Hill is a living tribute to—and sole survivor among—the synagogues built by Eastern European Jewish immigrants who arrived in Boston near the turn of the twentieth century.

Boston. The first were Sephardic Jews from Spain and Portugal, who followed Spanish trade routes to the New World in the colonial period. In the 1840s, German Jews made up a second, significantly larger wave. German Jews built Boston's first synagogue, Ohabei Shalom (Lovers of Peace) in the South End in 1851. They also benefited from vaguely liberalized laws in the commonwealth; in 1821, Jews were granted full citizenship rights in Massachusetts. But though they could live here, they still encountered troubles when they *died* here; until 1840, when new laws superseded the old, bodies of deceased Jews had to be sent to Newport, Albany, or New York City for legal burial.

The third wave of Jewish immigration to Boston was by far the largest, and it reflected a larger trend—so large, in fact, that America's Jewish population grew from 250,000 to 3.5 million between 1880 and 1920. Jews had lived in Eastern Europe since the twelfth century; by the seventeenth century the restrictions on their activities and periodic persecutions had grown significantly worse. In 1881, following the assassination of Tsar Alexander II of Russia, any remnants of freedom for Jews quickly evaporated. Alexander had actually been surprisingly liberal in his policies; his successors, however, loathed liberalism and reform and began vigorous persecution of all minority nationalities in a policy called Russification. New laws fostered official Russian anti-Semitism, harsh legal restrictions, and pogroms—mass anti-Jewish riots and killings—in Russia as well as other parts of Eastern Europe.

Ships carrying nineteenth-century Jewish immigrants arrived in America at Castle Garden or Ellis Island in New York, and later on at the Boston Immigration Building. If not poor before leaving the old country, the passengers were often impoverished by the costs of the trip. And though the established German Jews often headed charitable societies that offered them benevolent aid, they were frequently hostile to the new immigrants. (Such has often been the case in American history: immigrants who were themselves once considered second-class citizens settle in and prosper, enabling them to treat subsequent generations of newcomers as second-class citizens.)

In many ways, the Eastern European Jews who arrived at the turn of the century had a more difficult transition than their predecessors. They were poorer. There were many more of them—representing entire families and sometimes whole towns. Finally, according to the American Jewish Historical Society study *On Common Ground: The Boston Jewish Experience, 1649–1980,* they were not well received by Boston's other residents. "They were lumped together as Russian, as Orthodox, as ignorant, as speakers of that 'ugly' language called Yiddish, as uncouth."

Some of the new Bostonians moved to the South End neighborhood, following in the footsteps of the German Jews who had lived there before departing for "finer" neighborhoods. Some moved to the North End (the former home of Irish immigrants), which became 80 percent Jewish and Italian by 1910. Most of the newly arriving Eastern European Jews, however, moved to the north slope of Beacon Hill and the adjoining West End (an area later obliterated by urban renewal). When the Vilna Shul was built in 1919—as a synagogue and community center for its poor, hardworking congregation—it was one of more than fifty neighborhood synagogues erected from scratch or adapted from other buildings to serve Boston's newest citizens. In later decades, as these immigrants departed the area, their synagogues disappeared one by one—sometimes demolished, sometimes abandoned, and sometimes converted to other uses. Few people still remember that the African Meeting House on Beacon Hill, the Charles Playhouse in the theater district, and Boston University's Morse Auditorium were all once active synagogues.

Many of the new Jewish immigrants came from the city of Vilna. Vilna was located within or near Lithuania, Poland, or Russia, continually changing nationalities as border wars were resolved between those three countries. Despite the pogroms that plagued their city in the late nineteenth century, Vilna residents cherished their home as a center of Jewish intellectual, political, and cultural life—as "the citadel of culture" and "the Jerusalem of Lithuania."

Many of Vilna's Jews chose to come to Boston for a specific reason. "The streets of Boston reminded me of those in Vilna," wrote orator-preacher Zvi Hirsh Masliansky after his 1901 visit. "Large synagogues with truly Orthodox rabbis. Talmudic study groups . . . [and] almost all the stores are closed on Saturdays." Mira Jedwabnik Van Doren, an artist and filmmaker born and raised in Vilna, confirmed this assessment. "Most Vilna people that come to Boston say it reminds them of Vilna. In both cities, old and new coexist harmoniously. There's a pride and reverence in the life of the mind . . . the university, libraries, the pace. . . . A river runs through the city, and there is lots of greenery and parks. The crowded narrow streets and cobblestones were also similar."

Vilna immigrants, like most of the immigrant populations in the West End, were poor. Turn-of-the-twentieth-century West End residents often came to Boston in the steerage section of sailing vessels, where they were packed in like sardines. Once settled in Boston, they frequently lived in crowded tenement apartments with no baths or showers, no heat, no electricity, and no running water. Unheated toilets were found in a building's entry or hallway. Warmth was available only near heavy black stoves in the kitchen—stoves fueled by coal hauled up in buckets from the cellar. Children often shared a single bed, kept warm by a heated flat iron wrapped in a towel if they were lucky.

Both Edward Ross and Charles Smith were born in Eastern Europe in 1901, then immigrated to Boston. And both recalled, in interviews conducted in the early 1990s, the West End's primitive methods of refrigeration: poorer folks would simply cool their food by placing it out on chilly window ledges, while more solvent families had an icebox. Ross and Smith fondly remembered the West End's ice man, a one-armed black gentleman who carried treacherous-looking ice prongs and wore a sheet of rubber on his back, on which he hauled huge blocks of ice into the tenements.

"They were hard days, but fun," remembered Bill Cohen, who escaped Eastern European pogroms by moving to Boston. Many men and women earned just a dollar for a fifteen-hour workday, doing a variety of jobs including peddling, rolling pushcarts through the streets, tailoring, and butchering. Some did piecework at home, some toiled in larger shops, and others worked smaller mom-and-pop groceries, bakeries, delicatessens, and the like. Anti-Semitism still reared its head, even in the Golden Land. Still, snide comments, backward glances, tugs on older men's beards, or job competition with other minorities were nothing when compared to Old World pogroms. Meanwhile, Jews took good care of one another. "If a person was in want," explained Cohen, "the others would find some way to help him or her."

Part of that caring was channeled through the *shul* (*shul* is the Yiddish word for synagogue). In 1898, Vilna Jews living in the West End and the edge of Beacon Hill formed their own *landsmanshaft*, or religious group sharing common language, customs, and history. They prayed together in a rented, unheated one-room apartment at the corner of Cotting Street and Lomasney Way. In 1903, the group was granted a state charter as a charitable corporation, the Vilner Congregation. They continued to worship in various apartments until able to purchase the Twelfth Baptist Church on Phillips Street. When the city bought that property in 1915 and converted it to the Phillips School, the Vilner Congregation saved its money while renting space at 27 Anderson Street.

Finally, in 1919, they purchased two tenement buildings at 14–18 Phillips Street and hired Myer Feldman of Revere to demolish them. There they built the Vilna Shul, a lasting tribute to their heritage and a symbol of community pride. Throughout the construction process, neighbors offered services and contributed money toward the total cost of $20,150. Each time a holy Torah scroll was donated to or acquired by the *shul,* festive parades would erupt along Phillips Street.

Boston architect Max Kalman designed the *shul* as an L-shaped red-brick synagogue with two stories and a small basement below the entrance. The basic layout was probably inspired by the Touro Synagogue in Newport, Rhode Island, the Worms Shul in Germany, and the Altneushul in Prague. The building is set back twelve feet from the street, with a front courtyard surrounded by black wrought-iron fencing. At the top of the arched entrance doors are fanlights, while above those doors soars a large, round window depicting the Star of David in colored glass.

The architectural design aptly reflected the Vilna Jews' old life and new. The red-brick walls, wrought iron fencing, and sixteen-over-sixteen double-hung windows are Beacon Hill Bostonian, echoing the simplicity of colonial meetinghouses. The religious symbols and interior design, on the other hand, reflect the congregation's Eastern European heritage. The second-floor main sanctuary, for example, was filled with long rows of hard wooden pews, divided—in typical Orthodox fashion—into separate men's and women's sections of 150 seats each. Glass chandeliers, a raised square wooden *bimah* (reader's platform), and a magnificent, hand-carved, dark wooden ark all added to the sanctuary's warmth and charm.

To this day, the fifteen-foot tall, nine-foot-wide ark is the centerpiece of the Vilna Shul sanctuary. Possibly designed by local cabinetmaker Sam Katz, it was decorated with traditional religious symbols, many in gold bas-relief. Small replicas of the Ten Commandments tablets are flanked by lions of Judah. Two touching hands, with fingers parted to suggest the high priests' blessing, float below the symbolic eternal light and the Star of

David. Above the light is a spread-winged gilded bald eagle—the symbol of American freedom.

Recently, a whole new aspect of the interior has been revealed. Conservators have discovered remarkable painted decorations in the *shul*, long hidden beneath the plain white walls and blue ceiling. Three distinct paint schemes have been identified: the first and most elaborate represented architectural elements the congregation could not afford to build, including trompe l'oeil columns, landscape vignettes, and vases with flowers; two later schemes were each successively simpler, followed by the present-day spartan appearance.

The other most stunning architectural touches in the main sanctuary are three large skylights that seem to bring heaven to earth on sunny days. David Glater remembered attending services there for the High Holy Days during the *shul*'s last active years, between 1968 and 1985. "As part of the Yom Kippur [Day of Atonement] service, there is a late-afternoon prayer that essentially says, 'The gates of heaven are closing, get your prayers in now!' As the light gradually dimmed through the skylights at the Vilna Shul, you got the sense of gates closing. It was a remarkable feeling!"

In its heyday, the Vilna Shul, like dozens of other synagogues spread throughout the Boston community, was both a center for religious worship and study and a place for immigrants to find social and cultural activities and mutual support. Following the Orthodox tradition, men were expected to attend services several times a day, while women came only on the Sabbath and the High Holy Days.

Because of the poverty of its Eastern European membership, no full-time rabbi was ever hired at the Vilna Shul; a senior male congregant acted as daily leader, while visiting rabbis or cantors were hired to conduct important services. One unexpected advantage of the congregation's lack of monetary wealth was historic preservation: while wealthier *shuls* could constantly renovate to fit changing tastes and times, or could even move to more luxurious quarters, the Vilna Shul remained in its Phillips Street home virtually unchanged after 1919.

The building was kept in good repair through the 1970s, though the congregation itself declined. That decline was certainly no surprise. As far back as the 1920s, membership in Orthodox synagogues had suffered as Reform and Conservative movements gained in popularity. Also, as Jewish immigrants began to assimilate or gain financial stability, they moved from the South, North, and West Ends to roomier streetcar suburbs. Any remaining West End populations were displaced by federally funded urban renewal projects in the 1960s—projects that replaced the old West End tenements with the dull strip of commercial spaces, public buildings, and sections of Massachusetts General Hospital that are found there today. For those and other reasons, by 1985 the Vilna Shul had just one member, Mendell Miller. Though many other Jews continued to attend services there, Miller was technically the president, caretaker, and last official congregant of the Vilna Shul.

In 1985, Miller petitioned the Massachusetts Supreme Judicial Court to have the Vilner congregation dissolved, proposing to donate any proceeds from the sale of the building and land to Jewish charitable organizations. Miller initially tried to sell the land to a developer, who planned to raze the building and put a parking lot in its place. Because of soaring real estate prices, the sale was expected to raise more than a million dollars, and a number of local and overseas Jewish organizations and charities began competing for the anticipated windfall (in some cases their claims were based simply on their like status as Orthodox synagogues). Meanwhile, legal fees mounted as these claims were evaluated, the *shul*'s accounts with creditors settled, and other matters dealt with. Late in 1988, shortly before Miller died, the Supreme Judicial Court named a temporary receiver for the Vilner congregation so that its assets would not be wasted.

By that time, falling real estate prices were puncturing the dream of a great financial gain, while a variety of neighbors, abutters, and preservationists organized to protect the last intact early-twentieth-century Jewish synagogue in Boston. They sought and won Boston Landmark status for the sanctuary in 1989. (The exterior was theoretically already protected, since the Vilna Shul was listed in the National Register of Historic Places as part of the Beacon Hill National Historic District.) Finally, with the support and counsel of Historic Boston Incorporated and the formation of the nonprofit Vilna Center for Jewish Heritage in 1990 (renamed the Boston Center for Jewish Heritage in 2002), hope for preserving the Vilna Shul intact became a reality. Armed with a moving video about the *shul*'s place in Boston Jewish history (a video narrated by Leonard Nimoy, who was born of Jewish immigrants in the old West End), volunteers sought support from many sources and secured matching grants for restoration and programs.

In 1995, the group purchased the old *shul*, hired Claude Menders Architects to guide the building's preservation and renovation into use as a cultural center, and was awarded the first of several matching grants from the Massachusetts Historical Commission. In 1996 the Boston Preservation Alliance gave the Center its "Preservation-in-Progress Award"; by 1999, it had been designated an official project of Save America's Treasures. As a result of ongoing donations, volunteers, additional grants, and increased exposure, the exterior of the *shul* was completely renovated, including the brickwork, masonry, roof, sanctuary skylights, windows, and doors. The distinctive Star of David window, prominently facing the street, was restored with a grant from the George B. Henderson Foundation. Interior renovations—including restoration of historic features and introduction of accessibility—are the next step in rebuilding the *shul* as a living museum. To date, the interior has been fully studied, and examples of the remarkable interior decoration carefully exposed.

Starting in the mid-1990s and through the present day, the Vilna Shul has experienced another kind of renaissance as well—that of human activity. Despite the initially deteriorated condition of the building, the center encouraged people to enter the space and to feel its magical charm. Hence, events related to the *shul*, to its history and preservation, and to the Jewish community have been sponsored there, ranging from musical concerts by Josh Jacobson and Boston's Zamir Chorale and talks by author Anita Diamant (*The Jewish Wedding, The Red Tent*), to scholarly panels, walking tours, and press conferences. In 2002, a group of Jewish Bostonians formed the Havurah on the Hill, the young community division of the Boston Center for Jewish Heritage. Today, Havurah on the Hill gathers at the Vilna Shul for communal Shabbat meals, monthly Friday night and holiday learning services, classes, and lectures—events which incorporate educational, historical, communal, and spiritual elements of the Jewish experience in a warm, informal atmosphere.

Though its beautiful sanctuary was quiet for years—and, indeed, almost lost to the wrecking ball—the Vilna Shul rings out again with the sounds and songs of Jewish tradition. Its social hall, worn with years and awaiting renovations, nonetheless overflows with spirit, as Bostonians young and old enjoy programs and events celebrating the stories and the traditions of their forbears.

THE ESSENTIALS

Addresses: 18 Phillips Street, Beacon Hill, Boston. Boston Center for Jewish Heritage, Inc., 1 Financial Center, 40th floor, Boston, MA 02111. **Telephone:** (781) 416-1881. **Websites:** www.bcjh.org; www.vilnashul.com. **Visitor Information:** *Shul* currently closed to the public, except by appointment or for special events. For tour reservations and inquiries, please visit www.bcjh.org/contact. No wheelchair access at present.

40 The Peabody Museum's Hall of the North American Indian

AMID THE on-campus complex of Harvard museums lodged between Oxford Street and Divinity Avenue is the largest, most meticulously documented ethnographic and archaeological collection of Native American objects in New England. The gallery in which these objects are displayed, however, is hardly a staid, static, old-fashioned museum that only academics could appreciate. Instead, the Hall of the North American Indian—part of the Peabody Museum of Archaeology and Ethnology—is a modern, artfully arranged, beautifully lit gallery that's accessible to all—both physically and intellectually.

As visitors enter the hall's climate-controlled chamber, there is an immediate feeling of intimacy and involvement. Large paintings and photos, simply displayed handcrafts, and intricate dioramas engage the eye, as the sounds of native chants swell in the background. Visitors can push interactive buttons in the orientation area or wander a gently winding path through several color-coded areas representing ten different Native American cultural regions. For each region, bold copy tells of changing tribal lifeways over the past five centuries. Fascinating tales of kachinas, potlatches, the fur trade, and how horses came to the Plains are intermingled with displays of Navajo blankets, Sioux saddlebags, Apache cradles, Passamaquoddy canoe models, and towering Kwakiutl totem poles.

Detail from a
Kwakiutl pole, one of
more than 500 Native
American objects
beautifully displayed
and interpreted in the
Peabody Museum's
Hall of the North
American Indian.

The underlying theme of the hall's main exhibit is "Continuity and Change"—an exploration of how indigenous cultures coevolved with the European presence after 1492, sometimes for better, generally for worse. It also describes how some American Indian nations survived to this day, despite all odds, including the disease, enslavement, land theft, and genocide brought on first by European settlers and, later, by the government of the United States.

Like anthropological museums across the country, the Peabody has been very involved in the issue of repatriation—the returning of human remains, funerary objects of cultural patrimony, and sacred objects to tribes under the 1990 Native American Graves Protection and Repatriation Act. The Peabody's staff has also begun to engage Native Americans in other ways, through educational programs and special events that actively involve and support contemporary American Indian populations.

Understanding the historical context behind those current efforts, of course, requires a clearer picture of the Native Americans in the United States and how they have been studied over time. When Christopher Columbus and other European explorers first visited "the New World," the Americas were already inhabited by a variety of peoples. In the area we call

New England were an estimated 75,000 to 90,000 people, largely settled in the coastal regions and river valleys. The Wampanoag, Nipmuck, Pawtucket, and Massachuset lived on lands that would later be known as Massachusetts. Most spoke dialects of the Algonquin language, communicated their history through oral tradition, and spent considerable time hunting, fishing, and growing crops which included beans, squash, corn, and root vegetables.

By 1620, the first permanent English settlement in this region had been created at Plimoth Plantation, located on the coastal lands southeast of Boston. By 1630, the Shawmut peninsula—a name some claim meant "living waters" in one Algonquin dialect—had been settled and renamed Boston. Only six years later Harvard College was established in Cambridge. By 1646, "apostle" John Eliot and a small group of his Harvard colleagues had begun their mission to civilize, Christianize, and "save" the local "heathens." And by 1655, these English settlers had constructed an "Indian College."

From a modern perspective, Eliot's imposition of European culture and religion on the native peoples was misguided at best, imperialistic at worst. Yet it was arguably less horrendous than the actions of his peers; between 1492 and 1650, as much as 90 percent of New England's indigenous population had been wiped out by Europeans, primarily through disease and violence. In the most atrocious cases, people were hanged on Boston Common, their villages set aflame in the dead of night, their leaders' bodies desecrated and displayed on poles. White warriors were offered rewards for the delivery of American Indian scalps.

During the following two centuries, white settlers, often with the help of the U.S. government, gradually took away the land, the lives, the rights, and the identity of countless Native Americans. Then, in the nineteenth century, a new branch of science called anthropology began both to increase understanding of America's native peoples in advance of their anticipated vanishing, and, unfortunately, to impose another sort of loss on them.

On October 5, 1865, Professor O. C. Marsh of Yale College was digging in an ancient shell mound near Newark, New Jersey. Elated at the potential of his discoveries, Marsh wrote to his uncle, George A. Peabody (1795–1869) of Danvers, Massachusetts, a noted entrepreneur, financier, and philanthropist. Marsh knew that Peabody intended to make substantial gifts to Harvard College and other institutions, and he encouraged his uncle to establish a museum at Harvard to acquire and preserve material related to "primitive man." Peabody responded with a $150,000 trust. And on October 9, 1866, Harvard's Peabody Museum made its debut as the first American museum devoted specifically to archaeology and ethnology. (While the former discipline involved studies of extinct populations—analyzing physical remains of cultures for which no written records could be found— the latter focused on the life, behavior, and material culture of still-extant populations.)

According to their letters, nineteenth-century Harvard administrators had hoped to use Peabody's donation for the school library, the Museum of Comparative Zoology, or the general college budget. Still, they knew that anthropology was becoming a hot topic in Europe, in part because of Darwin's controversial new theories of evolution and the origin of species. James Walker, president of Harvard, acknowledged in 1866, "When a generous man, like Mr. Peabody, proposes a great gift, we should accept it on his own terms, and not on ours. . . . [Moreover, we] will have the best chance of securing those relics of our Indian tribes, which are now scattered in so many private collections." The Peabody was initially a separate institution allied with Harvard. But in 1897, its trustees formally transferred the property to the president and fellows of Harvard College. The association was appropriate, since the museum's collections grew side by side with the modern science (and the academic department) of anthropology at Harvard. From 1897 on, the museum was actively used to train students in archaeology, physical anthropology, and cultural anthropology. Boston-area art students, history students, teachers, and schoolchildren also regularly used the Peabody's collections for educational purposes.

Today, Harvard's Peabody Museum of Archaeology and Ethnology boasts an internationally known collection of about six million objects from around the world—a collection that occupies seven major galleries, plus a dozen storage areas. Though objects from Oceania, Central and South America, Africa, and Asia were eventually included, the Peabody's Native American materials have always been central to the collection. In their first annual report, curator Jeffries Wyman noted that "the collection consisted of crania and bones of North-American Indians, a few casts of Crania of other races, several kinds of stone implements, and a few articles of pottery—in all, about fifty specimens." The first specimen cataloged by the museum was "an Indian cranium from Chelsea, Massachusetts."

In 1866, the Peabody's collections were housed in a display case of the Museum of Comparative Anatomy, then located in Harvard's Boylston Hall. By 1876, those collections had so expanded that a permanent home was needed; so between 1876 and 1913, at a cost of $185,000, a five-story Victorian brick structure was constructed on Divinity Avenue. The Peabody remains in that same Victorian building today, sharing its galleries with the Department of Anthropology, classrooms, labs, workshops, storage space, and offices. The Peabody is also physically connected to the Harvard Museum of Natural History—comprising the Herbaria, Comparative Zoology, and Mineralogical collections—which are housed in adjoining Victorian buildings on 26 Oxford Street. (See Chapter 19 for information on Harvard's other museums.)

The original fifty items that composed the Peabody's collections in 1866 were rapidly augmented by other archaeological and ethnographic finds. Some were outright purchases. Many were gifts from individuals. Many others were "inherited" from other institutions that had surplus or duplicate specimens in their collections or other fields of expertise. Among those who gave or sold artifacts to the museum were the Boston Athenaeum, the Boston Museum of Natural History (the precursor to today's Museum of Science), the Smithsonian Institution, the Massachusetts Historical Society, the American Antiquarian Society in Worcester, and other Harvard collections.

The stories behind the 550 or more individual items now displayed at the Hall of the North American Indian—or the 1.2 million others kept in storage areas—are as diverse as the objects themselves. A certain Naskapi hat, for example, was originally collected by the explorer and adventurer William B. Cabot. A sculpted wooden beaver was received during the signing of the 1795 Greenville Treaty between the U.S. government and the tribes of the Illinois Confederacy. A group of ethnological objects brought back by the Lewis and Clark expedition was once displayed at the Peale Museum in Philadelphia.

Once individuals acquired these objects, they usually sold them to private collectors or various local, state, or federal repositories. The popular Charles Willson Peale Museum, founded in Philadelphia in 1785, was one such institution. When it closed in the middle of the nineteenth century, the Boston Museum purchased many of its precious objects. By the turn of the century, a number of those same items had been transferred to the Peabody, where they were used both for scientific study and public display.

Though they are not exhibited today, skeletal remains have always been a part of the Peabody research collections. As with other collection items, their sources varied widely. Peabody anthropologists often collected specimens from archaeological and ethnological expeditions led by museum staff and related Harvard faculty, particularly between 1870 and 1930. Beginning with curator Jeffries Wyman, who served during the Peabody's first decade, fieldwork and excavations at Indian burial mounds, shell heaps, caves, and village sites were led by scientists and educators like Frederic Putnam, Henry Gillman, Edwin Curtiss, Philip Phillips, and Stephen Williams. The Peabody also led efforts to protect archaeological sites through purchase or government action—resulting in the 1887 founding of Serpent Mound Park in Adams County, Ohio, and the passage of the Antiquities Act of 1906, which protected lands owned or controlled by the U.S. government from random excavation and appropriation of historic and prehistoric objects.

Another Harvard anthropologist, Alice C. Fletcher, gained renown for her ethnological studies among the Omaha (Nebraska) and Oglalla Sioux, the Winnebago, the Nez Perce, and the Ponca between 1882 and 1923. Though she was lauded by her peers, some of her acquisitions were deemed inappropriate by later generations. In 1989 and 1990, the Peabody returned many of the Omaha objects loaned to Fletcher a century earlier by an Omaha family, including a widely publicized sacred pole.

Well into the twentieth century, such scientific collecting was rarely seen as robbing Native Americans (neither is it today, if handled responsibly). Before easily portable still cameras, video, film, and digital imaging were widely available, collecting physical objects was the only practical way to study them. Furthermore, many researchers erroneously believed that American Indians were rapidly vanishing peoples whose artifacts and noble heritage should be saved for future generations. That intensive focus on collecting objects began to recede in the 1930s, as anthropology's interest in "material culture" gave way to study of other issues, such as rituals and linguistics. The results of that trend are apparent in the Hall of the North American Indian today; most of the objects displayed are from decades and centuries gone by, while the lives of modern Native Americans are alluded to in photographs, descriptive plaques, and recordings. Today's Hall of the North American Indian is the result of extensive re-thinking and the renovations that took place between 1981 and 1990. Be-fore those fundamental changes, the hall followed the quaint Victorian decor of most museums designed and developed in the nineteenth cen-tury—and featured a display method affectionately known in the industry as "cram 'n' jam." Dozens of seemingly redundant artifacts were displayed in row upon row of wooden, glass-sided cases, unprotected from the sun-light that streamed in through the tall windows. Tiny typed or handwrit-ten labels identified each ethnological item, sometimes giving no more in-formation than the object's name and donor. "There were once 6,000 objects on display here," remembered Catherine Linardos of the Peabody's development office. "So, if we had ten pairs of beaded moccasins, they were all exhibited. Every last pair."

To update the hall's exhibits and make other necessary renovations, then-director C.C. Lamberg-Karlovsky closed it down from 1981 to 1990. Since Harvard's museums have always been largely self-sustaining, funds for the major overhaul came from donations, grants, and sales of several museum paintings. Meetings with staff and consultants—who included several Native Americans—resulted in the exhibit theme of "Continuity and Change" and the choice of appropriate artifacts to display from a col-lection of 23,000. Meanwhile, designer Richard Riccio created today's en-gaging, accessible gallery from an awkward old space.

While, and in some cases *before*, those renovations were taking place, the Native American and civil rights movements were calling on the mu-seum to look anew at its collections. Certain items, especially those related to religious life, were deemed inappropriate for museums to display. As a result, several exhibits were changed based on advice from Native Ameri-can officials. In 2001, for example, the Peabody installed a new totem pole commissioned from Tlingit master carver Nathan Jackson, made from a red cedar tree donated by the Cape Fox Corporation of Alaska. The new Kaats and Bear Pole—which was dedicated in a special public celebration at the Peabody—replaced one repatriated to that same corporation in May 2001.

Since the Peabody's large-scale collecting of objects essentially ended with the 1950s, one more challenge faces the museum staff: celebrating and educating visitors about the lives of modern-day American Indians and their tribes while working to make the collections more accessible for anthropological teaching and research. Though they don't have the re-sources to replicate the contemporary Native American activities of Bos-ton's Children's Museum—or its spectacular permanent exhibit "We're Still Here"—the Peabody has developed new outreach programs that don't nec-essarily rely on the display of objects. Family events relating to modern Na-tive American culture are being held, featuring visiting artists and other tribal representatives.

Meanwhile, the Peabody's Hall of the North American Indian remains the best place in New England to absorb five hundred years of Native American adaptation and survival. "The Peabody Museum at Harvard is the only museum devoted to the art and artifacts of the indigenous peoples of the Americas, Africa, and Oceania," notes Peabody director Rubie Watson. "Its Native American and Maya collections are unsurpassed. And the museum remains, as always, one of the foremost research museums in the world." What better backdrop for dealing with contemporary concerns—concerns that ultimately reflect on, and affect, us all?

THE ESSENTIALS

Address: Peabody Museum of Archaeology and Ethnology, located on the Harvard University campus: 11 Divinity Avenue, Cambridge, MA 02138. **Telephone:** Reception desk and information, (617) 496-1027. **Website:** www.peabody.harvard.edu. **Visitor Information:** Peabody Museum open seven days a week, 9:00 A.M. to 5:00 P.M. Admission fee charged; includes entrance to Harvard Museum of Natural History. Free of charge Sundays 9:00 A.M. to 12:00 noon and from 3:00 to 5:00 P.M. Wednesdays, September through May. Closed Thanksgiving, Christmas Eve, Christmas Day, and New Year's Day. Teacher workshops, interactive programs for children, classes and special events for families, and public lectures are offered; call (617) 495-2341 or (617) 496-5402. Call ahead to arrange wheelchair access. Hall of the North American Indian and restroom both wheelchair accessible; wheelchair-accessible entrance through Tozzer Library at 21 Divinity Avenue.

41 Lowell National Historical Park

MOST CITIES and their citizenries would be thrilled to have one period of glory, one stretch of national recognition, in their historic past. For the city of Lowell, however—located thirty miles northwest of Boston—glory has emerged twice in the past two centuries, thanks largely to good fortune, wise investments, communal efforts, and long, hard work.

During its "golden years" in the nineteenth century, Lowell was a booming center of America's textile industry, renowned as the cradle of the American Industrial Revolution and home to a canal system considered a masterpiece of nineteenth-century engineering. In the late twentieth century, the city again came into the limelight—this time by hosting one of the first urban national parks in the country, and by offering the nation's largest free folk festival.

Despite the years of stagnation and decline that separated these two periods, Lowell looks none the worse for the wear today: its downtown streets are filled with bright, renovated mills, turn-of-the-century trolleys, canal boats, art galleries, cobblestone avenues, inviting parks and plazas, outdoor concerts, commemorative statues, free museums, friendly park rangers, and a wealth of multiethnic shops and restaurants. And locals are more than willing to boast of the city's famed sons and daughters—like actress Bette Davis, Beat writer Jack Kerouac, painter James McNeill Whistler (and his mom), the liberated mill girls, and comics Bob (Elliott) and Ray (Goulding), who began their radio career in Lowell, on WLLH-AM.

Historic "firsts" and "finests" do abound in downtown Lowell. Still, first-time visitors to the city and the Lowell National Historical Park are sometimes a bit confused, if only by the nomenclature. When many people think of national parks, they often picture forests, wildflowers, picnic areas, and campsites rather than buildings and sidewalks. But Lowell is an active city and an urban national park that commemorates and celebrates industrialization, labor, and ethnic diversity. That diversity is reflected in the annual Lowell Folk Festival, which runs the last weekend of every July and features street parades, six outdoor stages, and traditional folk music, dance, crafts, and foods by a variety of cultural and community groups.

While that festival is a weekend affair, the revitalized "historic Lowell" is a year-round adventure and includes a state park, a historic downtown district, and plenty of privately funded enterprises, all overlapping and supporting the National Park Service's work. In essence, the whole city of Lowell is like one of the constantly click-clacking looms in the Boott Cotton Mills Museum—it is a contemporary city-in-progress and historic park-in-process all rolled into one.

Stories and displays on the liberated "mill girls" of Lowell are among the fascinating exhibits at the Boott Cotton Mills Museum. The museum is one of many historic buildings that help visitors relive the days when Lowell was the center of America's textile industry and the cradle of the American Industrial Revolution.

Long before there was a park, long before there was a city, long before there were mills and canals, there was the Merrimack River. The Native Americans who lived by the river for 14,000 years—chasing woolly mammoths and mastodons in the earliest days, and being belligerently chased out by colonial settlers in the late 1600s—had named it Monumack, meaning "sturgeon." The river's name remains, with spelling changes, to this day; native members of the Independent Pennacook Confederacy, for the most part, did not.

The white settlers who began farming in the valley near the junction of the Merrimack and Concord rivers in the seventeenth century eventually called the area Chelmsford Neck, then East Chelmsford. They found the broad waterway a wonderful power source for their few small mills, but a mixed blessing for commerce; the Pawtucket Falls, with their precipitous thirty-two-foot drop, proved a major hindrance to boat traffic. Eventually the problem was solved by digging the Pawtucket Canal—a falls-bypass project completed in 1796 by a group of shipbuilders and merchants from Newburyport, Massachusetts, called the Proprietors of Locks and Canals.

Fame and fortune did not come to the area until wealthy Boston merchant Francis Cabot Lowell decided to create a "mill city" on its peaceful pastures. Until the early 1800s, Lowell had made a healthy living from capital investments in transatlantic shipping, which included picking up furs in the Pacific Northwest and trading them for teas, silks, and porcelain from the Orient. The ascendance of Emperor Napoleon Bonaparte in France, however, and Napoleon's imperialist efforts to regulate the economy of the European continent while crippling Britain's export trade, endangered Lowell's profitable business; as a result of the fighting in Europe, France was sinking or seizing neutral American ships, while Britain sometimes pressed American seamen into its service under the pretext that they had deserted from the Royal Navy. Rather than resort to war, in 1807 President Thomas Jefferson instituted an embargo forbidding U.S. vessels to sail to foreign ports. Understandably, Francis Cabot Lowell turned his attention to developing an industry that would minimize American dependence on European goods and overseas shipping.

Lowell had both a family and an ego to accommodate. Fortunately, the rich investor also had a plan and a remarkable memory. During an 1811 visit to the textile factories of England—where the Industrial Revolution was well under way—he literally memorized the complex mechanical elements of the power looms he observed there. With those images in mind, and with the aid of mechanical genius Paul Moody, Lowell returned to recreate the British power loom in America. Along with his colleagues, a group of businessmen-investors known as the Boston Associates, Lowell began planning a fully integrated textile manufacturing system—a system that could take raw cotton and turn it into finished fabric.

Though Lowell died in 1817, shortly after his bale-to-bolt system made a successful trial run in Waltham, Massachusetts, his vision lived on. In 1822, his partners began to build a textile mill city near the banks of the Merrimack River and Pawtucket Falls—together viewed as the finest source of water power in the area. They constructed machines and factory buildings, vastly expanded the existing canal system, recruited a unique new workforce, housed these workers in factory boardinghouses, and changed the course of American economic and social history. In the process, they created America's first major planned industrial city. And to no one's surprise, they named it Lowell.

Today, a variety of exhibits and interpretive tours in Lowell National Historical Park (and Lowell Heritage State Park, the offerings of which were significantly diminished after the massive state budget cuts of the early 1990s) tell the story of the city's origins and growth. A spectacular multimedia video presentation at the visitor center in the refurbished Market Mills complex provides an overview and introduction to the Lowell story. The nearby Queen Anne–style Mack Building now houses the National Streetcar Museum at Lowell, which presents the history of public transit in the city within the context of the broader American transit story.

Several specialized interpretive historic tours are also regularly available. One of the park's most popular ranger-led excursions is the seasonal boat and trolley tour, which has a nominal admission charge. Visitors travel by trolley, foot, and canal boat through working canal locks and to a canal sluice gate.

Throughout, well-informed rangers treat visitors to facts and anecdotes from Lowell's history. Some are tales about men at the top—like the arrogant, energetic company agent Kirk Boott (1790–1837), a colorful prime mover in Lowell's first decades who oversaw the construction and operation of Lowell's earliest canals and mills. Boott Mills was one of the ten original major textile corporations in Lowell, enduring from 1836 to 1956 and named to honor Boott, who was known as a heartless individual and hardworking business mastermind. Today the group of riverside buildings known as the Boott Mills Complex are the finest surviving examples of mill architecture in Lowell; they have recently been renovated in a multimillion-dollar public-private restoration project.

Boott Mill Number 6, built in 1873, houses the Boott Cotton Mills Museum. Since opening in the summer of 1992, the $15 million industrial museum has become the centerpiece of Lowell National Historical Park. It includes an ambitious exhibit of eighty-eight working power looms, plus interactive exhibits and videos about the Industrial Revolution, labor history, and the rise, fall, and rebirth of the city of Lowell. Also in Boott Mill Number 6 is the Paul Tsongas Industrial History Center (named for the former U.S. senator and presidential candidate), plus a museum store and the Lowell Historical Society. Nearby is Boarding House Park, with an outdoor concert stage that is actively used throughout the summer.

Though some of the tales told in these exhibits and tours are about men at the top, many others concern men at the bottom—like Hugh Cummiskey, who recruited and trekked hundreds of poor Irish immigrants up from Boston to dig the canals. Those immigrants cut through stone and swamp, using only small hand tools and deadly gunpowder to create the more than five miles of canals in place today. Their backbreaking work formed what's now renowned as the second oldest canal system in the United States. Cummiskey and his colleagues are commemorated in a downtown fountain, *The Worker,* and their stories are told throughout the park. Meanwhile, a new $15 million loop of walkways, called the Canalway, leads from the National Park Service Visitor Center at Market Mills through the downtown area.

Some of the best nineteenth-century tales of Lowell, of course, are about neither men at the top nor men at the bottom. They are about women—thousands of "female operatives," those legendary "mill girls"— who were the core of Lowell's labor force for the mills' first decades. Social historians confirm that Lowell was not the first city to employ young Yankee farm women in its factories. Still, the Lowell experiment—and the corporate paternalism at its core—became world famous, and set the standard for dozens of other American cities that eventually emulated Lowell's pioneering processes in industrialization.

Modern women workers would hardly find the lives of Lowell's early mill girls enticing. Their lives were controlled by the company they worked for, and rigidly scheduled. They rose at four-thirty A.M. to the sound of a clanging bell and reported to work by five. They had a quick breakfast back at the mill boardinghouse at seven A.M., then raced back to the humid, stuffy, noisy mill workrooms before seven-thirty. Their workdays would often run twelve to thirteen hours, with breaks only for breakfast and dinner. At day's end, seven P.M., the young women would return to their boardinghouse dorm rooms—where they slept several to a small room and usually two or three to a bed—to eat supper, then perhaps attend a lecture or concert, before retiring by the ten P.M. curfew bell. For their intensive labor, they were paid $1.00 to $1.50 per week—less than half of what their male counterparts were earning.

The mill girls got more than cash and exhaustion for their hard labors. Like the men who worked in the cotton mills, the women sometimes suffered deafness from the incessantly noisy looms and respiratory illness from inhaling cotton dust. Unlike the men, the mill girls—and most women of the period—were expected to wear stiff corsets, which often caused impairment of their internal organs. Working amid excessive heat and humidity was another job-related health risk, one considered relatively minor when compared to a scalping or a lost limb—the dangers of working too close to the power looms.

Still, the social, economic, and cultural benefits for young farm women —at least during the 1820s and 1830s, before factory conditions began to deteriorate—often made life in Lowell worthwhile. It gave many young women financial independence, friendships, cultural experiences, and certain freedoms they never would have found at home. Most of them worked in the mills for only two to three years, saving enough money for a dowry. (The greater the dowry, it seems, the greater chance a woman had of attracting a nonabusive husband.)

Even after working conditions worsened, there *were* long-term benefits for the mill girls. Perhaps ironically, the exploitation of women in Lowell led to their eventual empowerment. There was lots of female bonding— women taking care of women—and plenty of consciousness development. As a result, the Lowell experience became important to the later inclusion of working women in the women's movement of the nineteenth century.

The colorful two-floor mill girl exhibit at Mogan Cultural Center—

recreated in an actual Boott Mills boardinghouse and officially called the Mill Girls and Immigrants Exhibit—and the special tours with a women's history focus are excellent sources of more information about these pioneering workers.

The mill girls of Lowell were the first of many groups of laborers to work in the mill system during its century of peak operation. Visiting the immigration exhibit at Mogan Cultural Center or simply reading the ethnic names on varied downtown restaurants, groceries, churches, and shops—from Irish, French-Canadian, Greek, Polish, and Portuguese to Hispanic and Southeast Asian—gives visitors an idea of the rich tapestry of humanity drawn there over the decades.

In many ways, the story of artist Vassilios (Bill) Giavis is typical of the Lowell experience. His parents and other family members immigrated from Greece at the turn of the last century, enticed by "unskilled" jobs in the mills. As their confidence and education grew, they branched out into private enterprise. In the Giavises' case, the result was a family grocery that opened in 1911. Young Bill once ran that store, finally closing it in 1984 to pursue his dream of becoming an artist.

Today, Giavis is back in the mills again; he's one of several artists working in the Brush Art Gallery and Studios in the renovated Market Mills complex, across from the visitor center. Ninety percent of Giavis's artwork is about historic and modern Lowell—diners, churches, businesses, and buildings. The gallery is an artists' cooperative.

Dreams, of course, come and go. So, too, did the Lowell experiment. Eventually—after the Civil War, World War I, or the Great Depression, depending on whom you ask—the decline began. Competition from other cities, many of which had copied the Lowell industrial process, cut mill owners' profits, eventually driving salaries and working conditions down. Workers' unrest erupted into strikes. Some textile mills shut down. Others cut expenses by moving to the South.

As a result, "Spindle City" dwindled and almost died. For much of the twentieth century, in fact, Lowell was written off as a dreary has-been, a crumbling remnant of bygone days, full of boarded-up factories, empty row houses, high unemployment, and low morale.

What happened to bring about Lowell's rebirth is a book in itself. Perhaps the turning point began in the late 1950s and early 1960s, when the old Dutton Street boardinghouses were leveled—and part of the city's cultural heritage was swept away in the process. Perhaps it was in the late 1960s, when proposals to fill in Lowell's canals for parking lots were broached. In any event, the concept of creating a twentieth-century urban park from the decaying industrial city was originated by a local educator, Dr. Patrick J. Mogan. The result was the creation of Lowell Heritage State Park in 1974, and the establishment of Lowell National Historical Park and the Lowell Historic Preservation Commission, both on June 5, 1978. Their goals are being achieved, year after year, through a new "Lowell process": the cooperative support of federal, state, city, and private-sector resources. And save for the rigors of the recession, the city's economy and morale, as well as tourism, have been on the rise ever since.

THE ESSENTIALS

Addresses: National Park Visitor Center, Market Mills Courtyard, 246 Market Street, Lowell. Mailing address: 67 Kirk Street, Lowell, MA 01852. **Telephone:** Visitor center and National Historical Park offices, (978) 970-5000. **Website:** www.nps.gov/lowe. **Visitor Information:** Visitor center open 9:00 A.M. to 5:00 P.M. daily. Free. Park closed Thanksgiving, Christmas Day, and New Year's Day. Varied tours throughout the year; fees charged for selected offerings; reservations for tours suggested. Visitor center, Boott Cotton Mills Museum, Mogan Cultural Center, Suffolk Mills first floor, and restrooms all wheelchair accessible; tours require assistance; call for information. Tactile pedestrian maps, Braille and large-print literature, and printed narrations of audiovisual programs available on request.

PART SIX

The Green, Green Grass of Home

PARKS, PLAYGROUNDS, AND OPEN SPACES

THE CITY of Boston has long been known for its beautifully preserved historic structures, both secular and religious. Yet one of the true glories of wandering through its greater metropolitan area is discovering lands and open landscapes where few buildings exist at all.

There are dozens of such natural "escapes" in and around Boston—ranging from town and neighborhood commons to city parks, beaches, rivers, reservations, and other sanctuaries. Still, the fact that they remain intact and well tended today was hardly the result of a natural process. To the contrary: lands have always been preserved in the commonwealth of Massachusetts and the city of Boston with deliberate intent and vision. In the words of green-space advocate Mark Primack, author of the *Greater Boston Park and Recreation Guide*, "The people of Boston and Massachusetts have much to be proud of: no metropolitan area in the United States has done more to protect its natural resources."

The name most commonly associated with the Boston Park System per se is that of internationally acclaimed landscape architect Frederick Law Olmsted, Sr. During the last two decades of the nineteenth century, Olmsted and his Brookline-based firm helped develop what is popularly known as the Emerald Necklace of parks for the city of Boston, while simultaneously inventing the field of landscape architecture in America. Since 1981, Olmsted's home and office have been open to the public as the Olmsted National Historic Site. It's a perfect place to begin exploring the Olmsted firm and understanding how they molded in-town landscapes from Back Bay's Fens, Charlesbank Park, and the Riverway to the Jamaicaway, the Arnold Arboretum, and Franklin Park.

Still, Greater Boston's parks and open spaces neither began nor ended with Frederick Law Olmsted. As early as 1634, only four years after the settlement of Boston by the Massachusetts Bay Colony, Puritan leaders set aside a large site in the center of town as a "commonage" for its citizens. In early colonial days, the concept of a public park for strolling, socializing, and recreation was unheard of; Boston Common was initially used for more practical pursuits, like grazing cows, training the militia, and hanging heretics.

During the nineteenth century, both Boston and the new nation grew and changed, sometimes in an alarming manner. Across America and New England, rolling farmlands were giving way to towns, and cities were rapidly becoming overcrowded centers of industry and commerce. Unprecedented numbers of immigrants arrived from the Old World, creating new labor forces and new problems of space. Boston proper proceeded to build on many of its available open lands, including the farmlands of Beacon

Hill. When that ran out, the city created hundreds more in-town acres with the miracle of landfill.

Fortunately, many Bostonians acknowledged that urban congestion, pressures, and filth made public parks—as places for healthy escape and a breath of fresh air—essential to human survival. What became known as the parks movement of the nineteenth century was buttressed by other area events. In 1831, for example, scenic Mount Auburn Cemetery was founded in Cambridge, inspiring the development of rural garden cemeteries across the nation. In 1835, Concord philosopher Ralph Waldo Emerson published his *Nature*, expounding on the concept of nature as a thing to be nurtured and enjoyed.

Hence, as landfill was added to Boston's Back Bay, parks became an integral part of urban development. In 1837, a privately owned botanical garden was begun on the edge of Boston Common, and it soon evolved into today's Public Garden. As Commonwealth Avenue and its fine homes were built on landfilled marshes between 1857 and 1890, a long, tree-shaded walkway called the Commonwealth Avenue Mall was laid out as well. As a result, when Olmsted began designing his string of city parks, he had the existing Common, Public Garden, and Mall—as well as an early incarnation of the Arnold Arboretum—to work with, and on.

Meanwhile, other parts of the metropolitan area developed public lands and recreational facilities as well, thanks largely to the pioneering work of landscape architect Charles Eliot, the son of Harvard president Charles W. Eliot, and the apprentice (and eventual partner) of Frederick Law Olmsted, Sr. Due in part to pressures from Eliot and his conservation-minded colleagues, a Metropolitan Park Commission was created in 1892. Almost immediately, the commission began acquiring and developing parks and open spaces in and around Boston. By 1919, that agency evolved into the Metropolitan District Commission (MDC), which in its current incarnation—as the Massachusetts Department of Conservation and Recreation, Division of Urban Parks and Recreation (DCR)—continues to oversee and manage a host of parks and recreation sites, including those at Blue Hills Reservation, Georges Island, and Castle Island.

It's certainly noteworthy that as Boston's Central Artery project—the infamous Big Dig—winds toward completion, the decision has been made to create a greenway on some of the space formerly filled with whizzing highways. Quite appropriately, one segment will be named for a woman who once lived nearby in the North End—the late Rose Fitzgerald Kennedy.

42 Boston Common

IF YOU come to Boston, you really can't miss Boston Common. That's partly a matter of sheer mass: the sprawling public park is located at the hub of the bustling downtown area—near the shopping district, the theater district, and the State House. Down below the Common lies a cavernous public parking garage and the busy Park Street T stop. Above ground, visitors are frequently seen hopping onto tour buses or beginning their walking tours of the Freedom Trail, the Black Heritage Trail, or the Emerald Necklace of Boston parks.

All of this is meant to suggest not only that you *can't* miss Boston Common, but that you *shouldn't*. Boston Common, after all, is not just a busy thoroughfare. It's the oldest public green in America, and Boston's oldest, most actively used public area. And as such, it has several centuries of tales to tell.

In 1634, only four years after Boston was founded by English colonists, the Common was established as a cow pasture for the landholders of its first Puritan settlement. Since then, it's served as military training field, public punishment site, ball and game field, outdoor festival center, campground, swimming hole, performance stage, sledding hill, preaching pulpit, burying ground, balloon launching pad, public art gallery, deer park, rug-beating center, picnic ground, Victory Garden, recruiting office, lovers' lane, fast food stand, bucolic walkway, and haven for the homeless. You name it, it's been done there.

Unlike many other public and private parks, Boston Common's forty-eight acres have never been just a playground for the rich and famous. Today, these well-worn midtown lands reflect that democratic ideal more than ever. On any given day, you can find black and white, rich and poor, young and old wandering through—on foot, bike, skateboard, stroller, or wheelchair—sporting anything from three-piece suits to tattered cutoffs.

That's not to say that famous people haven't enjoyed the Common as well. Whitney Houston, Charles Lindbergh, Pope John Paul II, Martin Luther King, Jr., John Winthrop, Olivia Newton-John, George Washington, Benjamin Franklin, Willie Nelson, Frederick Douglass, the Marquis de Lafayette, Howard Zinn, Franklin D. Roosevelt, Colin Powell, Nelson Mandela, Arnold Schwarzenegger, and cast members of the television series *Cheers* have all held court there, drawing sizable crowds. Sometimes the occasions have been festive, like concerts, celebrations, and military parades. Sometimes they've been more somber: the day in 1979 when the pope celebrated a Mass, the day in 1965 when Dr. King cried out for racial equality, or the day in 1660 when Mary Dyer was suspended there on a hangman's noose.

The Common's history began in the seventeenth century, when Boston itself—called Shawmut by the American Indians who first camped and

Pigeons still regularly flutter through Boston Common, though cows have been banned from grazing there since 1830.

cleared land there—was a pear-shaped peninsula roughly half its present size. Native Americans had largely left the site by 1630, but Shawmut did have one white inhabitant that year: the reclusive Reverend William Blackstone.

When Blackstone (or Blaxton) heard that the British colonists who settled in nearby Charlestown were suffering from poor water, he allegedly invited them to share his peninsula and its cool, clear springs. John Winthrop and his Puritan followers accepted, officially moving their Massachusetts Bay Colony settlement there in 1630. They renamed the site Boston, after the English town in Lincolnshire that many had called home.

Interestingly, although the Puritans moved in search of cleaner water, they weren't planning to drink it straight. Experience in the Old Country had taught them that water-in-the-wild was generally unpotable. What they really needed was a plentiful water supply for making beer, which both adults and children quaffed daily.

Meanwhile Reverend Blackstone, feeling cramped by his new neighbors, decided to move on. Though he sold Winthrop and company much of his land for a sum of thirty British pounds, the Puritans reimbursed two local sachems as well, just to be safe. The 1634 transaction is commemorated in the Founders Memorial, erected in 1930 on the Beacon Street side of the Common, on the supposed site of an ancient spring.

According to Henry Lee, longtime president of the Friends of the Public Garden and Common, that Founders Memorial has a few curious quirks. The mural's representation of Blackstone, for example, bears a striking resemblance to James Michael Curley, Boston's mayor when the monument was erected. You may also note that the diminutive female figure behind Winthrop on the plaque looks like a girl, but it is actually a woman—a symbolic suggestion, perhaps, of women's second-class status?

The roughly forty-eight-acre parcel bought from Blackstone, essentially the same irregular pentagon we know as Boston Common today, was intended as common land for prominent Puritan householders. As in England, the new Bostonians wanted a centrally located open green, or "commonage," to share as cow pasture, military training field, and public punishment site.

Contemporary accounts suggest that Boston's seventeenth-century Common had at least four hills, three ponds, one grand elm, and a bathing beach. Though most of those hills were eventually leveled for landfill, vestiges of those early slopes can be seen on the upper Common's Liberty Mall, behind the stately Shaw/ 54th Regiment Memorial, and on Flagstaff Hill, where the Soldiers and Sailors Monument stands. Meanwhile, as the hills were leveled, the ponds and marshes were filled in, leaving only the shallow Frog Pond.

The Common's beach area began where Charles Street now divides the Common from the Public Garden. There, long before the Back Bay was filled and the Public Garden planted, Bostonians swam and boated during high tide and clammed in the mudflats at low tide. There young Ben Franklin fished. And there, on the night of April 18, 1775, British soldiers hopped into their boats as two lights flashed in the steeple of the Old North Church, warning colonial patriots of the enemy's departure "by sea" to Lexington and Concord (see Chapters 4 and 5).

Before and during the American Revolution, the Common played host to both colonial and British troops. Colonial soldiers mustered on the Common in 1745 on their way to the French and Indian War, a war that provided military training later used against the British. Patriots celebrated the repeal of the Stamp Act on the Common and hanged effigies there to protest the tax on tea. Under the boughs of the Common's Great Elm, the Sons of Liberty met and plotted revolutionary acts. And on the Common's open fields, General Washington reviewed his victorious troops.

The British, meanwhile, had used the Common for meetings, militia, and muster. From 1768 until their forced evacuation in 1776, in fact, British troops maintained a major encampment there. In 1775, 1,750 soldiers incensed the colonists by cutting down the Common's trees and fencing for firewood and spite and by digging trenches that would pockmark the terrain for decades after. Despite the danger, young Boston boys refused to let the British encampment interfere with their favorite winter pastime— sledding across the Common.

If American freedom rang from Boston Common, so too did American intolerance. In the seventeenth century, crowds regularly assembled there to ogle wrongdoers confined in the stocks or hanged on trees like the Great Elm. Hanging trees were later replaced by gallows, first installed in 1769. "Witches," American Indians, deserters, pirates, and ordinary criminals met the noose on Common grounds. So did many who didn't fit the strict Puritan religious mold—like four people strung up for the crime of being Quakers. One such victim was Mary Dyer, whose statue sits on the lawn of the State House, watching over her own execution site.

But the Common's long history includes public amusements as well as political history. In the nineteenth century, the traditional Feast of Squantum featured proper Bostonians performing "Indian rites" while mounted cavaliers rode about in spurs and white boots. In 1848, an extravagant Water Festival was celebrated, with a flurry of bells, rockets, and leaping fountains heralding the opening of the city's public water system. Soapbox orators regularly gathered crowds at Brimstone Corner, on the junction of Tremont and Park, throughout the nineteenth century.

Today, more than nine hundred permits are issued each year for events on Boston Common. Regular festivities include the popular holiday tree-lighting ceremonies; seventy-three trees are now illuminated throughout the winter holidays. During Boston's First Night celebrations on New Year's Eve, the park is filled with outdoor art and working artists, including mammoth ice sculptures. The summer finds the Common a-flurry with free classical concerts by the new Boston Landmarks Orchestra, the yearly Shakespeare Festival, the very much established Gay Pride March, and other special happenings. One of the greatest, and perhaps most surprising, public events occurred on September 21 and 22, 2002, when two free performances of *Carmen* by the Boston Lyric Opera drew an astonishing 125,000 audience members. (Producers were hoping for perhaps 5,000 fans per night.) Locals enjoyed putting on their best Boston accents and referring to the event as "*Caaah-min* on the *Caaah-min.*"

The Frog Pond, a favorite haunt of nineteenth-century Bostonians, is now a four-season attraction. It's a reflecting pool in the fall and spring, a skating facility in winter (attracting close to 100,000 skaters on a good cold winter), and a wading pool with water spouts in the summer.

Though modern Bostonians think of the Common as a park lined with trees, crisscrossing pathways, malls, and monuments, that look really wasn't established until the early 1800s. The original Common probably had only a handful of trees, the most famous of which was the Great Elm. Some twenty-two feet around and seventy feet high in 1855, the tree sheltered or supported many activities during its long life. Among them were the aforementioned public hangings, revolutionary gatherings, and a smoker's circle of rebellious young nineteenth-century men that formed and met there after smoking was banned from public places. The Great Elm was irreparably damaged by an 1869 storm and blown down completely in February 1876. Today, several paths converge on the marker that commemorates where the venerable tree is thought to have stood.

Like the nearby Commonwealth Avenue Mall, the nineteenth-century Boston Common eventually became a showplace of urban elms, especially the American and the English. And just as on the Mall, the Common's elms have suffered in recent decades, decimated by storms, pollutants from vehicle traffic, and Dutch elm disease. An 1891 history counted the Common's trees at 1,300, some 800 of which were elms. In 1977, there were a mere 822 trees left, 72 of which were dead. But today—thanks to increased city awareness and allocations, the Boston Parks and Recreation Department, and the volunteer Friends of the Public Garden and Common—a long period of deterioration is ending. Approximately 745 trees still stand, including 250 elms. Private tree "donations" are growing yearly, and in 1992 the Friends of the Public Garden and Common established a special fund to preserve the Common's mature trees.

On the Boylston Street side of the green sits the old Central Burying Ground, established in 1756 to relieve overcrowding in Boston's three other in-town graveyards. Overcrowding eventually became a problem in the new graveyard as well. In 1895, when excavations began under the Common for America's first subway, some 1,100 bodies were discovered beneath Boylston Street. They were soon reburied in a common grave in the northwest corner of the burial ground. The remains of three hundred Native Americans were discovered in late-twentieth-century archaeological digs there, sharing a space that "officially" housed dead British and colonial soldiers, many killed at the Battle of Bunker Hill during the American Revolution. Those official graves are still marked by 487 headstones, most of which face east, the best angle for hearing the trumpet call on Judgment Day. The Burying Ground's most famous resident is painter Gilbert Stuart. Though Stuart is commemorated by a marker, no one is really sure of the whereabouts of his remains—a typical dilemma for older urban cemeteries, where stones were often rearranged in total disregard for who lay beneath.

As with any such active outdoor stage, both the scenes and scenery of the Common have changed over the centuries. Though its 5,520-foot perimeter has remained fairly constant, its hills, ponds, and trees have diminished. Among other curious or significant changes are the following:

- Grazing cows, the first official residents of the Common, were gradually eliminated as Boston's population grew. (Young Ralph Waldo Emerson was among those who escorted the family cow there.) In 1830, with the Common generally acknowledged as a public park and recreation ground, cows were banned altogether.
- The early Common had wooden fencing around the perimeter. In the 1820s and 1830s, decorative iron replaced the wood. Much of that iron was taken for scrap metal in World War II, but since it was cast rather than wrought, it remained unused. As a result, the Common was largely fenceless for years. Today, however, Boston Common fencing is almost back to its pre–Second World War status, thanks to contributions from organizations like the Massachusetts Convention Center Authority (fencing and entrances along Charles Street) and Millenium Associates, owners of the new Ritz-Carlton (fencing on Tremont Street).
- In 1640, Boston's freemen voted that no one could ever build a "house" on the Common. The promise was rarely kept. Over the centuries

structures have included an almshouse, a workhouse, and a house for the insane and criminal. Today there are three mausoleum-like subway kiosks, four headhouses for the underground Boston Common Garage, a park ranger station, a new visitor center, and three new information kiosks. The Parkman Bandstand and the adjacent landscaping have been restored and are now used for numerous events—giving vibrant new life to a long-dormant facility.

The Common's collection of public art now includes sixteen statues, plaques, and memorials fabricated from granite, bronze, stone, slate, and even cast aluminum, commemorating everything from the first football club in the United States to the founder of the local Filene's department store.

- The finest work of art in the park is sculptor Augustus Saint-Gaudens's memorial to Colonel Robert Gould Shaw and his all-black volunteer 54th Regiment, many of whom died in the attack on Fort Wagner in Charleston Harbor during the Civil War. First installed in 1897, the memorial was refurbished in 1982, enjoyed a glorious centennial celebration in 1997, and is well maintained by the Friends of the Public Garden and Common (see Chapter 34).
- The most popular statue may well be the 1888 Boston Massacre Memorial, on Tremont Street near Boylston, nicknamed the "Crispus Attucks Monument" for the African-American who was the first to die in the 1770 event. The hand of one of the massacre victims, which protrudes from a bronze bas-relief, has a constant shine due to passersby's "good luck" rubbings. (He's also lost a finger to the well-wishers.) Though popular mythology says the hand belongs to Attucks, the latter's body is actually depicted lying on the ground below.
- The most controversial piece of public art is certainly the ominous *Partisans* statue, near MacArthur Mall on the Charles Street side of the Common. Hyperactive kids must love sculptor Andrzej Pitynski's somber depiction of five mounted Polish freedom fighters, since they try to climb it constantly, occasionally toppling off portions of the sculpture. The related controversy is twofold: the statue's connection to Boston history is obscure at best, and it was originally slated to stand on the Common for only one month in 1983. That statue stands on the section of the Common known as the Parade Ground.

Despite the wealth of history connected to Boston Common, the park is hardly a worn-out has-been. The city's Parks and Recreation Department continually raises funds for major capital improvements, like new lights, improved litter collection and maintenance, more visible city rangers, and construction of the new visitor center and information kiosks. While this work continues, the Common's strongest guiding light in recent years went out when Justine Mee Liff died in September 2002 after a lengthy, hard-fought bout with cancer. Liff was Boston's parks commissioner and, before that, director of capital development, who oversaw the physical renaissance of the Common and the rest of Boston's park system. The Friends of the Public Garden and Common, who were among Liff's biggest boosters, have continued to assist the city with much of the restoration work while sponsoring other vital projects like donating trees, saving statues, and monitoring nearby high-rise development. Such care and concern is well justified. Since 1972, this granddaddy of American public greens has been listed in the National Register of Historic Places. Moreover, Boston's 1822 city charter prohibits the sale of Boston Common, except by vote of its citizens. Since no one would be foolish enough to vote away those precious forty-eight acres, it's clear that the Common is there to stay.

THE ESSENTIALS

Address: Bounded by Beacon, Charles, Boylston, Tremont, and Park streets, Boston. Boston Common Visitor Information Center at 147 Tremont Street. **Telephone:** Boston Park Rangers, (617) 635-7383; Boston Common Ranger Station, (617) 635-7412; mayor's 24-hour hotline, (617) 635-4500; Boston Common Visitor Information Center, (617) 426-3115; Friends of the Public Garden and Common, (617) 723-8144, or (617) 227-8955. **Website:** www.cityofboston.gov/freedomtrail/bostoncommon.asp; go to Calendar section for current events. **Visitor Information:** Open 24 hours a day, 365 days per year. Free. Call city ranger station for information on free ranger-guided tours. Maps, brochures, and general tourist information available at Boston Common Visitor Information Center, on Tremont Street side of Common; open year-round, Monday through Saturday, 8:30 A.M. to 5:00 P.M., Sundays 9:00 A.M. to 5:00 P.M.; closed Christmas Day.

Paths throughout Common are wheelchair accessible. Beacon Street side more difficult to enter, due to several entrances with stairs and steeper slopes near the State House corner. Wheelchair-accessible bathrooms at the new visitor center and at the Frog Pond. Four pedestrian kiosks to underground Boston Common Garage have wheelchair-accessible elevators.

Boston Common is a site on the Freedom Trail (see Chapter 10), the Boston Women's Heritage Trail (see Chapter 36), and the Literary Trail of Greater Boston.

43 The Public Garden

IT'S ONLY half the size and less than half the age of its neighbor, the venerable Boston Common. Yet the Public Garden, neatly bound by black iron fencing along Arlington, Beacon, Charles, and Boylston streets, is an acknowledged gem with a personality all its own—a twenty-four-acre oasis of trees, flowers, public art, and paddling Swan Boats, in the middle of downtown Boston.

Though renowned worldwide as the first public botanical garden in the United States, life has never been easy for the Public Garden. First, there have been the enduring misnomers: no, it's not the Public *Gardens,* nor Boston Garden, where the Celtics and the circus historically held forth. Next have come the mishaps—a series of false starts, fierce controversies, and financial difficulties that have threatened the existence of the garden since its inception in the early nineteenth century.

The Public Garden, as it turns out, is a survivor—a survivor of foul-smelling ropewalk buildings, ill-conceived dams, and inadequate planning in the nineteenth century, and vandalism, hurricanes, and shrinking public funds in the twentieth. But for the grace of one Horace Gray, moreover, Boston's magnificent Public Garden might never have existed at all. To understand all that, we'll have to go back even before Gray's time.

In the beginning, there was water. During high tide, that meant colonial Bostonians could swim, fish, or skate on the area we now know as the Public Garden. At low tide, those same flats became soggy marshland, and a fine spot for digging clams or shooting snipe. Sometimes it was called Round Marsh, and at other times it was simply known it as the desolate shoreline on the western edge of the Common.

The grandest historic event to occur on Round Marsh in the eighteenth century took place on April 18, 1775. In the dark of that night, some seven hundred British troops embarked in barges and boats "from the foot of the Common" to cross over to Cambridge. From there they made a sunrise sweep into Lexington and then to Concord, initiating the first major battle

Founded by English immigrant and ship-builder Robert Paget in 1877, the Swan Boats were inspired by the newfangled bicycle and Wagner's *Lohengrin.*

of the American Revolution. The famous signal "one if by land, two if by sea" was made that night; thanks to two lanterns briefly lit in the steeple of the Old North Church, the colonists were warned of the soldiers' route across the flooding tides of the Charles River (see Chapters 4 and 5).

During those marshy days, the summit of Fox Hill, near the Charles Street entrance of the Garden, was the only segment of the future Public Garden not inundated by the river during high tide. In 1794, the City of Boston gave Fox Hill and the rest of this wasteland to rope manufacturers whose businesses had been burned out by fires in the old South End. Fires periodically broke out in this new land as well, but the ropewalks endured. Then, in 1821, Uriah Cotting's corporation built a dam across the adjoining Back Bay. Though the dam provided water power for mills and factories, it also created stagnation and stench—and became a favorite refuse dump. Looked at from any direction or perspective, the acreage that would some-day become the Public Garden was, to date, a mess.

In 1824, the city decided to repurchase the site for $55,000—land that they had given away only thirty years before—and then tried to sell it. Vended in small segments, the lots would presumably have been used for residential construction. The sale was stopped, however, by a citizens' vote to fill in the marsh and maintain it as public property.

Landfill was added here and there over the next decade, but nothing of note occurred until 1837. In that year, seventeen Bostonians led by wealthy iron manufacturer and horticulturalist Horace Gray leased the marshland under the name the Proprietors of the Botanic Garden in Boston. Using funds from private donors, they began reclaiming the mudflats and plant-ing on the site. The early flora included tulips, roses, camellias, and Bos-ton's first poinsettia. But when financing went awry in 1852, Horace Gray and his colleagues were forced to return the site to the city.

Again the city tried to sell the area, and again the public voted to hold on to their seminal downtown garden. They also voted to ban all buildings on the site, save those "expedient for horticultural purposes." In 1859, the city finally succumbed to the public will and set up a competition for a de-sign of the city's Public Garden. George F. Meacham, a young Boston ar-chitect, won with his English-style garden design and was awarded a hun-dred dollars for his efforts. The Public Garden as we know it had begun.

For many visitors, the first attraction of the Public Garden is clearly its flowers and trees. Depending on the time of year, the fifty-five flower beds and four rose beds may be showcasing laughing clusters of pansies, regi-ments of tulips, or burgeoning circles of brand-new roses—not to mention begonias, lantana standards, and various tropicals. Their ranks include 15,000 summer "bedding plants"—plants of the same species massed to-gether in pleasing combinations of complementary colors and textures. Most of the flowers, like those in public parks throughout the Hub, are grown in the city greenhouses at Franklin Park. They are maintained by the Boston Parks and Recreation Department and planted twice a year, in spring and summer.

The Public Garden's trees are some of its best-loved plants. Among local favorites are the huge Japanese pagoda, near the Beacon and Arlington street corner, of a species revered as the "scholar's tree" in the Far East; the looming metasequoia, near the entrance at Beacon and Charles, now strong and beautiful though only forty years ago it was believed to be near death; and, near the "Ether" monument, the unique ginkgo with its fan-shaped leaves, one of a species that evolved some 150 million years ago. The garden is home to more than 750 trees and shrubs in all, including about 125 varieties of trees.

Beloved too are the twenty weeping willows that surround the lagoon. The lagoon itself was completed in the summer of 1861 as part of architect Meacham's original design. This three-acre artificial pond, which averages three to four feet in depth, is drained and refilled each spring. Contrary to popular legend, the bridge spanning the lagoon is neither "the world's smallest suspension bridge" nor a replica of the Brooklyn Bridge. It looks like a suspension bridge, but that is a matter of deceptive design. And though it does slightly resemble its big Brooklyn cousin, Boston built the lagoon bridge in 1869, whereas Brooklyn's opened in 1883.

Since 1877, the public has been able to enjoy the lagoon through peaceful, fifteen-minute Swan Boat cruises. The unique Swan Boats were the invention of Robert Paget, a nineteenth-century English immigrant and shipbuilder, who ran the first boat-for-hire concession on the lagoon. In 1877, Paget scrapped his original fleet of rowboats and replaced them with foot-pedaled boats topped by man-made swans. He was inspired by the popularity of bicycles and by Richard Wagner's opera *Lohengrin,* in which a knight of the Grail crosses a river in a swan-drawn boat to defend his lady's innocence.

The Swan Boat experience has changed only slightly over the years. The five-cent fare of 1877 had grown to $2.50 by 2003 (though children 2 to 15 are still a mere $1.00), the boats in today's fleet are bigger than their predecessors, and the old copper swans have been replaced by fiberglass facsimiles. Still, owner Paul Paget sees a continuity in mood from the days when his grandfather founded the Swan Boat business. "It's almost like a fantasy land," he muses, noting the boats' and lagoon's enduring charm and ageless appeal.

Paul Paget's earliest memories, dating back to when his father, John Paget, was chief proprietor, include the day child star Shirley Temple requested a ride. "She was staying at the Ritz, and had a cold for three or four days. When she finally came over to ride the boats, she had a police detail with her—since twenty-five thousand people were out there watching. The police were worried that the public's affection for her might lead them to jump into the pond to greet her!" Thankfully, no such disaster occurred. Other celebrity Swan Boat riders over the years have included Will Rogers, Gary Cooper, Bette Davis, Lucille Ball, Maurice Chevalier, Xavier Cugat, Theodore Bikel, Barbara Walters, Howard Cosell, Sid Caesar, Lynn Redgrave, Carol Channing, Princess Grace of Monaco, President John F. and Jacqueline Kennedy, Rob Reiner, Howard Cosell, Huey Lewis, Steven Tyler, President Calvin Coolidge, Melissa Etheridge, Ted Danson, and Tyne Daly.

Paul Paget remembers another Swan Boat rider, affectionately known as Sally Mallard. Sally was a mother duck who, in the late 1950s, began laying eggs under the back seat of the Number 3 Swan Boat (the boats are numbered 1 through 6). Her cache of eggs increased daily, much to the delight of the fascinated local press corps, who closely followed the event. By roughly six P.M. of the last day, Paget recalls, thirteen ducklings were hatched. Sally picked them up one by one and plunked them in the pond. They swam just fine. Sally and two of her offspring returned to the Public Garden the following year, but they disappeared soon after. The mother duck was immortalized, though, when the Number 3 Swan Boat was renamed *Sally*.

Immortalized ducks were also added to the Public Garden's statuary—which constitutes another major attraction for visitors. Until the duckling statues arrived in 1987 (details below), the most famous figure was probably sculptor Thomas Ball's gargantuan equestrian version of George Washington, which greets visitors at the Arlington Street entrance. The oldest is the popular "Ether" monument, one of the few non-bronze memorials in the Garden. Emerging from a brick basin, the granite monument begins in a cube base, segues into decorative Venetian arches and columns, and is topped by a humanitarian figure administering aid to an ailing nude. It was erected in 1868 to commemorate the first successful use of anesthesia at Massachusetts General Hospital. Since a dispute arose as to just *which* doctor had first employed ether in surgery, the figure on top was made a generic Good Samaritan and the monument dedicated to the discovery of ether itself. (As a result, the bemused raconteur Oliver Wendell Holmes, Sr., dubbed it the "Ether Or . . ." monument.)

Near these two famous sculptures are statues of a host of other Boston-related luminaries, cast primarily in bronze. Among them are abolitionist orators Charles Sumner and Wendell Phillips, Civil War hero Thomas Cass, Unitarian preacher William Ellery Channing, and Polish-American Revolutionary War hero Tadeusz Kosciuszko.

Though all of the statues in the park represent men, the sculptures in the Public Garden's four circular fountains were all made by Boston women. Nevertheless, sexism certainly affected some art-related decisions in the nineteenth century. In a blind competition for the Charles Sumner statue, held shortly after Sumner's death in 1874, the work of talented sculptor Anne Whitney was chosen; but when the judges discovered the artist was female, they apparently reneged and named the top male competitor, Thomas Ball, the winner instead. Whitney's version of Sumner was eventually installed on the traffic island across from the Cambridge Common in Harvard Square.

The last statue commissioned for the Public Garden depicts a female, but not exactly a woman. Newton artist Nancy Schön's bronze sculpture, *Mrs. Mallard and Her Eight Ducklings,* was installed in 1987 to commemorate the one hundred and fiftieth anniversary of the Public Garden. The sculpture is based on a children's classic, Robert McCloskey's 1941 *Make Way for Ducklings.* The book has been reprinted time and time again and has helped familiarize thousands of children with the Public Garden. On any given day you can see several of them hugging, kissing, or riding the kid-sized duck statues—which serves to keep the bronze beautifully polished. The negative side to the sculpture's popularity is that duck-nappings have occurred several times since its installation.

In 1990, First Lady Barbara Bush visited the Garden with Raisa Gorbachev, wife of then president of the Soviet Union, Mikhail Gorbachev. Mrs. Gorbachev was so taken by the *Duckling* group that Mrs. Bush—with the permission of artist Schön—arranged to have a replica cast for the children of Russia; it was installed in Moscow's Novodevichy Park. (In 2003, fund-raising was well under way to erect a monument in the Public Garden to commemorate Massachusetts residents who were victims of the September 11, 2001, attacks.)

Throughout the Public Garden's history, cooperative efforts of the public and private sector have often been the key to its survival. And survival has generally meant protection from both natural forces and human activity. In recent decades, natural disasters there have ranged from hurricanes ripping through trees and fencing—as did the Great Hurricane of 1938 and Gloria in 1985—to Dutch elm disease, which has diminished the once-large elm population in a much quieter manner.

Meanwhile, man-made disasters—including insidious city pollution—have taken their toll as well. As far back as 1897, for instance, the building of America's first subway system took precious land from the Public Garden; fortunately, the old subway entrance near the Arlington-Boylston corner was finally plugged up in 1941. More recently, a coalition of Public Garden lovers fought to keep the Park Plaza building project, on the Boylston side of the Garden, a reasonable size; they were well aware that ill-considered development along the Garden's borders could create chilly, shaded corners and unduly high winds.

Today, members of the Friends of the Public Garden—a volunteer group that began organizing in 1971 in response to the Public Garden's decay—regularly step in to raise money and oversee projects that limited public funds cannot support. The Friends have recruited sponsors to help purchase and plant new young trees, replacing older ones that have died of age, disease, or exposure to the elements. Some of these older trees, of course, have succumbed to overzealous visitors who thoughtlessly tromp across roots or pick off branches. The Friends' Horticultural Planning Committee also works to keep identifying labels, with English and Latin names, both on the trees and out of reach of vandals.

Meanwhile, the Friends have collaborated with the City's Art Commission as well, on an ambitious project to return all the statuary to its original beauty. Thanks to the participation of generous donors, many of the once-green bronze statues are now brown—meaning that the patina caused by decades of oxidation has been removed. Color is not the only way to tell if a statue has been renovated, however, according to Henry Lee, longtime president of the Friends of the Public Garden. Some cleaning methods deliberately leave the look of patina behind, on the premise that such coloration is often part of the artist's long-term design.

The flagpole along the Charles Street border also represents a model of city, volunteer, and business cooperation. At the base of the flagpole is a memorial to architect Marvin Goody, a prominent Bostonian who was a director of the Friends, chair of the Boston Art Commission, and an important contributor to the Public Garden. The memorial and "pods" around the flagpole were designed by Goody's wife, architect Joan Goody. The flagpole itself predates the 1868 "Ether" statue; the Friends designed the surrounding paths and pavement in the 1970s, and the city provided the money to build them. Mr. and Mrs. Roger Saunders of the nearby Park Plaza Hotel donated the flag in 1986, in addition to funds for flagpole painting and lighting (protocol demands that the flag be illuminated, since it is never lowered).

Assuming the city, volunteers, and local businesses continue their support, Boston's beloved Public Garden should survive—and indeed prosper—for decades to come.

THE ESSENTIALS

Address: Bounded by Arlington, Beacon, Charles and Boylston streets, Boston. Telephone: Boston Park Rangers, (617) 635-7383; Swan Boat information, (617) 522-1966, or (617) 591-1150; Boston Parks and Recreation Department, (617) 635-4505; mayor's 24-hour hotline, (617) 635-4500; Boston Common Visitor Information Center, (617) 426-3115; Friends of the Public Garden, (617) 723-8144 or (617) 227-8955. **Websites:** www.cityofboston.gov (go to Calendar section for current events); www.swanboats.com. **Visitor Information:** Public Garden open 24 hours a day, year-round, free. Swan Boat rides open between Patriot's Day weekend (mid-April) through the third Sunday in September, weather permitting; Swan Boat hours 10:00 A.M. to 4:00 P.M. daily from Patriot's Day weekend through June 19 and from day after Labor Day through third week in September; 10:00 A.M. to 5:00 P.M. daily from June 20 through Labor Day; small fee. Call city park rangers for information on special Public Garden tours. No bicycling, skateboarding, automobiles, dogs without leashes, or game-playing on grass; no filming without a permit; no loitering after 10:00 P.M. Public Garden is wheelchair accessible throughout, with minor rerouting required due to steps near bridge area.

A perennial kids' favorite, the Make Way for Duckling Tour, is offered by the Historic Neighborhoods Foundation (617-426-1885).

44 The Commonwealth Avenue Mall

THE Pearly Gates may have Saint Peter, but the Commonwealth Avenue Mall—a thirty-two-acre promenade of shady elms, heroic statues, comfortable benches, and trod-but-true grass stretching from the Public Garden to Kenmore Square—has Stella Trafford. For the past three decades, the Back Bay resident and Mississippi native has chaired the neighborhood-based Commonwealth Avenue Mall Committee, a joint committee of the Neighborhood Association of the Back Bay (NABB) and the Friends of the Public Garden. In practical terms, that means that Trafford is the acknowledged Guardian of the Mall, the firm but friendly "Tree Lady" who watches out for the well-being of this public park as if it were her own backyard.

Trafford—along with committee cochair Margaret Pokorny, the Friends, the NABB, the city's Parks and Recreation Department, Art Commission, and Landmarks Commission—has helped preserve and replenish one of Boston's great urban treasures, an in-town park, walkway, and historic site that dates back to just before the Civil War.

Though most northeasterners are aware of this tree-lined path down Commonwealth Avenue, surprisingly few know it by name. The word *mall*, after all, has come to mean an indoor, air-conditioned shopping plaza. In the nineteenth and early twentieth centuries, however, when Back Bay was the preferred domain of Boston's rich and famous, the word meant a shaded walk or public promenade, an elegant enclave exclusively for pedestrians.

As malls went, the Commonwealth Avenue version was unprecedented in the United States. It resembled the spacious French boulevards of Napoleon III more than an American avenue. And though the Mall is somewhat less splendid today—pollution, vandalism, dogs, storms, rambunctious students, limited funds, Dutch elm disease, and changing Back Bay demographics have all taken their toll—it remains a vital link in Boston's famed Emerald Necklace of parks, joining the Public Garden and Common with the Frederick Law Olmsted–designed parks in the Fens and beyond.

Besides, with gentle warriors like Trafford and Pokorny on its side, it's getting better all the time.

The story of the Commonwealth Avenue Mall began in 1857, when trains and steam shovels began hauling gravel in a mammoth landfill project that eventually transformed the soggy Back Bay into terra firma. Before that time, Boston was a curious, pear-shaped peninsula, and today's Back Bay was exactly what its name suggests—the mudflat backside of Boston, which flooded twice daily when Atlantic tides swelled the lower reaches of the adjacent Charles River.

That was all well and good until 1821, when the Roxbury and Boston Mill Company built a poorly engineered dam across the bay. Though designed to harness tides to generate power for city industry, the dam was a financial failure. Even worse, added to the crisscross of railroad tracks laid nearby, it clogged up the bay's natural cleansing mechanism. By midcentury, the Boston City Council admitted that the Back Bay basin was "nothing less than a cesspool." Sewage and waste from surrounding areas accumulated, and the stench was appalling.

Though the state legislature ordered the Back Bay to be filled in 1852, the process was not begun for another five years. According to historian Walter Muir Whitehill, contractors Norman Munson and George Goss agreed to fill in the filthy expanse of marsh in return for parcels of the newly formed land. Since Boston's in-town hills had already been leveled— leaving no local landfill—the developers sent their thirty-five-car trains back and forth to Needham to haul in fresh gravel. Day and night the cars and crews ran, each averaging one round trip per hour, and depositing its load into the Boston basin in only ten minutes (thanks to the newly invented steam shovel). By 1871, the Commonwealth Avenue area was filled

The Boston Women's Memorial on the Commonwealth Avenue Mall honors three Boston writers who had progressive ideas and a commitment to social change—slave poet Phillis Wheatley, feminist editor Lucy Stone, and Revolution-era scribe Abigail Adams.

from Arlington to Exeter Street in some sections, and as far as Gloucester Street in others; by 1890, the Back Bay landfill was complete.

The eminent architect, wit, and bon vivant Arthur Gilman was chosen to improve and design the new lands in the 1850s. At that time, French architectural designs, gardens, and mansard roofs were all the rage in Boston's upper echelons. (The French influence held sway in the world of fashion as well, manifesting itself among wealthy Bostonians in the form of French phrases, Napoleon III mustaches, tall Second Empire coiffures, and crinolines.) Hence, the design for Back Bay, and for the hundred-foot-wide promenade that bisected Commonwealth Avenue, was in the French Second Empire grid-pattern style. Along with architect George Snell and landscape gardeners Robert Copeland and Horace W. S. Cleveland, Gilman proceeded to make the avenue the axial street of Back Bay. (Though landscape architect Frederick Law Olmsted is commonly associated with the Commonwealth Avenue Mall, his firm helped design only the last section, from the statue of Leif Eriksson at Charles Gate East to Kenmore Square; moreover, Olmsted's design was later changed and the roadway straightened by Arthur Shurcliff.) Elegant brownstone houses eventually rose on both sides of the street, tastefully and legally restricted in their height and distance from the roadway.

The plan called for the Mall itself to be flat, long, and symmetrical, with grass on each side, a walking path down the center, and four rows of elms—two on the left and two on the right, in decidedly soldierly ranks. Despite a few changes over the next century—new benches, new statues, fences, and gates, and new overpasses and underpasses to accommodate busy intersections such as Massachusetts Avenue—this pattern prevailed. Unfortunately, the graceful, seemingly sturdy elms did not. Those majestic, towering trees were logical choices for the Mall—to create shady, scenic archways down its center path. The trees planted were slender American elms, soaring and wineglass shaped, and heftier, lower-branching English elms. But the rigors of city life—including car exhaust, heavy foot traffic, and vandalism—gravely tested their endurance. Of the 182 elms planted between Arlington and Dartmouth streets during the Civil War, only 85 of them survived until 1909. Dutch elm disease—which first came from Europe to the United States in 1930 and officially arrived in Boston by 1941—dealt the trees an additional, often fatal blow. In 1968 alone, 90 of the 413 living trees on the Mall died of the disease. In 1969, alarmed Back Bay neighborhood residents mobilized and began vigorously spraying the trees; as a result, only one elm died that year. Over the past decade, the pace of elm loss has dropped dramatically, thanks to a new program of tree injections sponsored by the Friends and the Parks Department.

It's no coincidence that 1969 was also Stella Trafford's first year as chair of the Neighborhood Association of Back Bay's Commonwealth Avenue Mall Committee (the Association itself dated back to 1955). From 1969 on, the committee monitored incipient tree disease. One of its innovative fund-raising programs allows private donors to memorialize or celebrate loved ones with a new Commonwealth Avenue tree. As a result, to the remaining handful of century-old elms have been added leafy, disease-resistant Japanese zelkovas (cousins of the American elm), along with sweet gum, green ash, maple, Chinese scholar, and oak trees, as well as other strong, young hardwoods. All in all, a pretty and practical complement to the last great stand of urban elm trees in the Northeast.

Though trees are a primary attraction of the Commonwealth Avenue Mall, its monuments are clearly another. Until late in 2003, the seven statues located between Arlington and Charles Gate were all of men, save for two allegorical females guarding the Mayor Collins bust; however, women artists created fully one half of the sculptures. Anne Whitney molded Leif Eriksson; Penelope Jencks created Samuel Eliot Morison; Yvette Compagnion sculpted Argentine president Domingo Sarmiento; and TheoAlice Kitson shared credit for the bust of Boston mayor Patrick Andrew Collins with her husband.

The men immortalized on the Mall are an unlikely urban league of heroes. Most were not born in Boston, some never lived there, and one may have never even set foot within the city limits. It's no wonder, then, that the selections ignited protests beginning in 1865, the year the first statue was installed. Curious citizens have pondered many questions: Why was that brilliant sculptor Rimmer allowed to put his mediocre Hamilton on the Mall? What does Leif Eriksson have to do with Boston? Why is an ominous Argentinian blocking the path? Why is Samuel Eliot Morison wearing shoes instead of sneakers? Why can't we fit Gandhi's statue there?

All of which goes to prove that though the statues have frequently been controversial, they've never been boring.

Walking west from the Public Garden, we first find Dr. William Rimmer's vision of a flamboyant, stubborn Alexander Hamilton (1757–1804) staring out at the equestrian statue of General Washington in the Public Garden. The Hamilton monument—both the Mall's and America's first granite statue—depicts the man who won stateside fame as a Revolutionary War soldier, a signer of the Constitution, the first secretary of the treasury, and the face on the U.S. ten-dollar bill. Born in the British West Indies, Hamilton is also remembered as the victim of a pistol duel with Aaron Burr.

On the block between Berkeley and Clarendon streets is John Glover (1732–1797), a Marblehead, Massachusetts, fisherman and Revolutionary War general. Glover's "marine" regiment manned the boats at Washington's famous crossing of the Delaware River in 1776. The bronze statue by Martin Milmore was installed in 1875.

Another local hero memorialized on the Mall is beloved Boston mayor Patrick Andrew Collins (1844–1905), whose elevated bust is flanked by two mythic females: Erin, who represents Collins's Irish birthplace, and Columbia, the symbol of Collins's adopted home. Collins served the citizens of Boston as mayor, member of the Massachusetts state legislature and of the U.S. Congress, and counsel general—all that after years as a miner, upholsterer, and Harvard law student. While some of the other statues were gifts of philanthropists, the Collins bust was a gift from the people, paid for by funds collected within six days after his death. The Collins memorial was moved to this site in 1968 from its original 1908 Charles Gate location near Kenmore Square.

On June 17, 1972, fire broke out at the historic Hotel Vendome, on the corner of Commonwealth Avenue and Dartmouth Street. After the seemingly routine blaze appeared to be under control, disaster struck. A bystander described the conflagration in the next day's *Boston Globe:* "There was a tremendous rumble. It sounded like an earthquake. And then the wall facing Newbury Street collapsed from the top down. Everyone ran to get out of the way. As soon as the rubble had fallen, the firemen all ran quickly back in." Nine brave Boston firefighters died fighting the fire—the highest toll in Boston history. Twenty-five years later, in 1997, an unusual and moving memorial to these fallen firefighters was dedicated on the Mall, facing the rebuilt Vendome: crafted by artists Ted Clausen and Peter White, it is a twenty-eight-foot-long, polished, gently curving granite wall, draped with a fireman's hat, rubber jacket, and ax, and etched with dates, names, and the words of Boston firefighters.

Abolitionist William Lloyd Garrison (1805–1879) is the subject of the Mall's first seated statue, located between Dartmouth and Exeter streets. A celebrated orator, activist, and editor of the antislavery newspaper the *Liberator,* Garrison was once dragged through Boston's streets by an angry lynch mob and saved from an impromptu hanging by Mayor Theodore Lyman, Jr. By 1886, Garrison's liberal views were somewhat more acceptable, and Olin Levi Warner's superb bronze statue of him was added to Back Bay.

One of the most popular and modern monuments on the mall, of U.S. Navy admiral Samuel Eliot Morison (1887–1976), was added to the Exeter-Fairfield block in 1982. While Garrison sits on a chair, symbolically adorned with ink pot and papers, Morison's figure is perched on a twenty-ton granite rock, which was hand picked and hauled in from Rhode Island. Morison's list of accomplishments is impressive and long: a Boston native and lifelong lover of New England, he was a sailor, a maritime historian, a Harvard professor, the author of forty-eight books, and a Pulitzer Prize winner. His statue is the most natural and the most lavishly landscaped, and it was the first to be lighted at night. (The spotlights are mounted on opposite Commonwealth Avenue rooftops, to minimize shadows.)

Beginning in 1993, discussions were under way to add those conspicuously missing women's faces to the all-male cast of characters on the Mall. Representatives from City Hall, the Boston Women's Commission, the Neighborhood Association of the Back Bay, the Boston Women's Heritage Trail, and other interested parties met, processed, planned, fund-raised, and consciousness-raised for a decade before the Boston Women's Memorial was finally dedicated on October 25, 2003. One problem, of course, was how to choose a single female from the many worthy movers and shakers possible. The solution: a memorial featuring three Boston writers who had progressive ideas and a commitment to social change—slave poet Phillis Wheatley (1753–1784), feminist editor Lucy Stone (1818–1893), and Revolution-era scribe Abigail Adams (1744–1818). Like the women depicted, sculptor Meredith Gang Bergmann also broke from eighteenth-and nineteenth-century tradition: she made the memorial engaging and interactive, and placed the women in and around—rather than *on*—their respective pedestals.

If the Morison monument and the Boston Women's Memorial are the most inviting statues, the figure of Domingo Sarmiento (1811–1868), on the Gloucester-to-Hereford section of the Mall, is often called the most intimidating. The memorial to the Argentinean president, journalist, and diplomat, known in his country as the father of Argentinean public education, was offered to Boston in 1913. It was accepted as a free gift sixty years later. Depicted as a stocky, determined, rather brutish figure, Sarmiento was a dedicated disciple of celebrated Massachusetts educator Horace Mann.

Meanwhile, two blocks farther down stands that romantic Viking Leif Eriksson, staring off toward the fly balls of Fenway Park and the traffic jams of Kenmore Square. The picturesque statue was purchased by Boston chemist, manufacturer, and philanthropist Evan N. Horseford in 1887. Horseford believed Lucky Leif had landed in Cambridge in the year 1000, making him the true European discoverer of America. Needless to say, not everyone in Boston shared this belief, which may explain why an earlier plan to place Anne Whitney's statue of Eriksson in downtown Boston's Post Office Square never came to fruition.

The statues and trees of Commonwealth Avenue Mall can only truly be appreciated on foot. Automobiles have always been banned from the park. In 1906, an effort was made to eliminate automobiles from Commonwealth Avenue itself: eight worried horse-and-buggy drivers signed a petition claiming cars "traveled at such high rates of speed that there was grave danger to life and limb."

The battle of the buggies was lost, and modern traffic rushes by, faster than ever, on either side. But the Commonwealth Avenue Mall remains an oasis for amblers and ramblers—and a pleasant reminder of an earlier, slower time.

THE ESSENTIALS

Address: Center of Commonwealth Avenue, from Arlington Street intersection to Kenmore Square, Boston. **Telephone:** Boston Parks and Recreation Department, (617) 635-4505; volunteer maintenance and tree donations, Commonwealth Avenue Mall Committee, (617) 723-8144; mayor's 24-hour hotline, (617) 635-4500; Boston Common Visitors Center, (617) 426-3115. **Websites:** www.cityofboston.gov, go to Calendar section for current events; for info on the new Boston Women's Memorial, www.bwht.org (Boston Women's Heritage Trail). **Visitor Information:** Open 24 hours a day, 365 days a year. Free guided walks of Commonwealth Avenue Mall included in Boston Park Rangers tours of the Emerald Necklace and of Back Bay architecture, (617) 635-7383. Special tours may also be arranged through the Neighborhood Association of the Back Bay, (617) 247-3961. Passive recreation only; dog waste must be scooped, or owners will be subject to fines. Completely wheelchair accessible via long center path and curb cuts.

45 The Arnold Arboretum

THE SPRINGTIME view in Jamaica Plain's sprawling Arnold Arboretum is one of the more spectacular sights in town. As you wander down the 265-acre garden's main street, a winding paved path called Meadow Road, you can marvel at the glorious, colorful, and aromatic eruptions of azaleas, lilacs, honeysuckles, redbuds, dogwoods, and a host of other plants. And though May and June are prime blooming and viewing months for many trees, bushes, and vines, there's something fascinating happening on and around the Arboretum's rolling hillsides, ponds, meadows, and footpaths every month of the year.

Despite its well-known wealth of sensory splendor, the Arnold Arboretum is more than a beautiful parkland. An arboretum (from the root *arbor*, meaning "tree") is a specialized form of botanical garden. This one in particular has always been a place for scientific research and education, under the sponsorship of Harvard University. Founded in 1872, it was the first arboretum in the United States intended for both university and public use. Moreover, it's clear that putting diverse people and plants together— thereby aiding our understanding and appreciation of things botanical— has always been its central goal.

Case in point is the Arnold Arboretum's living plant collection, which includes 15,232 individual plants (including nursery holdings) representing 4,448 different kinds. For aesthetic reasons, the plants have been laid out with an eye for colorful sight lines and magnificent views. For educational purposes, however, they've also been arranged by evolutionary classification and grouped by their botanical families. American, Chinese, and Japanese maples, for example, are planted near one another, allowing researchers to make comparisons not made by nature. In addition, some 175,000 dried and mounted plants from around the world, which make up what might aptly be called the "dead" collection, are stored and studied in the herbarium in Jamaica Plain.

(Contrary to popular belief, an herbarium is not an herb garden. Instead, it's a place where plants are pressed, dried, identified, stored, and studied. Though the dried plant specimens—carefully mounted with linen tape on archival sheets of rag board—are stacked and stored in airtight cases, hungry insects are still a major threat. The Jamaica Plain herbarium, by the way, stores only cultivated plants. A larger, companion herbarium at Harvard University in Cambridge, which houses more than a million other specimens, contains wild plants native to New England.)

As you explore the Arboretum, you may notice that much of its flora comes from specific sections of Asia, Europe, and North America, rather than places like Australia, Africa, and Antarctica. The reason is that most of the Arboretum's plant life, though international in origin, is from the North Temperate Zone. "The Arboretum is situated in eastern North America," explains former horticultural taxonomist Dr. Stephen Spongberg, "so climatically, we are able to grow here what is natural to this climate."

Virtually all the plants at the Arboretum—with the specially treated bonsai collection an obvious exception—have to endure the traumas of New England weather on their own. Trees and other plants are neither covered nor brought inside during intense snows, rains, or winds. (Calamities do happen; the infamous hurricane of 1938, for example, reportedly destroyed some 1,500 trees.)

Although the inclusion of so many Asian plants seems contradictory at first, "some basic climatic patterns of eastern North America recur on the other side of the world . . . in Eastern Asia," adds Spongberg. "The two regions are almost mirror images of each other." Which explains why those Japanese, Chinese, and American maples can happily coexist on the gently rolling hillsides of Jamaica Plain.

More than a century ago, a variety of famous and not-so-famous men and women helped to conceive, build, and develop the Arnold Arboretum we know today. You can locate their names in local history books. Even better, however, is finding them commemorated in the names of buildings, hills, and trails, or on the labels attached to plants. Here's a quick who's who in Arboretum history:

The Arboretum began with James Arnold, a wealthy New Bedford whaler, land speculator, and Quaker pacifist. Arnold himself supported abolition societies and helped fugitive slaves in the pre–Civil War era, while his wife was beloved for her extensive charity work. James Arnold was a horticulturalist as well—a pastime affordable to few but the rich in nineteenth-century America. His New Bedford gardens were internationally renowned.

When Arnold died in 1842, his will allocated some $150,000 for "horticultural improvements." George B. Emerson, a trustee of Arnold's will, joined his colleagues in eventually deciding to invest this money in the

The Arnold Arboretum is a 265-acre parkland with a living and neatly labeled collection of 4,448 different kinds of plants.

Arboretum project. Among Emerson's supporters in developing that project was Harvard professor Asa Gray, director of the seven-acre Harvard Botanical Garden in Cambridge. (That garden was torn down to make way for a housing development during the era of the Second World War.)

For the new arboretum, Gray and Emerson sought a broad stretch of land that would enable trees as well as smaller plants to be grown. Among the sites they initially considered was the open turf by the Charles River, where Harvard Stadium now stands. Though it was eventually rejected as too expensive and too flat, Cambridge resident and poet Henry Wadsworth Longfellow continued to push for the Charles River site. Small wonder: it would have given him a marvelous (then unobstructed) view from his Brattle Street home, directly across the Charles.

Gray and Emerson eventually settled on land that had been donated to Harvard in 1843 by Benjamin Bussey, a wealthy gentleman farmer who pursued what his peers called "scientific farming" in the early 1800s. Bussey was famous within the community for a variety of reasons: he owned a fancy yellow coach, fought in the American Revolution, and donated bells to several area churches. He was also one of the first subscribers to Mount Auburn Cemetery in Cambridge, America's first rural garden cemetery, though he was not buried there. The Bussey lands were a superior place for an arboretum. They had native woodland, ecological diversity, and a fascinating topological contour. Charles Sprague Sargent, a distant cousin of the famed portrait artist John Singer Sargent, became the Arnold Arboretum's first director in 1872. Sargent was already director of the existing Harvard Botanical Garden and a horticulture professor at the Bussey Institution, Harvard's agricultural school, when he accepted the new position. (The Bussey Institution, incidentally, officially closed its doors in 1936.)

As director, Sargent worked with Frederick Law Olmsted—"the founder of American landscape architecture"—in an effort to include the Bussey lands in plans for the city's famous Emerald Necklace of Boston parks. Olmsted was enthusiastic about helping to design an arboretum in Boston, particularly since he was unable to include one in his well-known New York City project, Central Park.

The plan worked. In 1882, Harvard turned over the land bequeathed to them in the Bussey will to the City of Boston. Arnold Arboretum officially became part of the city's new park system, Olmsted became part of the design team, and the Arboretum eventually became known as the flagship of Olmsted's Emerald Necklace.

Though the city held the deed, which it continues to hold to this day, it leased the land back to Harvard for a thousand years, charging rent of one dollar per year. In practice, the city of Boston is financially responsible for walkways, walls, and security. Harvard pays for most of what happens inside the Arboretum's gates, including faculty and staff salaries. For other operating expenses and programs, the Arboretum depends on its own relatively small endowment income, plus gifts and grants.

In part because Sargent was involved in the first U.S. forest census, he initially concentrated on cultivating North American trees in the Arboretum. Soon, however, he began to exchange seeds and plants with gardens and nurseries around the world and mounted horticultural expeditions to faraway lands. Emissaries eventually brought back specimens of everything from the cedars of Lebanon to the pines of Rome. One of the most legendary of these plant explorers was Ernest (Chinese) Wilson, who traveled throughout China, Japan, Korea, and Taiwan in the early 1900s. Wilson, whose name appears on many Arboretum plants, successfully introduced to the Arboretum more than 1,500 trees and shrubs that were previously not cultivated in the West.

As noted before, much within the Arboretum—buildings, hills, trails, and plants—was named for people like Wilson, Bussey, Gray, and Sargent, who were directly involved in Arboretum history. Other hills, paths, and fields bear the names of old area families, or were simply labeled according to the plants or collections nearby—as with Hemlock Hill, Meadow Road, and Oak Path.

Just about everything at the Arboretum has a name or label, in fact, including the plants. Identifying plaques include each plant's common name, scientific name, native land, and a number, which is an index to that plant's history. Botanical Latin, the scientific language for identifying plants, can make even the most familiar stuff sound exotic: *Davidia involucrata,* *Ulmus americana,* and *Syringa vulgaris* are more commonly known as the Chinese dove tree, the American elm, and the common lilac, respectively.

If you want to find out more about any of your favorite plants inside the Arboretum or out, the Hunnewell Visitor Center is a marvelous resource. Pamphlets, regular classes, lectures, and walks providing information on special plant-related topics are all available there, and a free brochure chronicling all these activities is printed each spring and fall. Furthermore, the library inside the center contains more than 40,000 volumes and 25,000 photographs, and includes an archive that documents the Arboretum's history while serving as a repository for nineteenth-, twentieth-, and twenty-first-century horticultural and botanical collections. (The library is open Monday through Friday, 10:00 A.M. to 4:00 P.M.; on Saturdays the library is open the same hours as the Hunnewell Building; the library is closed on Sundays and holidays. Stacks are closed, and the collection does not circulate.)

Guided tours of the Arboretum's plant collections and landscape features are available throughout the year. Tours are led by knowledgeable docents and focus on seasonal interest and the history of the Arbor-etum.

There are obviously plenty of sights, stories, sounds, and smells that shouldn't be missed at the Arnold Arboretum. Perhaps the greatest single event, however, is the annual Lilac Sunday celebration in May—when thousands of guests arrive to revel in more than four hundred kinds of fragrant, multicolored lilacs reaching their peak bloom along Meadow Road. On that day, lilac lovers can also picnic—a recreation not usually permitted at the Arboretum. Local citizens began celebrating Lilac Sunday during World War I. They traditionally dressed up in their Sunday finest, then drove their horse-drawn buggies past the gloriously fragrant and vividly hued lilac collection.

A curious footnote to the Lilac Sunday story is that the lilac—the nostalgic harbinger of spring, so much a part of New England's heritage that it's the state flower of New Hampshire—is not native to New England, nor even to America. The shrub is actually Middle Eastern in origin, though it transplants easily. Lilacs were brought first to Europe, then to the New World by colonists.

By the way, you may notice that the Arboretum's lilacs are located near both forsythia bushes and ash trees. The reason? Though to the lay observer they don't look alike, all three are members of the olive family. So, of course, are olive trees, but the latter are not hardy enough to survive this climate.

On Lilac Sunday and any other time of the year, the Arboretum is a favorite setting for shutterbugs. If you plan to bring your camera, you may appreciate some tips from the late Al Bussewitz, expert photographer, longtime Arboretum guide, and unofficial Arboretum poet laureate:

- Early-morning or late-afternoon light is always the best for optimum color; midday overhead light is dull.
- Use the Arboretum ponds as reflective backdrops for pictures; drop a

pebble into the water to create a spiraling ripple. Breezes on the water give an Impressionistic feel.

• If your camera has sound, consider shooting near nightfall or on overcast days; during those times, a variety of frogs and toads trill, plunk, and peep, providing a veritable "Amphibian Overture."

Wedding photographers, incidentally, find a favorite bridal setting in front of the Eleanor Cabot Bradley Collection of Rosaceous Plants. You can find the rose garden by entering the main gate, then walking down Meadow Road to the intersection of three ponds, on the left.

THE ESSENTIALS

Address: 125 Arborway, Jamaica Plain, MA 02130. Main gates and visitor center in the Hunnewell Building, located 100 yards south of rotary at the junction of Routes 1 and 203. **Telephone:** (617) 524-1718. **Website:** http://arboretum.harvard.edu. **Visitor Information:** Grounds open sunrise to sunset every day of the year. No admission charge, but donations welcome. Parking available on Arborway and streets surrounding Arboretum; no parking inside Arboretum gates or grounds. Grounds closed to vehicular traffic except by permit for individuals with special needs; permits issued at visitor center in Hunnewell Building. Paved walking paths and visitor center, as well as restrooms, are wheelchair accessible.

Visitor center is open weekdays 9:00 A.M. to 4:00 P.M., weekends 12:00 noon to 4:00 P.M., March through October; 10:00 A.M. to 2:00 P.M., November through April. Visitor center is closed holidays, and on Sundays in January and February. Guided tours available seasonally. Dogs must be leashed at all times; owners are responsible for removal and disposal of waste. Picnicking, fires, and barbecues prohibited. Bicycling permitted on paved paths only.

46 Franklin Park

WHAT CONSTITUTES Boston's best-kept secret is a matter of conjecture. But Boston's *biggest* secret is unquestionably the beautiful, vibrant, green, and rolling 527-acre stretch of urban flora, fauna, and festivities known as Franklin Park.

Franklin Park? From the late 1950s through the early 1980s, the grand old parkland that straddles the neighborhoods of Jamaica Plain, Dorchester, and Roxbury was known as a home for abandoned cars, trash, and overgrown foliage; folks tended to mumble about its dilapidated old zoo and unusable golf course, or the illegal activities that transpired therein. But thanks to renewed public interest, increased funding, hard work—and an ample dose of pride and patience—the park once renowned as the finest green space in Frederick Law Olmsted's Emerald Necklace has come full circle.

As a result, the refurbished park offers visitors some of the most interesting and varied rural scenery found anywhere in Boston, along with well-tended facilities and a lot of community activity. Equally important is the revitalized sense of self-worth felt throughout this city treasure, evidenced by joggers, picnickers, cross-country skiers, maintenance crews, and city park rangers alike. And they're not the only ones by far. Every year, thousands of visitors flock to Franklin Park jazz and classical concerts, as well as Puerto Rican, Dominican, and Caribbean cultural festivals. The eighteen-hole, par-seventy Franklin Park Golf Course, which officially reopened in 1989 with $1.35 million in renovations, was voted one of the area's ten best public golf courses by *Boston* magazine in 2003. And the seventy-two-acre Franklin Park Zoo has been steadily moving forward on an innovative, expansive track that began in 1989 with the opening of the domed $26 million African Tropical Fores, and continues today with popular additions like Kalahari Kingdom, the Outback Trail, and Giraffe Savannah.

But this is all getting a bit ahead of our story, which begins a few hundred million years back.

It's called Roxbury puddingstone because that's a bit what it looks like—rounded plums floating in pudding. More important, it's Franklin Park's

Franklin Park
was considered
the largest and
most beautiful
gem in Frederick
Law Olmsted's
Emerald Necklace
of Boston parks.

most curious natural feature, manifested in massive outcroppings, or ledges, throughout the park.

Nineteenth-century Boston poet Oliver Wendell Holmes offered his own magical, mythical explanation of how this distinctive mottled rock came to be: Rude young giants from the northerly town of Everett, Massachusetts, had hurled lumps of pudding at some equally rude young giants from Roxbury. Since none of these insolent youth cleaned up the resulting mess, the land was left spattered with hardening clods of puddingstone.

Geologists, of course, explain Franklin Park's unusual rock motif in a slightly different way. The whole Boston basin, including the park, was once part of a drifting chain of volcanic islands that presumably formed near where Africa is today. Over a 900-million-year period, this archipelago drifted away from Africa, eventually crashing into and fusing with the North American continent. The massive collision left Himalayan-sized mountains in its wake.

About 600 million years ago, ancient streams began flowing from the foothills of these majestic mountain ranges, crisscrossing the Boston basin and leaving masses of sediment behind. That sediment eventually formed into "Roxbury conglomerate," popularly known as Roxbury puddingstone. In more recent times—a mere 10,000 years ago—the Wisconsin Glacier chiseled and eroded some parts of the area that became Franklin Park, leaving deposits of rock and sediment in others.

Today, giant dislocated puddingstone boulders, or "glacial erratics," are strewn throughout the park. In the Wilderness section, boulders range up to fifteen feet in diameter. Puddingstone also features prominently in some of the park's man-made structures, including the Ninety-nine Steps, the elegant Ellicott Arch, and numerous shelters, arches, walls, stairs, gates, and fountains.

By the time landscape architect Frederick Law Olmsted and his stepson and nephew John (Olmstead married his brother's widow) began designing Franklin Park for the Boston Park Commission in 1884, the land had evolved into rocky pastures dotted with about a dozen small farms, each with its own farmhouse, barn, and outbuildings. Many of these early landowners' names live on in the park today.

Joseph Ellicott's big white house, for example, stood near what we know as the Williams Street entrance at Ellicott Arch. Williams Street itself was named after Jeremiah Williams, who once owned the park's elevated center, with its splendid terraces and scenic view of surrounding meadows and the distant Blue Hills. Williams's hill became known as Schoolmaster Hill to honor yet another illustrious resident, Ralph Waldo Emerson, who lived nearby as a schoolteacher from 1823 to 1825.

Other names reflect even earlier times. The Nazingdale section of today's golf course was named for the English hometown of many of Roxbury's first European settlers. John Scarborough was one of those seventeenth-century settlers and the original owner of most of this area. He, too, was immortalized here, both in Scarborough Hill and the seven-acre, manmade Scarborough Pond. That pond, spanned by two graceful granite bridges, has become a favorite fishing, picnicking, and walking spot for all ages.

By the time Olmsted began designing Franklin Park, he had relatively little missionary work to do. The parks movement of the late 1860s and the 1870s had already attuned many Americans to the importance of urban wilderness (see Chapter 47). Most enlightened folks agreed that urban growth posed hazards to human health and sanity, and that large, natural "country parks" were an important solution. Moreover, Olmsted's work on New York's Central Park had proved a smashing success.

Olmsted was reportedly a charming, quiet fellow with a bit of a limp and a lot of ideas. He came to landscape architecture with a wealth of prior work experiences, ranging from ship's hand, farmer, and engineer to a newspaper correspondent and head of the precursor to the Red Cross. Working alongside Boston's new Parks Commission and Mayor Hugh O'Brien, Olmsted proceeded to design and develop what became known as the Emerald Necklace of Boston parks. The final gem in the necklace, the 527-acre West Roxbury Park, was considered his design masterpiece— comparable in excellence to his two famous New York creations, Central Park in Manhattan and Prospect Park in Brooklyn.

As planning began, the city opted to alter the park's name from West Roxbury Park to Franklin Park, in hopes that money left to the city by Ben Franklin a century earlier would be used to finance construction. The funds, alas, were directed elsewhere, though the name remained. (Folks have not yet given up on the Ben Franklin connection, by the way; in 2003, ParkArts and the American Composers Forum commissioned Boston composer Patricia Van Ness to write "Three Ben Franklin Dances" for an orchestral performance at the park by the Boston Landmarks Orchestra. The infectious, baroque-sounding tunes would surely have set Ben tapping had he not been dead since 1790.)

Unlike finely sculpted, symmetrical, "fussy" parks like the Public Garden, Franklin Park was meant to be pastoral, natural, and simple, creating the illusion of the rural New England countryside. To attain this effect, Olmsted employed "design by subtraction." He removed structures, walls, and other elements to reveal the land's native beauty, then used natural elements—like plantings and the plentiful puddingstone—to mold new functional forms.

Olmsted's favorite area was the gentle valley that rolled through the park's center. This section, composing two thirds of the entire site, was called the Country Park. It was intended for "passive recreation"—of the strolling and picnicking rather than football and Frisbee variety—as was the adjoining hundred-acre Wilderness. Home to more than wildlife, the Country Park was originally kept tidy by a flock of nibbling sheep. Peacocks also ran about, but were later removed when neighbors complained about their shrieking.

Olmsted died in 1903, so he never lived to see his beloved, psyche-soothing Country Park evolve from a passive to active center. The Ellicottdale portion of the Country Park erupted in forty lawn-tennis courts— which have dwindled to two courts today—while most of the meadow gave way to a sprawling golf course.

Golfers had actually been puttering and putting in Olmsted's sculpted rolling valley as early as 1896, though golfing wasn't officially permitted until 1915. In 1922 the eighteen-hole William J. Devine Golf Course (often called simply the Franklin Park Golf Course) was completed, making it the country's second oldest municipal golf course. By 1926, some 55,000 golfers were teeing off there annually. (One longtime Franklin Park Coalition member recalled learning to play golf there as a child and hearing neighbors brag about how legendary U.S. Open champion Bobby Jones used to practice on the formidable eighth—or maybe it was the twelfth?—hole.) Since reopening in 1989, the course—credited as the first racially integrated golf course in the nation—has enjoyed increased accolades and attendance. A new clubhouse was erected in 1998, with a well-stocked pro shop, a comfy lounge replete with fireplace, and a function facility that can seat 150.

Though Olmsted didn't plan it for his Country Park, he did realize that Victorian Bostonians wanted to engage in more than just passive recreation. Hence the famed landscape architect added an "Ante-Park" to his original design, including a children's recreation area called the Playstead. Teams of mules were brought in to level the land and to remove thousands of rocks. Once new turf had been planted and facilities added, Boston's first playground was ready for its gala opening, on June 12, 1889. Today the Playstead is still filled with youngsters, who use its ball fields, the rustic Overlook, and the ungainly, large White Stadium, which was added in 1949 and renovated in 1990.

Olmsted's original plan called for something he called the Greeting, intended as a formal park entrance and posh promenade. The latter never came to pass, however. Instead, former Olmsted apprentice Arthur Shurcliff was hired in 1910 to design a zoo for the undeveloped space. Over the next two decades, the zoo emerged, first with dens for cougars and bears and an enclosure for elk. Then came the elephant house, whose most famous residents—a gaily lumbering trio known as Waddy, Molly, and Tony—are still fondly remembered by senior Bostonians. The zoo's decorative touches included fluted granite columns, added to the entrance in 1917, and sculptor Daniel Chester French's statues of Commerce and Industry, placed at the far end of the zoo in 1929.

Though the Franklin Park Zoo suffered a long period of decline, beginning with the Great Depression and lasting through the 1960s, it has enjoyed new life and popularity since the mid-1970s. The completion and grand opening of the African Tropical Forest in 1989, with its cast of western lowland gorillas stealing the show much like the elephants of yore, added prestige and allure to both the zoo itself and the park as a whole. Managed by the city of Boston since 1911, then by the state's Metropolitan District Commission (MDC) after 1958, Franklin Park Zoo was privatized (along with the Stone Zoo in Stoneham) in 1991 as the Commonwealth Zoological Corporation. The name was changed to the hipper "Zoo New England" in 1997, which coincided with the development of a more contemporary zoo image and the flurry of innovative exhibits and ideas encountered at the zoo today.

Franklin Park remained a Boston showplace throughout the early part of the twentieth century. People flocked to it on foot, in trolley cars, on horseback, and in posh horse-drawn carriages on sunny Sunday afternoons. Kids reveled in the marvelous Refectory building and the toboggan slides on Schoolmaster Hill. By 1925 park officials were even letting motorcars tour about. The heyday of the park—and the zoo within it—was the 1930s. Certainly by the end of World War II a steady decline had set in. The reasons were many—including lack of funds, limited city input, official apathy, the onslaught of the automobile, competing interests, demographic shifts in area neighborhoods, Boston's racism, changes in tax laws (the infamous Proposition 2½), and changes in the "vision" for the park's future. Controversies erupted, for example, when open parklands were used for the construction of White Stadium in 1949 and for Shattuck Hospital in 1954.

By the 1960s and 1970s, the park's condition was downright dirty and dismal. And then reform efforts began to take shape, led by longtime Roxbury cultural activist Elma Lewis. Lewis created the Franklin Park Advisory Committee, corralled friends and supporters into cleanup projects, and began a decade of summer cultural events with her legendary Playhouse in the Park—a stage that welcomed both local talent and internationally known performers like Duke Ellington and Arthur Fiedler and the Boston Pops.

The Franklin Park Advisory Committee was a prototype for the Franklin Park Coalition, which emerged in 1975 with Richard Heath initially at the helm. For more than a decade the four-hundred-member volunteer coalition was a primary—and occasionally lone—force in helping to improve, maintain, promote, and police the park. By the mid-1980s, Boston's Parks and Recreation Department had joined with the coalition, consultants, a community-based task force, and the state Department of Environmental Management to bring new life, massive funding, and people back to Franklin Park, in part under the auspices of the Olmsted Historic Landscape Preservation Program. Beginning in the 1990s, Franklin Park and the rest of Boston's Emerald Necklace of parks shared some $60 million in improvements. The result: by the year 2000, the Trust for Public Land and the Urban Land Institute ranked Boston's green space as one of the three best urban park systems in America.

Today, Franklin Park is teeming with kids, adults, competitive runners, cross-country skiers, animal trackers, strollers, golfers, ballplayers, tennis players, cyclists, joggers, and festival-goers, as well as the scent of international foods and the sounds of music. Sure, Fenway Park has its formidable Green Monster, but Franklin Park is blessed to have its own Green Renaissance.

THE ESSENTIALS

Addresses: Bounded by Forest Hills Street, Walnut Avenue, Seaver Street, Blue Hill Avenue, American Legion Highway, and Morton Street, in the Jamaica Plain, Roxbury, and Dorchester neighborhoods of Boston. Zoo New England, 1 Franklin Park Road, Boston, MA 02121. Franklin Park Golf Course, 1 Circuit Drive, Boston, MA 02121. **Telephone:** Boston Park Rangers, (617) 635-7383; Boston Parks and Recreation program information, (617) 635-4505; Zoo New England's Franklin Park Zoo, (617) 541-LION; mayor's 24-

hour hotline, (617) 635-4500; Franklin Park Golf Course, (617) 265-4084; Franklin Park Coalition, (617) 908-4002. **Websites:** www.cityofboston.gov (go to Calendar section for current events); www.zoonewengland.com. **Visitor Information:** Park open dawn to dusk, 365 days a year. Free. Zoo open April 1 through September 30, Monday through Friday, 10:00 A.M. to 5:00 P.M.; Saturday, Sunday, and holidays, 10:00 A.M. to 6:00 P.M. Zoo winter hours, October 1 through March 31, 10:00 A.M. to 4:00 P.M. daily; closed Thanksgiving and Christmas Day. Admission charged to zoo. Call park rangers about Franklin Park tours and programs available through Boston Parks and Recreation Department. Wheelchair access difficult in Wilderness section with its many steps; no access in Humboldt tot lot; most other sites wheelchair accessible via paved paths or roads; zoo fully accessible, including restrooms.

47 Frederick Law Olmsted National Historic Site

WITH ITS stockade fence, stately foliage, and quiet unobtrusiveness, the Olmsted National Historic Site could easily pass for just another charming old Brookline homestead. But in fact, this pretty plot called Fairsted has been the center of a quiet little storm for more than a century now—a storm that changed the face of parks and public lands throughout Boston and across North America.

Fairsted began as the home and office of Frederick Law Olmsted, "the Founder of American Landscape Architecture," in 1883. Between 1857 and 1950, Olmsted, his sons, and his successors participated in some five thousand landscaping projects spanning forty-five states and Canada. Their most famous works—including New York's Central Park, Boston's Emerald Necklace of parks, and the Capitol Grounds in Washington, D.C.—became world-renowned landmarks, as well as prototypes in the development of the American public park.

Today, as many as eight thousand visitors come to the Olmsted National Historic Site annually to tour the beautifully restored office spaces and grounds, or to do research in the archives. What these visitors discover is a decidedly low-key but vibrant center. While park rangers are giving visitor tours, museum staff are processing numerous research requests and intensively cataloging and stabilizing close to a million plans and records in the Olmsted archives. Meanwhile, horticulturists are busy maintaining the newly restored grounds of Fairsted—a "living exhibit" of Olmstedian design principles and philosophy—while education staff challenge children to explore the stories embedded in landscape, to ponder the roles people play in shaping the green spaces around them, or to qualify as "Junior Rangers." Various new outreach and training programs are blossoming every day—including innovative student education activities, collaborative tours and workshops with partners like the Emerald Necklace Conservancy and Trustees of Reservations, and technical assistance to other national parks through the Olmsted Center for Landscape Preservation. In sum, the Olmsted Site balances a dual existence as a living museum and a working archive of American landscape architecture.

The man who initially instigated all this activity, the legendary Frederick Law Olmsted (1822–1903), has been heralded not only as the founder of American landscape architecture, but as the nation's premier park maker and proponent of urban planning. His early efforts to preserve Niagara Falls and Yosemite have even led some to give him a somewhat paternal status for the National Park system and the conservation movement. He was also the father of two men—his son, Frederick Jr., and his stepson and nephew, John Charles—who actually executed much of the later work that bears the Olmsted name. As the Olmsted Brothers, they brought the firm to its height of influence and activity in the 1920s and 1930s, three decades after their father's death.

Still, Frederick Olmsted, Sr., was the source—a fascinating figure who was in many ways as interesting as his designs. The elder Olmsted was born in Connecticut, the son of an upper-class merchant. His mother died when he was three years old. His brother John died when Frederick was

The sturdy old "Olmsted elm" still stands outside the famed landscape architect's former home and office, now a national park site.

thirty-five. Rejected by at least one true love, Elizabeth Baldwin, Olmsted remained a bachelor until he was thirty-seven, when he married Mary Cleveland Perkins Olmsted, the wife of his deceased brother.

As a child, Olmsted was sickly. As an adult, he suffered from an artistic temperament, perfectionism, and "workaholism," which were manifested in occasional depression, anxiety, and exhaustion. He was also known for his limp, which he acquired after an 1860 carriage accident in Central Park.

Olmsted never graduated from any grammar or high school, and his college studies at Yale lasted just a few months. Instead, his real education came from a series of travels and careers, including work as an engineer's apprentice, counter clerk, sailor, scientific farmer, journalist, publisher, and adventurer. During the Civil War, for example, he set up hospitals in the field, working with the U.S. Sanitary Commission, the precursor to the American Red Cross.

Olmsted himself called his early years "vagabondish and somewhat poetical." Whether one sees them as charmingly eclectic or merely haphazard, the result was positive. Olmsted was transformed into a Renaissance man.

Throughout his travels, Olmsted nurtured an appreciation of the land that would later serve him well. Since childhood, he had loved the natural landscape of New England, with its woodlands and meadows. As an adult, he worked occasionally as a farmer and wrote articles on the southern agricultural economy. In travels abroad, he observed parks in England and other European countries and was impressed by their growing importance for modern societies.

Perhaps most significant was that as Olmsted matured, so did nineteenth-century America—changing from a land of rolling rural farmlands to overcrowded industrialized cities. He had not yet found his calling, but the scene had been perfectly set.

In 1857, at the age of thirty-five, Olmsted stumbled into a career that would both define his life and change the urban landscape of America for decades to come. He was appointed the first superintendent of Central Park in New York City, a project that put all his experiences, skills, observations, neuroses, and energies to practical use.

Collaborating with architect Calvert Vaux, Olmsted designed and engineered a plan that eventually changed 840 acres of Manhattan swamps, rocks, pigsties, and slaughterhouses into a remarkable, varied, and world-renowned public park. Despite the frustrations of battling big-city politics throughout their tumultuous fourteen-year tenure there, Olmsted and Vaux essentially invented the American pleasure park in New York and the profession of landscape architecture in America.

During the next several decades, Olmsted's reputation grew. His major projects included Brooklyn's Prospect Park, the Riverside Subdivision in Chicago, Mount Royal Park in Montreal, and the Capitol Grounds in Washington, D.C. By the time the nascent Boston Park Commission hired him to design a new "Back Bay Park" in 1878, his concept of the function and fashion of public parks was well formed.

The ideal city park, as Olmsted viewed it, offered a fresh-air escape from urban pressures, creating a place where body and soul could be replenished. Olmsted rejected the exotic, sculpted European gardens that were monopolized by aristocrats—and frequently off-limits to ordinary people. His ruggedly naturalistic parks were meant to reflect America's democratic ideal; they would provide moral uplift, mental calm, and a unifying experience for both rich *and* poor.

According to C. Sue Rigney, chief of Planning and Communications at the Olmsted Site, "In Boston, and in Central Park, too, Olmsted was working to transform uninhabited, dead spaces into desirable ones. But he was just as concerned with improving the mental, spiritual, and physical health of people by providing these parks. Olmsted wanted to function as a social reformer. He believed in 'democracy in dirt'—creating public parks that were accessible to all classes of people. And that really sets him apart."

Olmsted based his designs on eighteenth-century English landscape gardens, mixing elements of the pastoral and picturesque schools into his own unique vision. His landscapes grew out of respect for the "genius of the place," the site's natural topography. He considered proper sanitation and drainage crucial, and subordinated detail to the overall design. In an Olmsted park, the visitor encounters "passages of scenery"—distinct environmental vignettes that might include a liberal use of plantings in a picturesque space, or a sense of spaciousness in a more pastoral one. Conscious separation is made between areas done in different styles, or those used for different purposes. The elm tree became Olmsted's personal signature on his landscapes; perhaps not coincidentally, the name Olmsted translates from Old English as "the place of the elm."

All of Olmsted's design concepts are in evidence in Boston's Emerald Necklace, from the Back Bay Fens to Franklin Park—and on the Fairsted grounds.

In 1883, Olmsted became a Boston-area resident, moving his home and offices from Manhattan to Brookline. Precisely why he relocated is a matter of conjecture. Olmsted was, of course, a New Englander by birth, and his disenchantment with New York bureaucrats may have contributed to his decision. Certainly, his work on a linear park system for Boston, begun back in 1878, was an enticement, as was the fact that the town of Brookline was home to one of his dearest friends, the architect H. H. Richardson. Brookline was also Olmsted's vision of a perfect suburb—beautiful, quiet, bucolic, and easily accessible to Boston by the trolley or by the road that eventually became Route 9. Although many of these factors may have played a role, some say that Olmsted's desire to relocate was based on a single event: awakening at Richardson's Brookline house one snowy morning to find the streets freshly, and impressively, plowed.

Whatever the reasons, Olmsted's move into the 1810 farmhouse once owned by the Clark sisters, Sarah and Susannah, was permanent. Over the decades, the house and office at Fairsted were enlarged by Olmsted and sons as their business and fame grew—the whole complex taking on a distinctly "Olmstedian" form. A curving, two-story office with a hodgepodge of rooms and half-staircases was attached to the original farmhouse, accommodating up to sixty employees from "sweep boys" to landscape architects. The house itself was expanded to include sleeping porches and a glassed-in conservatory for all-weather access to the outdoors. The original barn, moved from a nearby hill to hook in with the complex, served as a model-making shop.

Ranger-guided tours of Fairsted (every Friday through Sunday) give visitors an opportunity to view rooms in the historic design office, which now look much as they did during the firm's halcyon days. Particularly fascinating is the print processing room, where copies of original design drawings were made using a primitive "sun-printing" process—without benefit of Xerox or digital scanning. The "planting department" is furnished with original tables, stools, and lamps, plus a framed plan of George Vanderbilt's Biltmore estate in North Carolina, the last major project Olmsted worked on. Inside the historic house is a visitor information station, bookstore, orientation film, and exhibits that focus on the life and work of the Olmsteds and their Brookline firm.

Out on the Fairsted landscape, park rangers guide visitors through a small-scale sampler of typical Olmsted-designed spaces. Multiple "passages of scenery," distinct in style and character, were crafted with such skill and respect for nature that every shaded walk and rocky nook appears natural. Looming below Olmsted's master bedroom and the firm's drafting rooms is the shady, sunken Hollow, filled with an abundance of greenery in various forms, textures, and shadings of color. On the far side of the circular driveway is the picturesque Rock Garden, once a gloomy gravel pit. A miniature trail leads into a dense woodland adorned with mountain laurel, then opens magnificently into the rolling green of the South Lawn. This lawn was cluttered with trees and a driveway when Olmsted bought the property; he left just a single, tall elm at its center. Known as the Olmsted Elm, this carefully tended 150-year-old arbor has survived both the deadly Dutch elm disease and periodic hurricanes—including 1991's Hurricane Bob, whose death toll at Fairsted included a beautiful old red oak and a tulip poplar.

Since the Olmsted National Historic Site is an active research and outreach facility, destroyed plantings like those will literally rise again. With the aid of high-tech equipment and ongoing experiments, the National Park Service is learning to better understand, manage, and preserve culturally important landscapes of the past. Staff horticulturists periodically take cuttings from historically significant plantings on the site, which they root and grow to replacement size in a historic and native plants nursery. Hence, when a parent plant dies, genetically identical offspring can replace it. Also based at Fairsted is the Olmsted Center for Landscape Preservation—the Park Service's only center for cultural landscape preservation, training, and technology development. Olmsted Center staff work in partnership with national parks, universities, government agencies, and nonprofit organizations to undertake such collaborative projects as cultural landscape and historic plant inventories and inspection and stabilization of hazardous trees.

The house, grounds, and research facilities of the Frederick Law Olmsted National Historic Site were not always in such fine fettle as they appear today—having undergone both prosperous and lean periods since Olmsted's time. Frederick Law Olmsted himself died in 1903, after spending the last years of his life in McLean Asylum, a Boston-area psychiatric hospital for which, ironically, he had once submitted landscape plans. Though the senior Olmsted had supplied the enduring fame, it was his two sons, Frederick Jr. and John Charles, who brought in the bulk of Olmsted work and wealth, in the 1910s and 1920s. The last Olmsted left the firm in 1950, and the firm itself—known as Olmsted Associates—departed the Fairsted grounds in 1979.

Between 1979 and 1980, the National Park Service bought the old house, grounds, and voluminous archives. The good news was they had acquired a unique site—an artist's home complete with original artwork, both on paper and on the grounds themselves. The bad news was that all of the above were in nightmarish condition.

By 1980, when the Park Service moved in, the house was severely damaged. Most of the original landscaping was lost or overgrown—only the "bones" of the historic landscape were still apparent. The interior vault, where decades of precious drawings and documents were stored in rolls, was a downright disaster. "The vault had been unheated for more than ten years," explains site manager Lee Farrow Cook. "Environmental conditions were awful, because of the mold." When the initial dust had cleared, the prognosis was equally dismal: experts estimated it would take more than a century to conserve the Olmsted archives and make them accessible to researchers.

Thanks to decades of hard work, substantially increased funding from Congress, and support from the National Park Service, those dark days are past. Today, research requests that once took six months or more to process can be dealt with in a month. Jill Trebbe and her expanded museum staff are busy cataloging and stabilizing the last of nearly a million historic plans and associated records in the vast Olmsted archives. "We are finally reaching the finish line!" says Trebbe with a grin. This rescue from decay seemed unthinkable two decades ago. (In the historic landscape architecture stash are some 140,000 drawings, 60,000 photographs, and 30,000 negatives—accessed by research requests that come in at the rate of 1,000 per year.) Another exciting new development is the launch of the Olmsted Research Guide Online (ORGO), a searchable database program combining Olmsted design records at Fairsted with those located at the Library of Congress.

Since opening its doors to the public in 1981, the Olmsted site has attracted serious researchers and curious visitors alike. Visitor programs have been expanded to include not only tours of Fairsted but also a variety of partnership programs. "When we first began giving walking tours of Boston's Emerald Necklace parks in the early 1980s," remembers ranger Alan Banks, "as many as four hundred people would show up! Nobody seemed to know much about the history and design of these special places, but everybody seemed to want to." Now Banks and his ranger staff give regular tours of the park system, as well as organizing neighborhood walks and events, workshops, panel discussions, and slide programs. (The centennial of Olmsted's death in 2003 provided an opportunity for reflections on the man and his legacy that included several special events for children and adults.) The work of the Olmsteds has always been of particular interest to Massachusetts residents, since Olmsted's firm created 1,200 design projects in 150 Bay State communities between 1866 and 1950. Among these are parks in Lynn, Brockton, New Bedford, Fall River, Worcester, and Springfield; college and university campuses at the University of Massachusetts-Amherst, Mount Holyoke, Smith, Wellesley, and Harvard; community subdivisions in Brookline and Swampscott; the sites of the Massachusetts General Hospital in Boston, the Thomas Crane Library in Quincy, and Town Hall in Easton; Charlestown Playground; the Weld Estate in Dedham; the Tanglewood Estate in Lenox; Amherst Common; and World's End in Hingham.

As a result, the quietly dynamic Olmsted site is much more than a stop for knowledgeable Bostonians. "Frederick Law Olmsted's lifelong commitment to people, parks, and public spaces is our commitment as well," explains park superintendent Myra Harrison. "His interests and the involvement of his firm in creating green spaces stretched from 'sea to shining sea,' and this legacy needs to be understood and cherished by all people who love and respect the landscape."

THE ESSENTIALS
Address: 99 Warren Street, Brookline, MA 02445. **Telephone:** (617) 566-1689. **Website:** www.nps.gov/frla. **Visitor Information:** Open 10:00 A.M. to 4:30 P.M. Friday through Sunday for ranger-guided tours; groups may arrange tours other days by appointment. Free. Grounds and first floor of house are wheelchair accessible; office and one area of garden have multiple steps; ramps and accessible restroom are available.

48 Castle Island

NO TROOPS ever stormed its parapets, or rushed its sturdy earthworks with bayonets. No frigates were blown asunder by its cannon, and no fighter jets blasted down from its skies. No battles were lost, no wars won within in the confines of its shores. Indeed, volunteer summer guides from the Castle Island Association (CIA) proudly tell visitors that "no shot was ever fired in anger by American forces from this island." Still, as the oldest continuously fortified site on British North America, Castle Island played a long and vital role in American military history.

The name Castle Island itself is a bit confusing to those who first encounter the historic site. Though once an island in Boston Harbor, the area has been connected to South Boston by a causeway since the 1920s. Moreover, the largest structure on the island is no castle in the flowery, Disneyesque sense of the word. Instead, Fort Independence is an imposing, low-slung, pentagonal granite fortress built by Sylvanus Thayer, "the father of West Point," in the decades preceding the Civil War. Believed to be the eighth fort on this site, it's descended from a long line of harbor defense works built on the island since 1634.

Since those early colonial days, military activities on Castle Island have ranged from demagnetizing warships to confining prisoners of war, and from training artillery and infantry to burying the dead. The fort was also garrisoned during every major war from 1634 through World War II. Meanwhile, the site has played host to such diverse luminaries as Franklin Delano Roosevelt, Paul Revere, and Edgar Allan Poe. It has also been the scene of countless freak accidents, including deadly bolts of lightning, accidental explosions, fatal duels, overturned boats, and a drowning caused by a "killer" whale.

Castle Island has even been used to improve the quality of everyday Boston life. Once the site for various hospitals and the state's first penitentiary, it's now an active, twenty-two-acre public park with more than a million visitors each year. Today, the park and fort are owned and operated by the Massachusetts Department of Conservation and Recreation (DCR), in cooperation with the volunteer Castle Island Association.

Castle Island acquired its first fort in 1634, just four years after the founding of Boston. Although the Puritan settlement was well protected by the defense works on Fort Hill, not far from Rowe's Wharf, the Massachusetts Bay colonists wanted a second layer of security—to stop pirates, plunderers, and other enemies as they entered Boston Harbor. As a result, Governor Thomas Dudley and his advisors agreed to build a frontline fort on Castle Island. The hilly isle was a drumlin, a remnant of the last glacier to pass through these parts some twelve thousand years earlier. Its curious shape had inspired colonists to name it Castle Island even before a single fortress had been built on its shores.

That first "castle" was a rustic little structure consisting of two wooden-platformed earthworks and a small dwelling. The masonry was fabricated from crushed oyster shells. Four forts, all presumably called "the Castle," were built on the island that century. Since military action was minimal, the island's death toll was small.

The most unusual demise was that of Commander Richard Davenport, felled by a lightning bolt one summer night in 1665. The late Edward Rowe Snow, preeminent chronicler of Harbor Islands history and lore, wrote of another, equally strange death: in 1688, one John Evered became tangled in his own fishing line and was drowned by the whale snagged on the other end.

When the island's fifth fort was built around 1700, it was named Castle William after the English monarch. This particular incarnation of the Castle became a British refuge during the early stages of the American Revolution. When the incendiary Stamp Tax was levied in 1765, the hated stamps were hidden out in the island fort for protection. British regulars also fled to Castle William in the turmoil following the Boston Massacre of 1770. In the wake of the battles at Lexington and Concord, British troops sent out three unsuccessful expeditions from Castle Island.

Volunteers from the Castle Island Association offer seasonal tours and special events to visitors of the oldest continuously fortified site in British North America.

General George Washington, securely lodged on Dorchester Heights, finally proved too competent a warrior for the English enemy. Starting on March 17, 1776, the British were forced to abandon Boston altogether. This event is celebrated in Boston each year as Evacuation Day. (Falling on March 17, it ever-so-conveniently coincides with another of the Hub's favorite holidays, St. Patrick's Day.)

Determined to have the last word when they departed, the British mined and set fire to Castle Island and dumped some of its ordnance into the harbor. As an encore, they later blew up Boston Light in the outer harbor, the oldest lighthouse in North America. Undaunted, the resourceful patriots proceeded to build a sixth fort on the charred island. Among the construction supervisors were Richard Gridley, a renowned veteran of the Battle of Bunker Hill, and the ubiquitous Paul Revere.

By the end of the eighteenth century, this fort was transferred from state to federal ownership, renamed Fort Independence, and then replaced. The U.S. government was designing the first of many systems of coastal defenses, which eventually stretched from Maine to New Orleans. Having already built Fort McHenry in Baltimore, Jean Foncin was sent to construct a larger version of McHenry on Castle Island. By 1801, the first five-bastioned Fort Independence was well under way.

The Fort Independence that rests on the island today is the third by that name and the eighth defense work on the site. Designed by Braintree's Sylvanus Thayer, it was built between 1833 and 1851. Though Thayer's initial cost estimate was $255,574.66, expenditures had skyrocketed to $514,594.00 by 1851—with perhaps $10,000 more needed to complete the job. The new Fort Independence—with walls up to thirty feet high and five and a half feet thick—was the most formidable fortress in the island's history. Its pentagon shape was much like Foncin's previous structures, though Thayer replaced the old brick with Rockport and Quincy granite, doubling the earlier fort's height and constructing casemates within its walls. The newly enlarged Fort Independence was still relatively small when compared to another in Boston Harbor, Fort Warren on Georges Island, which Thayer built during the same period. Independence was about one sixth the size of Fort Warren—which basically meant you could fit the entire structure in Fort Warren's parade ground.

Though Fort Independence was garrisoned by the U.S. military during the Spanish-American and the two World Wars, its heyday was the Civil War period. Ninety-six cannon were mounted at the fort's height, including fifteen-inch Rodmans, which could lob a 300-pound shell or 450 pounds of solid shot more than three miles. More important to the fort's defense line was that by using all ninety-six cannon they could hurl more than 5,000 pounds of cannonballs at the enemy at any given time.

As it turned out, the cannon at Fort Independence did little more than fire practice balls at nearby Thompson Island. The cannon themselves were replaced over time, or sold for scrap during World War II. Of the seven cannons at the fort today, five were borrowed from places like Mount Hope Cemetery and USS *Constitution*. The two Rodmans are actually precise fiberglass replicas commissioned by the Castle Island Association for some $20,000.

As both a military fort and the site of Massachusetts's first state prison, Castle Island has housed its share of prisoners over the years, including Native Americans, French sailors, and British soldiers—and a fellow named Stephen Burroughs. Burroughs, true to his name, ingeniously weaseled out of the state prison there, then published his memoirs in a 1798 best-selling book. Castle Island's most famous prisoner was probably Sir Edmund Andros, the tyrannical royal governor of the northern colonies, who was held in the Castle during Britain's "Glorious Revolution" of 1688–89. Meanwhile, across the Atlantic, British citizens were successfully overthrowing King James II in favor of the less autocratic William of Orange.

Though the various incarnations of the fort have received the most attention over the centuries, they were far from Castle Island's only buildings. According to Bill Stokinger of the DCR, the island has had more than 120 structures over the years, including hospitals, barracks, officers' quarters, storehouses, powder magazines, and dungeons. Military graveyards were part of the island from the 1600s on. One such burying ground lay on the bluff behind where Sullivan's concession stand rests today. Both the British and Americans sculpted elaborate gardens on the grounds, echoed today in the well-kept flower beds maintained by the Castle Island Association.

New England's first marine hospital—a 1799 treatment center for sick sailors—was built on the island, as was an earlier inoculation center for smallpox. In 1721, Dr. Zabdiel Boylston, supported by the Reverend Cotton Mather, introduced the controversial new medical practice of inoculation to Boston. Though initially dreaded and resisted, the inoculations were ultimately effective in curbing the disease. In later years, the island was occasionally used as a smallpox isolation hospital, as during Boston's deadly outbreak of 1764.

Today, the only buildings left besides Fort Independence are a DCR-built restroom, several small structures associated with the McDonough Sailing Center, and a former U.S. Army Signal Corps facility—a remnant from the era of the World Wars. The latter is utilized as a Castle Island Association meeting place and a DCR field office. Meanwhile, the entrance to Castle Island has been guarded by Sullivan's, a popular local hangout and fast-food joint, since 1951. The current building, constructed in 1988, was designed to loosely resemble one of three officers' quarters that stood on the island more than a century ago.

The site where Sullivan's now stands—as well as the whole parking lot and approaching causeway—was under water before 1916. Prior to that time, Castle Island really *was* an island.

In 1892, a wooden pile bridge was completed, connecting South Boston to the island, in anticipation of extending Frederick Law Olmsted's Emerald Necklace of Boston parks out to the harbor. That Castle Island bridge, along with the decommissioning of Fort Independence in 1879, heralded the beginning of the area's life as a popular and accessible Boston park. Hydraulic dredging, begun in 1916, created enough landfill to complete a concrete walkway to the island by 1928. By 1932, a roadway had been laid. Boston had expanded a popular picnic area and given South Boston a new front yard.

Military personnel had long been memorialized on Castle Island, but once the roadway and circle were laid, prestigious local civilians began getting their due here as well. In 1933, a group of private donors—including Franklin Delano Roosevelt—contributed to the tallest monument on the island, a fifty-two-foot obelisk honoring Donald McKay, the famous nineteenth-century East Boston shipbuilder. Other names immortalized here reflect contemporary neighborhood heroes, as well as the area's Irish heritage. A lifelike bust and tot playground are dedicated to firefighter Robert M. Greene, and the fishing pier is named for another fireman, John J. McCorkle. The Harry McDonough Sailing Center is not far from Father Timothy J. O'Connor Memorial Walk. The island's most recent monument is South Boston's Korean War Memorial.

The Metropolitan District Commission (which became part of the D.C.R. in 2003) acquired the island and fort from the federal government in 1962—in totally dilapidated condition. Five million dollars' worth of renovations since that time has accomplished a great deal: the grounds have been improved and landscaped; seawall repairs have been completed; the fort has been made relatively safe and sound; and several interior rooms have been restored to their nineteenth-century appearance.

Today, Castle Island attractions include a summer sailing program, a beach on Pleasure Bay, a fishing pier, a tot playground, picnic areas, rambling walkways, well-kept flower beds, and free parking. The volunteer Castle Island Association, formed in 1977, has continually worked side by side with the DCR. Its members have given fort tours to summer visitors, outfitted the fort interior with dozens of historic and contemporary flags, and helped to organize special events, including a gala annual pre-Halloween bash.

Halloween is an appropriate time to visit the site, incidentally, since the most enduring legend about Castle Island is that it inspired Poe's classic tale "The Cask of Amontillado." According to historian-storyteller Edward Rowe Snow, a duel took place on the island on Christmas Day, 1817, between young Robert Massie and the fort bully, Lieutenant Gustavus Drane (called "Captain Green" in Snow's stories). When the other soldiers learned of Massie's cruel death, they were enraged. They got Drane drunk, hauled him into the fort's dungeon, chained him down, and sealed up the vault. Edgar Allan Poe enlisted in the 1st Regiment United States Artillery at Castle Island ten years later, heard the tale . . . and the rest is literary history.

In 1905, workers digging in the area allegedly uncovered a skeleton wearing the remnants of an old military uniform—a piece of evidence that seemed to support the story. But the finding was never supported by subsequent research. Moreover, although Drane's entombment allegedly took place twenty-nine years earlier, Drane didn't die until 1846, a time at which there were no interior chambers or subterranean dungeons in the island's fort.

Still, on Castle Island, truth has often been stranger than fiction, and other archaeological digs have spawned stories of their own. When a Brown University archaeological team collected artifacts on the island during the mid-1970s, more human remains were found. The workers first called it "Casper the Friendly Ghost," but later analysis by the Smithsonian Institute showed that the bones were actually the partly charred remains of not one but *two* individuals. Since one was a young male and the other an old female, they were affectionately dubbed "Harold and Maude," after the 1971 cult film starring Ruth Gordon in the tale of a May-December romance.

Who Castle Island's Harold and Maude were, when they arrived, and why they were there, are all still mysteries—or, better yet, a tangled web waiting to be unraveled by the right storyteller.

THE ESSENTIALS

Address: End of William J. Day Boulevard, on Boston Harbor, South Boston. Massachusetts Department of Conservation and Recreation, Harbor Region Office, 165 Day Boulevard, Boston, MA 02127. **Telephone:** Massachusetts Department of Conservation and Recreation, Harbor Region Headquarters, (617) 727-5290. **Website:** www.state.ma .us/DCR. **Visitor Information:** Island open 24 hours a day, 365 days a year. Free. Free tours of fort interior given by members of the Castle Island Association, on weekends and Monday holiday afternoons from Memorial Day to Labor Day, and on Sunday afternoons from Memorial Day through Columbus Day. Island, fort, and most facilities wheelchair accessible via flat or gently sloping walkways; upper sections of the fort interior require steep ramp for access; restrooms accessible.

49 Georges Island

WHEN BOSTON's temperatures hit their warm summer highs, some people seek relief in a cool drink and a canopied outdoor café. What fewer folks realize, however, is that a real escape from the sizzling city is only a short boat ride away. Seven miles east of downtown Boston lies a forty-acre park called Georges Island, one of the seventeen islands scattered throughout Boston Harbor that compose Boston Harbor Islands State Park, and one of thirty-four islands in Boston Harbor Islands National Recreation Area (a national park area). For the nominal cost of a boat ticket, Georges Island offers visitors fresh sea breezes, chirping birds, lapping surf, summer sun for tanning, picnic tables, shade trees, open space for light recreation, and regularly scheduled nature and history walks and talks.

Once on the island, visitors will also discover the unique role Georges Island has played in Boston history. One very visible reminder of that role is the site's magnificent "white elephant"—a sprawling Civil War–era fort that dominates the island, which guests can explore at will. A second reminder of days gone by is harder to see and impossible to verify; one of Boston's best-known ghosts, the mysterious Lady in Black, is said to stalk the island to this day.

Georges Island, like the other thirty-plus islands (and former islands) found throughout Boston's harbor today, was originally formed by glaciers. Native Americans had canoed in the harbor and camped, farmed, and fished on many of these islands for several thousand years before white settlers arrived in Boston; still, no evidence of any permanent native settlements on Georges has been found. Presumably, they came only from late spring to early autumn and set up temporary campsites, digging clams and catching fish there. (Though its official name is Boston Harbor Islands National Recreation Area, the thirty-four-island park, established in 1996, is often referred to as "Boston Harbor Islands, a national park area"; the altered wording evolved from sensitivity to modern Native Americans, who felt it disrespectful to associate sacred Indian grounds with "recreation.")

James Pemberton of nearby Hull is acknowledged as the island's first white settler. Pemberton claimed the island and began farming there by 1628. Farming and grazing remained major uses of Pemberton's Island under subsequent owners for almost two centuries. By 1690, the island was renamed George's in honor of one John George; it is assumed that he once owned or farmed the island as well. *George's*—meaning "of or belonging to George"—is theoretically the correct spelling of the name, though *Georges* is often used today.

Throughout the colonial period, and especially during the American Revolution, both the young nation and the prosperous city of Boston were aware of the need for seacoast defense from external enemies. Events of the War of 1812—especially the burning of Washington, D.C., by the British army—confirmed that notion and resulted in the establishment or improvement of a series of forts along the eastern coast, including Fort Adams in Newport, Rhode Island, and Fort Independence on Castle Island in Boston Harbor. In pursuing these seacoast defense plans, the U.S. government bought Georges Island in 1825. Several years later, they selected Lieutenant Colonel Sylvanus Thayer of Braintree, the illustrious "father of West Point," to oversee construction of a fort.

A seawall had already been completed on Georges Island by 1832. From 1833 to 1857 Thayer supervised the massive fort project, which included hauling huge, hand-hewn granite stones from Quincy quarries, then transporting them to the island on special sailing ships. The name chosen, Fort Warren, commemorated Joseph Warren, a highly respected colonial doctor, patriot, and Revolutionary War general who had been killed at the Battle of Bunker Hill. Although the commemorative block over the sally port (main entrance) gate reads, "Fort Warren, 1850," the date is not entirely ac-

From late spring to early fall, regular boat service takes visitors to Georges Island, part of Boston Harbor Islands, a national park area, and home to a fascinating Civil War fortress.

curate. Much of the fort's structure was completed by 1850, but the interior finish work and gun platforms were not. When the first battalions of Union soldiers arrived for training on Georges Island in 1861, in fact, the fort was still unfinished.

Thayer's design for Fort Warren was very French, very seventeenth century, very practical, and at the same time, very romantic. It has a lovely drawbridge that doesn't draw and a winding moat that was never filled with water. It also has a multitude of ingenious ways to thwart attacking enemies—from heavy bolt-studded oak doors and slamming portcullises (sliding wooden grates that could quickly close off entrances) to devilishly well positioned light-cannon embrasures designed to fend off intruding infantry. Other particularly fascinating features are the fort's dungeonlike casemates (fortified firing positions), spiral staircases, large fireplaces, and self-supporting arches.

All the good design and defense work by Thayer and his crew were never tested; Fort Warren was never attacked. When the Civil War began in 1861, several units of the Massachusetts Volunteer Infantry were stationed there for military training—often using the central parade ground to practice weapons drills, equipment maintenance, and marching techniques. Fort Warren's most important role during that war, however, was as a prison; some 2,300 Confederate soldiers and sympathizers were housed there in all. Unlike the infamous Confederate prison in Andersonville, Georgia, Fort Warren was renowned as a humane, well-kept jail—a credit to the fort's well-respected commander, Colonel Justin Dimick. Among its well-known inmates were Confederate ambassadors James M. Mason and John Slidell, and, at the war's conclusion, Alexander Hamilton Stephens, vice president of the Confederacy.

All kinds of legends, tall tales, and real historic events are intertwined in Georges Island's rich past—so inextricably, in some cases, that it's hard to tell fact from fiction. Among those stories, however, two stand out: one concerns the origins of the Civil War–era song "John Brown's Body"; the second relates to the island's resident ghost.

The John Brown was a zealous abolitionist, best known for the raid he led on the village of Harpers Ferry, Virginia, in 1859. When Brown and a tiny army of black and white men tried to incite a slave rebellion there, the federal government captured and hanged him, thereby assuring Brown the status of hero. Meanwhile, two years later, the 2nd Massachusetts Infantry Battalion arrived for military duty at Fort Warren in Boston Harbor. As one story goes, one of these Union soldiers was also named John Brown, which inspired some comrades to joke, "You can't be John Brown, 'cause he lies a-moulderin' in the grave." As an extension of that comment—part of which ended up in one of the song's verses—ordinary soldiers supposedly created the lyrics to "John Brown's Body" while they busily cleaned up rubble in the uncompleted fort.

According to the MDC's late, longtime archivist and military historian Al Schroeder, however, it was "Boston Brahmins" among the troops who wrote the song, in the evening, after work was done. Whatever the lyric's source, the tune the soldiers used was that of an old camp song, "Say, Brothers, Will You Meet Us." Most important was the final product, "John

Brown's Body," which quickly became the Union's favorite marching song as Fort Warren–trained troops marched south.

How did "John Brown's Body" inspire a patriotic hymn? Though abolitionist and poet Julia Ward Howe lived in Boston, she first heard the Massachusetts regiments singing "John Brown's Body" on a trip to Washington. Howe was so smitten by the catchy music that she had her carriage chase after the soldiers. Then, of course, she borrowed the tune, the chorus, and an image or two for her new anthem, "The Battle Hymn of the Republic." (Mrs. Howe's song was published in the *Atlantic Monthly* in February 1862. President Lincoln reportedly wept when he first heard the hymn; Howe was subsequently paid five dollars by the *Atlantic*.)

The second Civil War tale centered on Georges Island concerns the site's haunting presence, affectionately known as the Lady in Black. According to legend, a young woman named Melanie missed her new husband, a Confederate soldier imprisoned at Fort Warren. Disguised in a Union soldier's uniform, Melanie had friends transport her in a rowboat from Hull to the island. Once there, she hid, prowled about, and finally located her husband Samuel by whistling their favorite song outside the fort's windows, or musket loops. In some versions of the tale, their goal was simply to spring Samuel; others claim the couple meant to incite a rebellion in the fort's prison.

Unfortunately, the escape plan literally backfired. Melanie's antique gun exploded, killing her husband instead of the oncoming guards. Tried and convicted of treason, Melanie was allowed one last request before her hanging. She asked to die in women's clothing. Since there were no women or women's garments on the island at the time, they gave her a dark mourning shroud—made from Fort Warren's mess hall drapes—which was wrapped around her.

Many versions of the story, incidentally, identify Melanie and Samuel's last name as Lanier. A Samuel Lanier was indeed imprisoned at Fort Warren, which lent credence to the tale for decades. According to site spokespersons, however, Samuel Lanier died of kidney failure while imprisoned on the island, and the Lanier name has been deleted from modern tellings out of respect for the real—as opposed to the *surreal*—dead.

Although historical documentation for the Lady in Black's life is scant, records of her alleged afterlife are not. If you believe the stories, her hauntings have been many. Many journals and personal stories of soldiers stationed at Fort Warren through the World War II period, for example, have included frightening passages about a spectral presence: taps on the shoulder, or icy fingers around a soldier's neck; fresh female-size footprints appearing in the snow, with no body attached; and phone messages taken by a female voice, though no women were on the island.

After the Civil War, the technology of warfare evolved swiftly and the granite walls of Fort Warren became vulnerable to new weapons. The fort and its munitions were overhauled and updated for every foreign naval threat—including the Spanish-American War and both World Wars. Thanks to these upgrades, Fort Warren remained a vital link in America's seacoast defense system until after World War II.

The most interesting additions, around the turn of the twentieth century, were the so-called disappearing guns—including twelve-inch artillery rifles with ranges of eight to nine miles. (In an age before computers, hitting a moving target eight miles away was quite a feat.) The disappearing guns recoiled down into their concrete emplacements after firing, thus protecting the loading crew from returning volleys. Whenever the fort's two twelve-inch guns were fired during practice—and practice is all they did, since battle never came to the harbor—Quincy residents assumed an earthquake had struck.

Despite its impressive armaments, the military personnel stationed on the island during the twentieth century spent more time laying mines than firing guns. None of the guns remains to be seen; they'd become scrap metal by 1944, and other military artifacts were lost to vandals. The only cannon on the fort's grounds today—two three-inch saluting guns converted from old Civil War smoothbores—are probably not originally from Fort Warren.

Georges Island was a spotless, impeccably kept military installation for decades. Following World War II, however, the military abandoned it, retiring Warren as a fort in 1951. For a time both the land and the structure were sorely neglected. In 1957, a private company tried to acquire the island for a hazardous-waste dump site—an act that finally incited Bostonians to action. Led by storyteller-historian Edward Rowe Snow—whose books on Boston's Harbor Islands are the classics of the genre—a citizens group halted the sale and the dumpsters. Instead, the site was turned over to the Commonwealth's Metropolitan District Commission, and the park eventually co-run by the MDC and the Department of Environmental Management.

Today, the island's many activities are managed by the Massachusetts Department of Conservation and Recreation, as part of the Boston Harbor Islands National Park Area, with resident managers and interpreters providing educational programs and special events. Special trips, exhibits, cleanups, and other activities related to Georges and other Harbor Islands are also regularly sponsored by the nonprofit volunteer group the Friends of the Boston Harbor Islands and the Island Alliance. Ambitious renovation projects for the fort and island are in process as well. (Smaller ferries run from Georges to a half dozen other islands in the park, where visitors can also camp, picnic, swim, hike, explore forts, and enjoy nature.)

Since the military past of Georges Island included a series of levelings, clearings, and defoliations, the plant and animal life that survives there today must be hardy indeed. Resident plants include plenty of wild edibles—so many that an entire nature walk is devoted to this interesting topic. Nonpoisonous staghorn sumac, beach roses, wild apples, maple trees, and even a scarlet pimpernel are also found on the island. The wealth of birds that stop at Georges Island is one of its greatest attractions. Barn swallows are the most frequent visitors, though pheasants, snowy owls, and most migratory birds have also been sighted.

The most populous mammal on Georges Island is the occasional Norway rat, or "ship rat," an unpopular reflection of the island's military past. Muskrats have also been seen, and staff recall a big black "attack rabbit" who once roamed the island as well. Another famous rabbit was a white domestic bunny named Warren, who was fatally buzzed by a snowy owl in the winter of 1987. Warren was buried at sea; land burial was prohibited since Georges is a National Historical Landmark.

A fascinating footnote to Fort Warren's past is its connection to Baltimore socialite Bessie Wallis Warfield Simpson (1895–1986). In the 1990s, of course, tongues wagged around the world about the scandalous marital mistakes of various members of the British Royal family. In 1936, similar gossip surrounded Mrs. Simpson, the American divorcée who won the heart of the heir to the English throne, Edward VIII. Many remember that Edward abdicated to marry Wallis and that they became known as the Duke and Duchess of Windsor, but fewer recall that Wallis was named for two Confederate sympathizers who were imprisoned at Fort Warren. Henry M. Warfield and S. Teakle Wallis met while incarcerated at Fort Warren during the Civil War. Warfield became so attached to his friend Wallis that he named his son, and hence his granddaughter Wallis, after his former cellmate.

THE ESSENTIALS

Addresses: In Boston Harbor, seven miles east of downtown Boston. Massachusetts Department of Conservation and Recreation, Harbor Region Office, 165 Day Boulevard, Boston, MA 02127. Boston Harbor Islands, a National Park Area, 408 Atlantic Avenue, Suite 228, Boston, MA 02110 **Telephone:** Boston Harbor Islands National Recreation Area, a National Park Area, info line, (617) 223-8666; Massachusetts Department of Conservation and Recreation, Harbor Region, (617) 727-5290; Boston Harbor Cruises, (617) 227-4321; Island Alliance, (617) 223-8530. **Websites:** www.BostonIslands.com.; www.state.ma.us/DCR. **Visitor Information:** Island open 10:00 A.M. until dusk, May through September; exact dates vary yearly. Admission and tours free. Visit www.Bostonislands.com for extensive listings of events, opportunities, news, boat schedules, history, and other information. Accessible by private boat or forty-five-minute ferry ride, which runs late spring through early fall. The ferry charges moderate round-trip fares with specials for families, kids, seniors, and school groups; earliest boats leave Long Wharf at 10:00 A.M.; call for exact schedules and free inter-island shuttle information. Hour-long tours of Fort Warren take place as posted. Self-guided tours and nature walks available anytime. Fishing permitted; no swimming, camping, or alcohol. Most boats and island paths wheelchair accessible with some assistance; wheelchair-accessible restrooms in administrative building.

50 Blue Hills Reservation

FINDING A VAST expanse of nearly unadulterated nature amid the concrete jungle of urban development is a rarity. But the Blue Hills Reservation, with more than 7,000 acres of near-wilderness, is only nine miles—or an easy twenty-minute drive—from the center of bustling Boston. Spanning portions of Quincy, Milton, Canton, Randolph, Braintree, and Dedham, it's the largest reservation in Greater Boston's Metropolitan Parks

System. Moreover, Blue Hills's treasures include thirty-six holes, twenty-two hills, fifteen National Historic Sites, three national environmental study areas, and one of the oldest weather observatories in the United States. The thirty-six holes are found at the Reservation's Ponkapoag Golf Course, a well-worn championship green during fair weather and a good novice ski-touring spot when the snows arrive. The twenty-two hills—including Great Blue Hill, the highest and most popular peak in the metropolitan area—attract local hikers, rock climbers, and nature lovers.

The fifteen sites listed on the National Register of Historic Places tell the fascinating tales of inventors, explorers, farmers, quarriers, and Native Americans who once lived there. Meanwhile, three natural environmental study areas include the first bog boardwalk in the United States, built in 1949 and reconstructed in 1987. As for the weather, the observatory atop Great Blue Hill, now a National Historic Landmark, has been a post for professional and amateur weather watchers since 1885.

In its century of existence, Blue Hills Reservation has become many things to many people: a place to hike, swim, boat, fish, ski, picnic, ice skate, rock climb, snowshoe, bird-watch, mountain bike, camp, ride horses, or orienteer. Some folks go there to play tennis, golf, or softball, while others see it as the ultimate outdoor schoolroom, a place to study nature and natural history.

Still, there's a lot more "in them thar' hills" than recreation, as a glimpse into the area's past will quickly reveal. Carved by glaciers, the land is part of the highest coastal range on the eastern seaboard of the United States. Though calling the hills blue may seem illogical to those wandering through their vast greenery today, it wasn't to the folks who named them. Early European explorers who sailed along the coast three or four hundred years ago saw a bluish hue on the slopes when they viewed them from a distance.

More than ten thousand years before those Europeans arrived, Native Americans had camped and farmed in the Blue Hills. They even quarried there, seeking a brown volcanic rock known as Braintree hornfels, which they crafted into tools, spearheads, and arrowheads. These natives were known as the Massachuseuks, and the site they lived in as Massachusetts. This latter Indian word, translated as "the place of the great hills," is generally accepted as the origin of our state's name.

Native American words also live on in the Blue Hills Reservation. The Ponkapoag, whose name means "the place of the great or red spring," were among the "praying Indians" Christianized by the English; their name graces a pond, a bog, the golf course, and an archaeological site. (The reservation now includes more than fifty prehistoric sites.) The sachem Chickatawbut, who died of smallpox in 1633, is immortalized in the names of a hill, a road, and the environmental education center on today's Blue Hills Reservation. And Neponset, the name of the river reservation linked to Blue Hills by the Skyline Footpath, means "a place to have a summer vacation." The natives had different sites for spring, summer, and winter villages, and visited Boston's Harbor Islands during the warmer months. (Studies suggest that Calf Island, for example, was a special ritual island.) Houghton's Pond bears the name of the white settler family that farmed nearby for seven generations, but the site's Native American name was Wissahissic, translated as "beautiful still water." (Most modern histories still mispronounce that original name as "Hoosic-whisick," which, in the Algonquin Indian dialects spoken there, means absolutely nothing.)

The Native American population diminished quickly once white colonsts began settling and farming in the Blue Hills region. Diseases brought by the Europeans—including what is presumed to have been a virulent strain of chicken pox—were partly responsible for the Indians' untimely demise: while Europeans had built up immunities to many of these maladies, the natives had not.

These white seventeenth-century settlers and their descendants—whose names are still used for sites like Houghton's Pond and the historic Redman Farmhouse—introduced orchards and honeybees, built houses and barns, logged hillsides for lumber and grazing, and cleared fields for crops. The open fields were divided by the distinctive stone walls still found throughout Blue Hills today. Only after the fields were sold or donated for public parkland in 1892 did the forests begin to grow back again in abundance.

Many of the paths first walked by Native Americans became the trails

Among the treasures at Blue Hills Reservation are twenty-two hills, several national historic sites, a golf course, and the popular swimming area at Houghton Pond.

and roads the early Europeans used for their farm carts. A large number of those thoroughfares, large and small, are still used today. Archaeological evidence suggests that Sawcut Notch Trail, for example, may be some eight thousand years old.

The natural phenomenon that really put the Blue Hills area "on the map" in terms of history was its granite. Though Native Americans had quarried there for thousands of years, it was not until the early nineteenth century that granite quarrying in the Blue Hills, especially in the Quincy section, became a major, world-renowned industry. It was near today's reservation that Gridley Bryant created the first commercial railroad in 1826—a horse-drawn apparatus that hauled granite from inland quarries to the water. Among the famous structures constructed with Quincy granite were the Bunker Hill Monument, Quincy Market, King's Chapel, Fort Warren on Georges Island, and the Charles Street Jail.

Though some of the land containing these historic quarries was purchased for preservation within the Blue Hills Reservation in its earliest years, much more remained in private hands. Fearing that encroaching developers would build over these significant historic and recreational sites, concerned citizens engaged in a long and successful battle to preserve the remaining Quincy quarries. The famous Swingles Quarry, for example, which closed in the mid-1960s, has been refashioned into a recreation center, while Quincy Quarries Historic Site and Rattlesnake Hill are popular with rock climbers. During the late 1990s, both the Swingles Quarry and the Granite Rail Quarry were filled with dirt from Boston's Big Dig. At the Granite Rail Quarry, that landfill has proved superior to the water that used to be at its base; now, climbing walls reach some fifty feet above the fill line, making the site far more accessible and exciting to rock climbers— from beginners to quite advanced—and arguably the best climbing area in eastern Massachusetts.

In many ways, the recent efforts of concerned environmentalists to preserve and protect the Blue Hills from development and destruction resemble those of young Charles Eliot more than a century ago. Eliot, son of Harvard president Charles W. Eliot, was a landscape architect who worked with Frederick Law Olmsted, first as employee and later as a full partner. Though Olmsted has garnered most of the fame—partly due to his association with Boston's Emerald Necklace of parks—it was Eliot who was the true "father" of the Blue Hills Reservation. Eliot was a major force behind the creation of the Metropolitan Park Commission, which evolved into the Metropolitan District Commission in 1919. (Among the MDC's late-twentieth-century duties was overseeing a vast array of public parks, recreation areas, and other open spaces in the metropolitan Boston area, as well as organizing programs and special events on those sites; in July 2003 the MDC and the Department of Environmental Management [DEM] were combined into the new Department of Conservation and Recreation.) Eliot also helped create the Blue Hills Reservation itself, one of the first acquisitions of the Metropolitan Park System in 1893. The Eliot Footbridge, near the summit of Great Blue Hill, was erected in Eliot's honor in 1902, seven years after his death from cerebral meningitis at age thirty-seven.

There were well-thought-out reasons for Eliot's energetic crusades. "For crowded populations to live in health and happiness," he wrote, "they must have space for air, for light, for exercise, for rest, and for the enjoyment of that peaceful beauty of nature which, because it is the opposite of the noisy ugliness of the town, is so refreshing to the tired souls of townspeople."

The Civilian Conservation Corps, part of the Roosevelt administration's unemployment programs developed during the Depression, also played a major role in shaping the Blue Hills Reservation. CCC workers built, repaired, and improved many of the facilities, roads, footpaths, and trails still used today when they worked and camped on the reservation from 1933 to 1937.

The treasures of Blue Hills today include flora, fauna, and natural phenomena—from red foxes to rattlesnakes, dogwoods to orchids, and cedar swamps to Ice Age bogs. All are accessible to the public through a well-numbered trail system that crisscrosses the reservation in intersecting loops. There are one hundred miles of trails in all.

Moreover, partnerships with various organizations have enhanced and expanded the appeal of Blue Hills Reservation: the Appalachian Mountain Club, for example, sponsors primitive camping in log cabins; the YMCA runs a day camp; the Massachusetts Audubon Society operates the Trailside Museum and the Chickatawbut Educational Center; and Ragged Mountain Ski Resort runs the greatly improved Blue Hills ski area.

To begin any serious study of the nature, culture, archeology, and history of the Blue Hills, start at the Trailside Museum, managed by the Massachusetts Audubon Society. There you can get maps, orientation, and advice. One word to the wise: wear sturdy shoes, not sandals, for any hike.

The most popular hike is up Great Blue Hill, which offers a stunning view from the top, at 635 feet above sea level. Chickatawbut Overlook gives another magnificent aerial perspective. The best bird-watching is in Fowl Meadow. Try the walk though Ponkapoag Bog if you want to see what this area probably looked like soon after the Ice Age.

You may encounter some unusual wildlife along the way. For example, Blue Hills Reservation is the only place in eastern Massachusetts where those rare venomous serpents, copperheads and rattlesnakes, live. (You'll probably never see one, except in the reservation's museum displays, since they try to avoid contact with humans.) You may also encounter huge turkey vultures flying overhead; don't mistake them for pterodactyls, as some overimaginative motorists have done.

Among the historic sites on the reservation is the turreted stone weather observatory, known as one of the birthplaces of modern meteorology. The curious building, declared a National Historic Landmark in 1990, was the brainchild of Abbott Lawrence Rotch, an MIT graduate who pioneered weather experiments there beginning in 1885. The station once made weather forecasts for the area and wired these reports to daily Boston newspapers for publication. Today, daily temperatures are still collected, making the Blue Hill Observatory and Science Center the site with the longest continuous record of comparative temperatures in the United States. Its observations are no longer used for daily weather predictions but for studying climate trends. Most recently, the observatory has been an invaluable resource for thousands of visiting students and their teachers learning about meteorology.

As part of his landmark work in defining upper atmospheric flows, meteorologist Rotch conducted endless experiments there with kites and balloons. The kites were flown on expensive piano wire—the lightest, strongest cord available at the time—and sometimes caused disaster. One infamous incident occurred when a kite wire accidentally wrapped around an axle of a New York–New Haven railroad engine, bringing the train to a halt. The scientists lost some six miles of wire in that mishap. In another unfortunate incident, a cow accidentally ate a downed weather balloon and its instruments, then died.

Clearly, there are many tantalizing tales linked to the long history of the Blue Hills. One favorite bit of trivia involves radio transmissions: atop Great Blue Hill is the antenna that transmits the signal for WGBH-FM, a Boston public radio station, whose call letters stand for Great Blue Hill— not God Bless Harvard, as some folks like to believe.

THE ESSENTIALS

Address: Commonwealth of Massachusetts, Department of Conservation and Recreation, Blue Hills Reservation Headquarters, 695 Hillside Street, Milton, MA 02186. **Telephone:** Blue Hills Reservation Headquarters, (617) 698-1802 (extension 3 lists programs and gives a special events update); Trailside Museum, (617) 333-0690; William F. Rogers Ski Area on Great Blue Hill, (781) 828-5070; Blue Hill Observatory and Science Center, (617) 696-0389; Ponkapoag Golf Course, (781) 828-4242; Appalachian Mountain Club cabins on Ponkapoag Pond, (781) 961-7007. **Website:** www.state.ma.us/mdc/blue.htm. **Visitor Information:** Blue Hills Reservation open dawn to dusk, 365 days per year. Free. Trailside Museum open 10:00 A.M. to 5:00 P.M., Wednesday through Sunday; closed Thanksgiving, Christmas Day, and New Year's Day; small admission fee. Interpretive programs, hikes, lectures, and events sponsored by Massachusetts Audubon Society. Trailside Museum and its restrooms are wheelchair accessible, as is Houghton's Pond complex; rest of reservation is difficult, due to natural surfaces, steps, and slopes.

Acknowledgments

First and foremost, I want to thank three individuals at Beacon Press, without whom the 2004 edition of *Boston Sites and Insights* would never have existed: executive editor Joanne Wyckoff, who believed in the book and pushed to give it a new life; editor Brian Halley, who choreographed contacting all the sites as we began the mammoth updating process then kept me honest and on schedule throughout; and Beacon intern Kirsten Amann, who gently prodded site personnel time and again to get us corrections and clarifications and helped me juggle dozens of balls every week, making a seemingly impossible task possible.

I am grateful to all the personnel and friends at the fifty sites included in this book who generously offered their time, tales, opinions, criticisms, and expertise in the updating process. Since between one and four experts edited, commented on, or were interviewed for each chapter, there are more than one hundred people included in this thank-you. A few are mentioned or quoted in the stories herein, though many more simply gave their knowledge to the general fact pool of each story. Without your cooperation and enthusiasm, none of this could have happened.

There were certain individuals in particular whom I seem to consult time and again—both as sources of original information and as willing editors of portions of my manuscript. They proved to be expert resources on multiple historic sites whose judgment and advice I have come to count on, in this book and others. I am indebted to you all: Henry Lee, Marty Blatt, Ken Heidelberg, Nina Zannieri, Bill Stokinger, Amber Meisenzahl, and Ellen Lipsey. The resources of the Boston Public Library, the library of the Bostonian Society, and the Boston Athenaeum were essential tools in my process of discovery. We are fortunate to have such exceptional research libraries in our midst.

Heartfelt thanks to Jan Shepherd of the *Boston Globe*, without whom *Sites and Insights* would never have existed. In the spring of 1987, when she was still longtime editor of the *Boston Globe Calendar,* Jan helped me develop the idea of a feature column on Boston's historic landmarks and continued to support, encourage, and publish me as the series grew into the first edition of this book. Thanks also to the staff of the *Boston Globe* library, who helped me sift through antiquated clips, locate obscure files, and track down details for those original *Globe* stories.

Finally, to Rebecca Strauss, who advised, consoled, encouraged, and fed me throughout the months of writing and editing. And thanks, of course, to the city of Boston—for being there, surprisingly intact, for such a long, long time.

Index

Mogan, Patrick J., 270
Mogan Cultural Center, 269
Monet, Claude, 109, 122
Monis, Judah, 205, 253
Monthly Anthology and Boston Review, 167
Moody, Paul, 267
Moon Over Buffalo (play), 141
Moorhead, Agnes, 135
Morgan Memorial Goodwill Industries, 114
Morgan-Welch, Beverly, 212
Morison, Samuel Eliot, 71, 292; statue of, 293–94
Morris, Patricia C., 237
Morris, Robert, 221
Morris, William, 89
Morse, Edward, 113
Morse Auditorium, Boston University, 255
Mother Anna's restaurant, 245
"Mother Goose" (Elizabeth Foster Goose or Vergoose), 17, 93, 96, 235, 238
Mother's Day, 239
Mount Auburn Cemetery, 67, 95, 97, **98–103**, 129, 180, 276; birdwatching at, 101–2; chapels at, 101, 102; Washington tower at, 101, 102
Mount Auburn Hospital, 98
Mount Hope Cemetery, 315
Mount Royal Park (Montreal), 308
Mount Vernon (Boston), 75, 170, 194
Mount Vernon Proprietors, 213
MTA, *see* Metropolitan Transit Authority
Muello, Bill, 251
Muir, John, 199
Mulliken, Lydia, 31
Munson, Norman, 290
Murray, John, 244
Museum of Afro-American History, 211, 213, 216, 230, 231, 232; and Abiel Smith School, 218, 222, 234
Museum of Comparative Zoology (MCZ), 124, 262
Museum of Fine Arts, Boston (MFA), 15, 89, 107, 108, **109–15**, 170, 183, 240
Museum of Natural History, 262
Museum School, 115
Music Hall, *see* Boston Music Hall

Napoleon I, Emperor (France), 101, 267
Napoleon III, Emperor (France), 290, 291
National Association of Colored Women, 216
National Baseball Hall of Fame and Museum, 152
National Federation of Afro-American Women, 216
National Heritage Museum, 33

National Historic Civil Engineering Landmark, 155
National Historic Landmark, 98, 155, 179, 182, 211, 231, 323, 324
National Park Service, 10, 11, 16, 32, 55, 206; and Adams National Historical Park, 41, 42, 44; and Black Heritage Trail sites, 211, 222, 231, 232, 234; and Boston Women's Heritage Trail, 237, 240; and Bunker Hill Monument, 36, 38; and Freedom Trail, 57, 59, 62; and Lowell National Historical Park, 266, 269, 271; and Olmsted National Historic Site, 310, 311
National Park System, 307
National Portrait Gallery, 114, 170
National Register of Historic Places, 258, 283, 324
National Streetcar Museum at Lowell, 268
Native American Graves Protection and Repatriation Act (1990), 260
Native American(s), 11, 36, 112, 261, 267, 281; and Blue Hills, 324–26; and Harbor Islands, 318; Peabody Museum's Hall devoted to, 125, **259–65**; preaching Christianity to, 48, 67, 69, 70–71, 72, 261, 324; Schoolcraft collection of books in languages of, 170; and State seal, 48; and Walden Pond, 197
Navy, U.S., 51, 55
Needham, William, 42
Negro Freedom Trails of Boston, 230. *See also* Black Heritage Trail
Neighborhood Association of the Back Bay (NABB), 289, 290, 292, 294
Nell, William Cooper, 210, 221, 233
Nelson, Willie, 277
Neponset River, 324
New England Anti-Slavery Society, 210
New England Circle, 190
New England Holocaust Memorial, 246
New England Patriots, 149
Newman, Robert, 84
New North Meeting House, 243–44
New Old South Church, 21, 89
Newport Jazz Festival, 149
Newton-John, Olivia, 277
New Town House, *see* Old State House
New York Times, 142
New York Yankees, 151
Niagara Falls, 307
Nichipor, Mark, 30, 31
Nichols, Cushing, 220
Nimoy, Leonard, 258
No, No, Nanette (musical), 151
Nonack, Stephen, 171
Norma Jean Calderwood Art Gallery, 168
North American Review, 165, 167, 191
North Bridge, 28, 30, 31, 32, 33